MAKING INDIA

MAKING INDIA

COLONIALISM, NATIONAL CULTURE AND INDIAN ENGLISH LITERATURE

MAKARAND R. PARANJAPE

AMARYLLIS

AMARYLLIS

Copyright © Makarand Paranjape 2015

All rights are reserved by the Publisher, whether the whole or part of the material is concerned, specifically the rights of reprinting, reuse of illustrations, recitation, broadcasting, reproduction on microfilms or in any other physical way, and transmission or information storage and retrieval, electronic adaptation, computer software, or by similar or dissimilar methodology now known or hereafter developed.
All Rights Reserved

This edition first published in 2015

AMARYLLIS
An imprint of Manjul Publishing House Pvt. Ltd.
7/32 Ground Floor, Ansari Road, Daryaganj, New Delhi 110 002
Email: amaryllis@amaryllis.co.in Website: www.amaryllis.co.in

Registered Office:
10, Nishat Colony, Bhopal 462 003 - India

Distribution Centres:
Ahmedabad, Bengaluru, Bhopal, Kolkata, Chennai,
Hyderabad, Mumbai, New Delhi, Pune

ISBN: 978-93-81506-31-8

Based on the international edition of the Work:
*Making India: Colonialism, National Culture and
the Afterlife of Indian English Authority.*

This edition is a co-publication between Springer and Amaryllis and is for sale and distribution only within India, Nepal, Pakistan, Sri Lanka, Bangladesh, Afghanistan, Bhutan, and Maldives.

Printed and Bound in India by
Replika Press Pvt. Ltd.

For
Dr Manohar Shinde,
who is deeply committed to (re)making India

CONTENTS

Preface	ix
Introduction	1
'Usable Pasts': Ram Mohan Roy's Occidentalism	19
'East Indian' Cosmopolitanism: Henry Derozio's *The Fakeer of Jungheera* and the Birth of Indian Modernity	58
Michael Madhusudan Dutt: The Prodigal's Progress	93
Bankim Chandra Chatterjee: Colonialism and National Consciousness in *Rajmohan's Wife*	120
Subjects to Change: Gender Trouble and Women's 'Authority'	146
Representing Swami Vivekananda	186
Sarojini Naidu: Reclaiming a Kinship	239
'Home and the World': Colonialism and Alternativity in Tagore's India	284
Sri Aurobindo and the Renaissance in India	315
The 'Persistent' Mahatma – Rereading Gandhi Post-Hindutva	351
Conclusion: Usable Pasts, Possible Futures	372
Endnotes	384
Index	399

PREFACE

It would not be an exaggeration to say that this book has been more than twenty-five years in the making. As early as 1986 I began working on two of the chapters that find themselves here. Even earlier, during my research towards my PhD dissertation in "Mysticism in Indian English Poetry" (University of Illinois at Urbana-Champaign, 1985), I had encountered some of the personalities that populate the pages of this book. How was modern India formed? Who were the thought leaders that imagined it into being? What were the shaping influences and ideas that made this possible? What is the relationship between the formation of the Indian nation state and Indian modernity? And, most importantly, what role did Indian English texts play in this development? In one way or another, most of my work began to concern itself with questions such as these. They have preoccupied my intellectual exertions through most of my thinking life. Though it has taken the better part of my adult years to find out, I finally feel as if I have a sense of both the forces and the figures who made India what it is today. It has been a long journey, but one which I have not only found absorbing, but whose shape, direction, and outcome I finally find myself close to understanding.

Naturally, I have incurred so many debts over these years that it is impossible fully to acknowledge them. But, beginning with the latest, I am grateful to Manoj Kulkarni of Amaryllis who has overseen the Indian edition of this book to its completion. It has been a long and difficult journey, but he has been a courageous and steady partner.
I am grateful to the UGC Special Assistance Programme at the Centre for English Studies, Jawaharlal Nehru University for a publication grant to support this Indian edition, especially to my colleagues Professor G.

J. V. Prasad and Professor Saugata Bhaduri, the Coordinator and Deputy Coordinator respectively. Indeed, I owe a debt of gratitude to all my colleagues at JNU for their support. To my students, I offer a special word of thanks; my contact with them, especially in the classroom, has inspired so much of my thinking over the years. My greatest debt during the last stages of the manuscript is to Prayag Ray, my research assistant, student, copy editor, and friend. I cannot thank him enough for his prompt, efficient, and careful reading of the text as well as for his continuing loyalty and regard.

For the Springer international edition of this book which appeared in 2013, I wish to record my thanks to Dr. Purushottama Billimoria, the editor of the series. His timely encouragement saved this project from being consigned to oblivion. I would also like to mention Willemijn Arts, the then editorial director, for her patience, kindness, and tact in commissioning this manuscript. My special thanks are also due to Anita Fei van der Linden for guiding me through the Springer publication process from start to finish. I am thankful to the anonymous referee who read the manuscript and suggested valuable changes.

Work on this manuscript was begun in summer 2007 when I was a Visiting Professor at the Federal University of Minas Gerais (UFMG) and the University of Sao Paulo (USP). I am grateful to my colleagues Professor Carlos Gohn (UFMG) and Professor Laura I. P. Izarra (USP) for their solidarity and friendship. I reworked the whole book during my tenure as the inaugural Indian Council for Cultural Relations (ICCR) Chair in Indian Studies at the National University of Singapore (NUS). I would like to acknowledge both the ICCR and the NUS for facilitating my work. I am also grateful to Professor Fred Dallmayr and Professor Anthony J. Parel for reading the manuscript. and for their encouragement. Finally, I wish to thank all those who invited me to the conferences in which some of these chapters were first presented and to the journals or editors of the books in which earlier versions appeared.

Makarand R. Paranjape
29th July, 2014

1
INTRODUCTION

But if we were going to build the house of India's future, strong and secure and beautiful, we would have to dig deep for the foundations.

– Jawaharlal Nehru, The Discovery of India
(Nehru 1960, 28)

This book is about India's usable pasts as they impact us through Indian English authors and texts, shaping the national project all the way to the present. The phrase 'usable past' occurs in Van Wyck Brooks's *America's Coming of Age* (1915). It became evocative during the unstable and challenging decade of the 1930s when Americans began to reconstruct their past in a variety of ways, both textual and visual, to project a future in which the US would be the preeminent world power. Not just through books, pamphlets, posters and comics, but also public displays such as post office and court house murals, an attempt was made to depict the nation as secure, wealthy and powerful. I consider the present period of Indian history to somewhat similar – a time major transformations and possibilities, perhaps also of significant crises and challenges. India, too, for reasons quite different from the United States of the 1930s, needs some notion of a usable past to consolidate a stable state and viable civil society. This book explores the cultural and ideological possibilities of the pre-Nehruvian era to enable multiple ways of being Indian in the present times. Clearly, the prosperity and power of today's 'rising' India need to be undergirded by the cultural and ideological pluralities of our recent past. Without the notion of India as a democratic and diverse nation – commitment to social, gender and economic equity is unsustainable.

Michel Foucault offers us one way of structuring such a past – from the fragments and ruins still available to us. From the broken bits and remains, we might reassemble what the edifice of the past might have looked like (Foucault [1970] 1994). Foucault's concern is of course with the episteme – the conditions of knowledge and discourse in the selected epoch. In his later works Foucault combines his archaeological method with a Nietzschean genealogy to show us history developing out of twists and contingencies rather than rationally determined trends or necessities. It is by uncovering such discursive turns and their underlying conditions that Foucault makes sense of the past, showing us how we produce meaning. Thus he constructs not just a history of the past but a genealogy of the present. Influenced by Foucault, Joseph S. Alter in *Gandhi's Body* reconstructs the past in a manner significantly different from historians or anthropologists:

> The past is clearly in the present and the present is in the past. More to the point, however, the past is constituted of 'past presents' such that any given phenomenon at any point in time is simply the contingent manifestation – the apex – of an emerging pyramidal structure of meaning. The trick is not to undo the pyramid to discover truth but to show the dynamic interrelationship of its constituent parts as emergent myths. (Alter 2000, xiv)

It is precisely such 'emergent myths' and how they come into being that I wish to uncover by exploring the dynamic interconnections between the lives and works of select individuals of a specific period in India from approximately 1800–1950.

By re-examining the lives and works of historical figures from India's recent past, this book attempts not to re-write history, but to challenge the epistemic authority of historiography. History itself, as Dipesh Chakrabarty contends in *Provincialising Europe*, was a part of the civilising mission of the West consequent to imperialism and the Enlightenment (Chakrabarty 2000). Or, as Ashis Nandy puts it, history came in handy as 'a discipline and form of consciousness' that colonised people could be subjected to (Nandy 2001, 2). History, Nandy says, simplifies and flattens the pasts of colonised people: 'History tames time in a manner that myths, legends and epics do not' (4). Hence the attempt here is not to contribute to history but to break out of it. We may do so by examining the multiple ways in which the past is present to us and how it discloses new ways of being *in* the world, even changing it. I employ the illocutory force of textuality to do so, for before we can break *out* of history, we have to break *into* it. This is precisely the thrust of the rhetorical-literary here, to pry beneath and beyond the official histories to recover alternate and richer readings of the past. Reading texts and textualising lives helps us recuperate multiple and usable understandings of ourselves. This does not mean that the illocutory force of the text is to launch an escape from reality, nor is its hidden agenda merely to textualise the world; language does not merely create world-substitutes, but re-words the world in such a way as also to re-*world* it.

Hence, by recollecting historical figures, this book seeks to narrativize the contending epistemes that went into the making of the nation.[1] It is not just the past that is 'constituted of "past presents"' as Alter would have it. The present, too, is itself made up of 'present pasts' whose ruins or remnants we need to re-trace back to their times, even while their effects are slowly disappearing from our midst. This book is an exercise in such a retracing. The monuments from the past may be recollected textually here, but a text is not a bound or closed system of meaning. Rather, it is an area of endless play and signification, which from its moment of indeterminate 'origin' interpellates itself not only into our present, but also into the uncertain futures that dimly beckon to us.

This project seeks to explore in a direction contrary to the dominant school of post-colonial scholarship inaugurated by Edward

Said's discipline-altering *Orientalism* (1978). In an extraordinary but little-read early review of this book, the eminent historian of colonial Bengal, David Kopf says, 'Movements dedicated to human rights or national awakening are not inevitable and are certainly not possible without a very decisive change in the consciousness of those who suffer' (Kopf 1980, 501). In other words, native resistance was as important as British colonialism or Orientalism in creating the new India. That is why I am interested in not just how the material conditions changed, but the developments in the mentality or consciousness of Indians in the nineteenth century. In struggling with colonialism, they came to a new understanding of themselves. Out of this was born the possibility of a new India, the intellectual and aesthetic roots, which this book wishes to trace. My argument is that these roots are embedded in the cultural consensus that emerged through the nineteenth and early twentieth centuries in India.[2] Interestingly, some of the most important creators of this consensus were men and women of letters. They helped to bring the nation into being through language and textuality, thus imagining the community that became the modern Indian nation. What is more, many of these progenitors and shapers of new India wrote extensively or exclusively in English. The phrase 'Indian English Literature' in the subtitle of the book, thus, refers to the use of the English language by Indians to accomplish the project of the nation. Authorship conferred influence and authority upon them and their texts. Certainly, all the protagonists featured in this book are clearly 'canonical' in this sense: they were recognised, lionised and feted in India. They contended with one another as with themselves in the process, but in the end, helped shaped a broad, open consensus on what it meant to be Indian. To that extent, this book is about the 'great tradition' of the making of modern India or, at any rate, one of the ways such a tradition might be constructed.

The period that this book covers extends from the time when Ram Mohan Roy became active as a leader of public opinion in Calcutta to soon after India's independence when Gandhi was killed by a misguided zealot. This period, from roughly 1800–1950, was undoubtedly the crucible of modern India, a time during which the 'cultural consensus' that I have mentioned gradually emerged through debate, dialogue, conflict, confrontation and continuous struggle. India's tussle was not only with British colonialism and imperialism, but also with India's own self and its relationship with its past. Indian modernity no doubt emerged through resisting colonialism, but also through an active programme of religious and social reformation. In this process, the author(itie)s included in this book played a key role. To that extent, they formed the influential and formative, even dominant, tradition of modern Indian literature and history. Of course, there were many others too not considered here scientists, politicians, farmers, lawyers, activists and saints of diverse ethno-linguistic backgrounds and religious persuasions. The analysis has been confined to only a select, but crucial, sub-set of this larger group. From Ram Mohan Roy to Mahatma Gandhi, new continuities and connections have been established in the book, which have not been delineated as clearly or forcefully in the existing literature. Since this book is about exploring and re-examining the legacy of these canonical figures, I consider it the 'afterlife' of Indian English authority. This afterlife, as suggested earlier, is what makes them a part of the usable past, which we can turn through such re-readings, into a living present.

There may be some questions about the choice of those included in this book as about those excluded. As for the first, few could dispute the contribution of each of them to shaping the national consciousness. Many of those studied here – Henry Louis Vivian Derozio, Micheal Madhusudan Dutta, Bankim Chandra Chatterjee, Rabindra Nath Tagore, Sri Aurobindo and Sarojini Naidu – were primarily writers. I am concerned with the larger contribution they made, either through their literary texts or through the texts of their lives. They constitute a representative and open, not a complete or closed set. In a larger project others such as Subramanya Bharati or Mohammad Iqbal could have been included too. Similarly, the writerly aspects of the careers of other nation-builders such as Jawaharlal Nehru, Subhas Chandra Bose and Bhim Rao Ambdekar might also be considered. There are, in addition, several others that come to mind for a fuller application of the methods used here: Madhav Govind Ranade, Bal Gangadhar Tilak and Gopal Krishna Gokhale from Maharashtra; Srinivas Sastri and C. Rajagopalachari from Madras; or to return to Bengal, Akshay Kumar Datta, Krishna Mohun Bannerjee, Radhakanta Deb, Ishwar Chandra Vidyasagar, Brahmabandabh Upadhyay, Jagadish Chandra Bose and Subhas Chandra Bose. All of these might figure in a fuller and more extended exploration of 'Indian English literature.' The field is thus wide open and expanding when it comes to how textuality shaped mentality in nineteenth and early twentieth-century India, when the nation was being formed. A study of such figures would form a part of our 'usable past.'

Nehru, especially, might be thought as being absolutely central to a project like this, given his prodigious output as a writer in English. I too began this Introduction with a quotation from him. But Nehru has been the hero of many similar books, particularly *The Idea of India*. Its author, Sunil Khilnani, declares in the very first page of his Preface: 'I hope here to make clear why Nehru is so fundamental a figure in modern India's history' (Khilnani 1997, xvi). This book, on the other hand, is about the making of India *before* Nehru. In a sense, I wish to suggest that the imposition of a Nehruvian ideology was a flattening out and narrowing of the cultural and intellectual space of India by showing how rich the possibilities of India were earlier. There is also another reason Nehru does not fit into this narrative. As India's first Prime Minister, he ruled the country more directly, writing its story not so much in his books that came earlier, but more instrumentally through Parliament, by framing legislation, as also by directing the Executive to implement such writs. Khilnani's text is thus the history of the formation of a state, of the ruling ideology that sustained it in the four or five decades of its existence. Mine, on the other hand, is a narrative of the pre-conceptions of a nation. None of the characters in this book held positions of power, were ministers or heads of government. They were public figures, of course, and exercised considerable moral force through writings, which were either in English or translated into English. They were not statist intellectuals but helped shape the notion of a nation even before it was born. I am thus more interested in notions of national culture than in ideologies of the state. Gandhi represents the former, Nehru the latter. That is why the period covered in this book ends with Gandhi's death before Nehru becomes the dominant shaping influence of the newly independent India.

The literary and cultural encounters that constitute this book are, thus implicated in a special kind of phenomenology, an understanding of which is crucial to any notion of who contemporary Indians are or how they have come to be this way. What happened in India in the nineteenth and early twentieth centuries was nothing short of epochal in that it altered the entire mentality or consciousness of India. Moreover, at the very heart of this alteration was a contact, even clash of cultures – the collision between British imperialism and Indian civilisation, in which were foregrounded questions of autonomy, selfhood, or to use a Gandhian word, *svaraj* (literally, 'self-rule'). The whole project of imagining or forging a new nation was but a subset of this larger question of autonomy or svaraj. Power and resistance to power, which may be seen as the dominant tropes of the encounter between the colonisers and the colonised, also embody, in the final analysis, such a struggle for autonomy, for selfhood and for svaraj. These exertions over the meaning of a new individuality and collectivity were really about imagining into being the conditions for an economic, political, social and cultural order in which the humanity, dignity, equality and autonomy of Indian subjects could be safeguarded.

One of the main aims of this book is to retrieve and reassess what might be called Indian English literature. The phrase 'Indian English' has multiple meanings, but at its simplest it refers to Indians writing, reading and using English, a phenomenon that began to be more and more pronounced since the early nineteenth century. This was the by-product of the Indo-British encounter, which though it began earlier with the establishment of the East India Company in 1599, actually acquired a critical significance with the rise of British power in Bengal in the late eighteenth century. After Macaulay's

Minute of 1835 the Anglicisation of India, or at any rate, of Indian elites, became official colonial policy. Indian English also refers to the language, not just to its writers. The Indianisation of the English language produced, as several scholars and linguists have shown, a distinct variety whose standards and variables are seen in the wide range of registers and functions in which the language has been used over the last two hundred years.[3] Indian English is thus a composite adjective for both a language-variety and the literature produced by Indians in the English language.

Yet Indian English refers not just to a body of writing or the language in which it is written, but to a mindset or way of thinking, as to a class or community of those who arguably played the most important role in the modernisation of India.[4] In that sense, though overlapping with it, Indian English may be taken as referring to a group or body of people which, though related, is the obverse of Anglo-Indian and complementary to vernacular India. 'Anglo-Indian,' initially, meant the English in India and all things pertaining to them, including their literature. Later, it also came to mean of mixed race, Eurasian. The Indian English, as a class, were therefore perforce in direct contact, sometimes conflict and at other times in collusion, with the Anglo-Indian. Similarly, they both complemented as also at times, were in conflict with those who expressed themselves only in native Indian languages. It is remarkable to what extent these three sets interpenetrated and transformed one another over the period of their interaction. Eventually, after the transfer of power and independence, the Anglo-Indian had yielded to the Indian English as far as the authority over India was concerned, even as the vernacularists waited for a similar devolution that arguably never fully actually took place.

From this perspective, there were three kinds of authority at work in India in the last two centuries, the colonial – the Indian English and the vernacular – with some degree of overlap between them. These three authorities produced contending canons which clashed over the territorial and cultural control of India. Of course, India as we know it today did not exist then but had to be imagined into existence through the struggle between these traditions and imaginations. In response to the colonial canon and in opposition to it, developed a national canon constituted of the protagonists and makers of modern India. The Indian canon borrowed, incorporated, deflected, resisted and eventually possibly even overthrew the colonial one. But what is fascinating is that their common link and even the site of a contentious and continuous tussle, remained the English language. English thus became *Inglish* and, later, even *Hinglish* – and some other varieties such as *Tamlish, Bonglish, Punjlish* and so on, that combined English and Indian linguistic and cultural codes. Indian self-expression and affirmation, no doubt, also took place in many languages, the so-called vernaculars in which the native elite articulated themselves and helped to constitute new identities. Yet, because most these elites were bilingual and because English remained the link language, it was through the latter that Indian opinion was mediated and conveyed to the British authority and vice-versa. It is clear, therefore, that implicit to Indian English is some form or the other of translation. Indian English is thus a hyphenated space where the vernaculars in translation and original writing in English by Indians co-exist and meld to create a medium for transition and transgression. This medium breaks out of the confines of monolingualism to create a heteroglossia that absorbs and engulfs colonial power, colliding and collaborating with it and ultimately breaking free of it.

Indian English canons and the accompanying processes of canon formation, are therefore crucial to the understanding of modern India. This book examines one such canon, starting with Raja Ram Mohan Roy and ending with Mohandas Karamchand Gandhi. Included are several of the defining figures of that period such as Henry Derozio, Michael Madhusudan Dutt, Bankim Chandra Chatterjee, Swami Vivekananda, Rabindranath Tagore, Sri Aurobindo, Sarojini Naidu and several other women writers. This, as clarified earlier, is a representative, not exhaustive list, articulating a certain vision and telos for India that continues to speak to our times. This vision was a way of resisting power and ensuring plurality, of fighting for human dignity and justice without succumbing to the pulls of fanaticism or fundamentalism. It was a way of dealing with the Other without hatred or othering the Other, without, ultimately, even thinking of it as the Other. The Other was clearly the colonial West, with its vast military might and cultural power. The self was the defeated and humiliated civilisation of India, which had a dim memory of another past. The object was to forge a new nation out of the almost impossible diversity that made up India. The result – at least partial success? This book seeks to map how the Indian English literary enterprise was deeply connected, even implicated in this project.

English itself played a rather curious role in India, both culturally and politically. Macaulay had intended for it to create a 'class who may be the interpreters between us and the millions we govern – a class of persons Indian in blood and colour, but English in taste, in opinions, in words and in intellect,' (Young 1952, 729), yet as Modhumita Roy puts it, 'it was the English-educated who led the nationalist movement from its very inception' (103). In other words, English did not quite serve the purposes that the colonial administrators had set for it; on the other hand, it was not a panacea for all of India's ills. The role of English was more complex. As Roy observes: '"English" neither pacified Indians nor did it by itself infuse the population with nationalist fervour. The role of English, like colonialism itself, was contradictory in its outcome' (ibid.). This book explores this complication that English wrought on the Indian mind. The authority that the writers in the book exercised came largely, though not exclusively, through English. Indian English literature, thus, is seen in this book in a more specialized sense as Indian English *authority*.

My use of the word 'authority' for how these writers and leaders affected society, perhaps, needs further explanation. The original Latin word *auctoritas* goes back to the proto Indo-European root 'aug,' meaning 'make grow'. The word thus has connotations of both origination and increase. Both these senses are appropriate to my purpose of tracing the origin and growth of modernity in India, especially through the fostering of national culture. The persons or institutions to whom we ascribe authority thus become the source, inspiration, or cause of our own ideas, beliefs, thoughts and actions, even after they are dead. In the context of this study, they live on in their texts, which exert an influence right up to present times.

Max Weber's discussion of the three types of authority is relevant here. Both traditional and legal-rational authority may be the origin of the thoughts and actions of large numbers of people. In the first instance, we believe or do things merely because they are expected of us, because that is how we are conditioned to think, behave and act (Weber 1947, 130–132). In such authority, the sanctions against disobedience are subtle and certainly not enforceable. But in the latter case of legal-rational authority, non-compliance may result in punishment or prosecution. According to Weber, it is the legal and rational features of the bureaucracy legitimize its authority. Foucault's analysis of institutions like the prison, hospital, or school, all of which serve to discipline and manage citizens, may be seen as extensions of Weber's method. Thus a nexus of knowledge and power comes into operation, affecting a regime of psychological control.[5] But translating the original German word *herrschaft* as authority in English only gives it a legal-juridical flavour, thus equating it with legitimacy. However, authority is not always hostage to legitimacy. Certainly, in colonial India, all the figures discussed in this book lacked this kind of legal, bureaucratic or administrative sanction. On the contrary, they were often seen as trouble-makers, offenders and in Gandhi's case, spent several years of their lives in jails. All the same, by going contrary to colonial authority, they acquired a certain legitimacy in the eyes of the people as did their own kind of counter-authority.

Perhaps, it is Weber's third category of charismatic authority that is most applicable here. Weber categorically states that that authority (*herrschaft*) is also a kind of power (*macht*) but the compliance relationships involved are various and different. So far as the figures and the texts that I study, authority is neither legally sanctioned nor coercive; rather it is manifested in a wide-ranging influence over large sections of the people. Issues of command, compliance, reward or sanction are, thus, less important. As Weber himself put it, 'every true relation [entails] a certain minimum of voluntary submission'(14). It is this element of unforced compliance that is magnified in charismatic authority, which operates quite differently from traditional and rational legal authority. As the Rudolphs describe it, charismatic authority 'erupts' in times of severe crisis or rapid change as its bearer attempts to establish a new normative orientation and social order (1979, 196). Such authority nevertheless serves the function of unifying and centralising a narrative, in this case the narrative of Indian nationalism and modernity. One of the key arguments of this book is that the very act of writing, especially in English, was charismatic for Indians. Regardless of who the writers were, such writing gave them a sort of magical power and reach. Yet the specific authors I cover here were especially charismatic and powerful. Some, like Gandhi, made an incredibly forceful charismatic text of his life, but the in the case of others, their writing both added to as well as derived in some measure from the aura that surrounded them.

The special kind of charisma that writing in English became endowed with during this time is what 'Indian English literature' primarily means in this book. Considering the way I use the word, literature essentially hinges on two notions of authority. The first is that of authorship. Authority is a form of authorship just as authorship is also a kind of authority. It is the act of becoming an author that confers the most primary forms of authority to the person who exercises it. Such an authority, no doubt, comes with its own dangers, threats and risks, but these are directed at the person of the author and do not necessarily diminish his or her authority. An author may, for instance, receive a death threat for a certain work, but the work will outlive even the successful execution of such a threat. Authority, thus, is an accumulation and circulation of power that exceeds the person of the author. The author, we will remember, was declared dead by Roland Barthes and was reduced to a function by Michel Foucault, but such deconstructions do not necessarily curtail the authority of the author. Authority far exceeds and outlasts the author, which is why I am concerned with it more than with authors.

Another sense of authority in traditional Indian epistemology refers to the *apta* or the reliable expert as a valid source of knowledge apart from direct perception and inference. Therefore we may to ask what kinds of knowledge does Indian English 'authority' afford us today? To the extent that such authority can form a living tradition or *parampara* it must embody not just received ideas or conventional prestige. A breathing (if not smoking) canon consists of exemplars rather than ideologues, those who lived a certain kind of life and practiced what they preached. A consistency in thought, word and deed is, according to K J Shah, the test of an exemplar.[6] Even if all the authorities in this book do not qualify to be considered exemplars, some, such as Vivekananda, Tagore, Aurobindo and Gandhi probably were. The tradition is sustained by such incandescent exemplars. This too, acquires salience after decades of post-colonial bashing and debunking of authority.

As opposed to a hierarchical, linear, massified great tradition-producing authority, my concern is with the 'collective assemblages of enunciation', that went into forming 'a whole micropolitics of the social field' as Deleuze and Guattari put it (Deleuze and Guattari 1987, 28). Even Indian English is not just a language but a field of difference and cross-pollination between the vernacular on the one hand and the master's tongue on the other: 'In fact, there is no language in itself, nor are there any linguistic universals, only a throng of dialects, patois, slangs and specialised languages' (ibid.). The attempt here is to discover 'connections between semiotic chains, organisations of power and circumstances relative to the arts, sciences and social struggles' (ibid.). Despite the apparently chronological progression of the book, its internal movements are meant to suggest a multiplicity of determinations and supplements, not a consistency of development or outcome. The disruptive energy of these writers and their texts, especially in how they relate to their world, is quite aptly described by Deleuze and Guattari (1987, 33) :

> ...the book is not an image of the world. It forms a rhizome with the world, there is a parallel evolution of the book and the world; the book assures the deterritorialisation of the world,

but the world effects a reterritorialisation of the book, which in turn deterritorialises itself in the world (if it is capable, if it can).

I would hope that this is how this very book relates to its milieu today.

One of India's renowned living writers U. R. Anantha Murthy says: 'whatever one can truly say about India, one can also say the exact opposite with equal truthfulness' (Anantha Murthy 2000, 37). That is why, must resist the temptation of foisting any artificial sense of unity on what is a heterogeneous terrain. The cultural consensus that is described herein must itself be seen as open, plural, field of difference, a texture of multiplicities rather than any artificially imposed uniformity that is derived from erasure of diversity. To quote Anantha Murthy again:

> If you overstress unity in India and maintain that there is only one India, then diversities begin to appear.... On the other hand, trying to emphasise diversity, arguing that Indians are all very different and that they have nothing in common, makes me uneasy and I start to feel that there something common after all between a Bengali and myself and everyone else.... So unity and diversity appear true only in actuality.... (42)

In other words, unity and diversity are in a constant and never-ending dialogue when it comes to India. That is what this book attempts to show.

'History is always written,' Deleuze and Guattari warn us, 'from the sedentary point of view and in the name of a unitary State apparatus, at least a possible one....' (Deleuze and Guattari 1987, 44). That is why this very attempt to take flight from history, may actually resemble a history, with its tree-like structures of roots and shoots. If so, it ought to be read not as a history but as a melange of narratives, not as a tree, but as a rhizome, operating by 'variation, expansion, conquest, capture, offshoots' (42).This book is about culture and may therefore seem like a set of tracings, 'a tracing of the previous book by the same author, a tracing of other books however different they may be, an endless tracing of established concepts and words, a tracing of the world present, past and future' (45). But if it seems so at times, it should not be taken merely as such; because what seems like a trace here is actually an attempt to blaze a new trail; the tracing, in this case, is only a reinscription of a map of endless possibilities, just as Buddha's tree itself becomes a sort of rhizome. The reader is expected to make the leap of faith, as Deleuze and Guattari remind us, in 'perceptual semiotics' (44). The method, the invitation to the reader, should be clear: 'this is not a new or different dualism' but if 'we invoke one dualism' it is 'only in order to challenge another' (41). Always, the attempt is not to restrict but to expand understanding, not merely to ground oneself, but to break into flight: as Deleuze and Guattari say, 'the line of flight or deterritorialisation' is 'the maximum dimension' (42).

Afterlife best expresses the spill over, the surplus, the never-ending chain of signification implied in the texts and lives as texts that I wish to explore. It refers, quite plainly, to the persistence of 'authority' after the death of authors. It also indicates the periodic renewal that a tradition undergoes after periods of fracture and rupture. To write the afterlives of authority is thus to attempt to suture a tradition whose strands have been ripped apart by the engines of history. Of course, in a culture where transmigration and rebirth are not foreign, afterlife ought to have an added resonance. Afterlives imply continuities and resistance to easy closures. Release, liberation is of course desirable, but not merely cessation or death. Instead of terminations, we have transformations. The 'lives' of these canonical figures have come under great scrutiny and have been written and re-written. But their 'afterlives' have not yet been considered, at least in the manner in which I have tried to. An afterlife is not just what remains after a life is over, but also how its traces and fragments continue to live in and influence the present, generation after generation. To me, afterlife is actually a question of the usable past: it is the present that animates the afterlife, while it was the past that defined the life.

That is why it would be apposite to return to the idea of 'usable pasts.' After World War II, the US became an acknowledged superpower.

While Britain, already weakened by its heroic but debilitating war efforts, was soon to lose its colonies then subsequently recede from its pre-eminence in world affairs. The assumption of a dominant role by the US was, at least partly, prepared by harnessing the usable pasts of America. Similarly, a critically negotiated recovery of Indian English literature can be the basis for strengthening the forces of democracy, pluralism and social justice within India. The ensuing fortification of both state and civil society is not just so that India can assume the mantle of a global leader or super power as some are predicting or wishing, but more so that it can fulfil the promise of the freedom struggle by its arrival into a unique modernity that is neither a reaction against nor an imitation of the West. To be truly post-colonial, India must outgrow its subordination and apprenticeship, but to do so it must retrieve its usable pasts to confirm its best present and most hopeful future.

WORKS CITED

Ahmad, Aijaz. 2005. 'The Making of India.' *Social Scientist*. 33. 11/12 (Nov-Dec): 3-13.

Alter, Joseph S. 2000. *Gandhi's Body: Sex, Diet and the Politics of Nationalism*. Philadelphia: University of Pennsylvania Press.

Anantha Murthy, U. R. 2000. 'Towards the Concept of a New Nationhood: Languages and Literatures in India.' In *Contemporary India: Transitions*, ed. Peter Ronald de Souza, 37-48. New Delhi: Fundacao Orient and Sage Publications.

Barthes, Roland. 1977. 'The Death of the Author.' In *Image, Music, Text*, trans S. Heath, 142-148. New York: Hill and Wang.

Chakrabarty, Dipesh. 2000. *Provincialising Europe: Postcolonial Thought and Historical Difference*. Princeton, NJ: Princeton University Press.

Dasgupta, Probal. 1993. *The Otherness of English: India's Auntie Tongue Syndrome*. New Delhi: Sage Publications.

Deleuze, Giles and Felix Guattari. 1987. (1980). *A Thousand Plateaus: Capitalism and Schizophrenia*. trans. Brian Masuni. Minneapolis and London: University of Minnesota Press.

Foucault, Michel. 1977. 'What is an Author'? In *Language, Counter-Memory, Practice*, trans. Donald F. Bouchard and Sherry Simon, 124–127. Ithaca, New York: Cornell University Press.

———. (1970) 1994. *The Order of Things: An Archaeology of the Human Sciences*. New York: Vintage.

Kachru, Braj B. 1983. *The Indianisation of English: the English Language in India*. New Delhi: Oxford University Press.

Khilnani, Sunil. 1997. *The Idea of India*. London: Hamish Hamilton.

Kopf, David. 1980. 'Hermeneutics versus History.' Review of *Orientalism* by Edward W. Said. *The Journal of Asian Studies*. 39.3 (May): 495–506.

Nandy, Ashis. 2001. *An Ambiguous Journey to the City: The Village and Other Odd Ruins of the Self in the Indian Imagination*. Delhi: Oxford University Press.

Nehru, Jawaharlal. 1960. *The Discovery of India*. 1946. New York: Anchor.

Paranjape, Makarand R. 2006. 'Indian Anglophony, Diasporan Polycentricism and Postcolonial Futures.' In *Peripheral Centres, Central Peripheries: India and its Diaspora(s)*, Martina Ghosh-Schellhorn and Vera Alexander, eds. 101–112. Berlin: Lit Verlag.

Paranjape, Makarand R. and G. J.V. Prasad 2010. eds. *Indian English and Vernacular India*. New Delhi: Pearson Longman.

Poddar, Arabinda. 1970. *The Renaissance in Bengal Quests and Confrontations 1800-1860*. Shimla: Indian Institute of Advanced Study.

Roy, Modhumita. 1994. '"Englishing" India: Reinstituting Class and Social Privilege.' *Social Text*. 39: 83–109. Earlier version published in 1993 as 'The Englishing of India: Class Formation and Social Privilege.' *Social Scientist* 21.5/6: 36–62.

Rudolph, Lloyd I. and Susanne Hoeber. 1979. 'Authority and Power in Bureaucratic and Patrimonial Administration: A Revisionist Interpretation of Weber on Bureaucracy.' *World Politics* 31.2 (Jan): 195–227.

Said, Edward. 1978. *Orientalism*. New York: Pantheon Books.

Shah, K. J. 1977. 'Dissent, Protest and Reform: Some Conceptual Clarifications.' In *Dissent, Protest and Reform in Indian Civilisation*, S. C. Malik ed., 70–80. Shimla: Indian Institute of Advanced Study.

———. 1981. 'Of Artha and Arthasastra.' *Contributions to Indian Sociology*. 15.1/2: 55–73.

Uphoff, Norman. 1989. 'Distinguishing Power, Authority & Legitimacy: Taking Max Weber at His Word by Using Resources-Exchange Analysis.' *Polity*, 22. 2 (Winter): 295–322.

Weber, Max. 1947. *The Theory of Social and Economic organisation*. Trans. A. M. Henderson and Talcott Parsons. New York: Oxford University Press.

Young, G. M., 1952. Ed. *Macaulay: Prose and Poetry*. Cambridge, Mass: Harvard University Press, 1952.

2
'USABLE PASTS': RAM MOHAN ROY'S OCCIDENTALISM

2.1 USABLE PASTS, OCCIDENTALISMS, DISCIPLINARY BOUNDARIES

That many have considered Ram Mohan Roy (1772-1833) one of the progenitors of Indian modernity is well known, but few have asked what the value of such a reconstruction is to us today. Behind this specific question is the broader issue of how we make meaning out of texts, or in this case, how we interpret and understand historical figures and their careers. If Ram Mohan Roy's life is itself a kind of text which is open to interpretation, its different ideological and theoretical underpinnings tell us not only something of Ram Mohan, but also of how we reconstruct our own pasts. Ultimately, these questions boil down simply to what is our 'usable past' and how do we retrieve it? Whether Ram Mohan was actually the founding father of modern India is another issue, but that there is a need to make a strong and persuasive case for such a figure is clear. That is because contemporary India, from the various possibilities available, requires a genealogy for its present that may also predict a course for its future. Ram Mohan gives us the wherewithal to construct such a genealogy, allowing us to trace the vital trajectory of a socially shaping rationality from our recent history and thereby helping us to reinforce those aspects of the past which are imperative to constructing a modern state and civil society.

In the discussion that follows, my agenda is threefold: first, to define Ram Mohan's response to the West and argue that it was, considering the limitations of his time, a way of dealing with British colonialism which we may still find 'usable'; secondly, to examine more specifically Ram Mohan's positions on religious issues and on education so as to illustrate the above proposition; and, finally, to speculate on some of the biographical factors which made such a response possible.

The study of the life and works of Ram Mohan Roy is valuable, indeed empowering, also because it highlights India's intellectual response to the West on the eve of the colonial era. It helps not only to open up the whole territory of India's colonial encounter with Britain via the English language, but also shows us that there was reflection and resistance, leading to alterative possibilities, at the very beginning of the encounter, not only at the end, as we are often led to believe. The Indo-British encounter is not simply one of capitulation-reaction-transformation, but much more complex both ideologically and historically. Neither a simple evolutionary pattern nor 'pilgrim's progress' culminating in the triumph of, say, Gandhian nationalism, it is a story of continuous contestation and negotiation, not of conquest and capitulation. Furthermore and closer to my own interest, if the language and the works produced during this encounter are sites for a struggle between the coloniser and the colonised, then Ram Mohan Roy, in his use of English and his responses to the 'superior' knowledge of the West, can serve as a key figure, even an inspiring exemplar, who affords us a resisting space at the very 'originary' moment of this encounter.[1] Studying Ram Mohan Roy in this fashion, as the 'first' in a line of similar, even if heterogeneous figures might alter the entire map of post-colonialism in India. From Ram Mohan Roy to Mahatma Gandhi, we might see a continuous, if contentious, *tradition* of engaging with and resisting the West of which we would otherwise be unaware. The construction of such a tradition is how we can make the past usable.

It is this face-off with the West that I call Ram Mohan Roy's Occidentalism. I must clarify that I do not use the word in the negative sense that Ian Buruma and Avishai Margalit endow it in their book. Unlike Buruma and Margalit, I do not think that Occidentalism is of Western provenance, nor do I agree, contrarily, that the idea of the West was a non-Western 'invention' as Alastair Bonnet (2004) contends. Instead, I think that both India and the West emerge through a continuous engagement, and therefore are contingent and relational. By Occidentalism I do not mean demonised fantasies and stereotypes of the West by non-Western people, but instead, a way of studying, appreciating and dealing with the West. This is why it is a history of this engagement that concerns me, more than its polemics. Ram Mohan Roy is crucial to India because he inaugurates the familiarisation of the West in India, as he does India's attempt to understand it on its own terms. It is this study and the knowledge that it produces that I call Occidentalism. It is this kind of Occidentalism that later, in fuller ripeness and self-expression, enabled Indians to overthrow colonialism.

This chapter is also, necessarily, about genres, disciplines and their boundaries. I understood this when I began to read Ram Mohan Roy's life and works more than twenty years back.[2] In 'Little Gidding' T. S. Eliot said 'History may be servitude, History may be freedom' (Eliot 1968, 43). Bankim in the nineteenth century considered History (or the lack of it) as the cause of India's servitude while Gandhi, half a century later, demurred. However, both recognised its value, either to seize control over one's past and therefore shape one's present and future, or to deliberately and ethically opt out of history into a radical and ethical present. Taking a Gandhian position, historian Vinay Lal in his impassioned and erudite critique says,

> History is the new dogmatism; and as a dogma, as well as a mode of conquest, it is more unremitting and total than science, which has had its detractors from the very beginning. (Lal 2003, 67)

Without quite going so far, I can only humbly submit that the disciplinary policing, if it went unresisted, only leads to servitude.

Ram Mohan Roy who was a writer, critic, polemicist and religious leader is himself hard to classify. He opens himself to a variety of disciplines and genres, including literary and cultural criticism. Ram Mohan Roy's life and works may thus be regarded as cultural texts.

But my biggest discovery in the process of my work was that the academic clique at work in India was actually at odds with the great nomadic tradition of Indian intellectual and cultural life, the legacy of which helped to shape modern India. Such Indian English authority as I sought to recuperate was, in fact, actively against both internal narrow-mindedness and external oppression. In those days, the former was embodied in pernicious aspects of tradition, mostly in religious intolerance. The external tyranny, which was not fully in place in Ram Mohan's life, was colonial hegemony. The situation in India today is similarly marked by the dominance of Western scholarship, refracted and distorted through its local brokers.

Especially when the very structure of an argument is predicated on certain premises about how we make meaning out of texts or interpret the careers of historical actors, I realized that this work on Ram Mohan Roy was the beginning of a larger project. The ultimate aim of this project, if successful, would be nothing short of a re-examination of the history of the Indo-Western encounter, especially of colonialism and nationalism. Ram Mohan Roy was simply one in a larger sequence of leaders from the past, ancestral voices, who were willing, when respectfully coaxed, to whisper their secrets to us. Moreover, this was a history that was waiting to be written, somewhat like a civilisation finding its own voice, looking for a suitable channel to narrate it.

The initial exercise on Ram Mohan Roy was not just the beginning of the engagement with this story of Indian English authority, but also an initiation into the larger project of writing the history of India's quest for swaraj, a story which was nothing short of an account of India's recent intellectual history and the narrative of the decolonisation of the Indian mind.[3] As time passed, it became apparent that this loneliness was illusory; there were many other scholars and thinkers who were working along the same lines, had been doing so for generations and would continue much after this work was completed. The delusion of singularity passed, but not the sense of purpose that drove my research. The world outside changed substantially too; this way of reading the past suddenly seemed much more feasible.

2.2 TEN THESES ON RAM MOHAN ROY

From such a vantage point of improved self-knowledge and confidence, I came to spell out the following ten theses on Ram Mohan Roy:
1. Ram Mohan Roy's life can be read as an exemplary encounter of the East with the West.
2. This encounter is exemplary because it is the 'originating' type of all future encounters. Ram Mohan Roy's placement in history is strategic and unique – he arrives at the very beginning of the colonial period in a rather spectacular and unprecedented way.
3. The encounter is also exemplary because it is a kind of 'right' response to the West. It is 'right' because it shows a way for the less powerful to cope with the more powerful, for the conquered to stand up to their conquerors, for the colonised to face their colonisers, with the least loss of dignity or self-respect. It shows a way for the subject to retain his sanity and psychological wholeness in the face of overwhelmingly unequal encounters.
4. Ram Mohan Roy's response is enabling because it involves neither denial nor capitulation, neither yielding to the West nor rejecting it. Ram Mohan Roy's is the way of the comprehension of the Other and of responding from one's strength rather than from insecurity.
5. The way of comprehension consists in using knowledge to counter power. It enables the subject to cease to see the adversary as a unitary monolith or the struggle purely in binary terms. Ram Mohan Roy seeks alliances with those aspects of the West that he finds liberating in order to resist the dominant West.
6. At the same time, he criticises and seeks to reform aspects of his own traditions instead of being totally defensive or apologetic

about them. The sanity of his position lies in its ability to deconstruct the oppressive and dehumanising opposition of the colonised and the coloniser implicit in the structure of British rule in India, that was yet fully to unfold.
7. Ram Mohan Roy's response to the West foreshadows and points to the Indian consensus on how to deal with the West, a consensus which Mahatma Gandhi was instrumental in consolidating. It is his prescience that is thus truly radical.
8. Ram Mohan Roy's response proves that within every colonised people is the space for someone who can embody the strength of its indigenous culture and thus resist the coloniser from an alternate centre, a centre that is not itself already co-opted.
9. It proves, therefore, that whoever dismantles the false logic of colonialism belongs not to one nation or people, but to the human race. And Ram Mohan Roy was such a one, as much a universalist as a 'proto-nationalist.'
10. If the ideology of colonialism is false because it suggests the superiority of one race, nation on culture over another, then there must be a renewed and palpable demonstration of its falsehood. By implication, the struggle for justice and dignity proceeds from the assumption that all of us human beings belong to one family, one tribe, one nation, one earth, one planet, which is why all ideologies which divide and separate people are false. Ram Mohan Roy, in the ideals of the Brahmo Sabha that he founded, clearly enunciated such ideals.

When I started studying Ram Mohan Roy's life, what was truly liberating was that I was not 'inventing' such a narrative or such a figure out of thin air but that there were concrete proofs and precedents for it in both the primary and the secondary literature on Ram Mohan Roy. I found that readings cognate to mine were already prevalent in the initial accounts of his life written by his close followers and admirers such as Mary Carpenter and Sophia Dobson Collet. Rather than a resister of colonial supremacism, however, these writers saw Ram Mohan Roy as embodying the great synthesis between the West and the East. Versions of this theme were later popularised by English historians such as Vincent Smith too, but for their own reasons. Ram Mohan Roy, like other significant figures of recent India, had become the site of a struggle between the colonised and the colonisers. The latter wished to show in him the example of an enlightened native created by benign colonial authority, while the former wanted to project him as a champion social reformer and leader of indigenous thought in strategic partnership with the liberal West. Later Indian historians had to debunk such a cosy closeting in order to undertake a more 'critical' view of Ram Mohan Roy, seeing him as flawed and compromised by colonialism, already a collaborator. The controversies of historians are, however, of little consequence compared to the more urgent need to reconstruct the past in terms of the needs of the present – to discover if there was a native tradition of modern Indian thought.

That I was untroubled by whether such a reading would fit into the schools of colonial, national, Marxist, or subaltern historiography only helped me focus on what was 'useful' in Ram Mohan Roy's life, even if such a narrative was ideologically open-ended. Beyond a point therefore I was not interested in finding out if Ram Mohan Roy was a collaborator of colonialism or whether he was the first native resister. Perhaps, he was a bit of both, but still one of the 'fathers' of Indian modernity. Ram Mohan Roy, like all of us, was a product of his times, limited by his circumstances – he was neither omniscient nor trans-historical. Yet, unlike his other contemporaries, he was able uniquely to articulate a new zeitgeist that came from understanding two contending epistemes, those of Indian tradition and Western modernity. What is more, he was able to negotiate between these two worlds with great fluency and effectiveness. He thus rose above his times to enable his influence on generations to come, by his power to hew a new path for an ancient country on the threshold of a major upheaval. It is this path that we are still treading and which enables us to recover his life today.

2.3 INDIA, BRITAIN AND SVARAJ

The words 'India' and the 'West' recur many times in this book, I should like to clarify, at an early stage, what I mean by them. Both these terms are unstable, but still necessary; I use them in a variety of senses which the context will make clear. Generally speaking, by India I refer not just to the modern nation-state, but also to what used to be called the Indian sub-continent and, in an even broader sense, Indian civilisation. The West, on the other hand, is Europe, North America, but more specifically Britain, in the context of this book, which was a great imperial power and ruled India for more than 150 years. Culturally and intellectually, the West means those knowledge traditions that came from the Greeks, from Christianity and from post-Renaissance Europe. It is of course clear that the West is not a homogenous monolith, but a conglomeration and coalescing of shifting interests and desires, as is India itself. The latter, during the period that this book covers, was being constructed by the West, but was also trying to assert itself through self-discovery and self-assertion, displaying contradictory pulls and tendencies.

In Ram Mohan Roy's time, India included both native states and the territories under British influence. A year after Ram Mohan Roy was born in 1772, though Warren Hastings became the first Governor-General of the Bengal Presidency, much of India still remained outside direct British rule. Yet, by the time he died in 1833, in a short span of about fifty years, Britain not only gained control over vast areas of the sub-continent, but was the leading power in India. Even so, right till independence in 1947, India also meant non-British territories, independent or semi-independent kingdoms. Although Ram Mohan Roy probably did not clearly articulate an idea of this larger India, the proto-nation, he did live outside Bengal, travelling considerably both at home and abroad to gain a sense of its existence. In addition, he certainly had a notion of a larger and longer civilisational continuity that was India. His writings do reflect a consciousness if not of the nation then certainly of a bigger cultural, religious, political and geographical entity. That there was a crucial encounter, if not clash, taking place between the two, right before his eyes, was something Ram Mohan Roy was acutely aware of.

My narrative of this encounter is admittedly svarajist, which is to say, concerned primarily with India's quest not only for intellectual and cultural parity, but also with issues of selfhood, autonomy and liberty. Svaraj is not just political independence, although without political independence, no society can hope to have personal liberty. But svaraj is also concerned with selfhood and self-realisation, as it is with cultural sovereignty and social justice. Svaraj yokes the personal and the political in a transformative, even revolutionary, process. Svaraj stands for an ideal of individual spiritual evolution which simultaneously leads to an ideal social order, as it does for the harmony between inner self-development and outer order. It is such a visionary horizon of (im)possibility towards which Gandhi strove and with which India's modern project is irrevocably intermeshed. I would like to argue that Ram Mohan Roy's life-work also contributed to it, especially in the manner in which he shows us how to stand firm, both intellectually and culturally, against the onslaught of the colonial West.

Implicit in the considerable volume of literature available on Ram Mohan Roy, there is a constant concern with his response to the West in general and to British imperialism in particular. Yet, rather surprisingly, rarely has a historian or critic made it explicit. As a consequence, one seldom finds a satisfactory and effective evaluation of his attitude to the West. Admittedly, Ram Mohan Roy is not just an important historical figure, but also the founder of a religious movement. He is thus praised lavishly by successive generations of his followers, both in English and in Bangla works.[4] On the other hand there are those who, in an attempt to re-examine his contribution, have tried to show how this idolisation of the great reformer is exaggerated, if not misplaced. Both these views underscore the preoccupation of the secondary literature on Ram Mohan Roy to arrive at the 'true' estimate of his achievement.[5] Today this fixation seems somewhat misplaced, if not irrelevant. It would be far more valuable to see him as the progenitor of a new hermeneutics, the pioneer of a uniquely Indian response to the West – what I have called Ram Mohan Roy's occidentalism. I consider such an attempt not just heuristic or expedient, but historically persuasive. But it is in its aesthetically imperative form that it most appeals to me – a sort of moral allegory of the Raja's actual life that satisfies our demands for a rich, coherent and convincing narrative of India's engagement with Western imperialism.

The underlying case for attempting such a narrative is to offer a counter-imperialistic model, one which I believe is still useful in dealing with the West as an ideological system. When we make Ram Mohan Roy a torch-bearer of svaraj we immediately put him in dialogue with those who stood up for the autonomy and dignity of Indian culture even in times of adversity. Ram Mohan Roy, as the father of the Indian renaissance or the first modern Indian – to use two of the by-now-clichéd canonisations of him – is the ideal person with whom to begin the construction of such a narrative. It is in Ram Mohan Roy that we find the very first significant, coherent response of the modern Indian mind to the impact of the West and therefore an exemplar of how to cope with and counteract this impact.Furthermore, we might posit a continuity from Ram Mohan Roy to the present, a continuous tradition of a counter-imperialistic intelligentsia that provides us with the requisite history as also patrimony to counteract – on our own terms – colonialism and other such oppressive systems. This genealogy, I suggest, is like the underground or mythical river, Saraswati.[6] One keeps searching for it everywhere only to find that it is not a real river at all, but system of ideas which flows not 'out there' but 'in here.' It is only with the discovery of this hidden, secret river of Saraswati that the 'Triveni' the triune stream of Ganga, Yamuna and Saraswati, becomes the sacred confluence – *prayag* – that can offer us absolution from the sins of cowardice and slavery. Saraswati, who is also the Goddess of knowledge, is the only one who can liberate us from both our mundane and spiritual bondage. Saraswati, the ever-flowing one, is however 'underground,' not visible on the surface; she must be excavated, discovered, allowed to flow once more. My reading of Ram

Mohan Roy is meant to do precisely this, to enable the flow of the secret and self-empowering tradition of svaraj through our darkest hours to the present, rather more propitious times.

2.4 THE MIDDLE GROUND BETWEEN REDUCTIVE OPPOSITIONS

My aim in this section is not only to re-state Ram Mohan Roy's response to the West, but also to show how we may arrive at it. To begin with, we find that some of the earliest commentators on his life were able to place him as the great synthesiser who was able to transcend the binaries of capitulation and rebellion in order to arrive at a more considered response to the West. Vincent Smith, a well-known British historian, sums up such a position very aptly: 'His [Ram Mohan Roy's] attitude towards the West was neither that of surrender, or withdrawal or conflict. It was one of comprehension' (quoted in Crawford 1984, 33). Bengali historians repeated this assessment but without the acute political import that Smith was able to inject into it. For instance, Sushobhan Sarkar says: 'In his outlook, Ram Mohan worked out a synthesis of the best thought of the East and the West' (1970, 5). However, merely or every primarily, I do not see 'synthesis' as the chief meaning or contribution of Ram Mohan's life. Rather, Ram Mohan was able to find an integrity which came not from any synthetic combination of incommensurable elements, but through a rigorous and rational application of his energies to the problems of his times. My 'return' to Smith is thus not a simple reiteration, but a recovery through a long and contentious journey through nineteenth century sources and commentaries. We can arrive at this juncture only after we contextualise Ram Mohan's approach, comparing it with the other Indian attitudes toward the threat that the British held out to India during the early part of the nineteenth century.

Let us first consider the response of the feudal ruling elites of India to British imperialism. On the eve of the British conquest of India, the country was divided into many small principalities, often ruled by a price or potentate whose token allegiance to the Moghul emperor in Delhi did not hide the fact that the latter's empire had severely declined. The British manipulated these divided, mutually distrustful, warring states to their own advantage. These feudal classes which were supplanted by the British, expressed their resentment in the Great Revolt of 1857 by making common cause with the mutinying soldiers of the East Indian Company army. When the opportunity came, they reacted violently but haphazardly in a desperate effort to overthrow the British. But, disunited, demoralised and technologically outdated, they were defeated and destroyed. Bahadur Shah Zafar, the last Moghul emperor, was captured and exiled to Rangoon, Burma. Baji Rao II, the last Peshwa or head of the Maratha confederacy escaped, it is believed, to Nepal, never to be found. A new class of princelings, all of them loyal to the British crown, were created to prop up British authority. With the Queen's Proclamation of 1858, Victoria became Empress of India. The rule of the East India Company ended. India became formally a part of the British Empire.

An impetus of an entirely different type would be required to overthrow the consolidated might of the British Raj. Nothing short of a mass movement, which understood the entire colonial system that the British had assembled and placed led by a new intelligentsia – equipped with different tools – would be needed to provide this impetus. This new elite was drawn from the prosperous and educated new middle class, to which Ram Mohan Roy belonged. What is important to note, however, is that this class owed this class owed its very existence, its social formation, ideals, values, and mentality to the colonial encounter, of which it was a product. While Dacca and Murshidabad declined, Calcutta prospered with the growing might of the British commercial and imperial power, giving rise to a new native bourgeoisie, who naturally professed loyalty to their patrons. As Arabinda Poddar observes, 'whoever was engaged in trade or commerce in whatever proportion or of whatever status was not only subservient to the British rule but prayed for its perpetuation' (1970, 236). Yet, eventually, this native bourgeoisie was also the class that led the freedom struggle against the British, fashioning tools derived from the colonisers themselves, but turning them on their masters.

The native bourgeoisie, not the feudal classes or the working classes, would eventually overthrow British authority.

The response of this class to the British impact is usually classified as belonging to one of three types – 'Orthodox, Radical and Liberal' (see, for instance, Crawford 1984, 31–33; Joshi 1975, 97). The orthodox or the conservative factions were the proponents of status quo, especially in religious and social matters. As Crawford puts it:

> The Orthodox group clung tenaciously to the old ways and traditions. Political submission must not be followed by cultural submission. Hindu society, regulated by the caste system, was well-suited to stand aloof from foreign encroachments. (31)

We know how this group founded the Dharma Sabha in 1830 under the leadership of Radhakanta Deb to combat anti-sati legislation. Indeed, the number of such organisations formed to 'save Dharma' was so numerous during that time that a widespread sense of threat and challenge was endemic to Hindu society.

Similarly, it is argued that diametrically opposed to the orthodox faction was the Radical group or those who formed the 'Young Bengal' movement. Constituted by those who were deeply influenced by English education and Western ideas, this group included students and followers of Henry Derozio. Derozio had the reputation of being a free thinker who encouraged his students to question everything. Reared chiefly on European rationalist thought and English poetry, these students become famous for their supposedly outrageous behaviour, which included eating beef and drinking wine, not to mention their attacks on orthodox Hinduism. Some converted to Christianity. They thought that the best recourse was to obliterate the threatened Indian self under attack from the triumphant Western culture and refashion themselves in the image of their masters. These anglophiles, who, by and large, accepted the superiority of Western culture and tried to emulate it, did not enjoy widespread support.[7]

If such a method of understanding nineteenth-century Bengal is pursued further, we naturally have a third group in between these two extreme responses. Ram Mohan Roy becomes the prime architect and representative of this group. He embodies the so-called 'liberal' and 'reformist' approach. According to Crawford, 'He rejected the cultural isolationism of the Conservatives and the cultural abdication of the Radicals' (32). He neither opposed the West unthinkingly, nor did he capitulate to it. Moreover, through his intensive and tireless public campaigns on a variety of issues, he created considerable space for this enlightened and intelligent approach to the British impact. Around him gathered some of the leading minds of his time, who despite differences of opinion could form a broad consensus. These included Dwarkanath Tagore, Prasanna Kumar Tagore, Kali Nath and Baikuntha Nath Munshi, Brindaban Mitra, Kasi Nath Mullick, Raja Kali Sankar Gosal, Annanda Prosad Banerji and Nanda Kishore Bose. I would argue, furthermore, that in time, the intellectual and biological descendants of these men would help constitute our national consensus on British imperialism, culminating in our victorious freedom struggle under the leadership of Mahatma Gandhi.

It may not be inappropriate to take the trouble to sketch, briefly, how we might construct such a tradition. I would posit a direct link between Ram Mohan and Gandhi through the following, albeit unorthodox, construction of a *guru-sishya parampara* or teacher-student tradition. The influence of Ram Mohan and the Brahmo Samaj can be seen clearly in the formation of the Prarthana Sabha in Bombay in 1867. One of the leading lights of the Sabha was Justice R. D. Ranade. Ranade strongly influenced Gopal Krishna Gokhale, the 'moderate' Congress leader, whom Gandhi regarded as his political guru. It is interesting to note that what Gokhale saw in Ranade was not only an intellectual and a social reformer, but a saintly man.[8] It is this model of saintly politics and spiritual activism that Gokhale and Gandhi too followed. Ram Mohan Roy is the first prototype of this in modern India. He was intensely practical and yet highly evolved spiritually: in him we see an outward, public, constitutional application of dharma. Sushobhan Sarkar himself offers a slightly different genealogy bringing us up to Surendranath Banerjee from Ram Mohan Roy via Dwarkanath, Debendranath, Keshub Chandra

Sen and Vidyalankar. Bannerjee, of course, was one of the founders of the Indian National Congress and its President from 1895–1902. He knew Gandhi personally and was considered a moderate in politics. These links fill up gaps in the leap from Bengal to Maharashtra and Gujarat.

Returning to Ram Mohan Roy, the middle path that is ascribed to him has been affirmed in diverse religious and secular texts – the *Bhagavad Gita* and Hegel – to name one odd pair. Indeed, in one form or another, the middle path becomes the symbolic instrument of undoing the duality that binary categorisation imposes upon us. By identifying Ram Mohan Roy's position with this path, we can privilege him enormously over his other contemporaries. However, such a neat characterisation of human beings into three positions is bound to be somewhat reductive. Certainly, both Radhakanta Deb and Krishna Mohun Banerjee, to name a representative each from the orthodox and radical factions respectively, are seen to be much too complex and multidimensional to be slotted merely as 'orthodox' or 'radical.' The complexities of both historical and psychological realities resist such easy typification. In addition, the idea of life-cycles too bears out the difficulty in classifying historical figures ideologically. A person may start being a radical and end up being a conservative. Moreover, he/she may have a radical response to one issue and a liberal response to another. To entirely classify him/her as 'radical' or 'conservative,' therefore militates against both historical and psychological complexity.

If so, what options do we have when it comes to reconstructing Ram Mohan Roy's life? We have, on the one hand, the somewhat simple formulation of Ram Mohan Roy as the splendid hero, the great reformer, the grand harmoniser of East and West, the father of modern India and so on. On the other, we may see him as more complex, imperfect, flawed, not a prophet of Indian modernity, but a creature of his own times. From the point of view of psychological or historical verisimilitude, the latter reading is naturally preferable. A hagiographical portrait such as produced by the official Brahmo accounts fails to offer an engrossing or compelling account of a complex figure. However, I am interested neither in the 'greatness' of Ram Mohan Roy, nor even, beyond a point, in his 'complexity.' The latter may actually take us to a realm of indeterminacy in which no 'usable' past may remain available to us. This chapter attempts, instead, to ask if some lessons may be derived from Ram Mohan Roy's response to the West. If so, we must jettison the principle of the post-structural indeterminacy to propose a new allegory of Ram Mohan Roy. Unlike a hagiography, our allegory need not evoke awe and adoration, but critical scrutiny. Yet, it may also allow us enabling pointers to our present-day dilemmas, where the path of comprehension with reasoned engagement is preferable to either imitation or rejection of the West.

Hence, neither the indeterminacy of post-modernist deconstructions nor the promised certitudes either of hagiographies or pseudo-scientific histories alone and by themselves help solve the riddle of Ram Mohan Roy. Rather, the middle path, steering between a professed anti-foundationalism and a reductive master-narrative may best serve our purposes. Given this context, neither extreme scepticism which affirms nothing but our inability to understand our past, nor dogmas of ideologically committed historiography help; instead, both severely hamper any indigenous search for alternatives, besides being inimical to plurality.

If we do not allow for such a position theoretically, we find ourselves doomed to be in one of the binary and mutually destructive categories of slave/victim, master/servant, oppressor/oppressed, coloniser/colonised. However complex the combination of these elements in our dialectic, if we do not create or posit a space for an alternate mode of being, which escapes these equally disastrous options, our outlook will remain partial and flawed. Ram Mohan Roy's response to colonialism allows the colonised self to survive the onslaught of a system that not only alienates peoples, but also breaks the spirit of the subject race. A positive response to colonialism is one which would enable the individual and society to retain their integrity, dignity and sanity – without letting the mind lapse into hatred or torpor.[9] Ram Mohan Roy demonstrates such a response, as we shall see, in his engagement with Christian missionaries and with the issue of English education.

As an example of how Ram Mohan Roy's life is a part of our usable past, I offer the following narratives of his response to the designs of Christian missionaries as also to the proposal to introduce English education. This two-theme retelling is underpinned by the ten theses already spelled out that remain at the same time, their source. If our knowledge of the world comes to us through narratives, then these stories are worth being told and retold. Though their truth-claims and yardsticks of verifiability may be different, both histories and stories are valuable epistemologically and need to be persuasive on their own terms to win adherents.[10]

2.5 RAM MOHAN ROY'S INTEREST IN THE CHRISTIAN MISSIONARIES

Ram Mohan Roy's interest in religion goes back to his upbringing in a staunch Vaishnavite family. After receiving rudimentary education at home, he was sent to Patna at the age of nine. There he studied Arabic and Persian and achieved expertise in Islamic learning. At the age of twelve he went to Banaras where he studied Sanskrit and the sacred books of Hinduism. When he returned home after spending four years in Banaras, his non-conformism, love for truth and rational method of enquiry were already in evidence. In his reminiscences to William Adam, Ram Mohan Roy narrates how after listening to his father's arguments quietly and respectfully, he would always respond with the 'adversative participle, "But," (*kintu*)' (Kotnala 1975, 17; Crawford 1984, 4).

That Ram Mohan Roy rejected dogma and superstition and introduced a healthy and liberating scepticism into religious enquiry cannot be merely ascribed to his having imbibed the values of the Enlightenment. His contact with the West came much later. The Enlightenment that Ram Mohan Roy represents is indigenous and its roots can be traced to India's own self-questioning at this period. An example of this phase of Ram Mohan Roy's work is his book

Tuhfut'ul Muhawahhiddin or 'Gift to Monotheists,' composed around 1793 and published in 1803. It is written in Persian with an Arabic Preface and is a polemic against idolatry. The discovery of this text and its indigenous sources proves that international movements like the Enlightenment or Romanticism are not mono-genetic, but polycentric, emerging at many different places around the same time. It would seem that we all participate in a larger human culture even if we are not fully aware of it. *Tuhfult'ul Muhawahhiddin* was written before Ram Mohan Roy's contact with the West, indeed before he learned English. The advocacy of rationality as the supreme arbiter must have had native precedents and adherents, even in the largely Islamic, Persio-Arabic intellectual climate that was dominant in those times.

But hence to Ram Mohan Roy's encounters with the missionaries. Religious life in Bengal was stirred by the arrival of William Carey, a Baptist evangelist, on 11 November, 1793. He was soon joined by Joshua Marshman and William Ward. They set up their mission at Serampur, near Calcutta, under the Danish flag on 10 January, 1800. This is because the East India Company did not encourage religious activities in its territories to begin with. It is only later, with the consolidation of empire, that the attempt to convert the natives was openly encouraged. During its incipiency, British imperialism was cautiously mercantile, driven by profit, averse to risking a violent reaction from the natives as the Portuguese had met with their Inquisition and forcible conversion of native subjects to Catholicism. That is why missionaries set up shop in the more hospitable Danish territories, although that was merely their beachhead to British India. In the meanwhile, Ram Mohan Roy had learned English from John Digby, with whom he had a profitable business and personal relationship. By 1815 he began to have frequent contacts with the Serampore missionaries. He supported their educational and social efforts and made a sincere attempt to understand Christianity.

The fundamental difference between Ram Mohan Roy and the missionaries was ideological: whereas Ram Mohan Roy was interested in reforming his society, the missionaries were interested in prosyletisation. The latter saw in Ram Mohan Roy a useful tool in their grand design of Christianising India. Ram Mohan Roy, on the other hand, applied the same rigor and scepticism upon Christian doctrines as the missionaries directed at Hindu scriptures. His attitude confused the Christian missionaries who took the superiority of their faith as self-evident and could not understand Ram Mohan Roy's hesitation, which they took as a sign of his imminent conversion. Thus William Yates, with whom Ram Mohan Roy corresponded during 1815-1816, hopeful of winning him over, said of him:

> He is bewildered and questions whether any religion can be right, though he acknowledges, as far as he knows, that the Christian religion is superior to any other. I pray that Lord may open his eyes to understand and his heart receive the words of life. (quoted in Kotnala 1975, 80)

Yet, even such a sanguine assessment cannot fully hide Ram Mohan Roy's resistance to any easy capitulation. Not only the Serampore missionaries, but the less fundamentalist Anglican clergy of Calcutta too wished that Ram Mohan Roy would convert. Sophia Dobson Collet narrates how Dr Middleton, Bishop of Calcutta, inviting Ram Mohan Roy to his house, tried to offer him 'the bribe of world-wide fame' to induce him to accept Christianity (1962, 125). There was a grand design in such attempts. If the leaders of Indian society, the Brahmins – of which Ram Mohan Roy was one – could be won over, it was only a matter of time before the rest of the populace would capitulate. Ram Mohan Roy, however, resisted such blandishment; he never met the Bishop again.

Yet, Ram Mohan Roy continued to study Christianity seriously, even learning Hebrew, Greek and Latin to read the original texts. In 1820 he published under the pseudonym of Prusunnu Koomar Thakoor, his understanding of Christianity in *The Precepts of Jesus – The Guide to Peace and Happiness*. This is his selection of Jesus's words from the Gospels, containing what Ram Mohan Roy considered the core teaching, shorn of its dogmatic and miraculous passages. So read, Christianity ceases to contradict any other religion in the world;

Jesus's words assume the power and authority of an enlightened being without being tied down to institutional Christianity. In his Preface Ram Mohan Roy says:

> I feel persuaded that by separating from the other matters contained in the New Testament, the moral precepts found in that book, these will be more likely to produce the desirable effect of improving the hearts and minds of men of different persuasions and degrees of understanding. (*Selected Works* 1977, 206)

This book, the first study of and selection from the Bible by any Hindu was nothing short of pathbreaking. It shows a uniquely Hindu reading of the life and teachings of Christ. Implicit in it is the *sanatani* plurality that is enshrined in the Vedic declaration *ekam sat vipra bahuda vadanti* – 'truth is one; the wise call it by various names'. In this encounter between a monotheistic prophetic faith and a pluralistic wisdom tradition, we find the latter reread the former so that the former's own inherent possibilities are liberated. Christian totalitarianism is shown to be inferior to the religion of compassion, love and moral rectitude, which the life of Christ illustrates. Ram Mohan Roy not only made Christ accessible to Indians, but, in effect, added another hero or god to the Hindu pantheon and also offered Christians a new way to be Christian, to regain the Christ that had been lost in their dogmas of organised religion. The so-called colonial pupil had subverted the teacher's intention, teaching the latter a lesson or two. The proposed brisk make-over and Christianising of an ancient civilisation was to be neither as brisk nor one-sided as desired or expected.

Ram Mohan Roy's service to Christianity was, however, far from appreciated or welcomed. The reactions were rather opposite of the 'Peace and Happiness' that he hoped to produce. Rather, he became embroiled in a protracted and sapping controversy stretching through several polemical works. A critical response, penned by Marshman, to *The Precepts* was published by the Serampore missionaries in their journal *Friend of India* (February 1820). Ram Mohan Roy responded almost immediately with *An Appeal to the Christian Published in Defence of the Precepts of Jesus by a Friend of Truth*, again published under the assumed name of Ram Dass. Joshua Marshman published his rejoinder in the *Friend of India* (May 1820). By now the battle lines were clearly drawn. Ram Mohan Roy published his *Second Appeal* in 1821, a well-reasoned essay of 173 pages. The *Friend of India* carried a 128 page rebuttal in June 1821. The protagonists of colonial and missionary Christianity began with a sense of complacency, thinking that they could easily refute a native novice's objections. After all, they were schooled precisely in such argumentation, being trained theologians. What they did not understand is that Ram Mohan Roy also came from a very long and once vigorous tradition of *sastrartha* or scholarly debate on religious issues. Ram Mohan Roy was, thus, our first 'argumentative Indian' of modern times. That he debated with the European Christian missionaries not in Sanskrit, but in their own language, English, makes him an even greater cultural hero. Since his times, many a debate on behalf of India has been carried out in English by Indians, including Gandhi much later, who brought the world's most powerful empire to its knees. Ram Mohan Roy was alone, without the kind of institutional and financial means that his adversaries had. They had the power of the organised Church behind them; he, on the other hand, did not even have the help of his own co-religionists, most of who neither knew English nor had studied Christianity. On the other hand, many of the orthodox Hindus had boycotted him for his social reformist agenda.

The Baptist Mission Press of Calcutta refused to print Ram Mohan Roy's *Third and Final Appeal*. This was a deliberate ploy to shut him up when they found that they were not winning the argument. Undeterred, Ram Mohan Roy purchased the typesetting equipment and printed it himself at the Unitarian Press. This *Final Appeal* published in January 1823 was 379 pages long and was divided into seven chapters. *The Indian Gazette* described Ram Mohan Roy as the 'most gigantic combatant in the theological field' in their review of the work (Kotnala 1975, 92). Though Marshman penned two essays in reply, the controversy had ended from Ram Mohan Roy's side with an amicable parting of ways.

By the end of this exchange, Ram Mohan Roy was famous as a religious controversialist not only in Calcutta but abroad as well. He had started his own newspapers, *Sambad Kaumudi* and the *Mirat-ul-Akhbar* in Bengali and Persian, respectively. He also started the *Brahmanical Magazine* in English with a Bengali version, *Brahmana Sevadhi*. *Sambad Kaumudi* was the first newspaper owned, edited and published by any Indian. In 1821 Ram Mohan Roy's cause received an unexpected boost when Rev William Adam, one of the Serampore missionaries, converted to Unitarianism, which was close to Ram Mohan Roy's own position. Ram Mohan Roy's religious reformism culminated in the founding of the Brahmo Sabha in 1830, which later changed its name to the Brahmo Samaj. The establishment of the Brahmo Samaj marks a watershed in the history of Hinduism. This was India's first modern reform sect, followed by several others such as the Prarthana Samaj, the Arya Samaj, the Theosophical Society and so on. The Brahmo Samaj's constitution is unique for its liberalism and openness. Its theology, based on the Upanishads, rejects idol worship. In the evolution of modern Hinduism, the Brahmos played a vital role though they were later reabsorbed or overtaken by 'mainstream' Hinduism inspired by the likes of Sri Ramakrishna.

Ram Mohan Roy and the Serampore missionaries clashed on several doctrinal issues, but the real clash was, in my opinion, not just theological or ideological, but civilisational. The missionaries did not wish that an Indian should scrutinise their scriptures; equality among religions was totally antithetical to their world-view. They only wished to convert Ram Mohan Roy; when they found him arguing with them instead, they were disappointed but accepted the challenge; finally, finding themselves discomfited by his logical rigour, Biblical exegesis and tenacity, they found their own dogmas questioned if not undermined. At last, they gave up on trying to convert Ram Mohan Roy and attacked him instead as an adversary. What had begun as an amicable 'inter-faith dialogue', ended in a bitter denunciation by the missionaries of Ram Mohan Roy's ideas. When their policy of conciliation was shown to be ineffective, they escalated their propaganda engine against Hinduism. In a sense, this confrontation shows the difficulties with inter-religious dialogues to this day. Semitic faiths, convinced of their superiority and God-given monopoly to Truth, often used the ruse of dialogue to worst their opponents. Dialogue is only possible if both sides are open, not when inherent to the very theology of one side is their assertion of a superior, even exclusive claim to truth.

Ram Mohan Roy was curious about Christianity, especially given that it was being projected as the supreme revelation by the missionaries. At first he thought that perhaps Christianity with its moral emphasis would be a better religion than the superstition ridden Hinduism of his time. But a closer examination revealed several superstitions and dogmas within Christianity to his discerning eye. When he attempted to separate the miraculous and the doctrinal from the essential teachings of Christ, he was surprised to find the missionaries tenaciously clinging to their dogmas. Instead of the welcome he expected for his 'appeals,' he was called a heathen; his credentials and sincerity were questioned. Finding the missionaries intransigent and narrow-minded, Ram Mohan Roy undertook to defend himself. He claimed that the missionaries wanted him to exchange one set of superstitions for another, something he found irrational and illogical. Finally, at the end of the controversy, he understood why there could be no conciliation with the missionaries on religious issues. Now, Ram Mohan Roy decided to turn his attention to reforming his own society and to defending Hinduism against erroneous propaganda. Explaining his position, he said in his *Final Appeal*:

> After I have long relinquished every idea of plurality of Gods, or of the persons of the God-head taught under different systems of Modern Hinduism, I cannot conscientiously and consistently embrace one of a similar nature, though greatly refined by religious information of modern times.... (quoted in Kotnala 1975, 93)

Ram Mohan Roy's own attitude to those professing other faiths was in marked contrast to that of the missionaries. In his 'Humble Suggestions to His Countrymen Who Believe in the One True God' (1823), he says:

> When anyone ... endeavours to make converts of us, the believers in the only living and true God, even then we should feel no resentment towards them, but rather compassion, on account of the blindness and errors into which they themselves have fallen.... ([1906] 1982, 211)

The trust deed of the Brahmo Sabha dated 8 January, 1830 too testifies to Ram Mohan Roy's all-embracing pluralism and breadth of acceptance. The building and the land of the Sabha were to be open to 'all sorts and descriptions of people, without distinction, as shall behave and conduct themselves in an orderly, sober, religious and devout manner' (Crawford 1984, 81).

Ram Mohan Roy stood in sharp contrast not only to the missionaries but to his other co-religionists as well. The orthodoxy rallied against him. They attacked him relentlessly, even tried to get him excommunicated. His family members were set against him. The orthodox groups not only opposed the abolition of sati but supported the various other ills of Hindu society such as animal sacrifice, child marriage, denial of inheritance rights to women, Kulinism and so on, which Ram Mohan Roy campaigned against. They organised themselves into several groups such as the Dharma Sabha, the Sanatan Dharma Rakshini, Ranaghat Sanatan Dharmarakshini Sabha, the Jashohar Dharma Rakshini Sabha, the Faridpur Kaulinya Pratha Samshodhani Sabha and so on (see Sen 1979, 12). The orthodox could little understand what Ram Mohan Roy was trying to attain as he advocated a more rational and humane religion. The Young Bengal radicals, on the other hand, went to the other extreme, completely denouncing their ancestral religion, without understanding fully what it stood for. In the manuscript of Baboo Huro Mohun Chatterjee on the history of the Hindu College, we have a description of one of their meetings:

> The principles and practices of the Hindu religion were openly ridiculed and condemned and angry disputes were held on moral subjects....The Hindu Religion was denounced as vile and corrupt and unworthy of the regard of rational beings. The degraded state of the Hindus formed the topic of many debates; their ignorance and superstition were declared to be the causes of such a state and it was resolved that nothing but a liberal education could enfranchise the minds of the people. (quoted in Edwards 1884, 68)

Though this portrayal may not be considered as entirely reliable, it does indicate the temper of the times. As Sushobhan Sarkar says, 'Radical politics of a Western type were hardly possibly in Bengal a century ago and the rich promise we see in the Derozians never matured into anything solid' (1970, 25). Yet, the attack against Hinduism mounted from the dual platform of liberal modernity and evangelical Christianity did have serious repercussions. The conversions of Krishna Mohun Banerjee and Michael Madhusudan Dutt and later of the famous Dutt family of Cassipore took place precisely in such a climate because of the acceptance in some quarters of the superiority of Christianity as the revealed religion versus the superstitions of Hinduism. Doubtless, the conflation of Western religion with European political, economic and cultural domination resulted in many such conversions, even if they did not always result in a change of faith. The acceptance of the superiority of the West, the desire to emulate it and finally, to belong to the Western narrative as the only universal narrative were nothing short of a conversion, whether secular or religious. At the same time, we cannot deny that Hindu society of that period did need reform. The challenge that Christianity posed was important in that it offered a way out of the caste-ridden, oppressive society. In a way, reformers like Ram Mohan Roy and Krishna Mohun were working not against one another, but in tandem, the former reforming Hindu society from within and the latter exerting a pressure from the outside.

Yet, as I have tried to show, it is the 'middle path' of Ram Mohan Roy that offered the most to the future in contra-distinction to the extremes of orthodox upholding or radical rejection of tradition. Ram Mohan Roy's approach was quite different because he was among the first modern Indians to study systematically the original texts of other religions so as to make a comparison and start a dialogue. His ideas of tolerance and validity of all religions in the pure form, again, anticipate the Indian consensus reflected in the mind from Sri Ramakrishna to Mahatma Gandhi.

Ram Mohan Roy believed in a religion which would serve man and improve his life, not one which kept him enslaved to ignorance. He wanted a rational religion which could satisfy the doubts of the seeker rather than enforce submission to authority. Ram Mohan Roy believed that religious texts had to be interpreted like any other texts and though 'divine,' they had to make sense to human beings. When in doubt, he always accepted what appealed to common sense or reason, setting aside the fabulous, the miraculous, the spectacular. It has been pointed out that his religion was rational, not devotional or mystical. Also that it merely reconstructed Hinduism in terms that were understandable and acceptable to the West. His was, in other words, a Christianised Hinduism, shorn of idol worship, polytheism, pujas, rituals, caste and other components of what was thought to be essential to Hinduism. Yet, the Brahmos too believed in karma, dharma, rebirth and, above all, in the possibility of self-realisation as enunciated in the Upanishads. In the context of the inequalities of the Indo-Western encounter of the early nineteenth century, the Brahmo Samaj did seem like the 'right' answer, even if not the 'best' one. Ram Mohan Roy's approach helped stave off imperialistic Christian evangelicism that was threatening to defeat and convert the Indian intelligentsia. The best minds of that time became attracted to Brahmoism, preferring it as a more culturally and emotionally satisfying alternative to conversion and Westernisation.

2.6 RAM MOHAN ROY AND ENGLISH EDUCATION

Ram Mohan Roy's position on English education is more complex and ambivalent. It would be very hard to argue today that the introduction of English education was an unmixed blessing. For one, we know that unlike the myths later perpetuated by both the English and the Indians, indigenous forms of education were extensively available. Also, the position of the Orientalists in the Orientalist vs Anglicist controversy preceding the Macaulay-powered victory of the latter, had much to offer in support of the continuation of traditional forms of education. Finally, we must not forget that the controversy was really three-cornered with one offshoot arguing for vernacular education. Without going into the entire controversy in detail, we know that Ram Mohan Roy is normally considered to have supported the Anglicists in their demand for English education. But was the case so straightforward?[11]

William Carey, the Serampore Baptist missionary, was a staunch advocate of vernacular education. He opposed the elitism of the Orientalists who wished to reinstate Sanskrit knowledge. Also, in June 1814 long before Ram Mohan Roy's letter to Lord Amherst, Carey advocated his plan for 'Instructing Native Inhabitants of India in European Sciences' (Kopf 1969, 149). Carey was a Calvinist; before he came to India, he had already spelled out his mission in his 1792 tract *An Enquiry into the Obligations of Christians, To Use Means for the Conversion of the Heathens. In which the Religious State of the Different Nations of the World, The Success of Former Undertakings and the Practicability of further Undertakings, are Considered.*[12] This book contained the germ of his subsequent ideas, including using the native languages of the heathens in order to convert them. Ram Mohan Roy resisted conversion, but agreed with Carey's basic thrust that Hindu society was fallen and in dire need of reform. His advocacy of vernacular school education, followed by English higher education, not only appears to be a compromise between the Anglicists and Carey's vernacularism, but looks ahead to what independent India also adopted in its three-language formula.

In a remarkable letter dated 14 October, 1826, William Adam, Ram Mohan Roy's friend and the manager of his Anglo-Hindu school, makes a case for combining the traditional educational system with the fruits of Western liberal education. Adam is so important because, as mentioned earlier, he came over to Ram Mohan Roy from the side of Serampore missionaries and so was among the first reverse converts in the history of Indo-British relations. Referring to traditional Indian schools, he says:

> To whatever extent such institutions may exist and in whatever condition they may be found – stationary, advancing or retrograding – they present the only true and sure foundations on which any scheme of general or national education can be established. We may improve, enlarge and beautify the superstructure; but these [indigenous institutions] are the foundations on which the building should be raised. (quoted in Reena Chatterjee 1983, 9)

The point that I have been building up to is that though Ram Mohan Roy welcomed the new education, his idea of it – if Adam's views can be considered to be in consonance to his – was very different from Macaulay's. This is also evident simply by comparing his letter of 11 December, 1823 to Governor-General Lord Amherst with Macaulay's notorious Minute of 2 February, 1835. The heavy sarcasm of Ram Mohan Roy's letter is unmistakable:

> Humbly reluctant as the natives of India are to obtrude upon the notice of Government the sentiments they entertain on any public measure, there are circumstances when silence would be carrying this respectful feeling to culpable excess. The present Rulers of India, coming from a distance of many thousand miles to govern a people whose language, literature, manners, customs and ideas are almost entirely new and strange to them, cannot easily become so intimately acquainted with their real circumstances, as the natives of the country are themselves. We would therefore be guilty of a gross dereliction of duty to ourselves and afford our Rulers just ground of complaint at our apathy, did we omit on occasions of importance like the present to supply them with such accurate information as might enable them to devise and adopt measures calculated

to be beneficial to the country and thus second by our local knowledge and experience their declared benevolent intentions for its improvement. (*Selected Works* 1977, 300)

Ram Mohan Roy's intentions are fairly clear. First, he stresses that his countrymen are to face the brunt of Governmental policies without any opportunities to participate in the decision-making processes. Secondly, that the British come from a distant isle and are hence more or less ignorant of Indian customs, manners and culture. Ram Mohan Roy is thus questioning, though indirectly, the very right of the British to rule and make decisions on behalf of Indians. But he has to concede that they are, at present, the rulers and that their professed intentions, he will allow, seem honourable. Deftly, he hints that he is offering his views unasked not only because he wants to help his countrymen, but because he does not want to give the British a chance of later accusing Indians of failing in their duty to themselves. The whole tone and attitude of this passage contrasts with the self-arrogated authority to dictate other peoples' lives which Macaulay's minute displays. I would argue that in Ram Mohan Roy's letter the process of decolonisation is already underway even as colonialism is revealing its true colours.

True, that in the paragraphs that follow, Ram Mohan Roy is unremittingly harsh, even dismissive, towards Sanskrit education, but only because it appears that he found it hidebound and narrow-minded, completely unsuited for the 'improvement' of Indians. The word 'improvement' is repeated often, not so much because Ram Mohan Roy was influenced by the Utilitarians as some have argued, but because he had, in my opinion, imbibed their vocabulary to impress the rulers to take his words seriously. He accuses the Sanskrit system of being 'best calculated to keep this country in darkness' (*Selected Works* 1977, 302). What he wants instead is a 'more liberal and enlightened system of instruction, embracing Mathematics, natural philosophy, chemistry and anatomy with other useful sciences' (ibid.). In a word, as Reena Chatterjee has argued, he wished to usher in modernisation, not necessarily westernisation (Chatterjee

1983, 61). There is no reference to the medium of education here, nor to the inclusion of western literature, philosophy, history and religion into the curriculum.

The moot point is whether we needed to learn modern sciences and mathematics from the West at that time. The answer, clearly, is yes, we did. India was materially inferior to the West and its knowledge systems had not been able to deliver the wherewithal to face the onslaught of the West. The only recourse was to learn from our masters. Does this mean that the traditional knowledge was useless or had to be denigrated? Probably not; Sanskrit knowledge systems did not have to be rejected or ridiculed in order to promote or accept modern, Western science. But it is equally true that the traditional knowledge system could not deliver what Western science did. Not only could it not offer jobs and means of livelihood to its practitioners, it was also unable to reinvent itself or reassert its utility in the changed circumstances. As Macaulay himself pointed out, those who were educated in Sanskrit learning had to be subsidised while those who acquired English education were highly in demand. The market was predisposed in favour of English given that the English were our new rulers, while Sanskrit learning was less and less viable.

Ram Mohan Roy, himself well-versed in Sanskrit, made a plea for modern education through the English medium. Yet, I believe that what he asked for was indeed very different from the heavily literary type of education which Macaulay had in mind and imposed upon India. Ram Mohan Roy wanted Indians to be as well equipped as the free nations of Europe in order to participate in a larger world of learning and life-making. Instead, what was imposed on the natives was a system of education which served the interests of the colonisers and which kept many of its recipients in a state of slavish apathy or outright subordination.

Macaulay's Minute, though it has its supporters, is a record of imperial arrogance coupled with evangelical fervour. Macaulay claims that 'a single shelf of a good European library was worth the whole native literature of India and Arabia' (Sharp 1965, 109). In the same breath he admits that he has not read any of the literatures he dismisses so easily (ibid.). Macaulay betrays ignorance not just of Indian literature, but also of the efforts of the Orientalists over the several preceding decades to systematically study ancient Indian culture. He ignores the tremendous impetus this knowledge gave to European scholarship and literature itself.[13] Macaulay actually threatened to resign if his views were not accepted. This shows the extent of his fervent belief in himself and the imperialist mission. Macaulay saw India in terms of the passive, the pliable Orient, waiting to be both defined and acted upon by the superior, masculine West – he was thus in the classic Orientalist mould that Edward Said has exposed so brilliantly. Macaulay, we must not forget, wished to create 'a class of persons Indian in blood and colour, but English in tastes, in opinions, in morals and in intellect' (Sharp 1965, 116). Would Ram Mohan Roy have supported Macaulay's views? Even his worst detractors would have to admit that Ram Mohan Roy's position was somewhat different. As Sumit Sarkar says:

> The negative, alienating, aspects of the English education which Ram Mohan Roy and his generation so ardently welcomed are of course fairly obvious today. In fairness to Ram Mohan Roy, certain qualifications should be made here. The traditional Sanskrit or Persian educated literati were also utterly alienated from the masses; the 1823 letter pleaded for Western scientific values, not necessarily for English as the medium of instruction; and there were elements of a kind of mass approach in Ram Mohan Roy's pioneer translation of the shastras into the vernacular, his promotion of Bengali journalism....(Quoted in Joshi 56)

Yet what is equally important is that both Ram Mohan Roy and Macaulay were actually reflecting trends rather than producing them. The demand for English education, whether inclusive of sciences or exclusively of them, was so great in Calcutta that it could simply not be attributed either merely to colonial policy or aberrant native anglophilia.[14] Incidents of Bengali boys offering themselves to be 'taken' for absorption, adoption and assimilation into English, both as a language and a cultural system, abound. As the influential missionary Alexander Duff records, the natives pursued and supplicated him with 'pitiful earnestness' craving for 'English reading' and 'English knowledge'; in broken English they cried 'Oh take me'(quoted in Poddar 1970, 91). The desire to be taken was so great that only the selected candidates, who were given tickets, were admitted, while men stationed at the door of the school kept out the throngs of disappointed applicants (ibid.), a practice which, in a slightly different form, continues to this day with entrance exams, quotas and other ways to manage a demand that so exceeds the supply in education. Macaulay's biographer and nephew C. E. Trevelyan in his book *On the Education of the People of India* published in Calcutta not long after Macaulay's Minute of 1835 recounts how Englishmen on the steamboats plying the Ganges were besieged by troops of Bengali boys clamouring for English books. In one instance, a gentleman so beset hit upon the 'expedient of cutting up an old *Quarterly Review*' to distribute the articles among the boys (Poddar 1970, 93).

Ram Mohan Roy's championing of modern education, inclusive of science, was thus far more sensible and balanced than the craze for things English that was sweeping through Bengal. Moreover, as has already been shown, his advocacy of English was neither at the cost nor to the exclusion of native Bengali. Actually, Ram Mohan Roy did much to promote the language. He was not just the pioneer of Bengali journalism, he also wrote the first grammar of modern Bengali (Tagore 1983, 30-31). In addition, he started at his own expense, a Vedantic college to impart traditional scriptural learning (Crawford 1984, 111), merely two years after his famous letter to Lord Amherst. Was this a reversal of his earlier position in favour of English education? Collet sees this move as a further illustration of Ram Mohan Roy's belief in Vedanta as a bridge of continuity between old Hinduism and New Hinduism, between 'Hindu Polytheism' and 'Hindu Theism' (1962, 191). He also founded an Anglo-Hindu school in which Bengali would be the medium of instruction, even to teach science subjects (Tagore 1983, 29). David Hare and William Adam assisted in its management, Lal Behari Dey was one of its teachers and Maharshi Debendranath Tagore, a student of this school (Reena Chatterjee 1983, 69-73).

All this shows that Ram Mohan Roy was not a simple-minded Anglicist as some have supposed him to be or an intellectual 'pigmy', as Gandhi was mistakenly accused of calling him[15]; instead, he was not only a pioneer of vernacular education and journalism, but one of the founders of the modern Bengali language. In addition, he retained his links to traditional knowledge by translating and making available to the masses the Vedantic texts. Finally, as a qualified proponent of Western learning, he showed that he was capable of combining and reconciling tradition and modernity, Indian and Western thought in the most challenging and illuminating manner.

CONCLUSION

While Ram Mohan Roy was sagacious and perceptive about many aspects of the Indo-Western encounter, recent criticism has shown that there are several doubtful and problematic positions that Ram Mohan Roy assumed including the encouragement of the colonisation of India by European settlers and his advocacy of the Zamindari system in his depositions before the Crown Council. My intention has been only to present Ram Mohan Roy's as a remarkably prescient and enabling response to colonialism, not to suggest that it was perfect in all areas. I have tried to argue that he can be constructed as a pioneering figure in the history of our resistance to colonialism, especially in that he tried to understand the West on its own terms and to preserve what was best in his own society even as he tried to reform both. Furthermore, his life has a continuing heuristic value to us and to others in the postcolonial world who are continuing the struggle against intellectual imperialism. Clearly, reasoned and persistent engagement, countering knowledge with knowledge, rather than with irrational fanaticism, is the way even today.

Ultimately, though, it will not do to regard Ram Mohan Roy from the viewpoint of Indian interests alone. What makes him an outstanding figure of the eighteenth century and early nineteenth century was his breadth of vision. It will not be an exaggeration to say that Ram Mohan Roy was one of the few intellectuals of his time to be worried about the human condition itself and about the future of the human race. While in England he sent a representation to the French Foreign Minister, which is now an important document. In it he said:

> It is now generally admitted that not religion only but unbiased commonsense as well as the accurate deduction that all mankind are one great family of which the numerous nations and tribes existing are only various branches. (*Selected Works* 1977, 317)

It is in this letter that he proposes a 'Congress composed of an equal number from the Parliament of each country' to solve political differences arising between them. This was nearly a hundred years before the formation of the League of Nations. Ram Mohan Roy was far ahead of his time. It is no wonder then that almost any modern social, political, religious, or economic movement in India can trace its origin to him. Along with other prominent figures like Dwarkanath Tagore, he was among the early Indian cosmopolitans in modern times.

He was also probably the first Brahmin and prominent Indian of modern times to 'cross the black water' against the prevailing prejudices of the times. He went to England in 1831 as a representative of the Moghul Emperor to plead the latter's cause with the Crown and Parliament. He never returned to his native land but died of meningitis in Bristol in 1833, where he was buried. Ten years later, Dwarkanath Tagore, one of his followers, built a mausoleum for him in the Arnos Vale Cemetery in Southern Bristol. His epitaph bears recollection and repetition:

> Beneath this stone rest the remains of Raja Rammohan Roy Bahadur, a conscientious and steadfast believer in the unity of Godhead, he consecrated his life with entire devotion to the worship of the Divine Spirit alone.

To great natural talents, he united through mastery of many languages and distinguished himself as one of the greatest scholars of his day. His unwearied labour to promote the social, moral and physical condition of the people of India, his earnest endeavours to suppress idolatry and the rite of suttie and his constant zealous advocacy of whatever tended to advance the glory of God and the welfare of man live in the grateful remembrance of his countrymen.[16]

As Kotnala says, 'he dared to break the spell which the sea had laid on the Hindu mind for ages' (1975, 140). In his life and death he literally bridged the two continents and cultures.

As one of the founders of modern India, it is no surprise that he coined the term 'Hindooism,' introducing it into the English language in 1818 (ibid.). Though he is best remembered for his campaign against the barbaric practice of sati or forced immolation of widows on their deceased husbands' funeral pyre, he also questioned many other superstitions and oppressive traditions, pushing Indian society to new frontiers in almost every sphere of life. Yet, he never compromised his own identity; in many ways he remained quintessentially Indian. Certainly his death as Crawford reports it, puts him in touch with a very ancient tradition whose vital springs he tried to rejuvenate: 'With his last breath Ram Mohan Roy uttered the imperishable sound – Om!' (170). Ram Mohan Roy was thus one of the makers not just of modern India but of the modern world. Moreover, he may be regarded as the foremost representative of the Indian enlightenment.

I began this paper by examining Ram Mohan Roy's response to the challenge of the West. Now, at the end of the paper, I shall extend this idea to his response to the challenge of life itself. This is to be expected in the kind of 'biography' I am presenting; the significance of the exemplar must be pushed as far as possible so as to yield the widest possible application. We must examine if he can be seen as a type of *satpurusha*, one who wins not small battles or skirmishes, but triumphs in the very game of life itself. In other words, Ram Mohan Roy is not only a prototype of how an Indian can respond intelligently to the overt material superiority of the West, but also how one might make a success of life, living sanely, wholly and richly.

It remains for me to speculate upon those factors which went into the making of such a life. What enables Ram Mohan Roy to survive, even succeed, where many others end in bitter disappointment and failure? Perhaps, his birth and parentage were of some importance. Ram Mohan Roy was born into a *kulin* (high caste) Brahmin family; perhaps, he did not have a sense of inferiority to begin with. Then, his education was most definitely significant. Unlike the others who lost their way, Ram Mohan Roy had a solid foundation in his own traditions. No one could be more 'Indian' than he was when he reached adulthood. Moreover, his education showed familiarity with multiple traditions; he was well-versed in both the Islamic and the Hindu traditions of learning, which constituted the twin streams of Indian heritage at that time. To this he added the third stream of English education and Western learning, thereby equipping himself better than the best of his peers, whether Indian or Western. Thirdly, he was fairly prosperous. This allowed him to rub shoulders with members of both Indian and British high society as their equals. His material position also released him from working to earn his living, freeing him to devote his tremendous energies to more worthwhile pursuits. Ram Mohan Roy used all these factors to develop himself to the fullest. His was a penetrating and profound mind, always going to the source of things, never content with superficialities.

His talents were prodigious – he knew, in varying degrees, ten languages – and so was his capacity for work. How is his extraordinary life to be explained ultimately?[17] Genius? Chance? Or, simply, historical circumstance? Ram Mohan Roy was certainly a very gifted individual, one of those who seem to be born with more than a normal share of greatness. But we are not really concerned with cracking the riddle of his genius so much as in understanding how he managed to respond with such confidence and self-assurance to the challenge of the West. Yes, all the above mentioned factors helped, but I think the key to it all is somewhat mystical and in that sense very Indian – I think it is a deep understanding of oneself that is the source of confidence. As J. Krishnamurti says:

> What is it that gives dignity to man? Self-knowledge – the knowledge of what you are? The follower is the greatest curse. (quoted in Jayakar 1987, 151)

From this standpoint, Ram Mohan Roy, having achieved his own svaraj, tried to work for the svaraj of his countrymen and women too.

WORKS CITED

Bonnett, Alastair. 2004. *The Idea of the West: Culture, Politics and History.* Houndmills, Basingstoke, Hampshire; New York: Palgrave Macmillan.

Buruma, Ian and Avishai Margalit. 2004. *Occidentalism: A Short History of Anti-Westernism.* London: Atlantic.

Carey, William. 1792. *An Enquiry into the Obligations of Christians, To Use Means for the Conversion of the Heathens. In which the Religious State of the Different Nations of the World, The Success of Former Undertakings and the Practicability of further Undertakings, are Considered.* Leicester: Ann Ireland.

Carpenter, Mary. 1976. *The Last Days in England of the Rajah Rammohan Roy.* Swapna Majumdar. Ed. Calcutta: Riddhi.

Chatterjee, Kalyan K. 1976. *English Education in India: Issues and Opinions.* Delhi: Macmillan.

Chatterjee, Ramananda. 1972. *Rammohan Roy and Modern India.* 1918; Rpt. Calcutta: Sadharan Brahmo Samaj.

Chatterjee, Reena. 1983. *Impact of Raja Rammohan Roy on Education in India.* New Delhi: S. Chand.

Collet, Sophia Dobson. 1962. *The Life and Letters of Raja Rammohan Roy.* Dilip Kumar Biswas and Prabhat Chundra Ganguly. Eds. 1900; Reprint. Calcutta: Sadharan Brahmo Samaj.

Crawford, Cromwell S. 1984. *Ram Mohan Roy: His Era and Ethics.* New Delhi: Arnold-Heinemann.

Das, Sisir Kumar, Ed. 1996. *The English Writings of Rabindranath Tagore.* Volume II. New Delhi: Sahitya Akademi.

Drew, John. 1986. *India and the Romantic Imagination*. Delhi: Oxford University Press.
Dharmpal. 1983. *The Beautiful Tree*. New Delhi: Bibla Impex.
Edwards, Thomas. 1884. *Henry Derozio, the Eurasian, Poet, Teacher and Journalist*, Calcutta: W. Newman and Co.
Eliot, T. S. 1968. *Four Quartets*. New York: Mariner Books.
Fanon, Franz. 1976. *The Wretched of the Earth*. Harmonsworth: Penguin.
Gandhi, Mohandas Karamchand. 1999. *The Collected Works of Mahatma Gandhi*. Electronic book. 98 vols. New Delhi: Publications Division Government of India.
Jayakar, Paul. 1987. *J. Krishnamurti: A Biography*. New Delhi: Penguin.
Joshi, V.C. 1975. Ed. *Rammohan Roy and the Process of Modernisation in India*. Delhi: Vikas.
Kearns, Cleo Mcnelly. 1987. *T.S. Eliot and Indic Traditions*. Cambridge: CambridgeUniversity Press.
King, Thomas. 2003. *The Truth About Stories: A Native Narrative*. Minneapolis: University of Minnesota Press.
Kopf, David. 1969. *British Orientalism and the Bengal Renaissance: The Dynamics of Indian Modernisation, 1773-1835*. Berkeley: University of California Press.
Kotnala, M.C. 1975. *Raja Rammohan Roy and the Indian Awakening*. New Delhi: Gitanjali Prakashan.
Lal, Vinay. 2003. *The History of History: Politics and Scholarship in Modern India*. New Delhi: Oxford University Press.
Majumdar, J.K., 1983. Ed. *Raja Rammohan Roy and Progressive Movements in India*. Volume I 1941; rpt. Calcutta: Brahmo Mission Press.
Martin, Wallace. 1986. *Recent Theories of Narrative*. Ithaca, New York: Cornell University Press.
Nag, Mamuna. 1972. *Raja Rammohan Roy*. Delhi: Orient Paperbacks.
Paranjape, Makarand. 2009. *Altered destinations: Self, Society and Nation in India*. London: Anthem Press.
_____. 1993. *Decolonisation and Development: Hind Svaraj Revisioned*. New Delhi: Sage Publications.
Poddar, Arabinda. 1970. *The Renaissance in Bengal: Quests and Confrontations 1800-1860*. Shimla: Indian Institute of Advanced Study.

Ranade, Ramabai. 1963. *Ranade: His Wife's Reminiscences*. Tran. Kusumvati Deshpande. Delhi: Publications Divisions.

Roy, Raja Rammohan. 1977. *Selected Works*. New Delhi: Publications Division.

———. 1982. *The English Works of Raja Rammohan Roy*. J.C. Ghose. Ed. 4 Vols. 1906; Rpt. Delhi: Cosmo Publications.

Said, Edward. 1978. *Orientalism*. London: Routledge and Kegan Paul.

Salmond, Noel A. 2004. *Hindu Iconoclasts: Ram Mohan Roy, Dayananda Sarasvati and Nineteenth-century Polemics against Idolatry*. Waterloo, Ont: Wilfrid Laurier University Press.

Sarkar, Sushobhan. 1970. *Bengal Renaissance and Other Essay*. New Delhi: People's Publishing House.

Schwab, Raymond. 1984. *The Oriental Renaissance: Europe's Rediscovery of India and the East 1600–1880*. 1950. Trans. Vicor Reinking and Gene Patterson-Black. New York: Columbia UP.

Sen, S.P. 1979. Ed. *Social and Religious Reform Movements in the Nineteenth and Twentieth Centuries*. Calcutta: Institute of Historical Studies.

Sharp, H. 1965. Ed. *Selections from Educational Records. Part I 1781–1839*. 1920; Rpt. Delhi: National Archives of India.

Tagore, Saumyendranath. 1983. *Raja Rammohan Roy*. New Delhi: Sahitya Academy.

Urmson, J.O. 1975. Ed. *The Concise Encyclopedia of Western Philosophy and Philosophers*. 1960: rpt. London: Hutchinson.

Viswanathan, Gauri. 1989. *Masks of Conquest: Literary Study and British Rule in India*. New York: Columbia University Press.

White, Hayden. 1978. *Tropics of Discourse. Essays in Cultural Criticism*. Baltimore: Johns Hopkins University Press.

Zastoupil, Lynn. 2010. *Ram Mohan Roy and the Making of Victorian Britain*. New York, New York: Palgrave Macmillan.

3
'EAST INDIAN' COSMOPOLITANISM: HENRY DEROZIO'S *THE FAKEER OF JUNGHEERA* AND THE BIRTH OF INDIAN MODERNITY

3.1 INTRODUCTION

Henry Vivian Louis Derozio (1809–1831) was born more than thirty-five years after Ram Mohan Roy, but died very young, a couple of years before the latter. Derozio was Eurasian or Anglo-Indian, of mixed descent; his father was a native Indian of Indo-Portuguese ancestry and his mother's antecedents are not clearly identified.[1] Though his surname, Derozio, which his first biographer Thomas Edwards claims was originally DeRozario (1884, 2), indicates a Catholic past, his parents were Protestants, with their baptismal records in St. John's Church in Calcutta.[2] His father worked in the trading firm of J. Scott and Company and was fairly prosperous. The family home on Lower Circular Road, was a spacious colonial bungalow in a large compound, with its own tank. Derozio's brief, but illustrious life is crucial to the narrative of making India. Though he lived for less than twenty-two years, his accomplishments are astounding: he was an influential teacher, a leading poet and one of the pioneering Indian English journalists of his time. He owned and edited a newspaper called *The East Indian*, where he wrote and commented extensively on contemporary issues. He was, without question, one of the early participants, even creators of a modern public culture in India.

In this chapter I wish to reassess the legacy of Derozio through an extended interpretation of *The Fakeer of Jungheera* (1828), his 2050 line poem, published when he was barely nineteen.[3] I propose to look at the style, structure, idiom, as well as the content of the poem to show how it represents a special moment in early colonial India. What makes this poem unique, even extraordinary, is that it is the first long poem written by any Indian in the English language. More remarkably, it is also an intriguing conjuncture of a complex set of relations that went into the making of modern India: British colonialism and local resistance, the English language in India and Indian vernaculars, native and European miscegenation, Christian missionaries and Hindu reform, proto-nationalism and the imagining of India, gender and patriarchal norms, Hindu-Muslim relations, *sati* and colonial power, to name a few. Though the poem is justifiably famous, it has hardly received the attention that it deserves.

Our purpose here, however, extends beyond a reading of *The Fakeer of Jungheera*. It is to argue that the conventional ways in which Derozio is understood – as a pioneer of Indian modernity and a proto-nationalist – are actually insufficient if not misleading. They throw, as it were, a blanket over not only his singular career, but over the whole phenomenon of what we can call 'East Indian cosmopolitanism.' Though evanescent in the shifting identity politics of its time, this category, short-lived like Derozio himself, was actually a significant forerunner to more stable models of emerging Indian identity such as the varieties of liberal, anti-colonial nationalism which became more fully instantiated in the later part of the nineteenth century. East Indian cosmopolitanism, thus, is one of those 'lost' modes of being which were replaced and overwritten by others. By recovering them, we add a vital component to our knowledge of how colonialism in its early days shaped a new society and consciousness in India.

3.2 THE FAKEER OF JUNGHEERA

The Fakeer of Jungheera (henceforth referred to as *FJ*) is the longest and most challenging of Derozio's poetic works. Given that neither a single work, nor a poet's entire oeuvre, may be read in isolation from a tradition or history of reading, it is noteworthy that for a poem like *FJ*, we lack such a narrative. As Rosinka Chaudhuri, Derozio's definitive editor, observes, 'the nineteenth-century idiom in which much of Derozio's verse is written may be compared to the Sanskrit in its often remote English literariness' (2008, xxii). Whether the comparison with classical Sanskrit is apt or not, Derozio's remoteness from our tastes is obvious. Chaudhuri claims that contemporary literary sensibility, shaped as it is by 'the Romantic turn to inwardness and the Modernist turn to the quotidian' tends to look at poems in isolation, apart from 'the political, cultural and aesthetic values' of their time; the result is that 'Derozio's poems ... remain remote and unresponsive' (xxiii). Perhaps, this is one reason why *FJ*, though so important, is rarely read, let alone taught. Even those who are considered experts on Derozio appear to have given it wide berth. This despite the fact that most critics find it a poem of crucial importance. As Milinda Banerjee puts it:

> *The Fakeer of Jungheera* is universally acknowledged to be Derozio's most important literary work. In fact, it would not be an exaggeration to say that Derozio's reputation as a poet largely rests on this work. What is often neglected is the political and chronological import of this poem. In his most famous creation, Derozio, to articulate his nationalism and social message, harks back to the world of the Fakir rebellion, in other words, to the early modern oecumene of lower-class empowerment.... *Jungheera* is the missing piece in our puzzle, the element which ties up all the threads we had been pursuing so far, the connection between guru Derozio, the early modern Indic Perso-Islamic oecumene and lower-class militancy on the one hand and Western-modern Derozio, the nineteenth

century Bengal Renaissance and modern Indian nationalism on the other. (2009, 71-72)

Regardless of such lofty claims, the paradox remains that there is not a single detailed analysis of the poem, not even in Banerjee's essay cited above.

It would seem that we simply don't know *how* to read it as yet – or haven't *really* tried. Indeed, in the entire history of Indian English criticism, it is difficult to find more than a few paragraphs here and there on this poem. The fact is that *FJ* is not just unprecedented in its length, scope, prosodic virtuosity and subject matter, but it is also without a suitable successor. It comes across as a sort of one-off marvel, along with other such singular literary sports as Dean Mohamet's *Travels* (1794), purportedly the first Indian English published book and Bankim's unfinished debutant romance, also supposedly the first Indian English novel, *Rajmohan's Wife* (1864).

Not only is *FJ* the first Indian English long poem, it is also an impressive achievement for a poet not yet twenty. Published in 1828, a year after Henry Derozio's first volume, *Poems*, it consists of two cantos of 1010 and 1040 lines respectively, composed mostly in couplets of rhyming iambic tetrameter, but also in a variety of other metres to suit the occasion. It comes many decades before other long poems that Indians have written in English, including *Savitri* by Sri Aurobindo, which at nearly 24,000 lines and one of the longest in the language, which its author continued to work on till close to his death in 1950. Though Indian English poetry is nearly two hundred years old, very few Indians have written successful long poems. In the modern period, especially, we find few long poems. Even R. Parthasarathy's *Rough Passage* or Vikram Seth's *The Golden Gate* really consist of a series of interconnected short poems. Closer to Derozio's own time, Behram Malabari's quaint long poems, too, lack the poetic punch that *FJ* has.

The long poem poses special challenges to any poet, but especially to a non-native writer of English. Traditionally, the epic, with its long history and complex literary conventions, has been considered the highest poetic genre. Apart from *Savitri*, there are few other well-known or recognised epics by Indians in English. While K. R. Srinivasa Iyengar did write in the epic mode, the verse is too prosaic to really have the feel or heft of significant poetry. This is also true of other more obscure attempts. A long poem not only requires great poetic gifts so that the verse can be sustained over enormous lengths, but it also requires a loftiness of subject and ambition. Derozio's *FJ*, though uneven, does show that he had the poetic gifts with the inspiration to attempt a long poem even, indeed, the requisite aspiration. While the poem, arguably, lacks a subject that is commensurate with its ambition. While its execution may be imperfect, what is important to establish is the substantial achievement that it actually embodies. Not the least of these is an exceptional poetic talent that displays itself in innovative rhymes, soaring verses, inspiring lines including consistent erudition.

3.3 THE PLOT OR ACTION

One of the main difficulties with *FJ* is its plot, which is not only far-fetched, but full of diversions and miscellaneous elements. As its earliest reviewers also noticed, it cannot therefore be considered an unqualified success. Of course, among the deficiencies pointed out, we may discount some, such as 'defective rhymes' that the long review in *India Gazette* (Chaudhuri 2008, 400) points out. In fact, Derozio's rhymes are much more 'modern' in their variety and vivacity; far from being defective, they may actually constitute one of his strengths. But the same review also observes, quite perceptively, that 'the story is not entirely to our taste: the transition of a beautiful and modest widow from the funeral pile which had all but blazed around herself and her husband's corpse, to the arms of a stalwart swarthy Dacoit, appears rather violent. Neither were we quite prepared to find in the compass of six lines ... 'the meek Fakeer' ... at once bristling into "a bloody man,/The chieftain of a robber clan"' (ibid.). What the reviewer highlights are the sudden shifts in character, motivation and plot which render the narrative implausible.

To appreciate this more fully, we need to understand what actually comprises the 'action' of the poem. Indeed, to put it bluntly, *FJ* consists of a rather thin and far-fetched plot-line embellished by many diversions. Perhaps, this is one reason, accordingly to modernist canons of poetic perfection, it does not quite measure up, therefore is seldom taught in classes. The poem is made up essentially of two kinds of poetic passages. One of these consists of narrative verse that furthers the plot; the other of various kinds of passages and exercises meant to offer delight and relief. In a fundamental sense, then, the main story-line does not hold the poem together; *FJ*, more properly, consists of a patchwork of compositions of different sorts, many of which are not only self-contained, but quite independent of the main plot. It is, thus, very much an implausible tour-de-force composed of a melange of styles, ideas, plot-lines with devices. Yet together, though impressive and dramatic, do not quite amount to a coherent or deeply moving literary accomplishment.

3.4 THE PREFATORY SONNET AND DEROZIO'S 'ORIENTALISM'

A good example of such stand-alone elements is the famous sonnet which prefaces the poem. In this fine composition, the poet, somewhat self-consciously, reflects on his own purpose and possibilities as a poet. He speaks of the fall of India, invoking the image of an idealised past when India was 'worshipped as a deity' with a 'a beauteous halo' circling her brow (quoted in Chaudhuri 2008, 173)[4]. In this image, Derozio is not only drawing on Orientalist material on the golden past of India, but also anticipating the deification of India by Bankim in *Anandamath* much later. The second movement of the octave laments the fall of India, 'grovelling in the lowly dust' (ibid.). Given this fall, the minstrel has nothing to sing of except the tale of the country's misery. The octave thus sets up the task for the present poet, which he spells out in the sestet. In an attempt to redress his country's inability to inspire anything but sad songs, the poet promises to 'dive into the depths of time' to 'bring from out the ages that have rolled/A few small fragments of those wrecks sublime/

Which human eyes may never more behold' (ibid.). In return, all he wishes from his 'fallen country,' 'one kind wish' (ibid.). The last line is quite poignant, if not prophetic. The celebration of Derozio's bicentenary, as other such earlier celebrations, with many a kind wish for the poet would imply a fulfilment, at least in part, of the poet's yearning for acceptance from his countrymen and women.

The fate of *FJ* is that this sonnet, which was supplied the title 'To India – My Native Land'[5] by a later editor, has been excerpted, anthologised and widely taught in schools in India, while the long poem it prefaces is entirely forgotten or neglected. Nevertheless, a moot question remains: is the agenda that the poet sets out for himself or even the explanation of his intentions at the start of his labours *sati*sfied or fulfilled by *FJ*? The story is not a well-known historical or mythological one, neither is it from the so-called glorious past of India. Rather, it is set in much more recent times, to be precise, during the reign of Shah Shuja (1639–1660), when the latter made Rajmahal in northern Jharkhand his capital, less than 150 years before Derozio's own times. What is more, as Bannerjee has argued, Derozio was superimposing upon this tale aspects of the *Pagolpanthi Bidroho* (literally, 'rebellion of the followers of madness') in Eastern Bengal, a rebellion of Sufi *fakirs* or renouncers with the Hindu-Muslim peasantry, against the colonial state (2009, 71). Yet, despite attempts to lend it ideological gravitas, the story is nothing if not a sad and melodramatic saga. Ironically, then, Derozio ends up casting himself in the very same mould as those minstrels who merely lament the 'sad story' of their country's plight. If, as I shall try to show at greater length later, Nuleeni's story can be read as a political allegory for the story of India herself, all we see is thwarted desire and death. Instead of breaking out from the stereotype as he promises to, Derozio only reinforces it. Similarly, he is unable to offer an idea, metaphor, model, or paradigm of the India of the future. It is for this reason that I would argue that attempts to consider him a proto-nationalist or a pioneer of modernity are somewhat farfetched. *FJ* embodies not so much a plan of action or even a prophecy for the future as *Anandamath* later does; instead, it reflects the fragmentary state of early mixed-race elites, still groping to articulate a viable alternative to colonialism. It is this consciousness that I call 'East Indian cosmopolitanism', which I propose to elaborate later.

3.5 CANTO I

Just as the opening sonnet can be read independently of the main story of the poem, so can the italicised moral with which Canto First opens:

> Affections are not made for merchandise. –
> What will ye give in barter for the heart?
> Has this world wealth enough to buy the store
> Of hopes and feelings, which are linked for ever
> With Woman's soul? (174)

These lines containing a sentimentalised generalisation about the nature of woman's soul, somewhat typical of the cult of English sensibility of that time, are the first among many which suggest that love, especially in a woman, is irrational, impractical and eventually fatal. It is, in other words, nothing short of a sort of disease, especially in that it appears to go contrary to interests of class and capital, which were dominant in both capitalism and colonialism. Other poems of Derozio, including 'Ada', also play on such a notion. A woman in love, according to such a portrayal, will behave in a manner that contradicts her class and economic self-interests and, eventually, pay the heavy 'price' of her life for her transgression. Love is construed, thus, not only as a mystic force that escapes the regime of capital, but which, ultimately must succumb and sacrifice itself to the latter. It is the story of the spiritual being defeated by the material, of the female by the male, of the weak by the strong – but somehow, in its own defeat, love emerges burnished and effulgent in its melancholic, even tragic end.

With such an ominous beginning, the poem quickly shifts gears in Section 1, to the vocation of the young poet. There is an enchanting world of nature in which our Eastern bard lives, sought to be made attractive to Western readers more acquainted with the more conventional beauties of nature known in cooler climes. This section is remarkable for its celebration of the Indian landscape, which though semi-tropical, is lush and sunny. Derozio harks back, perhaps unconsciously, to Kalidasa and the great tradition of Sanskrit poetry in which the flora, fauna and landscape of India were celebrated. But making this landscape fit for English poetry is, in effect, creating a new aesthetic space. It is such an aesthetic move that is, perhaps, more 'political' than the more overt political action that Derozio's admirers seek in his work. This, perhaps, is the most 'usable' aspect of his work. What follows is the first of the many tributes to the sun, which emerges almost as the tutelary deity of the poem:

> The sun is like a golden urn
> Where floods of light for ever burn,
> And fall like blessings fast on earth,
> Bringing its beauties brightly forth. (174)

Later, the 'Hymn to the Sun' is another magnificent tribute. Quite unlike later colonial descriptions of the maddening heat of India, Derozio's notion of the Indian sun is quite mild and more pleasant. While there is a sort of precedent in William Jones 'Hymn to Surya,' Derozio's sun is no mythological abstraction, but a very real, Eastern phenomenon that actually affects the climate and vegetation of the land.

What we notice in these lines is also a curious hybridity which characterises the style and sensibility of the entire poem. While the portrayal and idea of the young and hedonistic poet is derived from the conventions of Western poetry, especially the Romantic idea of the poetic genius, the setting is perforce Indian. Like other Romantic poets, Derozio is a careful observer and worshipper of nature, in this case, the bounties of the Indian, sub-tropical environment, teeming with animal and vegetal life. At the same time, Derozio is also drawing on Persian ideas of the '*shair*,' or the poet, which was a living tradition in India, but was also entering English for the first time through translations by Orientalists. The idea of the *shair* proclaims itself in the title of the very next book of poems written by an Indian in English and the first by a native Bengali, Kashiprasad Ghose's *The Shair and Other Poems* (1830). Ghose was, in a sense and not surprisingly, a product of Presidency College and a sort of Derozian himself. Yet, to revert to my point about the non-essential elements, this section of *FJ*, too, can be read independently of the rest of the poem and, indeed, has little to do with the main narrative.

Section 2 of the first canto begins with a description of the setting of the sun but ends with the alarming disclosure that sets the plot into motion: 'Fore ere the evening shadows fly,/ Devoted woman here must die' (175). The compression and dire portent of the couple are brilliantly chilling after the languorous and expansive passages celebrating the poet's vocation and Indian landscapes.

The next section shifts to the craggy rocks of Jungheera, an island in the middle of the Ganges near Monghyr, which was known to British travellers as being picturesque. Derozio tells us in his notes that he lived in the vicinity for the three years (Chaudhuri 2008, 228) he spent with his maternal uncle, who was an indigo planter. Here Derozio acquaints us with his protagonist, who is first described as 'holy man' more hallowed not just than mortal and impure eye, but even the moonlight. The Fakeer is purer than the 'brightest angel's blissful dreams' (ibid.). But before the section ends, we are suddenly told that this same holy man may actually be the cause of 'deeds of death,' his 'blood stained hands' responsible not only for 'hamlet burned,' 'plundered swain,/The peasant forced his home to flee' but also of 'princely maiden's treachery,/Her youthful lord's untimely fall – /And he, the demon – cause of it all!' (ibid.). Such an utter and unconvincing reversal is typical rather than unusual in the poem. With almost equal poetic gusto, the poet seems paint a portrait, then undo it entirely.

Here we have in a few lines the gist of the story – Nuleeni, of noble birth, in love with a robber-chieftain, whose main disguise is that of a Fakeer or holy man. Though the poem never quite tells us this part of the story in full, he is somehow to blame for Nuleeni's husband's 'untimely' death. When the poem opens, Nuleeni is preparing for the rite of *sati* or concremation. Rather than depict the rite as barbaric or horrific, Derozio produces some of the most moving passages in the first canto on his heroine's preparation for self-immolation. Several sections describe not only her stately progress to the pyre, but also her inner conflict. On the one hand her decision is 'a heroine's choice' (182) and in her song, she contemplates the greater joy that awaits her as a *sati* (the true one) when she will attain 'The Glorious kingdom of our God!' (187); on the other hand, her thoughts also wing their way to her lover, rather than her dead husband and the 'blissful hours/That flew on odorous wings in those bright bowers/ Where erst she met him!' (183). The sections leading up to her swift rescue effected in a few lines in Section XXII, are interspersed with several other 'pull outs' such as the Chorus of Women (178-179), the Chorus of Brahmuns (179-180), the speech of The Chief Brahmun (180), Nuleeni's own near swan-song, which is a lengthy poetic peroration on the verge of her mounting the pyre (185-187), in addition to the 'Hymn to the Sun' (188-190). In fact, even after her rescue, there follows, almost Bollywood-like, a 'Song' (Section XXIV; 192-193) in which the victorious the bandits celebrate their 'treasure won' (192). The lovers then have lengthy poetic parlays (194-198), sighing to each other in picturesque settings, before finally retiring to 'their rocky home' in the concluding section of the first canto.

3.6 CANTO II

Canto 'Second' also starts with an italicised moral similar to the one in the first. This time, the canker in a rose, bright lightening and young love are likened – they are beautiful, yet they are blighted. If the sun is the presiding god over the first canto, it is the moon that dominates now, especially the brief moments of honeymoon-like bliss, that the lovers enjoy in each other's arms in the bandit's hilly fastness. The opening sections, which begin at night, show a huge party in progress at Prince Shuja's palace in Rajmahal, complete with a *nautch*. The dancer is Kashmiri and sings a lay about her native land, almost like an item girl in a Hindi movie on the one hand, but so like a Derozian who celebrates her place of birth, on the other. This is followed by another performance in which the court minstrel entertains the audience with 'The Legend of Shushan' (204–210). The latter, incidentally, is an example of the Orientalism that Chaudhuri is at pains to show in her earlier work, *Gentlemen Poets in Colonial Bengal* (2002), as being constitutive of early Indian English verse. Derozio draws on the story-cycle *Vetal Panchavimshati*, which had become recently available in English translation. In his learned footnote, the poet speaks of one of the students of Hindu College bringing him a translation of the Betal Puncheesa (Chaudhuri 2008, 235). Shushan, of course, is *smashan,* the cremation ground, which is the setting of the story: 'I thought of writing a ballad, the subject of which should be strictly India' (ibid.) says Derozio. Needless to say, this whole section is totally extraneous to the main plot of Nuleeni and her *fakeer*/bandit-lover.

Interestingly, this is the only section of the poem in which Derozio actually presents to his readers 'a few small fragments of those wrecks sublime' 'from out the ages that have rolled' as he promised in his prefatory sonnet. At first this digression seems as dispensable as the others that I have already mentioned, a ballad that can be taken out of the poem and read as if it were an independent composition. Yet, a careful reading shows that it may be seen as a counter-narrative to the main story in its depiction of love's progress, in union and happiness rather than loss and death. Here, the Prince Jogindra, mourning for his dead beloved Radhika, inhabits the ghoulish *smashan* for three days and nights. At the behest of a *sannyasi,* he assays to win back his dead lady-love by keeping vigil over her lifeless body. If he can emerge triumphant in his trials, the *sannyasi* tells him, he will have her revived. On the third day, he is accosted by an exquisitely beautiful temptress-sprite who beseeches him to accept her (instead of the dead Radhika). After a moment's hesitation, however, he repudiates the ghostly seductress, thus demonstrating his fidelity to his dead wife. The very next moment, the 'dark Shushan is a palace bright' and Jogindra sits high on a 'throne of azure and gold' with his bride seated by his side, leaning on his arm. Derozio concludes,

> O! Love is strong and its hopes 'twill build
>   Where nothing beside would dare;
> O! Love is bright and its beams will gild
>   The desert dark and bare. (210)

Love, in other words, will triumph over death.

In the minstrel's song at Prince Shuja's court, then, we see something quite different from what actually happens in the more corrupt, fallen time in which Nuleeni's tragedy is enacted. Here, youth and love emerge triumphant, in the face of all odds. They even overcome death. Jogindra keeps his faith, resisting the seductions and blandishments of an ethereal temptress, thereby winning his dead bride back. In contrast, Nuleeni is almost sacrificed at her dead husband's burning pyre and, if we jump to the end of the story, will meet an end not too dissimilar on the battlefield where her dead lover, the bandit chief, lies. I shall return to this important inner commentary and counterpoint to the main story later, when I discuss how the poem depicts *sati*.

But, to return to the story in canto two, at the end of the carousing, Nuleeni's father cuts through the throng to ask Shuja to avenge his daughter's dishonour and kidnapping. Nowhere does Derozio seem to be aware of the incongruity of the request or indeed the oddness of the inter-religious dimensions of his story. *Sati* was a rite for Hindu widows. Not only is Nuleeni's abductor-rescuer and lover a Muslim, so are Prince Shuja and his "Moslem chivalry" (212). A Hindu father's appeal to a Muslim ruler to avenge his daughter's failure to commit *sati* is, to say the least, rather improbable, if not impossible. But what is even stranger is that this is narrated without any awareness or acknowledgement of the dynamics of differing faiths or the ensuing politics of such affiliations. Chaudhuri has written about the anti-Muslim rhetoric in Derozio's poems, but there seems little evidence of it his longest and most ambitious composition. Though the story affords ample opportunities to express prejudice against either Hindu 'superstition' or Muslim 'barbarism,' Derozio refrains from both. Even so, his refusal to touch upon the inter-religious tensions inherent in his story suggests that his main purpose was not so much to be realistic as amusing to his audience, which was at that time chiefly British and Eurasian. To a Western(ised) readership, the exoticism of the poem would only be complicated if not dimmed by the inter-religious confusion.

If *sati* was the dreaded subject of the first canto, war seems to the dire outcome of the second. After their brief honeymoon, young Nuleeni and her 'Robber-love' must, alas, part. Disregarding Nuleeni's request not to leave her side, the bandit seeks 'but one hour' away from her for his last escapade, after which he promises that he will 'quit for ever and be all thine own' (215), allowing another leader to lead the band. Of course, the Fakeer does not tell her that he goes to fight her father and Prince Shuja's troops, but claims that 'A daring conquest my band achieve' (215), 'the spoil before us,' (218) that he must 'stretch to grasp' (ibid.).

'Farewell!' – with that 'melancholy word' (218) the Fakeer leaves Nuleeni, rowing across the river from his 'rocky hold' (219). The battle cry of the Muslim chivalry sounds 'The dreadful herald of madness and war' (220). As the fierce battle rages, Derozio almost turns into a critic of war, portraying its senseless violence and waste. A warrior dies 'with burning, slakeless, maddening thirst' (222) drinking the blood of a 'fallen comrade' lying by his side (223). 'A father hung o'er his perishing child/Whose breath heaved thick and whose gaze was wild' (ibid.). It seems at first as if the bandit and his band will get the better of their adversaries:

> The royal ranks are weak they find,
> They waver like mountain reeds in the wind –
> And though each steps where his comrade fell
> The work of destruction prospers well!
> Now Robber-chief! Once more, once more
> And the field is thine and the triumph o'er! (222)

But then Nuleeni's 'father returns on the robber-band' 'Like a comet fierce with floating mane,' 'Still madly directs the madder storm'; 'sabres clash' and 'lances ring' (223). At last, 'Behold he falls – the curse of the land!' (224). The man whose 'own right arm had strewed the plain,' is felled by 'An unseen hand with a glittering lance' (224).

As the poem comes to an end, Nuleeni descends on the battlefield to look for her lover:

> She bends her form, beholds, stands fixed and mute:
> Is it a dream, or does the night deceive ? –
> She looks again – she trembles – must believe.
> 'Tis he – that robber – not victorious now –
> The cold death-damp descending on his brow,
> The filmy curtain gathering o'er his eye
> But vainly fixed – (235)

When morning dawns the peasant sees 'Steed and rider slain' but what arrests his gaze is Nuleeni's form 'fondly ivying round' her lover, dead (227).

In the end, it is almost as if Nuleeni commits *sati* twice, the first time unsuccessfully with her dead husband in the traditional manner, the second time in more successful if less fiery fashion sanctioned by the conventions of Western romanticism. In either case, the outcome is the same: thwarted or brief fulfilment, the victory of Thanatos over Eros. If one were to read the poem post-colonially, one would see in it the impossibility of the full blossoming of a productive love and life-affirming narrative under colonialism. It is only in the golden 'mythical' past of the 'Legend of the Shushan' that love survives and triumphs even over death. Elsewhere, it is the touch of what *FJ's* reviewer called Derozio's compulsive *morbidezza* (Chaudhuri 2008, 400, 412), the sense of melancholy and doomed fatality, that pervades not only this poem, but much of Derozio's work. One might be tempted to see in this Derozio's veiled critique of colonialism – Nuleeni is India herself, almost forced to ascend the funeral pyre of her first, Hindu husband, then wrested or rescued by a Muslim bandit, only to be abandoned yet again by him. Nuleeni's second expiration on the battlefield with her arms around her lover suggests an abrupt and untimely termination of her life. India as Nuleeni really has few choices and no hope of real fulfilment. Her father, husband and lover – all three men who control her life, turn against her happiness. She has, needless to say, no son or daughter, so dies without reproducing and thus, in effect has no viable future. Even if somewhat farfetched, such an interpretation does give us the opportunity to look at the poem from a different angle, as a political allegory.

3.7 CRITICAL RECEPTION AND CONTEMPORARY READINGS

As this overview of the poem shows, *FJ* contains many passages which might be inessential if not extraneous to the central plot-line. That is why I called this poem more a collection of fragments than a coherent whole. Perhaps, this is why the reviewer in *India Gazette* whom I cited earlier, hails 'this performance ... rather as an earnest of what we have still to expect, than as of itself constituting a complete monument of his poetical powers' (quoted in Chaudhuri 2008, 398). This emphasis on promise rather than achievement, potential rather than accomplishment, is something we cannot forget when discussing Derozio's work. As the then Governor of West Bengal and Mahatma Gandhi's grandson, Gopal Krishna Gandhi put it in his inaugural address at the Derozio Bicentennial Celebrations,[6] a part of the young poet's mystique derives from the fact that he was 'pinnacle to penultimacy.' What might have been had he lived a long life is impossible to tell, but certainly the probabilities of great literary output are certainly likely. Derozio, a prodigy, left behind a huge volume of works though his life ended in his early twenties, when most careers are likely to begin. Nonetheless, much of his work must perforce be considered juvenilia, something he himself perhaps anticipates in his pen name 'Juvenis.' *FJ*, thus, need not, indeed *cannot*, be considered as an adult work. Its inconsistencies, unevenness and inner instability are as likely a measure or function of the youth of its author as they are of the disjointed times in which he lived. Though the life-cycles of men in early nineteenth century India were much briefer and more compressed in comparison to what we now enjoy, Derozio's lack of maturity cannot be overlooked.

It is this immaturity that also clouds the real contribution of Young Bengal, the movement that came to be associated with him. By the time its main actors attained maturity, if not majority, they no longer represented what we normally understand by that term. Some became pillars of society, others established poets or scholars. many even turned pious, remaining in their own ancestral faith or converting to Christianity.

The second crucial observation in the review cited earlier is the somewhat derivative nature of Derozio's poetry, reminiscent of Matthew 'Monk' Lewis, the author of the gothic extravaganza *The Monk* (1794), of Thomas Moore, author of *Lallah Rookh* (1817) and L.E.L or Letitia Elizabeth Landen (1802–1838) (Chaudhuri 407; 413). The reviewer asks the young poet to 'forget Moore and L.E.L. and Magazines and Weekly Reviews and devote those occasional hours of leisure to the pages of the Elizabethan as well as those of what has been called the Augustan age' (413). The following year, *The India Gazette* reprinted a review that had appeared in the July–September 1829 volume of J. S. Buckingham's *The Oriental Herald* (414). Chaudhuri speculates that the review might have been penned by Buckingham himself, who was deported out of Calcutta for practicing freedom of speech (ibid.). This reviewer also accuses Derozio of being derivative, drawing too much on the 'Byronic school, high into the perilous realms of exaggerated passion and falsetto sentiment' (419). The other influences mentioned include 'mad' Charles Taylor Maturin (1782-1824), L.E.L. (ibid.) and Moore (420). More specifically, the reviewer in *India Gazette* says,

> *The Fakeer of Jungheera*, is a personage lineally descended from 'The Corsair' and near of kin to the 'Veiled Prophet of Khorassan': and his lady-love, Nuleeni, is as 'warm and wild,' and woe-begone, as one of L.E.L.'s ecstatic damsels, whose only occupation is to kiss – and die. (421)

Again, he exhorts the young Derozio to improve his reading, to look for better models such as Shakespeare, Milton, Spencer, the old dramatists and Robert Burns (ibid.), concluding that 'He is capable

... of something better than inditing 'wild and wondrous lays' such as his "Fakeer'" (ibid.).

The charge that Indian English poetry is imitative has been with us for more than 150 years. In the 1960s and 1970s when Indian English literature began to be studied and taught in Indian universities, critics like David McCutcheon and M. K. Naik discussed this issue. In fact, one of the standard arguments in favour of modern Indian English poetry was that it was not imitative like the earlier poetry written by Indians in English. That it was possibly imitative of *different* models is, of course, another matter. In the case of *FJ*, it is clear that its influences and sources include a streak of Orientalism, especially of the type represented by *Lallah Rookh*, which draws on Persian sources, the late-18th century Gothic tales represented by Charles Maturin or 'Monk' Lewis and the cult of sentimental romanticism of L.E.L. This is an additional reason for its strangeness to us – none of its sources or models is a part of our reading today.

But it is not possible to explain or understand a poet like Derozio merely by speaking of influence and imitation. Actually, whatever he borrowed, he superimposed on his local, Indian material, creating a new idiom in Indian English poetry. The result is not mere imitation as these early reviewers or later Indian English critics claim, but the start of systematic and structural hybridisation. Sometimes artistically successful, sometimes, as in *FJ*, perhaps, less effective, this process was to become central not just to Indian English literature, but to the fabrication of Indian modernities. Unlike the hybridity of the coloniser that Homi Bhabha focuses on in *The Location of Culture*, Derozio's work shows the hybridity of the colonised, which creates radical alterity and thus offers itself as a locus of ambivalence. If (post-)colonised modernity is marked but such hybridity, then Derozio was certainly leading the way. It is in his pioneering this kind of 'vernacular modernism' that his achievement may really lie. Applying such ideas to visual practices, Christopher Pinney remarks that 'vernacular modernism' is a 'provincialising strategy, for it relocates the historical agency and centrality of Western representational practice in a new space,' (12) in Derozio's case, non-metropolitan

Kolkata. What Pinney identifies in visual culture, I would like to suggest, was already prevalent in the textual practices inaugurated by Derozio and his kin.

Though neither of these early reviewers paid much attention to the depiction of *sati* in the poem, later readers returned to the poem quite often on account of this. Though the rite of *sati* forms a crucial element, most readers have recognised that the poem is *not* primarily about *sati* at all. Had *sati* truly been its subject, I think Derozio would perhaps have had a really significant theme, fit for a major work. But in *FJ sati* is merely the exotic setting of the story and the poet's treatment of it evidently rather romantic.

Rajeswari Sunder Rajan in an influential essay, 'Representing *Sati*: Continuities and Discontinuites,' considers Derozio's *FJ* as representing 'the male indigenous reformist/liberal position on women's issues' (2001, 175). She shows how the 'paradigm of rescue' that *FJ* inaugurated was repeated in several texts that followed including Rabindranath Tagore's short story 'Saved' and Gautam Ghosh's *Antarjali Yatra* (ibid.). Sunder Rajan also points out how in spite of not submitting to *sati*, the woman dies in all three texts (ibid.). She considers such an end to the story as an outcome of the reluctance to show an afterlife of 'romantic/sexual fulfilment' for the widow (176). This, clearly, does not apply to *FJ* where Nuleeni consummates her relationship with the Fakeer, albeit in a brief interlude before the latter's death. Sunder Rajan is also wrong about a number of other details of the poem. For instance, she says that the poem 'runs to a thousand lines' (176), when it is clearly more than twice as long. She then says that she has been forced to 'marry a rich old man' (176), whereas the poem makes no such claim and actually describes the husband as her 'youthful lord' (Chaudhuri 2008, 228). Sunder Rajan also calls Shah Shuja 'Soorjah,' showing no awareness that he was an actual historical figure. But she is right in pointing out that Derozio's *FJ* is not an 'anti-*sati*' tract': what Derozio condemns is a 'loveless marriage' as he extols 'romantic love' in its place (176). It would appear, she says, that the poet would not have objected to Nuleeni's *sati* if she had married for love in the first place (ibid.). In fact, 'to die of love,' Sunder Rajan asserts, 'is to die of a recognised Western disease' and it is this death that Derozio reserves for his heroine at the end of the poem (ibid.). She also shows how Derozio exoticises *sati*, making it a 'set piece' which it later became. But despite these drawbacks, Sunder Rajan finds some agency in Nuleeni, who seems to choose death earlier and then life with her lover before finally dying over her slain lover's body. In the end, 'Nuleeni's death is sanctioned by the conventions of romantic poetry and the social status quo is preserved by the cautionary death of both the lovers. However heroic the rescuer's death, it defeats the purpose of the rescue' (ibid.). Sunder Rajan's take on *FJ*, though peppered with insights, fails to do justice to Derozio's treatment of *sati*. As I shall try to show, Derozio's position cannot be considered identical to that of male reformers like Ram Mohan Roy who called for its abolition. His was not the sort of hidden conservatism of the liberal reformers springing from a sentimental clinging to traditions that she wishes to unmask, but a more straightforward conformity to the dominant colonial position on the matter.

Indeed, it is this tendency to place Derozio too easily among the radicals and reformists that I question. While Derozio was clearly a liberal and cosmopolitan public intellectual, one cannot credit him with too many well-worked out positions and agendas. When it came to *sati*, as Chaudhuri shows us, his own attitude was ambivalent. After *sati* was abolished by William Bentinck in an act passed on 8 November 1829, Derozio published a laudatory poem 'On the Abolition of Suttee' in *India Gazette* on 10 December 1829. While he is emphatically opposed to *sati* in this later poem, his position in *FJ* which was published just the previous year, is quite different. In the former, which Chaudhuri calls an 'official' poem (2008, 284), Derozio portrays Bentinck as the savour of the wronged and wretched Indian widow: 'Nations unborn shall venerate thy name,/...Thy memory shall be blest, as is the morning star' (287). In his notes to *FJ*, on the contrary, Derozio does not wish it banned. He starts by saying that a 'Suttee is a spectacle of misery, exciting in the spectator a melancholy reflection upon the tyranny of superstition and priest-craft' (229). Yet he is against its proscription because, first of all the life of a Hindu widow is often worse than death. Then he quotes an unnamed writer at length from *Indian Magazine* who argues against the prohibition of *sati* and leaves it at that. The writer quoted claims that the burning of Hindu widows, though 'criminal in itself,' is not injurious to society because Hindus are brought up to believe in its virtues. Because the life of Hindu women in general and widows in particular is utterly degraded. Until the Hindus are educated out of 'the bitter gloom of ignorance and superstitions,' the writer is 'convinced of their right to the peaceable enjoyment of this their particular, though inhuman ceremony' (230). Thus he asks, 'How then can we stand acquitted from the charge of intolerance, if we exercise our power in violently suppressing so popularly respected a ceremony among the Hindoos?' (230; 286). He then goes on to quote an even longer extract from the *Bengal Chronicle* which describes an English eyewitness account of the peaceful and voluntary self-immolation of a Kayastha widow (232-233). Chaudhuri explains Derozio's toleration of *sati* as an 'articulation of a dislike of authoritarianism, even if that is the authoritarianism of benevolent reform' (286). But if this were true, then how or why did Derozio change his stance after Bentinck abolished the rite? Chaudhuri does not offer us an explanation.

To me, it seems that contrary to her view, Derozio seems rather compliant to authority than disrespectful of it. His view on *sati* is, in fact, the official colonial one – of non-interfering repugnance to begin with and a triumphant assertion of benevolent colonial intervention afterwards. That is why I question the stereotypical construction of Derozio as a rebel. If he *was* a rebel, as he has been painted to be, then what did he rebel against? He cannot not be accused of rebelling against Hindu superstitions because they were not his to begin with. That was a charge levelled against Young Bengal, allegedly tutored by him. But he himself denied it. There is no evidence that he took a position either against established Christianity or against colonial authority. That, like Drummond, he was a rationalist and somewhat of a free-thinker cannot be denied, but a careful examination of his religious beliefs shows, though he was not a conventional Christian, he did believe in a Christian God. Though not clearly articulated, his religion seems to resemble that of the Deists and other rational schools that emerged out of the European Enlightenment.

As it should be fairly clear that from the discussion so far, I have tried to show that *FJ* is romantic rather than reformist. Rationalism, if not reform, is more characteristic of some of Derozio's prose writings, which I shall come to shortly. In *FJ* he 'Orientalises' the rite of *sati*, making it an exotic spectacle, complete with Choruses of women and Brahmin priests, addresses to the sun by the chief priest, a pseudo-Vedic hymn to the sun and other such corybantic exertions. If poetry is Derozio's primary medium of expression, then his only claim to being the progenitor of Indian modernity must rest on his creation of a new poetic idiom and aesthetic rather than on a political, social, or religious intervention. But as a poet Derozio is more a one-off phenomenon than the creator of a tradition. His hybridisation was but one of the many types possible for Indians writing in English before this literature found some stability and depth. Moreover, he died young, so his writing, as I have already said, does not fully overpass the juvenile. A poetic career marked by partially fulfilled promise, exercises in an Orientalist, romantic exoticisation and a hybrid poetic discourse in English, rather than by reform or radicalism of the native traditions, would not appear to support the claim that he helped form the Indian modern or imagine the Indian nation into being.

3.8 DEROZIO AND INDIAN MODERNITY

As this reading of *FJ* shows, the poem speaks to several crucial issues pertaining to early nineteenth century colonial India including *sati*, Orientalism, literary and cultural hybridisation, Indo-British relations, ethnic Eurasians, the beginnings of 'national' public culture and so on. However, I have also tried in my analysis to modify the somewhat conventional view that Derozio's writings are 'formative, providing the foundational basis of the coming Bengali literary modernity' (Chaudhuri 2008, xxxv), that 'as a self-consciously nationalist poet' he was 'imaging a nation into being' (lxxx) and finally that his 'vocabulary and iconography of patriotism constructs a notion of indigeneity... often...emphatically and unprecedentedly, Indian' (lxxxi).

These claims reiterated by Chaudhuri and underscored in the very title of her volume, '*Derozio, Poet of India*,' are by no means new, let alone unprecedented. Indeed, the construction of Derozio as a patriot-nationalist may be traced back to the very notice in the *India Gazette* of 17 July 1828 announcing the forthcoming publication of *The Fakeer of Jungheera*: 'The East Indians in particular, we hope, will give their Indian Poet staunch support – evincing thereby their admiration for kindred genius and their patriotic feelings" (Chaudhuri 2008, 395). The longer two-instalment review of *FJ* in *India Gazette* that followed on 30th October and 3rd November 1828, declares even more emphatically that Derozio 'has some title to be considered as a national poet' (399).

The theme of Derozio's nationalism came to be developed along two lines, nationalist and Eurasian or Anglo-Indian, ethnic markers that succeeded and replaced the term 'East Indian' which was more common in Derozio's own time. This latter line was advanced by his earliest biographers Thomas Edwards and Eliot Walter Madge. While both took pains to argue that he was patriotic and nationalist, they also added another, racial twist; the titles of both their works emphasise Derozio's identity as 'Eurasian.' But it was Francis Bradley-Birt, the editor of the 1923 Oxford University Press selection of his poems, who really underscores Derozio's ethnicity. Starting with the very title of his book '*A Forgotten Anglo-Indian Poet*,' he goes on in his Introduction to read Derozio's life as an allegory of the racial tragedy of the Anglo-Indian community. In the annals of Anglo-Indiana, he claims 'there is no more brilliant and pathetic figure than the boy-poet' ([1923] 1980, i). This edition was published when the demand for independence was well-articulated; in such a context, the Anglo-Indian community, traditionally aligned with the British, found itself, as Bradley-Birt puts it, 'fallen helplessly between them, failing to win acceptance from either' (ii). If his Introduction begins thus, it also ends on the same note: 'What might not his genius and enthusiasm have done for his neglected race?...In his early death there is written the tragedy of his race' (lv-lvi). Bradley-Birt considers Derozio's early death as an 'inherited' outcome of 'the weakness of constitution that but too often descends as a legacy of mixed European and Indian parentage' (v). Calling Derozio 'the only poet of real distinction that the Anglo-Indian community has produced' (iii), Bradley-Birt attempts to recuperate his legacy as its representative. In fact, Derozio's cause as an Indian patriot was championed by the Anglo-Indian community, who, several years after one failed attempt, finally gathered the money to build a memorial on his grave in the Park Street cemetery. Similarly, his prefatory sonnet to *FJ*, was widely taught and anthologised because it was prescribed in the Indian Certificate of Secondary Education (ICSE) English syllabus conducted by the Indian School Certificate Examination (ISE) Board, which was founded and directed by ethnic Anglo-Indian educators. The appropriation of Derozio's legacy by his community was thus, at least in part, a political strategy, used to shore up the claims of the community to be patriotic Indians in a post-colonial nation.

Developing the other, nationalist, line E. F. Oaten, in *Anglo-Indian Literature*, the first scholarly monograph on the subject originally published in London in 1908, calls Derozio 'the National bard of modern India' (1908, 57). Unlike Edwards, Madge, or Bradley-Birth, Oaten uses 'Anglo-Indian' not a racial or ethnic term but to denote both Englishmen and Indians who wrote in English in India. Following suit, K. R. Srinivasa Iyengar in his monumental *Indian Writing in English* says, 'Derozio loved India' ([1962] 1985, 34). Similarly, John Alphonso-Karlaka asserts that Derozio 'identified himself with his native land and wrote purely on Indian themes with a reformer's zeal' (1970, 43). M. K. Naik in his *History of Indian English Literature* adds that 'A noteworthy feature of Derozio's poetry is its burning nationalistic zeal' (1970, 23). C. Paul Verghese observes that 'His poems breathe the spirit of patriotism and may be regarded as an important landmark in the history of patriotic poetry in India' (1984, 1). Even R. K. Dasgupta's Foreword to the 1980 reprint of the

Bradley-Birt edition calls him 'modern India's first patriot...the first to contemplate an intellectual renaissance for an ancient civilisation' (1980, 'C'). Manju Dalmia in her perceptive essay 'Derozio: English Teacher' adds: 'He is regarded as a proto-nationalist, one who created a critical awareness of modes of government and representation, but at the same time reflected the contradictions surrounding English higher education at the time' (1992, 43). Almost summing up this thread, Vinay Dharwadkar says, Derozio 'developed a passionate love for an 'imagined' India (in Benedict Anderson's sense of the term) that can only be described as the first expression of romantic nationalism in Indian literature' (2003, 225).

Both lines of appropriation, thus, impute a modern, nationalist role for Derozio after the fact, as a result of the compelling uses of such narratives in literary historiography itself. It is the dominance of these narratives that actually makes it difficult to see the rather more cosmopolitan, if tentative and fragmentary space that Derozio actually inhabited. It was the shrinkage of this public sphere wrought by the rise of British paramountcy and the consolidation of the empire in India which then gave rise to the colonial-national discursive binary and made it so attractive to see Derozio as a proto-modern, nationalist cultural hero.

I have already argued that Derozio's modernity lay in his aesthetic practices, more specifically in his vernacularising his Western sources and influences, grafting them upon local material to create a new, hybridised idiom of expression. This Indian English idiom later became a sort of *lingua franca* of Indian nationalism and identity. It lacked one essential feature, though, that of bilingualism, which I shall address shortly, but it did provide in English a new way for Indians to express themselves. In other words, Derozio's contribution to Indian modernity and nationalism was more aesthetic than intellectual, more artistic than ideological, more creative than political.

Indeed, in so far as his intellectual temperament or the tenor of his beliefs, he was more an East-Indian cosmopolitan than a proto-modernist or nationalist. This becomes more and more evident if we examine the 'the well-defined public arena that Derozio inhabited in the early nineteenth century' as 'the precondition of the birth of the modern in India' (Chaudhuri 2008, lxviii). Chaudhuri explains how the city that Derozio inhabited was 'Polyglot and multi-ethnic, in a period of enormous change' (lxx). Most importantly, she demonstrates how 'The nationalism espoused by these men at this time was internationalist in character' (lxxv). This was a special moment in the history of India, these three decades from 1800 to 1830, when, quoting C.A. Bayley, she indicates how 'a *conjunctural* liberalism prevailed (lxxvi).

3.9 EAST INDIAN COSMOPOLITANISM

While such a narrative is plausible, it is not entirely persuasive. It restricts the field of the forces that went into the formation of the Indian 'modern.' I believe that it is more productive to invoke the idea of cosmopolitanism than proto-nationalism to understand the importance of a figure like Derozio. The substantial recent body of work in this area, Sheldon Pollock's magisterial discussion of both the cosmopolitan and the vernacular, *The Language of the Gods in a World of Men* (2003) not only goes farther than the earlier volume *Cosmopolitanism* edited by him and others, but perhaps remains unsurpassed. Early in his argument, Pollock says that 'cosmopolitan transculturation' is concerned with 'how and why people may have been induced to adopt languages or life ways or modes of political belonging that affiliated them with the distant rather than the near, the unfamiliar rather than the customary' (2003, 10). However, the crucial point that Pollock makes in this section of his book is that 'Premodern space, whether cosmopolitan or vernacular, is not the nation-space – and yet it was no less filled with political content than it was with cultural content' (17). This is because the national is 'a second-generation representation' that is informed by 'a very different logic that nationalism often seeks to elide' (ibid.).

A more straightforward, political explanation such as I have offered of the shrinking of the public sphere explains why Derozio's cosmopolitanism is harder for us to understand and why it is easier to slot him into a modernist-nationalist narrative as its precursor. However, the latter reading actually simplifies, if not distorts, the nature of Indian modernity, which is characterised not as much by a linear trajectory of expansion and consolidation, as by a fuzzier logic of alternate phases of expansion and contraction, cosmopolitanism and vernacularisation. As it happened by the time of Derozio's death, Britain's hegemony over India, its rather swift *realisation* in a matter of decades, also caused the demise of the decades of possibility in the late eighteenth century which engendered a Ram Mohan or a Derozio. It was not until the Company's decisive victory over the Marathas in the third Anglo-Maratha war in 1818 that the British became the dominant power in India. From here on, the divisions between the rulers and the ruled changed radically. Not only were these much more rigidly enforced, but came to be defined in terms of race, power, superiority and the colonising mission. Similarly, we might propose that this period of possibilities was not only unique to Calcutta, but was available elsewhere – for instance in Pondicherry as the diaries of Ananda Ranga Pillai show, or in Hyderabad, as portrayed so movingly by William Dalrymple in *White Moguls* (2002). We might add that the period begins earlier than 1800 as Chaudhuri thinks, perhaps as early as the start of the Company rule in 1772, with Warren Hastings as the first Governor-General, or even with Robert Clive in the South with the Anglo-French wars.

Race and cultural relations just prior to Britain's decisive victories were far more fluid and flexible, allowing the creation of a truly unprecedented English cosmopolitanism in India. For the first time, through the medium of the English language for which they had developed an avid, almost insatiable appetite, Indians from a new middle class suddenly found themselves a part of a larger world, a world outside India and its traditional neighbourhood of which they had little more than the dimmest notions earlier. This world was in fact the post-Enlightenment Europe, expanding not just economically, but culturally to far territories of the globe, having discovered new continents and dominions. A class of Indians came to the forefront, which a mixed-race native of India such as Derozio found himself, albeit for a short time. Later, the Bengali Hindu elite would bring a new consolidation of the nationalist bourgeoisie ranged against a colonial regime. In that later consolidation, the short-lived East Indian cosmopolitanism of Derozio would have little place.

Partha Chatterjee calls this a 'heterogeneous time of modernity' which contained within it the 'co-presence of several times – the time of the modern and the times of the premodern' (quoted in Chaudhuri 2008, lxxxvii). If so, to construct a singular beginning for Indian modernity and to place Derozio at its foundational moment is, surely, to misconstrue the nature of the Indian modern. No wonder, those who do so do not speculate on whether Derozio knew Bangla and whether he participated in the local non-English culture in any measurable way. While we know that Derozio translated from the French and so must have had some acquaintance with the language, we also know that he read the Vetal Pacheesa because a student from Hindu College could translate it to him. Perhaps, he knew some Hindustani, in addition to Bangla, having lived in Bhagalpur for three years. Yet, there is no direct evidence of his forays into local cultures or into languages other than English.

In this regard, Dharwardkar contends that 'Literatures and literary cultures are located ... most often at the intersection of multiple, crisscrossing histories' (2003, 201). According to him, Derozio 'emerged from the zones of interracial marriage and Christian upbringing in India, the one early Indian-English writer to grow up monolingual in English' (224). Derozio, Dharwardkar adds, 'thus positioned himself squarely inside the Indian critical discourse put into circulation by Ram Mohan Roy ... and aestheticised the Indian criticism of India as well as the Indian counter-critique of the British discourse that disparaged the histories and cultures of the subcontinent' (226). This adds a further limitation to Derozio's contribution: not only was it confined to the largely colonial and European sphere in India, but it was also exclusively devoted to the English language. Dharwadkar thus identifies Derozio as emerging from a space which in itself was rather restricted in the context of polyglot and multi-cultural India. His limitation was underscored also by his monolingualism, juvenility and early death. As such, he was marginal to the construction of Indian modernity.

A quick comparison with Ram Mohan Roy will be illustrative. Ram Mohan, like Derozio, was not only cosmopolitan, but also participated, much more actively, in the public sphere. But unlike Derozio, he not only wrote and functioned in several indigenous languages, in addition to English, but much more daringly so than Derozio. Besides being at the heart of major developments such as the founding of the Brahmo Samaj, the start of the vernacular press, the translation of the Upanishads into Bangla and a long-drawn out controversy with the Christian missionaries, Ram Mohan actually travelled to England and the continent and, of course, lived for a fuller term. Derozio's career, in comparison, is much more restricted and limited to the literary, rather than the social, political, economic, religious, or cultural. Unlike Derozio, Roy was not only conversant in English, but fluently productive in Bangla, Sanskrit and even Persian. He intervened in all the three spheres – classical, vernacular and English (*marga, desi and videsi*) that had to be transformed before the Indian modern could emerge.

If we believe that though English is crucially constitutive of Indian modernity, the latter cannot be constructed solely in English, then we will immediately understand Derozio's limitations. English, in other words, though arguably necessary, is not sufficient. When English monolingualism or English-dominant multilingualism seems to be the chosen medium of the Indian elites, then the championing of a figure like Derozio as a key creator of Indian modernity is only to be expected. It is the English-wallas, at the end of the day, who are the biggest champions of Derozio. Nevertheless such sponsorship is not without its dangers. It amounts to the exaltation of 'English India' and 'Indian English' over all other modes and registers of cultural formation. English, it should be obvious, is not just a language, but a mode of representation.[7] It may be dominant, but not sufficient. Nor does it cover the entire spectrum of the Indian experience or become constitutive of all of Indian reality. The narrow space that it occupies cannot be equated with the whole public sphere of

India, especially in its early years of English ascendancy in India. While it may have provided some models for the conducting of public discourse in other languages, it is in the latter that the really transformative process of modernising India was and is still taking place. This is a two-way process which entails the Indianisation of English on the one hand and the Anglicisation of the vernaculars on the other. What we need, therefore, is a much more carefully calibrated placement in which Derozio's liminality and limitation are clearly spelt out rather than glossed over. Clearly, it would not do simply to assert that he was our first nationalist poet as Dharwadkar or Chaudhuri proclaim.

That is why it is also necessary to disengage the strands of modernity with those of nationalism. Even if Derozio's contribution to the making of Indian modernity is acknowledged, it would be hard to consider him, in the same breath, as a nationalist or even someone who through his poems 'imagined' (Dharwadkar 2003, 225) 'a nation into being' (Chaudhuri 2008, lxxx). I would contend that Derozio and his reviewers used the word 'nation' and 'national' in a rather loose way, synonymous with indigenous and native, as opposed to British and foreign. They used it, moreover, in the specific context of Derozio's writings in English, a language few Indians were proficient in and fewer still capable of versifying in. These terms, were then used without any clear notion of a state or political entity. Surely the Britishers who first employed them were far from thinking of India as an independent political entity, a nation state. Even Ram Mohan had no idea of an Indian nation, coming to terms as he was with the decline of the Moghul empire and the rise of British power in India. Clearly, the early reviewers and Dharwardkar or Chaudhuri mean very different things when they use 'national' to describe Derozio's poetry. The post-Anderson sense of imagining a community into being, which the latter have in mind seems more a back projection without solid evidence than a convincing and carefully documented case. Clearly, the idea of the nation was a late if not final product of Indian modernity, it emerged many decades after Derozio's death. Patriotism or love for the land of one's birth is not the same as the idea of a nation. The national imaginary would only emerge in India only much after Derozio's death.

If I consider both the modern and the national as inadequate signifiers, a better way of defining Derozio's location, whether ethnic or aesthetic, would be to consider him as an East Indian cosmopolitan. The term 'East Indian', which Derozio used to describe himself in his contributions to *India Gazette* as early as 1826 (Chaudhuri 2008, xxvii) and which name he gave to his newspaper – started a year before his death – is I believe, a good way to define his special locus. My argument, however, is different from the earlier 'Anglo-Indian' appropriations of Derozio that I have already discussed. To me, the phrase East Indian is not the same as Anglo-Indian or Eurasian. Taken by itself, it only makes sense if we can contrast it with, say, West Indian. Why did Derozio not simply say 'Indian'? It stands to reason that he wished to distinguish himself from the 'merely' Indian and also from all the others peoples that the Europeans had (mistakenly) labelled 'Indian.'

The East Indian, in those days, was a phrase used to designate Europeanised people of mixed race in India. According to one estimate there were over 11,000 such Eurasians or 'mestizos' in Calcutta alone by the end of the eighteenth century. It would not be inconceivable to someone in Derozio's situation to think of these as forming if not a nation, then at least a distinctive cultural and social group. Along with the colonisers, they could constitute the basis of a new community. Therefore, his own specific ethnic identity was 'East Indian.'[8]

After being associated with numerous periodicals, Derozio started a paper called *The East Indian* about a year before his death. In its prospectus, he says it would 'advocate the just rights of all classes of the community' (Chaudhuri 2008, xliii). As Derozio's participation in the two public meetings of the East Indians shows (342-356), the community regarded itself as distinct from Hindus and Mahommedans, both of whom had their own code of civil law (349). The East Indians, on the other hand, asked to be tried under European law claiming that the East Indians in 'Their conduct, habits, thoughts, usages and feelings were totally dissimilar' (ibid.). In the draft of the Second Petition of the East Indians to the British Parliament, they identified themselves as 'natives of and residents in, British India; Christians in religion; and acknowledging subjection to the Crown of Great Britain' (351). This self-definition with Derozio as a signatory clearly shows him not so much as a proto-nationalist but as a loyal subject of colonial India, aligned more closely with the imperial than native interests.

The zone of 'interracial contact and acculturation,' to use Dharwadkar's phrase (2003, 206), that he inhabits is thus, more properly, somewhat on the sidelines of the main thrust of Indian modernity and nationalism, although, it must be admitted that in its own time it was rather more significant than it came to be later. The very term 'East Indian,' as we know only too well, disappeared from our vocabulary, giving way to the more ambiguous and imprecise 'Anglo-Indian.' East Indians included other forms of mixed race people than only those born of the union of the English and the natives of India. With the establishment of British paramountcy, the frequency and importance of Portuguese, Dutch, Danish and French mixed marriages with native women also declined. From being a pre-colonial *entrepot*, with a large migrant trading community that included Jews, Armenians and other foreigners, Calcutta became the second city of the British empire. The scope and power of the East Indian community was subsequently reduced.

While the East Indian defines Derozio's ethnicity and identity, it is merely one side of it. Derozio's work shows his interest in and familiarity not only with European thought and literature, but also with Persian texts, particularly Hafiz, whom he translated. That he participated in a larger intellectual and cultural world is also quite clear. To that extent he was not just East Indian, but certainly cosmopolitan. East Indian cosmopolitanism in Derozio, thus, signifies a special, even crucial moment in the formation of modern Indian literary culture. *FJ*, despite being fragmentary and unintegrated, is a unique instantiation of it, somewhat like in Dean Mahomet's *Travels*, another outstanding if singular achievement which inaugurates Indian writing in English as an instance of a Bihari-Muslim early-colonial diasporic cosmopolitanism.

Both these texts are singular and unreplicated accomplishments, with nothing like them before or after. From several such contributory fragments, many of them unrelated to one another, a more solid base for Indian modern gradually begins to take shape. This foundation, however, is formed by a more cohesive group of vernacular and English texts, mostly by native Indians who have much more in common, notably a shared vision of what the India of the future may be after it is free from the colonial yoke. It is texts such as these that go on, in their own polyglot, heterogeneous and complex manner, to imagine – then actually to fabricate modern India.

3.10 CONCLUSION

The manner in which Derozio's brief albeit remarkable, career has been read, shows the curiously paradoxical ways in which different cultural elites have tried to reinterpret and appropriate his legacy. The earlier interpretations tried to highlight his marginalisation and neglect, attributing it to his status as an ethnic Anglo-Indian and hence a member of a disappearing minority, more contemporary scholars like Chaudhuri have tried to relocate him at the very heart of India's nationalist and modernist project. Through a detailed reading of his greatest literary accomplishment and India's first long English poem, I have tried to argue that while Derozio played an important role in the making of modern India, he did so from a special, now unavailable space, which I have termed East Indian cosmopolitanism. Kumari Jayawardena in her book *Erasure of the Euro-Asian: Recovering Early Radicalism and Feminism in South Asia* has looked at several mixed race pioneers in South Asia and elsewhere who, like Derozio, played crucial roles in every 'progressive' movement in the region, including the production of the 'modern' and the 'national.' In Derozio's case, however, his monolingualism and closeness to European ideas made his contribution to the reshaping of Indian traditions somewhat marginal. In addition, his brief life, cut off in the bloom of youth, presents truncated promise rather than fully-realised accomplishment. Derozio impacted a small, but influential section of his times, those Europeans, Eurasians and Indians to whom English was the main if not sole medium of communication and being. Naturally, it is the English-knowing elite of today's India who considers him of the greatest importance. In the bigger multi-lingual, multi-cultural and multifaceted project of modern India, he remains a significant, but liminal figure. Now he remains an increasingly accepted, familiar ancestor whose words still speak to us with urgency as well as power across the gulf of two centuries.

WORKS CITED

Alphonso-Karkala, John B. 1970. *Indo-English Literature in the Nineteenth Century*. Mysore: Literary Half Yearly.
Banerjee, M. 2009. 'The Trial of Derozio, or the Scandal of Reason.' *Social Scientist* 37 (7/8, Jul-Aug): 60-88.
Bhabha, Homi K. 1994. *The Location of Culture*. London: Routledge.
Bradley-Birt, Francis Bradley. (1923) 1980. *Poems of Henry Louis Vivian Derozio: A Forgotten Anglo-Indian Poet*. Reprint. Delhi: Oxford University Press.
Chaudhuri, Rosinka. 2002. *Gentlemen Poets in Colonial Bengal: Emergent Nationalism and the Orientalist Project*. Kolkata: Seagull Books.
_____. Ed. 2008. *Derozio, Poet of India*. Delhi: Oxford University Press.
_____. 2010. 'The Politics of Naming: Derozio in Two Formative Moments of Literary and Political Discourse, Calcutta, 1825-31.' *Modern Asian Studies* 44 (4): 857-885.
Dalmia, Manju. 1992. 'Derozio: English Teacher.' In *Lie of the Land: English Literary Studies in India*, edited by Rajeswari Sunder Rajan, 42-62. Delhi: Oxford University Press.
Devy, G. N. 1998. *'Of Many Heroes': An Indian Essay in Literary Historiography*. Mumbai: Orient Longman.
Dharwardkar, V. 2003. 'The Historical Formation of Indian-English Literature.' In *Literary Cultures in History: Reconstructions from South Asia*, edited by Sheldon Pollock, 199-267. New Delhi: Oxford University Press.

Edwards, Thomas. 1884. *Henry Derozio, the Eurasian Poet, Teacher and Journalist, with Appendices.* Calcutta: W. Newman and Co.

Jayawardena, Kumari. 2007. *Erasure of the Euro-Asian: Recovering Early Radicalism and Feminism in South Asia.* Colombo: Social Scientists' Association.

Iyengar, K. R. S. (1962) 1985. *Indian Writing in English.* 5th ed. New Delhi: Sterling.

Madge, Elliot Walter. (1905) 1967. *Henry Derozio: The Eurasian Poet and Reformer.* Reprint. Calcutta: Metropolitan Book Agency.

McCutcheon, David. 1968. 'Must Indian Poetry in English always follow England?' In *Critical Essays on Indian Writing in English,* edited by M. K. Naik et. al., 164–180. Dharwad: Karnataka University.

Naik, M. K. 1970. 'Echo and Voice in Indian Poetry in English.' *Indian Writing Today* 4 (1): 32–41.

———. 1982. *A History of Indian English Literature.* New Delhi: Sahitya Akademi.

Oaten, Edward Farley. 1908. *A Sketch of Anglo-Indian Literature.* London: K. Paul, Trench, Trübner.

Paranjape, Makarand R. 2011. '"East Indian Cosmopolitanism": *The Fakeer of Jungheera* and the Birth of Indian Modernity.' *Interventions: International Journal of Postcolonial Studies.* 13.4: 550–569.

Paranjape, Makarand R. and GJV Prasad, Eds. 2010. *Indian English and Vernacular India.* New Delhi: Pearson Longman.

Pollock, Sheldon. 2003. *The Language of the Gods in the World of Men: Sanskrit, Power and Culture in Premodern India.* Berkeley: University of California Press.

Pinney, C. and Nicolas Peterson, (2003) 2005. Eds. *Photography's Other Histories.* Durham, NC: Duke UP.

Sunder Rajan, R. 2001. 'Representing *Sati*: Continuities and Discontinuites.' In *Postcolonial Discourses: An Anthology,* edited by Gregory Castle, 167–189. Oxford: Blackwell.

Verghese, C. Paul. 1984. 'Henry Derozio: An Assessment.' In *Perspectives on Indian English Poetry,* edited by M. K. Naik, 1–9. New Delhi: Abhinav.

4
MICHAEL MADHUSUDAN DUTT: THE PRODIGAL'S PROGRESS

> *'Knowledge is power': that is the slogan of Western civilisation.*
> *'Knowledge is salvation' is the slogan of Hindu civilisation.*[1]
>
> — BANKIM CHANDRA CHATTOPADHYAY
>
> *This century has shown that in every situation of organised oppression the true antonyms are always the exclusive part versus the inclusive whole – not masculinity versus femininity but either of them versus androgyny, not the past versus the present but either of them versus the timelessness in which the past is the present and the present is the past, not the oppressor versus the oppressed but both of them versus the rationality which turns them into co-victims.*[2]
>
> — ASHIS NANDY

4.1 INTRODUCTION

In 1837, six years after Henry Derozio's death, a bright young pupil joined Hindu College. Thus, Michael Madhusudan Dutt (1824–1873) – celebrated as Bengal's first modern poet – was not strictly speaking, a Derozian. But the atmosphere in which he came of age was deeply influenced by intellectual currents in which Derozio played a stirring, even stellar, role. One of Derozio's direct disciples,

Krishna Mohun Banerjee, whose conversion to Christianity caused a furore, wrote thus about the activities in the Academic Association, the freethinking club that Derozio presided over:

> The authority of the Hindu religion was questioned, its sanctions impeached, its doctrines ridiculed, its philosophy despised, its ceremonies accounted fooleries, its injunctions openly violated and its priesthood defied as an assembly of fools, hypocrites and fanatics. (Cited in De 1962, 480)

Krishna Mohun, who became a Christian priest, was not only one of the most prominent Indian Christians of his time, but being a Brahmin, also induced deep anxiety in the Bengali *bhadrasamaj*, the middle-class elite, to whom it was left to bear the brunt of the colonial impact. Krishna Mohun took a path quite different from Ram Mohan Roy, though he shared the latter's sense of mission to reform Indian society. Incidentally, it was to the Rev Krishna Mohun that Madhusudan betook himself when he decided to flee – from his home, parents and ancestral faith – admitting himself to the ranks of the newly converted upper-class and upper-caste Christians of Calcutta. In Madhusudan's case, the civilising mission of colonialism found an eager respondent. No persuasion was needed. He not only believed what the colonisers were trying to preach, but went a step further: 'It is the glorious mission, I repeat, of the Anglo-Saxon to renovate, to regenerate or in one word, to Christianise the Hindu,' he declared unabashedly in his essay 'The Anglo-Saxon and the Hindu' (Gupta 1980, 638).

This chapter which, in a sense, must be finished not by its author but by its reader, contains two sections, one set in the present and the other in the past. The first is an argument, while the second is a narrative. However, I hope they are related by a common anxiety that has preoccupied many Indians over decades, if not centuries. The two sections have the intention of clarifying the entire phenomenon of colonialism, particularly how India responded to the impact of the West in its formative period. My concern, as evidenced in the previous chapters, is less with the economic and political as with the psychological and cultural effects of colonialism. Of course, both these sets are related in what might be thought of as the overall structure of domination-subordination that colonialism imposes and which makes its operation so complicated and destructive. In other words, I want to ask: first, how do we cope with colonialism (or neo-colonialism) or indeed, with any situation defined by asymmetrical relations of power? Secondly, what can we learn from our history of the last few hundred years that can help us in this project?

4.2 THE COLONISERS AND THE COLONISED

It seems only appropriate to begin the exploration of this problematic in the here and the now, not in the distant past as it is usually done. A reading of Madhusudan's life depends on how we view the history of the colonisers and the colonised. From the fifteenth century right up to the twentieth, the spread and triumph of European peoples and cultures over the rest of the world seemed an irrevocable fact. In the process, many peoples, races, civilisations were destroyed, overcome, or absorbed. India, reduced to starvation and backwardness, survived by the skin of its teeth. Despite a bloody partition and truncated nationhood, we managed to take tenuous hold of our destiny.

From this vantage point, we may regard colonialism as a matter of the past; we are now in the age not of colonialism, or even of de-colonisation, but, as some might go to the extent of venturing, even of a sort of reverse colonialism.[3] The very process of decolonisation, it is believed, was possible partly because the older imperialistic ideology was defeated both externally by the various movements for independence and nationalism in the colonies and internally within the imperium – by the two world wars. Subsequent to all these changes, especially in the last twenty years, the former colonial powers have themselves been occupied by vast numbers of people from their colonies, so as to face a severe crisis. This crisis is not so much that of multiculturalism as it is sometimes thought to be, but of liberal society itself. That liberalism carried with it a fundamental contradiction was always known in the colonies because they bore the brunt of imperial despotism, while the metropoles both ensured and vaunted their liberty to the rest of the world.[4] Now, that contradiction has returned to haunt these societies, forcing them to subject racially or ethnically profiled citizens to surveillance, thereby trampling on those very liberties to protect which such acts of repression are ostensibly carried out. Somehow, our former colonisers have been better even at dealing with some of these challenges, moving on from the past without as much trauma or tribulation as we have and continue to go through.

Another possible assumption is that as academics we belong to an international community which, in spite of our differences, has shared goals. The hope is that the largely political and economic vested interests that divide the world into various blocks do not matter quite as much in academics, that academics is somehow neutral and immune to their influence.[5] Hence, we can make alliances and affiliations with those among our former colonisers who are sympathetic to our cause and can help us in our quest for decolonisation or for greater justice in our world. Or to put it slightly differently, after Theory, it is the quest for equity that unites the West and the rest of us.

Those who might consider the above premise as naïve would, on the other hand, contend that because academics is shot through with the politics and economics of neo-imperialism, we of what used to be called the Third World and what people nowadays call the South, must be ever vigilant and resist the new hegemonies of the post-colonial world. But even to those who hold such views, the question of what sort of contacts to maintain with the West still remains. Should we form alliances with the progressive sections of the West, to use the West to fight the 'oppressive' West? With their readings against the grain, with the politics of opposition and with their well-organised literature of protest, these post-colonialists have created a space for themselves within Western critical discourse. In either case and underlying both types of view is the idea that the West itself is divided – to put it simplistically – into the what we might call the 'good' West and the 'bad' West, or the enlightened, humane, progressive, anti-oppressive West and the reactionary, conservative, vested-interest controlled, aggressive and militaristic West.

Thus, our definition of our own role in the process of decolonisation depends a good deal on how we view the West, whether we see it as a monolithic entity, as the evil 'Other' whom we are fighting, or as divided against itself, both oppressor and partner. I have tried to show above that no matter which position we take, most of us would see the West in the latter, more complex terms unless we wish to walk with the *jihadists*.

On the face of it, the radicalisation of criticism in the Third World has served us well, by helping us to create for ourselves a special space, which only we – with our unique record of suffering and oppression can occupy. Also, it has given us post-colonialists a sense of purpose, amounting in some cases, almost to a missionary zeal. However, to retain this critical space, we are forced constantly to reiterate the rhetoric of opposition and confrontation, always to harp on our oppressed status and hence to perpetuate the dualism that colonialism itself created and exploited. Once, the East was a career; now post-colonialism has turned the East into a career, but in the West, materially benefiting people from the colonised world, especially as they located themselves in the world of the colonisers. In the Western academy, this has resulted in the splitting of the academic community into several small constituencies, each with its separate flag, creed and armoury, fighting for its own dearly won and evidently fragile identity. Each group finds itself saddled with the problem of defining its own unique ground which no one else can claim, usually defined on the basis of gender, race, nationality, ethnicity or sexual preference. However, no group is stable because no group can stake its claim to a unique, non-oppressive experience as exclusively its own; there will always be smaller or more specific groups, while each group also shares several experiences with others, thereby undermining its claim to uniqueness. Thus, while reacting to the authoritarian and universalistic tendencies of earlier modes of criticism, we have now created our own alternative prison houses.

I want to question this dualism, whose origin, as I have suggested above, is in the old dichotomy of the West and the rest and whose impact has registered itself strongly on Indian criticism as well. Particularly, I want to deconstruct those sets of opposing categories that are primarily associated with colonialism: the coloniser and the colonised, the oppressor and the oppressed, the masculine and the feminine, the West and the East and so on. Why should the burden of decolonisation fall only upon the colonised alone? We know very well that it affects the colonisers 'as much' as the colonised. This point has already been stressed by a whole host of sensitive critics like Manoni, Cesaire and even Fanon. We know that violence directed outward, comes back to haunt its perpetrators as internalised violence. The aggression, greed, violence and destruction that Europe exported to its colonies, it may be argued, returned as its own *karmic* nemesis in the shape of the two World Wars. One cannot destroy the Other without destroying oneself. One cannot brutalise the Other without becoming a brute oneself. One cannot oppress the Other without becoming an oppressor oneself. To project oneself as strong, superior, masculine, aggressive – the West had to pretend not only that the Other was servile, passive, feminine, inferior and so on, but also to suppress these qualities within itself. The West had to split itself first, repressing precisely those traits that it saw in its Other, though these qualities could have saved the West from untold damage to itself. By redefining itself so as to exclude the softer side of its own nature, it had to renounce important qualities that it had valued greatly itself. There is, within the West, a continual history of the brutal suppression and liquidation of several smaller groups and defeated people. In its great march towards rationality and modernity, we might assume that much that was valuable was also lost.

What is more, we must resist the old dualisms without equating the colonisers with the colonised, without pretending that colonialism never happened, or without cynically critiquing the West only to find a comfortable place within it. We can do so not by substituting old dualisms with new ones, but by an altogether different kind of reasoning. We must resist the privileging of the oppressor over the oppressed, the coloniser over the colonised, the masculine over the feminine. We must question the logic that considers being exploited, oppressed, colonised, emasculated, 'worse' than being an oppressor, exploiter, coloniser and so on. It would be foolish to assert that going hungry is as good as being well-fed, but we may well question whether stealing others' food is better than starving. Doing harm to others, in other words, is no more desirable than having harm done to oneself. The real question, though, is whether doing harm to others is actually preferable to suffering oneself. Is the coloniser really superior to the colonised or is he in actuality a victim too, albeit a different kind of victim than the one whom he oppresses? Is he really more civilised as he claims to be when that is merely an excuse to rob, rape and wipe out others?

To all appearances, the ethical onus on the colonisers is the greater because their actions have involved them in a conscious commission of evil, while their victims cannot be held equally responsible for what was done to them. Yet, is it not possible for the victims, even at the point of extinction, to have pity for the colonisers because despite being in such dire straits, they would be loath to exchange places with the colonisers? Colonisation, thus, is as much the business of the colonisers as it is of the colonised, even if the latter must take up cudgels on their own behalf, while the former move on as if they were washed clean of the sins of their past, having atoned for them with the adoption of more politically correct ideologies in keeping with changing times.

Thus, the more desirable state is being neither the coloniser nor the colonised. This is a third and if I may say so, 'higher' state. In it, one owns up to not just one's own special history of oppression or suppression, but the whole history of the human race with all its terrible cruelties, bloody wars, horrible sufferings and also its magnificent achievements and triumphs. This state of mind is sane and whole, not fragmented; it is neither in conflict with itself nor at war with the Other. Asymmetrical power can only be addressed from a position in which equality is claimed on some *a priori* assumption or the falsehood and unsustainability of the inequality is taken for granted. What cannot be resolved at the level of the coloniser-colonised, can only be addressed by a level of consciousness that is born out of a higher order of cognition.

Our age has been characterised by extreme scepticism and anxiety, especially in Western thought. What has been demonstrated, with great logic and sophistication, is the frightening vision of the ultimate irrationality of reason itself. Even if the old false god, Logos, in his avatar of the sole arbiter of human knowledge in Western civilisation, did not have much to offer in the first place, his substitution by the anti-foundationalist 'non-entity' has not done us too much good either. Similarly, those who worship history, valorising it over all other human narratives, also genuflect to another false god because history is not equally available or applicable to all of us. Perhaps, we live in and experience several worlds, each with its own logic and internal coherence, existing simultaneously and, to a large extent, consistent in itself.

All of this brings us to a series of points to ponder:

- To be strong is not necessarily better than to be weak; sometimes the strong destroy themselves while the weak survive.
- The suffering of being oppressed is not necessarily 'worse' than the guilt and inhumanity being an oppressor.
- Life and its enjoyments are not necessarily superior to a death that is the outcome of virtuous resistance to oppression or injustice.
- To be extinct, to be superseded by history, to be left behind by evolution may be preferable to being the destroyers, slaughters and killers of the weak, the conquered, or the defeated. Perhaps the extinct races are the blessed; we do not mourn for them as much as for ourselves who systematically destroyed them.
- To be aggressive, strong, powerful, confident and rich, especially at the expense of others, is not necessarily the aim of human existence.
- Winners are not always winners; losers are not always

losers – colonisers are not always winners, colonised are not always losers.
- To be backward has its own rewards as being forward has its own penalties.
- The quest for power destroys; the quest for truth liberates. Of course, power has its own 'truth,' just has truth has its own 'power.'

4.3 THE LOSS AND RECOVERY OF MADHUSUDAN DATTA[6]

It is now time to recount the life history of Michael Madhusudan Dutt. It is not as if his story has not been told earlier. It has. What is more, long ago, Madhusudan's life has already been narrated as an allegory of cultural loss and recovery. For instance, over fifty years back, the renowned Bangla poet Bishnu De wrote this about Madhusudan:

> Madhusudan's private and poetic life is a noble tragedy of which the other name is England's work in India. He is to us a symbol of genius. His tragedy is a drama of running after false analogies in the gloom of Indo-British history. (quoted in Poddar 1970, 194)

Such a tribute coming from Bishnu De is all the more striking because De is in the direct line of descent of modernist poetry at the head of which stands Madhusudan. Indeed, one might examine numerous such representations of Madhusudan before or after De's. Instead, is it not better to participate in its poignancy rather than to stand apart or outside in order to examine its structures or patterns? To me such participation is part of the ancestral debt that modern Indians owe to their predecessors.

Unlike modern history or literary criticism, much of traditional Indian storytelling was preoccupied with recalling or narrating the lives of 'heroes' or gods in order to commemorate them, to mourn or celebrate their lives. My story may be considered a part of this tradition. I see the task of telling this story as valuable for two reasons: first, on account of what we learn from the effort required to put it together, but also as a sort of atonement in one more attempt to recover that part of our past which has unconsciously gone into the shaping of what we are today. My purpose is not to pass judgement on Madhusudan's life, but to accept it as one version of the making of modern India.[7]

Madhusudan started writing poetry in English around 1841, when he was about seventeen (Murshid 2003, 33). He also began an extremely fascinating correspondence in English with his friend Gaur Dass Bysack, which is today one of the most valuable sources on his life. These letters are now available in the bilingual (Bengali-English) edition of his complete works called *Madhusudan Rachnavali* edited by Kshetra Gupta. In one of his early poems, we find the clear symptoms of the incurable obsession, which was to later prove to be his undoing.

> I sigh for Albion's distant shore,
> Its valleys green, its mountains high;
> Tho' friends, relations I have none
> In that far clime, yet, oh! I sigh
> To cross the vast Atlantic wave
> For glory, or a nameless grave!
>
> My father, mother, sister, all
> Do love me and I love them too,
> Yet oft the tear-drops rush and fall
> From my sad eyes like winter's dew.
> And, oh! I sigh for Albion's stand
> As if she were my native-land!
>
> Kidderpore, 1841 (Gupta 1980, 438)

Nostalgia for a place one has never been to! This, I think, is the first and best articulation of a pathology that colonialism created and whose symptoms are still evident today. The poem embodies what might best be called colonised desire. Colonial desire longs to conquer, occupy and possess a distant, often inhospitable land, for power and for glory. Similarly colonised desire wishes to capture, own and occupy both the space and the land of the coloniser as well as to be captured, owned and occupied by it. Such desire is neither retaliatory nor even reactive to begin with, but actually characterised by great innocence and self-confidence – wanting to be like the master, wanting to live where the master lives, wanting to *be* the master and to be accepted as such. Like a transmigrating soul, the colonised wishes to be 'translated' into the body of the coloniser.

One might say that these verses show that Madhusudan suffered from a severe maladjustment which resulted in transference of emotional attachment from the 'natural' mother (India) to a surrogate object of desire (England). This is not surprising considering that Madhusudan was a devotee of both the English language and of Western culture even before he became an adult. At the age of eight (in 1832) he was admitted to an English medium school in Calcutta and at thirteen (in 1837) he entered Hindu College. The environment at Hindu College worked to reinforce and institutionalise the superiority of Western culture. British imperialism seemed omnipotent as Madhusudan himself admitted later in 'The Anglo-Saxon and the Hindu,' a lecture he delivered in Madras in 1854, published subsequently as a booklet. Clearly, the Anglo-Saxon whites were a superior race, destined to conquer and rule the world, trampling on inferior people and places, leaving their stamp wherever they went: 'it is the Solemn Mission of the Anglo-Saxon to renovate, to regenerate, to civilise, or in a word, to Christianise the Hindu!' (Gupta 1980, 638). The only option was to be strong like the colonisers, to despise one's own past and detach oneself from one's pathetic countrymen.

Yet what is also important is that unlike others who were filled with resentment at this state of affairs, Madhusudan, far from resisting the West, welcomed its influence. No special persuasion was required to convert him; he took the initiative himself. He *loved* the West; its poetry, history and culture inspired him like his own never did. This is important because those who take the initiative themselves – in whichever direction – are not easy to control or contain.

In 1842 Madhusudan had already started sending his poems to English periodicals. In this, he prefigures many of his compatriots to this day, similarly aspiring to find acceptance in the great heartland of the advanced world. The Cinderella-like 'discovery' of an unknown author from the colonies, who then achieves fame and fortune in the great metropolis, is the stuff of which dreams are made of even today.[8] Madhusudan's poems were nearly always rejected, but his repeated attempts at seeking acceptance are instructive. In his letter of 7 October, 1842, he says to Gaur Dass:

> I have sent my poems to the Editor of the *Blackwood's* Tuesday last: I haven't dedicated them to you as I intended, but to William Wordsworth, the Poet: My dedication runs: 'These Poems are most respectfully dedicated to William Wordsworth Esq., the Poet, by a foreign admirer of his genius – the author.' Oh! To what a painful state have I committed myself. Now, I think the Editor will receive them graciously, now I think he will reject them (Murshid 2004, 23).[9]

The pathos of such hope, anxiety, expectation and final ultimate humiliation are familiar to us even today. With what naïve hope Madhusudan sent his work and with what lively expectations did he crave for an early acceptance and how innocently he changes his dedication of them from his unknown but dear friend to one of the most celebrated English poets of his time. Let me quote one more of Madhusudan's letters, this time to the editor of *Bentley's Miscellany*, London, written in October 1842:

> Sir,
>
> It is not without much fear that I send you the accompanying productions of my juvenile Muse, as contribution to your periodical. The magnanimity with which you always encourage aspirants to 'Literary Fame' induces me to commit myself to you. 'Fame,' sir, is not my object at present; for I am really conscious I do not deserve it – all that I require is Encouragement. I have a strong conviction that a Public like the British – discerning, generous and magnanimous will not damp the spirit of a poor foreigner. I am a Hindu – a native of Bengal – and study at the Hindu College in Calcutta. I am now in my eighteenth year, – 'a

child' – to use the language of a poet of your land, Cowley, 'in learning but not in age.' (Murshid 2004, 21)

The poor foreigner only begs for 'encouragement,' not daring to aspire to 'fame.' He expects support almost as his rightful due for being colonised. Yet the metropolis is not a charity; its purpose is not to extend sympathy and compassion to those who knock at its doors. It is, instead, run as a business, where profit and the ability to create wealth are what determine decisions.

Not surprisingly, the colonial heartland refuses to recognise its own accidental offspring or regard them as anything other than exotic objects of curiosity and amusement. The spirit of the poor foreigner must be dampened because cultural imperialism does not function on the basis of generosity, magnanimity, pity or even discernment. Simply put, in Madhusudan Dutt, we have an early example of the double alienation and marginalisation of the Westernised Indian. He first rejects his own community and creed, thereby alienating himself from them. Next he turns full of hope to his newly embraced masters' mores, but finds himself turned away for not being up to scratch. Now he is neither at home in India nor abroad.

Almost as if he was destined to work out such a life term, on 9 February, 1843, Madhusudan suddenly embraced Christianity. This event has puzzled biographers because there seems to have been no clear motivation for it. Madhusudan was not a religious person so he did not convert for theological reasons as had the Rev K. M. Bannerjee earlier or Rev Lal Behari Dey around the same time. In fact, Bannerjee himself noticed this when Madhusudan had gone to see him a couple of times before the event: 'I was impressed with the belief that his desire of becoming a Christian was scarcely greater than his desire of a voyage to England. I was unwilling to mix up the two questions...' (see Bose 1981, 24). Amalendu Bose uses this and other passages in Madhusudan's letters to suggest that the latter became a Christian because he felt that it would help him go to England. To me it seems that once Madhusudan had accepted the superiority of Western culture, his becoming a Christian was merely a logical step towards his goal of acquiring a new identity. He would do whatever was necessary to accomplish his makeover from Indian to English. The reasons for Madhusudan's conversion were essentially secular and profane, not religious or spiritual. Once he did convert, however, he did consider briefly going so far as to consider a career as a clergyman.

Madhusudan's instrumental approach to 'becoming English' is revealed in his letters of this period, albeit ironically. In October 1942, the previous year, he wrote to his friend Gaur Dass from a mufossil place, Tumlook: 'I am come nearer that sea which will perhaps see me at a period (which I hope is not far off) ploughing its bosom for "England's glorious shore"' (Murshid 2004, 26). In the same letter, he goes on to say: 'I am reading Tom Moore's *Life* of my favourite Byron – a splendid book upon my word! Oh! how should I like to see you write my "Life" if I happen to be a great poet – , which I am almost sure I shall be, if I can go to England' (ibid.). Madhusudan's prophecy did come true, but in a manner almost as if to spite his words. He did become a great poet, but in Bengali and at home, in Calcutta, not in English or in England. And his going to England did take place, but long after, in fact subsequent to his having already attained this distinction in his motherland. Sadly, after being recognised as a great poet at home, he has to spend his days abroad in abject penury, both his family and himself on the brink of starvation and destitution. Gaur Dass did not write Madhusudan's life, but did the next best thing by preserving his letters and works for posterity.

Biographers speculate that what hastened Madhusudan in his conversion to Christianity was the plan of his parents to get him married. In a letter dated 26 November, 1842, he writes to Gaur Dass: 'I am now plotting against my own parents. (I won't explain this, understand it yourself)' (Murshid 2004, 30). Then in a letter written at midnight the very next day, 27 November, 1842, he writes:

> At the expiration of three months from hence, I am to be married; dreadful thought! It harrows up my blood and makes my hair

stand like quills on the fretful porcupine! My betrothed is the daughter of a rich zemindar; poor girl! What a deal of misery is in store for her in the inexplorable womb of futurity.

In the very next sentence, he writes:

You know my desire for leaving the country, is to[o] firmly rooted to be removed. The sun may forget to rise, but I cannot remove it from my heart. Depend upon it – in the course of a year or two more, I must, either be in England or cease 'to be' at all – one of these must be done! (Murshid 2004, 33)

The die had been cast; Madhusudan could not turn back from an experiment in identity-swapping which would forever change his life. He not only began wearing western clothes, but got himself a 'European' haircut at the extravagant price of a gold mohur (Murshid 2003, 48).

The next sequence of letters, which is not precisely dated, was written some time in 1843 from the Old Mission Church after his conversion. Madhusudan had to be given police protection owing to the sensation which his conversion caused in the city. His father, who was a well-known lawyer, set hired *lathials* or goons to dissuade him. Madhusudan, however, was set on his course. He was baptised by Archdeacon Dealtry of the Church of England. Apparently, he did not assume his new name Michael upon conversion but only on seeking for himself a new identity in Madras later.[10] This event really shattered his parents, who were forced to disinherit him officially, but continued to support him covertly. He could now no longer live with them.

This period of his life shows just how great a risk Madhusudan had taken and how severe its consequences were going to be. His father, reconciled gradually to Madhusudan's great leap of faith, tried his best to get his son back, even promising to send him to England. In order to return home, Madhusudan would have to perform a penance, which he haughtily refused. Worse, he also had to drop out of Hindu College, whose rules did not permit his return. Again, his father tried his best to keep his son in the College, even paying his fees for months until the College made up its mind what to do (Murshid 2003, 54). D. L. Richardson had relinquished charge of the College, returning to England in April 1943. His successor, James Kerr and the College authorities, ruled against Michael. The implications of conversion slowly began to sink in.

Michael had no place to stay. At first he had been welcomed into the home of Dealtry, who baptised him. But after a few days, he could no longer avail the Archdeacon's hospitality, nor could he return home. None of his friends went to see him. Even Gaur Dass, the exception, relented only on Michael's pleading: 'Well I'm "in need" and if you are my "Friend indeed" show it now.... Alas! I am *Alone!* And am "in need" that is I want company' (Murshid 2005, 36). Michael had expected the whole world to go on as before, but how naïve and mistaken was he. Unable to find lodgings with any Hindu family, he was forced to live in the Old Church, the site of his conversion, before a kindly priest from another denomination offered him shelter.

Unwilling to go back to the Hindu fold, Michael joined, as a lay student, Bishop's College, an institution to train Indian Christians to become missionaries or teachers. He resided there from 1844 to 1847, completing his interrupted studies. In 1847, English replaced Persian as the official court language. Michael's father Rajnarain's income from his legal practice dwindled. Also, by now Michael's parents had lost all hope of recovering their son. Rajnarain married a second time, hoping to produce another male heir; then, when the second wife died soon after marriage, he married a third time, but still failed to produce another male heir. Madhusudan, however, was now on his own, cut off from his inheritance.

So, to try his prospects elsewhere, he set sail for Madras in South India in 1847, remaining there for the next nine years, till 1856. He worked first as an usher in the free Day School for boys attached to the Madras Male and Female Orphan Asylum run by the Church of England. His salary was Rs. 46 a month. Soon thereafter, in July 1848, he married Rebecca Thompson McTavish. She was then seventeen, while he was twenty-four. Murshid has painstakingly traced who she was. An orphan who lived in the female Asylum where Madhusudan worked, Rebecca's father was a British gunner, while her mother was an 'Indo-Briton' named Catherine Dyson, whose father had been English (hence Dyson) and the mother a native South Asian (Murshid 2003, 77). Michael, for this is the name he assumed when their marriage was entered in the Baptismal register, himself described the event to Gaur Dass as follows:

> Your information with regard to my matrimonial doings is quite correct. Mrs D. is of English parentage. Her father was an indigo-planter of this Presidency [Madras Presidency, one of three such administrative units in British India at this time – Calcutta Presidency and Bombay Presidency were the others]; I had great trouble in getting her. Her friends as you may imagine, were very much against the match. However, 'all is well, that ends well!' (Murshid 2005, 62)

Michael and Rebecca had four children. Later, in 1851, he became a Second Tutor in the Madras University High School, drawing a monthly salary of Rs. 150. These sums were considered quite adequate, if not handsome in those days, when entire families of peasants lived on 1 rupee a month, yet Michael was always short of money, a trait that dogged him to the end of his life.

To this period belong several of his English works such as *Visions of the Past*, *King Porus* and the more famous, *Captive Ladie* (1848). The latter poem did not launch Michael's career the way he thought it would. Indeed, it is quite an unconvincing, if not pathetic composition. The poet himself was not unaware of its shortcomings. In his letter of 6 July, 1849, Michael tells Gaur Dass: 'I am sure you are disappointed by my poem! I feel it. Remember, my friend, that I published it for the sake of attracting some notice, in order to better my prospects and not exactly for Fame' (Murshid 2005, 75). Though circulated in the limited circles of Anglo-India, the poem brought neither fortune nor fame for its author.

Michael's mother died in 1850 and his father in 1855. He now returned to Calcutta in January 1856 to try to reclaim his property, which his relatives were fighting over. What is amazing is that he left his wife and four children behind in Madras. The gap in his letters from 1849, when his first daughter was born, to 1855, when he had already resolved to return to Calcutta, leaves us with very few clues as to why he separated from his wife and children. This remains as one of the puzzles in the story of his life. But we do know that he travelled under an alias of 'Mr. Holt' from Madras to Calcutta (Murshid 2005, 103-104). Did he abandon them and run away, fearing that bringing them with him would jeopardise his prospects in Calcutta? Or did he leave them to start a new life with Henrietta Sophia White, whom he had known in Madras and who followed him to Calcutta.

Michael's second 'wife,' Henrietta, who was also from Madras, came to Calcutta about two years after his arrival there, in 1858 (Bose 1980, 90). Actually, they were never legally married because Rebecca did not divorce Michael, but kept the name Dutt till she died. According to Murshid, Henrietta must have been about sixteen, less than half Michael's age, when they must have first met around 1852 (Murshid 2003, 102). Amelia Henrietta Sophie was the eldest daughter of George White, who had been Michael's colleague at the Asylum. Michael's first daughter from this union, Sarmishtha, named after his first Bengali play, was born in 1859. This period of his life in Calcutta lasted till 1862, during which another son was born, whom he named Milton. Michael enjoyed a fairly secure and highly creative life during these six years. He first worked as head clerk and then as Chief Interpreter in the Court. He also recovered some of his property from his squabbling relatives.

It was in this brief span that Michael not only returned to Bengali, first as a dramatist and then as a poet, but established himself as the 'father' of modern Bengali poetry and one of the great poets in the language. He wrote *Sarmishtha* (1859), *Padmavati* (1859), *Ekei Ki Boley Sobhyata* (1860) and *Buro Shaliker Ghare Ron* (1860). The last two plays were satirical comedies which attacked the hypocrisies of his contemporaries. They didn't go well with his patrons and virtually brought his career as a dramatist to an end. He wrote one more play, *Krishna Kumari* (1860) and another play, *Maya Kaman*, was discovered to have been written nearly twelve years later (1872), after his return to India (Bose 1980, 47).

The poetical works, *Tilottama Sambhava Kavya* (1861), *Meghnad Badh Kavya* (1861), *Brajagana Kavya* (1861) and *Veerangana Kavya* (1862), which made him renowned in Bangla literary circles and at last earned him the 'Fame' he aspired for, were written within the next three years. What Michael wrote in these two to three years secured his position in the literary history of modern India, while the remaining years of his life seem to have been filled with unceasing restlessness and turmoil. A lot has been written about these compositions, especially *Meghnad Badh Kavya*, which is considered his masterpiece. Michael introduced, almost on a dare, blank verse into Bengali poetry. What is more, he made the villains, Ravan and Meghnad (Indrajit) the heroes, while turning Ram and Lakshman into effete and scheming cowards. One might argue that only a convert to Christianity, someone who had broken from his ancestral faith, could have done so.

In June 1862, Michael at last left for Europe to fulfil his cherished childhood dream when he was thirty-eight years old. It is unclear what made him decide to take this extreme step so late in his life, but he had at last wrested control over his ancestral properties and decided to use them to go to England to become a Barrister-at-Law. He reached his beloved Albion towards the end of July 1862 and entered Gray's Inn shortly thereafter. In February 1867, about four and a half years later, he returned to Bengal as Bar-at-Law with his wife and three children. These years abroad were marked by unmitigated agony and humiliation for him and his family. Before leaving Calcutta, Michael had made arrangements for his own allowance in England and for his family's expenses in Calcutta. Their arrangements did not work out. Henrietta found herself penniless without her husband and somehow managed to buy herself and her children a passage to join him, collecting whatever she could of Michael's inheritance. She reached England on 2 May, 1863. To save money, they moved to Versailles, France, which was then much cheaper than England. Living in terrible poverty and misery, they were saved from utter ruin only by the generous intervention of Ishwarchandra Vidyasagar, who periodically raised money on Michael's behalf. Every single letter of this period is filled with woeful and beseeching pleas to Vidyasagar to send more money to keep the Dutts alive. Michael probably even spent time in debtor's prisons in France before Vidyasagar made him solvent again. I shall quote only one example of the Dutts' distress. In his letter of 8 June 1864 to Vidyasagar, he cries:

> If we perish, I hope our blood will cry out to God for vengeance against our murderers. If I hadn't little helpless children and my wife with me, I should kill myself, for there is nothing in the instrument of misery and humiliations, however base and low, which I have not sounded! God has given me a brave and proud heart, or it would have broken long ago. (Murshid 2005, 207)

What is most interesting, however, about this European period, is that it was here that the recovery of self which began with Michael's return to Bengali, was completed, with Madhusudan Dutt's disillusionment with Europe. In one of his Bengali sonnets, 'Banga Bhasha,' the language, personified as a Goddess, tells the poet:

> 'You have, my child, a mass of jewels in your mother's lap; why then should you be in a beggar's garment? Go back home, you foolish child.' The poet responds: 'I obeyed this maternal command and presently found in my mother-tongue a mine of gems.' (Bose 1980, 73)

The sense of nostalgia is now reversed and corrected: no longer does the poet sigh for 'Albion's distant shore,' but for the sound of the river Kapotaksha, in the village Sagardanri, Jessore, where he was born:

> Constantly, O River, you come to my remembrance,
> Constantly I think of you when I am alone:
> As men in slumber dream of magical music,
> So I hear spell-bound the rippling sound of your flow. (Bose 1980, 74)

The last phase of Dutt's life belongs once again to Calcutta, where he returned in February 1867. He was admitted to the High Court as an advocate only upon the intervention and support of his influential friends because the notoriety he had acquired by now had allowed his enemies to bring up the question of his 'character.' Datta, however, continued to live extravagantly, incurring debts and soon found himself in dire financial straits once more. By 1872, his health was shattered. On 26 June, 1873, Henrietta, his wife, died. We find him telling his barrister friend, Manmohan Ghose,

> You see, Manu, my days are numbered, my hours are numbered, even my minutes are numbered....If you have one bread, you must divide it between yourself and my children; if you say you will, I depart with consolation. (Bose 1980, 81)

On 29 June, a few days later, as he had predicted, he himself died.

Already, during his last days, there was some question about whether he would ever get a decent Christian burial, because his co-religionists of Calcutta were unwilling to accept him as one of their own. Datta himself didn't care for such ceremony (Bose 1980, 81), but as it happened, there was no trouble. He was buried in the famous cemetery on Lower Circular Road and four hundred people attended his funeral. Some years back, I went to his grave to look at the memorial erected on it. His epitaph, which he had himself composed, is still legible. Here is its inscribed English translation:

> Stop a while, traveller!
> Should Mother Bengal claim thee for her son.
> As a child takes repose on his mother's Elysian lap,
> Even so here in the Long Home,
> On the bosom of the earth,
> Enjoys the sweet eternal sleep
> Poet Madhusudan of the Dattas.

Or in another more accurate translation by Bose:

> Pause a while, O passer-by;
> If born you have been in Bengal.

> In this grave, as a child resting
> In his mother's lap, here sleeps at the feet
> Of Mother Earth, Sri Madhusudan,
> The poet born in the family of the Dutts,
> A native of Sagar Danri, on Kapotaksh bank;
> His father, the noble Rajnarain, the mother, Jahanvi.
> (Bose 1980, 82)

This epitaph written not in English, but in Bengali, signals his final reintegration and return to the mother culture. We should note that he identifies himself as only, Sri Madhusudan, defining himself as a Bengali, a poet, born in the family of Dattas, native of Sagar Danri and the son of his parents in that order. The epitaph marks the complete recovery of the lost Indian self of Madhusudan.

4.4 A PRODIGAL'S PROGRESS?

This narration of Madhusudan's emblematic life will, I hope, serve as an allegory of sorts for the whole process of colonisation, at least in the cultural and literary sense. Madhusudan was the first of the many Indian poets who started writing in English, only to return to their mother tongue later. He thus anticipates, over a hundred years earlier, the typical structure of 'Exile,' 'Trial,' and 'Homecoming' that R. Parthasarathy enunciates in *Rough Passage*. I believe that all of us Westernised Indians go through his process, in one way or another. The return to an Indian identity need not always be through the medium of the mother tongue: even those of us who continue to write in English have to recover some of the lost portions of our identity through some other means, usually by owning up those configurations of thought and culture that are sub-linguistic, which enable us to derive strength from our traditions.

Madhusudan's obsession with the West ended as such compulsive addictions do – with calamity, if not destruction. Madhusudan sacrificed his parents, his religion, his ancestral property, his family, his health and all that he held dear, to capture the West, but he ended up rejected and bereft. I am reminded of Krishna's injunction in the *Geeta* about *svadharma: svadharme nidhanam shreyaha paradharmo bhayaavahaha* (better death following one's own nature for another's path is full of fear) (Bhagavad Gita 3.35) However, what is one's *svadharma* or true self? Also what is the duty most appropriate to it? Perhaps, Madhusudan's career suggests what it is *not,* even it does not help us define what it is. Certainly, for us post-colonials, our *svadharma* does not lie in rejecting or repudiating someone like Madhusudan, even if we do not wish to emulate him. Indeed, we owe him a debt of gratitude in his showing us the consequences of his type of career. On the other hand, we might argue that it is only by breaking the boundaries of his own society and traditions that Madhusudan could liberate himself to create and pen his kind of literary works. Whether hailed as our first modern poet or as an errant prodigal, Madhusudan's life needs to be restored to the larger narrative of the making of modern India, a narrative which is complex, contradictory as also contested, both from within and from without.

I had said earlier that it is possible to see Madhusudan as a person both made and unmade by colonialism. But having seen how he was unmade, we should also see how colonialism made him. That no one but a Westernised Indian could write poetry such as his is obvious. He introduced the blank verse into Bengali. This gave a new impetus as well as direction to it. He also gave a modern, even Western twist to the epic, *Meghnad Badh*. By depicting the gods as evil and the *rakshashas* good, the poem becomes a commentary of Madhusudan's own times. The poet's sympathies are with Meghnad, the honest, courageous, masculine, Western, Rakshasha who is done in by the deceitful, weak, cowardly, feminine Lakshamana. Was Madhusudan merely imitating Milton who, according to some, had made Satan more attractive than God? Or was Meghnad a projection of Madhusudan himself? Did he see himself done in by a weak, snivelling, cowardly and hypocritical Hindu society? More importantly, in the defeat of Meghnad and his ideology in the mythical past, did Madhusudan see an explanation for the fallen state of Hindu society in his own times? Or was Meghnad a prototype of Indian civilisation overpowered by the chicanery of the British? Or might we argue that what Rama and Lakshmana represented was neither weakness nor cowardice, but true strength and bravery, something that Madhusudan could not recognise because of his accepting the Western ideal of power over knowledge. In the end, it was another 'frail' and 'feminine' Mahatma who stood up against the might of the British empire. Any way we read the poem, the questions it raises cannot be silenced, nor can its subversive force be easily tamed.

To consider Madhusudan's life merely as the tragedy of someone who imitates the West is to reduce and over-simplify its significance. His biographers, like Murshid, resort to a sort of sentimentalism to win our sympathies for him. Clearly, this will not do either. We must own up Madhusudan as much as we accept Ram Mohan, because his life is as valid an experiment on how to deal with the West as was Ram Mohan's. While may need to choose between these two paths, we must do so with a rectitude that withholds either reductive condemnation or maudlin admiration.

Perhaps it would be appropriate to end this story with an interesting anecdote about him that is available in the literature on Sri Ramakrishna. It seems that Madhusudan met Sri Ramakrishna in the company of a devotee, Narayan Sastri, at the house of Dwarikanath Biswas. Madhusudan had arranged the meeting and wished to listen to Sri Ramakrishna. The latter, however, was unable to utter a word. Madhusudan wondered if this reluctance was because of his conversion. Sri Ramakrishna reportedly said, 'Not that. Believe me, I want to speak. But my chest is being pressed as it were by someone and I am prevented from speaking.' It was Sastri who spoke to Madhusudan instead, asking him in the course of the conversation why he gave up his religion. Pointing to his stomach, Madhusudan said, 'It was for this.' Sastri was very upset by this, but Sri Ramakrishna felt sorry for his visitor. He sang for him a few songs composed by Ramprasad and other Baul poets. It is reported that Madhusudan felt much better after listening to the songs (Prabhananda 1987, 46-50). Sri Ramakrishna offers Madhusudan not intellectual discourse or disputations, but the solace and transcendence of poetry and song. This non-judgemental acceptance of those who are our own, prodigal sons thought they may be, seems to me an appropriate note on which to bring to a closure this rendition of Madhusudan's story.

Though Madhusudan failed as an English poet and returned to Bangla, today, as a modern Indian, I have access to his life mainly, if not exclusively, through English. In trying to recover his life, I am forced to resort to the language he himself abandoned. Clearly, it is not only the direct route that works, but often it is the indirect, roundabout even paradoxical way that leads to the goal. Those who are literal-minded cannot cope with such contradictions and complications so would like to rewrite a simpler, more direct history, a history which will not trouble them with insecurity. Actually, history doesn't work that way: one can pursue the most un-Indian path to recover one's Indianness or use the most Indian methods to Westernise oneself. Hence what appears to be Indian, need not be Indian: what appears to be Western, need not be Western. In terms of what I have said earlier: the Self and the Other are not all that distinct or discrete. Whatever we call ourselves – Indian or Western – the Other, that which we are not, is also included in what we are.

4.5 CONCLUSION: COLONISER, COLONISED – OR NEITHER

One legacy of colonialism is a great transfer of populations. A time of scattering, as Homi Bhabha suggests, is also a time of gathering – albeit elsewhere:

> ...the scattering of the people that in other times and other places, in the nations of others, becomes a time of gathering. Gatherings of exiles and émigrés and refugees; gathering on the edge of 'foreign' cultures; gathering at the frontiers; gatherings in the ghettos or cafes of city centres; gathering in the half-life, half-light of foreign tongues, or in the uncanny fluency of another's language; gathering the signs of approval and acceptance, degrees, discourses, disciplines; gathering the memories of underdevelopment, of other worlds lived

retroactively; gathering the past in a ritual of revival; gathering the present. Also the gathering of people in the diaspora: indentured, migrant, interned; the gathering of incriminatory statistics, educational performance, legal statutes, immigration status.... (Bhabha 1994, 139).

This elsewhere is the space neither of the nation nor of exile, but, supposedly of diaspora, an in-between space, which as a supplement, alters the main text of a nation's history. Thus the history of Britain cannot be written without the inclusion of the history of its empire. Yet, are these two histories the same? They may be overlapping, but they are not the same. Though we see that the colonisers and the colonised co-mingle to create hybrids, both biological and cultural, such hybridities themselves are not identical or equal. Indeed, it is unwise to collapse entirely the distinction, even the division, between the colonisers and the colonised even if we refuse to see them as binaries. The assertion of difference is crucial to the cry for justice. No doubt, the colonised have now 'invaded' the coloniser, but they are neither fully integrated nor equal citizens in these societies. Often they live in ghettos, small enclaves or internal colonies of the metropolis, forced to do the least-paid and hardest jobs. Divided by race, national background and religion, they are unable to form a cohesive group within their new nations so as to fight for their rights.

The post-globalisation world does not take very kindly to nation states. Larger conglomerates such as the European Union are seen as more in the present economic world order. Big states such as the US, China, Japan, India, Brazil, Russia and South Africa and of course, entities like the European Union play a dominant role in today's world. Even so, global inequality is as much a problem as is global warming. Inequality, economic, political, cultural and ecological, is built on structures not dissimilar to colonialism and imperialism. These forces persist in our times; hence the struggle against them must also continue. The solution is not to destroy the dominant as the counter-systemic forces of religious bigotry seek to do nor, indeed, to join it as Madhusudan first tried to do, but to find a third way.

This third way is not necessarily Bhabha's interstitial space between the colonisers and the colonised, but perhaps Gandhi's, which seeks *svaraj* (self-rule) and *sarvodaya* (the welfare of all). This way can be found neither through capitulation nor through retaliation, but through principled self-expression and dialogue with the Other. Neither dominant nor subordinate, neither coloniser nor colonised, this truly third space is the natural habitat of all of us who belong to one human family.

WORKS CITED

Bhabha, Homi K. 1994. *The Location of Culture.* London: Routledge.
Bose, Amalendu. 1981. *Michael Madhusudan Dutt.* New Delhi: Sahitya Akademi.
Chakrabarty, Dipesh. 2000. *Provincialising Europe: Postcolonial Thought and Historical Difference.* Princeton, NJ: Princeton University Press.
Chatterjee, Partha. 1986. *Nationalist Thought and the Colonial World: A Derivative Discourse?* London: Zed Books.
Datta, Michael Madhusudan. 2005. *The Slaying of Meghanada : A Ramayana from Colonial Bengal.* Translated and with an introduction by Clinton B. Seely. New Delhi: Oxford UP.
De, Sushil Kumar. 1962. *Bengali Literature in the Nineteenth Century, 1757–1857.* Kolkata: Firma K. L. Mukhopadhyay.
Gupta, Kshetra ed. (1974) 1980. *Madhusudan Rachnavali.* Reprint. Calcutta: Sahitya Sansad.
Murshid, Ghulam. 1977. *Ashara Chalane Bhuli: Maikela-jivani* (Duped by Hope's Trickery: Michael's Life). 2nd ed. Kolkata: Ananda Publishers.
———. 2003. *Lured by Hope: A Biography of Michael Madhusudan Dutt.* Trans. By Gopa Majumdar. New Delhi: Oxford University Press.
———. Ed. 2004. *The Heart of a Rebel Poet: Letters of Michael Madhusudan Dutt.* New Delhi: Oxford University Press.
Nandy, Ashis. *The Intimate Enemy.* 1983. Delhi: Oxford University Press.
Parthasarathy, R. 1976. *Rough Passage.* Delhi: Oxford University Press.
Prabhananda, Swami, Ed. 1987. *First Meetings with Sri Ramakrishna.* Madras: Sri Ramakrishna Math.

5
BANKIM CHANDRA CHATTERJEE: COLONIALISM AND NATIONAL CONSCIOUSNESS IN *RAJMOHAN'S WIFE*

> Sri Ramakrishna (smiling): 'Bankim![1] Well, what has made you bent?'
> Bankim (smiling): 'Why, sir, boots are responsible for it. The kicks of our white masters have bent my body.'
>
> (GUPTA 1985, 667)

5.1 INTRODUCTION: THE PARADOX OF REPRESENTATION

Bankim Chandra Chatterjee (1838–1894) followed a course that was apparently the opposite of Madhusudan Dutt's, even his fame as a writer far exceeding the latter's. Bankim was a product of Hindu College, which in 1855, the year before he joined, was renamed Presidency College. When India's first modern university was established in January 1857 in Calcutta, Presidency College came under its jurisdiction. Bankim was one of the first two graduates of this university, earning a Bachelor of Arts degree in 1858. Soon thereafter, he was appointed as a Deputy Collector by the colonial administration. After he passed the Bachelor of Law (BL) exams in 1869, he was promoted to Deputy Magistrate. He served in the same position till 1891, retiring at the age of fifty-two, after having served under British officers for thirty-two years.

As his quip to Sri Ramakrishna above shows, Bankim knew a good deal about colonialism first hand. Unlike Madhusudan, he was no enthusiastic proponent of things Western or Christian. Instead, he is regarded as one of the great modernisers of Hindu traditions, in the line of Ram Mohan Roy, but of a somewhat more conservative, some even say, revivalist ilk. Bankim was no doubt reacting to the more aggressive and blatant forms of imperialism and racism which had come to the fore during Edward Robert Lytton Bulwer-Lytton or more simply Lord Lytton's term as the Viceroy from 1876-1880. This period was notorious for the great Bengal and South Indian famine (1876-1878), which starting in Bihar and Bengal, soon spread to central and south India, claiming over five million lives.[2] *Anandamath* (1882), though set a hundred years earlier, during another food crisis which coincided with the first years of British rule in Bengal when Warren Hastings was Governor-General, is clearly a famine text. It begins on bleak, hot day in rural Bengal in 1770, when the landlord of the village, Mahendra Simha, his wife Kalyani with their child, decide to take the high road to Calcutta because they have been starving. All about them, death, disease and utter destitution stalk the land. It is this 'fallen' state of India that the *santan* rebels in the novel wish to rectify. The novel went through several versions, as Chittaranjan Bandyopadhyay shows in his study (Bandyopadhyay 1983): Bankim's original criticism of the British colonisers was toned down and some of the harsher passages of the text directed against the Muslim rulers of Bengal inserted.

Around this time, Bankim also directed his energies at reconstituting Hindu traditions so that they could face contemporary challenges. Both *Krishnacharitra* (Life of Krishna, 1886) and *Dharmatattva* (Principles of Religion, 1888) were efforts in this direction. Attacking the eroticised and effeminate Krishna of the Gaudiya Vaishnava cult popularised by Chaitanya in Bengal, Bankim seeks to resurrect the Krishna of the Mahabharata, the Godhead incarnate who is also a prince, counsellor, warrior, master of Yoga and Karma and, above all, a practical man of the world (see Kaviraj

1995). If Chaitanya had reinterpreted the Gita as a text of devotion from Sankara's reading of it as a text of knowledge, then Bankim was the first among the moderns who tried to shift the emphasis from devotion to action. After him, a long line of political interpreters of the Gita, including Bal Gangadhar Tilak, Sri Aurobindo and Gandhi, would also see the song celestial as a call to action.

In September 1882, Bankim found himself embroiled in a heated public debate with the Reverend William Hastie, the Scottish missionary and Principal of the General Assembly's Institution (which was later renamed Scottish Church College). In a series of six letters published in *The Statesman*, India's leading English language newspaper, Hastie attacked Hindu idolatry, especially in the educated classes, some of whom had attended the worship of Krishna at the *sraddh* or funeral ceremony organised by Raja Radhakanta Deb of Shobhabazaar, Calcutta:

> Notwithstanding all that has been written about the myriotheistic idolatry of India, no pen has yet adequately depicted the hideousness and grossness of the monstrous system. It has been well described by one who knew it as 'Satan's masterpiece... the most stupendous fortress and citadel of ancient error and idolatry now in the world'... With much that was noble and healthy in its early stages, the Sanskrit literature became infected by a moral leprosy which gradually spread like a corrupting disease through almost all its fibres and organs. ... Need we seek elsewhere for the foul disease that has been preying upon the vitals of the national life and reducing the people to what they are? 'Shew me your gods,' cried an ancient Greek apologist, 'and I will show you your men.' The Hindu is just what his idol gods have made him. His own idolatry and not foreign conquerors has been the curse of his history. No people was ever degraded except by itself and this is most literally so with the Hindus. (quoted in Chatterjee 1969, 192–3)

In his spirited defence, Bankim responded by questioning Hastie's knowledge of Sanskrit, pointing to the inadequacy of translation and unmasking the imperial and missionary arrogance which underlay such rhetoric, thus concluding that Hastie's position was 'the logical outcome of that monstrous claim to omniscience, which certain Europeans ... put forward for themselves....Yet nothing is a more common subject of merriment among the natives of India than the Europeans' ignorance of all that relates to India....' (ibid.). Incidentally, Bankim 'cheerfully admit[s] the intellectual superiority of Europe' but he denies that 'intellectual superiority can enable the blind to see or the deaf to hear' (ibid.). This exchange has been much discussed. Tapan Raychauduri, for instance, considers it Bankim's 'first uncompromising avowal of faith in Hinduism' (Raychauduri 1988, 146) while Tanika Sarkar sees it as marking a major shift from the earlier radical, liberal, egalitarian Bankim of *Samya* (Equality, 1879) to a conservative, authoritarian as also intolerant stance (Sarkar 2001, 156).[3] It seems to me, however, that Bankim's project involved both a critique of his own traditions as well as the defence of these very traditions from external attack. While Madhusudan had internalised the missionaries' criticism of Hinduism, Bankim, like Ram Mohan Roy before and Sri Aurobindo after, entered the lists in defence of his culture.

The complexity of Bankim's position is all the more evident in his approach to literary questions which Amitav Ghosh, one of our most accomplished contemporary writers, explores in his essay 'The March of the Novel through History.'[4] Not only was Bankim Bengal's leading literary personality before Tagore, but he is also credited as being the founder of modern Bangla prose. Nirad C. Chaudhuri, for instance, hailed him as 'the creator of Bengali fiction and...the greatest novelist in the Bengali language' (Chaudhuri 1987, 156). However, Bankim accomplished this by forging a new path for himself as well as for Bangla, not by following older models. Like Madhusudan before him, Bankim broke from the Sanskritic literary conventions of his time, just as the early novelists in Europe repudiated the conventions of medieval romances to forge a new medium of realism for the new form that was the novel. Bankim openly admitted learning from Western models arguing that 'Imitation...was the law of progress; no civilisation was self-contained or self-generated, none could advance without borrowing' (quoted in Ghosh 2005, 114). Furthermore, he divided his fellow Bangla writers into two schools, Sanskritic and English, clearly indicating that he belonged to the latter:

> Those who are familiar with the present writers in Bengali, will readily admit that they all, good and bad alike, may be classed under two heads, the Sanskrit and the English schools. The former represents Sanskrit scholarship and the ancient literature of the country; the latter is the fruit of Western knowledge and ideas. By far the greater number of Bengali writers belong to the Sanskrit school; but by far the greater number of good writers belong to the other.... It may be said that there is not at the present day anything like an indigenous school of writers, owing nothing either to Sanskrit writers or to those of Europe. (ibid.)

Today, the Sanskritic school is, to all appearances, totally eclipsed, only its residual traces showing here and there, except in rare cases like Raja Rao who actively seek a reconnection with it. Moreover, one might argue that even the vernacular tradition of modern literature that Bankim helped to establish has today been overrun and overshadowed by Indian English writing.

Curiously, like Madhusudan, Bankim too began trying to write in English, before switching to Bangla. His first fictional experiment, *Rajmohan's Wife* (1864), remained unfinished and is considered by most to be a false start. Ghosh revisits this text in his essay to ask why Bankim embarked upon this laboured and unsuccessful attempt at writing a novel in English. In trying to find answers to his own questions, Ghosh speculates, 'I don't think Bankim was writing for anyone but himself. I suspect that Bankim never really intended to publish *Rajmohan's Wife* .... *Rajmohan's Wife* was clearly a rehearsal, a preparation for something else' (Ghosh 2005, 118). Yet what is this preparation for? It is, Ghosh believes, Bankim's attempt to domesticate the European novel into Bangla, 'to mount a springboard that would allow him to vault the gap between two entirely different conventions of narrative' (ibid.). The radical 'dislocation' of writing in English was necessary in order to lay claim to the all-too-familiar location of his fictional world that lay all about him in the countryside of Bengal which Bankim knew so well. But to transform it into fiction he had to see it again, as it were, through the foreign eyes of English: 'To write about one's surroundings is anything but natural: to even perceive one's immediate environment one must somehow distance oneself from it....' (Ghosh 2005, 119). Ghosh does not quite answer how this 'very loss of a lived sense of place that makes their fictional representation possible' (ibid.) works when Bankim shifted from English to Bangla. Did he, perhaps, like Madhusudan, who introduced blank verse into Bangla or who turned villains into heroes, use the unfamiliar mode of English realism to write about his recognisable surroundings in order to create a 'sense of place' which we so expect from modern novels?

It is now time to examine the actual text, which is the subject of this chapter, for answers to such questions.

5.2 ASIA'S 'FIRST' ENGLISH NOVEL?

The recent reprintings[5] of Bankim Chandra Chatterjee's abruptly abandoned or (un)finished English novel, *Rajmohan's Wife*, originally published in 1864, makes available an important nineteenth century text for renewed consideration. Professor Meenakshi Mukherjee, the editor of one of these reprints (Chatterjee [1864] 1996), in her Foreword and Afterword, highlights several important areas for debate and discussion: the implications and consequences of writing in English as opposed to Bangla, the 'realistic' mode of representation used in the novel and the entire question of 'Woman' in the nineteenth century. The text, as Mukherjee says, is 'a potent site for discussing crucial questions about language, culture, colonisation and representation.' While this is true, Mukherjee does not provide a framework within which these issues may be read productively if problematically.

I believe the latter is possible if the novel is read as a sort of national allegory.

Frederic Jameson, it may be recalled, claimed that:

> All third-world texts are necessarily, I want to argue, allegorical and in a very specific way: they are to be read as what I will call *national allegories*, even when, or perhaps I should say, particularly when their forms develop out of predominantly western machineries of representation, such as the novel. (Jameson 1986, 69)

Aijaz Ahmad's incisive and relentless interrogation of 'Jameson's Rhetoric of Otherness' (see Chapter 3 of *In Theory: Classes, Nations, Literatures*) notwithstanding, national allegories are common to both Western, canonical and other post-colonial literatures, I think it would be useful to see if *Rajmohan's Wife* can be read in this manner. We would, of course, do well to question binary oppositions between the so called 'First' and 'Third' worlds, not to speak of singular and reductive ways of theorising their literatures.

Indeed, it is not at all unusual to read Bankim as one of the creators of Indian nationalism, who used devises such as allegory and personification extensively to convey his ideas. Sri Aurobindo made such an interpretation in the essays that he wrote as early as 1894, the year of Bankim's death, in *Indu Prakash,* arguing that what Bankim was trying to create was nothing short of 'a language, a literature and a nation' (Aurobindo [1894] 1972a, 102). That *Anandamath* (1882), despite Bankim's additions of pro-British statements in the second edition of 1883, inspired generations of Indian freedom fighters, is a historical fact. Both a national song and a battle cry, it influenced thousands of revolutionaries as well as millions of more moderate Indians. In a later essay, 'Rishi Bankim Chandra,' Sri Aurobindo, writing in a nationalist newspaper also called *Bande Mataram,* said that Bankim in his later works 'will rank among the Makers of Modern India' (Aurobindo [1907] 1972b, 345). Sri Aurobindo claimed that Bankim not only fashioned a new language which could 'combine the strength, dignity or soft beauty of Sanskrit with the nerve and vigour of the vernacular' (ibid.), but, what was more important, practically invented 'the religion of patriotism' (346). Bankim was able to do this by giving the country 'the vision of our Mother':

> It is not till the Motherland reveals herself to the eye of the mind as something more than a stretch of earth or a mass of individuals, it is not till she takes shape as a great Divine and Maternal Power in a form of beauty that...the patriotism that works miracles and saves a doomed nation is born. To some men is given to have that vision and reveal it to others. It was thirty-two years ago that Bankim wrote his great song and a few listened; but in a sudden moment of awakening ...and in a fated moment somebody sang *Bande Mataram*. The Mantra had been given in a single day[,] a whole people had been converted to the religion of patriotism. The Mother had revealed herself....
> A great nation which has had that vision can never again bend its neck in subjection to the yoke of a conqueror. (347)

Sri Aurobindo's eulogy, written in the heady days of his revolutionary activism is not exaggerated. For decades, several martyrs to the cause of India's freedom went to the gallows with the cry '*Bande Mataram*' on their lips. The novel *Anandamath* was itself translated into all the major Indian languages and widely circulated long after Bankim's death. One indication of its impact is the fact that there are seven different translations of the book in Hindi alone (Bose 1974, 125).

I would like to suggest that though the pronounced nationalism of *Anandamath* belongs to a later phase in Bankim's career its beginnings may be found in *Rajmohan's Wife*. This is because Bankim's larger project was nothing short of the task of imagining a nation into existence through his fictional and non-fictional writings. Consciously or unconsciously, that is what he strove to accomplish. As Sudipto Kaviraj puts it:

> An imaginary community can only have an imaginary history. The actual history of Hindus and Indians could, by definition, never capture what was wanted of it, a history of mobilised action. Only a fictional history can show such reconstructed Hindus or

Indians, putting men of the future inside events of the past. That is why the task wanted of this historical discourse could never be accomplished by a discourse of facts, but by a discourse of truth, or poetry, of the imagination. (Kaviraj 1995, 131)

It is only in the 'mythic discourse' of novels that such a task can be accomplished. Kaviraj calls this discourse Bankim's 'imaginary history,' after Bhudev Mukhopadhyay's famous phrase '*Swapnalabdha Bharatvarser Itihas*' (A Dream-derived History of India) the title of an influential book. The phrase is felicitous because of its multiple semantic possibilities: not only does it mean the more obvious 'history of India as revealed or obtained in a dream', but it also suggests that the Bharatvarsha or India that it refers to is itself revealed or obtained in a dream – and therefore imaginary.

There are many other reasons to tempt us to read *Rajmohan's Wife* as an imaginary history of modern India. For long, *Rajmohan's Wife* has been considered the *first* Indian English novel. Some years ago, Subhendu Kumar Mund claimed that Paunchkouree Khan's *The Revelations of an Orderly* first published in *Benares Recorder* in 1846 and later reprinted in London by James Madden in 1849 is the first Indian English novel (Mund 1997, 9). More than one edition of the book is available. The earliest that I could find was published in London by James Madden and Co in 1849. The webpage where the book opens indicates that Panchkhouree Kahn is a pseudonym.[6] The actual author, I suspect, was not Indian, but an Englishman. Also, the book consists of the revelations of an Orderly or lower court functionary, a device used by its author to expose the abuses in the mofussil courts, which is what the subtitle indicates: 'BEING AN ATTEMPT TO EXPOSE THE ABUSES OF ADMINISTRATION BY THE RELATION OF EVERY-DAY OCCURRENCES IN THE MOFUSSIL COURTS.' This is a reformist and satirical tract, not by any stretch of imagination a novel in the commonly understood sense of the term. To claim this as the first Indian English novel is, therefore, unfounded; Mund seems to have been duped.

For all practical purposes therefore, Mund's or other similar claims have not robbed *Rajmohan's Wife* of the glamour attached to first texts. By setting itself up as a sort of originary type of a certain cultural encounter, the novel seems to promise much. However, the only exemplary value that most critics have derived from it is to regard it as a 'false start,' the road that should not have been taken. Sunil Kumar Banerji's and Kaviraj's books on Bankim do not even mention the book. Mukherjee cites Sri Aurobindo, Nirad C. Chaudhuri, Sisir Kumar Das and Jogesh Chandra Bagal in support of the view that the novel was a sort of 'mistake'; Bankim himself advised Romesh Chandra Dutt to write in Bangla (Chatterjee 1996, 151-154). Mukherjee argues that though Bankim accepted English as a valid medium for political and polemical writings, the mother tongue was the preferred language for imaginative literature. The parallel with Michael Madhusudan Dutt, the first modern Bangla poet, is too obvious to reiterate. In the latter's case, the repudiation of English was not just more categorical, but more moving and pathetic (ibid.). All this evidence supposedly goes to show that the only thing that *Rajmohan's Wife* exemplifies is a wrong cultural turn, which Bankim himself rectified when he switched to Bangla with *Durgeshnandini* two years later.

5.3 NATIONAL CULTURE AND COLONIALISM

It is not my purpose to oppose the 'false start' view merely on grounds that a hundred years later Indians have proved that they can write complex and satisfying novels in English. In fact, I would argue just the opposite: that however 'good' or 'successful' these English novels are, they can't accomplish what novels written our own region in Bangla, Hindi, Marathi, Kannada and so on, do. The kind of Indian experience that can be represented in English is different from what is available in other Indian languages. That Bankim was well aware of these limitations is obvious; therefore his switching to Bangla was not just accidental or fortuitous, but deliberate and felicitous both aesthetically and politically. And yet, I think *Rajmohan's Wife* cannot be dismissed merely as a false start. It is much more than an indirect commentary on the limitations of writing a novel about India in English. What the novel actually offers is a way of mapping the Indian society of that period on a complex grid of ideological, political, social and cultural coordinates. The novel accomplishes this through its richly textured negotiation of cultural choices for a newly emergent society, which for the sake of convenience, we may call modern India. In other words, *Rajmohan's Wife* may perhaps be read as an allegory of modern India, of the kind of society that can rise out of the debris of an older, broken social order and of the new, albeit stunted, possibilities available to it under colonialism. The novel shows both the glimmer of hope and a more realistic closure of options towards the end.

In order to read the novel in this manner, we shall have to agree that each character is much more than the portrayal or representation of an individual. That the characters are individuals cannot be disputed, but for the kind of reading that I have in mind, their typical and collective features must be teased out and highlighted. Viewed in this light, each character becomes an embodiment of social conditions and ideological configurations. Each is not merely individual moral agent, but carries larger socio-cultural thematic baggage. Such a reading will not seem implausible when we bear in mind that the latter half of the nineteenth century was a period of intense cultural reformation during which nothing short of what Frantz Fanon called a national culture was to emerge. As Fanon put it in *The Wretched of the Earth*:

> A national culture is the whole body of efforts made by a people in the sphere of thought to describe, justify and praise the action through which that people has created itself and keeps itself in existence. (Fanon 1976, 188)

For Fanon, this struggle for the creation of a national culture mobilises what is the best as also the most energetic in a society:

> It is the fight for national existence which sets culture moving and opens to it the doors of creation. Later on it is the nation

which will ensure the conditions and framework necessary to culture. The nation gathers together the various indispensable elements necessary for the creation of a culture, those elements which alone can give it credibility, validity, life and creative power. (197)

That much of Bankim's life and certainly most of his writing was employed in the creation of such a national culture is now well established, as we have already seen. To read *Rajmohan's Wife* as a part of this larger project is therefore to accept an invitation that the author and his texts so clearly extend to us.

At the heart of such a culturalist-allegorical reading of the novel is, of course, Matangini, the heroine of *Rajmohan's Wife*. We see her first in the opening pages of the novel as an eighteen-year-old 'perfect flower of beauty':

> The dainty limbs of the woman of eighteen were not burdened with such an abundance of ornaments, nor did her speech betray any trace of the East Bengal accent, which clearly showed that this perfect flower of beauty was no daughter of the banks of the Madhumati, but was born and brought up on the Bhagirathi in some place near the capital. Some sorrow of deep anxiety had dimmed the lustre of her fair complexion. Yet her bloom was as full of charm as that of the land-lotus half-scorched and half-radiant under the noonday sun. Her long locks were tied up in a careless knot on her shoulder; but some loose tresses had thrown away that bondage and were straying over her forehead and cheeks. Her faultlessly drawn arched eyebrows were quivering with bashfulness under a full and wide forehead. The eyes were often only half-seen under their drooping lids. But when they were raised for a glance, lightening [sic] seemed to play in a summer cloud. Yet even those keen glances charged with the fire of youth betrayed anxiety. The small lips indicated the sorrow nursed in her heart. The beauty of her figure and limbs had been greatly spoilt by her physical or mental suffering. Yet no sculptor had ever created anything nearly as perfect as

the form half revealed by the neat sari she wore. (Chatterjee [1864] 1996, 3)

This carefully drawn portrait is a unique contribution of the traditional and the radically new. As Ganeswar Mishra shows, it uses several elements from both classical and folk forms. For instance, the heroine is always shown with a companion who serves to highlight the former's beauty; besides, several of the images used are taken from long-standing literary conventions (Mishra 1990, 10). Bankim's overtly stated departure from classical conventions was not entirely successful, after all. But, given that Bankim's dissatisfaction with literary conventions was well known, the question that arises is what was new or different about Matangini? Mishra says 'It is characteristic of the Sanskrit school that they seldom venture an original composition' (Mishra 1990, 5). What we realise is that the description of Matangini may be typical in certain respects, but her actions are not. She's an entirely new kind of heroine, someone who is not timid and weak, but strong and spirited. She carries the plot forward with her own kinetic energy and though thwarted, does not end up entirely defeated. It is such selective retention of tradition coupled with innovative departures that characterises the strange familiarities of Indian modernity. We may term this our unique double-vision or hybridity, but it becomes constitutive of the whole mentality of our times.

Matangini, then, is not just Rajmohan's wife, but the 'spirit' or personification of modern India itself. This is an emergent, hesitant, yet strong-willed and attractive India. It is not the India of villages or the old India of feudal ossifications. This India has been born near the capital, Calcutta and is full of new possibilities. But, this beautiful and powerfully drawn image of India is also shown as burdened by sorrow and anxiety. It is neither free nor happy, but its energies and powers are under the control of an unworthy 'husband.' No wonder, the very first chapter begins with a temptation and a transgression. Matangini, who has been forbidden from going to fetch water from the river, is cajoled by her friend Kanak into doing so. Matangini, thus, crosses the threshold, thereby exposing herself to Madhav, her brother-in-law and setting the plot into motion. What Malashri Lal called 'the law of the threshold,' thus, seems to operate in the very first Indian English novel (Lal 1995). Once Matangini has stepped 'over the bar,' she can never return to her 'designated first world' but must make the 'irretrievable choice of making the other world [her] permanent home' (Lal 1995, 12). The defining features of modern India are thus its energy, its adventurousness, its unwillingness to be confined by tradition with its desire to break free. Yet, especially in the way modernity in this text is engendered, its transgressivity is attendant with serious risks of irrevocable displacement and rupture. The restlessness, vitality, charm and drive of an emerging society, with all its anxieties, fears and threats are thus embodied in Matangini.

The next chapter is symmetrical to the first in that it introduces us to two male characters, one of whom is clearly a foil to the other. The older man, Mathur, is crude, vulgar as well as corpulent. Tall, stout, dark, 'he had something positively unattractive about him' (Chatterjee [1864] 1996, 7). Almost bald, his fat body oozes out of his Dacca muslin shirt. He has a gold amulet, a gold chain, gold studs on his shirt with rings on all the fingers of his hands. This is the picture of a corrupt unscrupulous landlord, one of the first of many such portraits to follow in Indian fiction and cinema and the villain of this novel. He is described as 'an exceedingly apt scholar in the science of chicane, fraud and torture' (17). It is not surprising that it is he who wishes to steal the will from Madhav and who later imprisons Matangini in his cellar, 'determined to gratify at once both revenge and lust' (119).

The other man, the hero of the novel, is Madhav, 'a remarkably handsome young man of about twenty-two' (8). In both Matangini and Madhav, physical appearance is an index of moral character. Madhav is from Calcutta, an English educated, progressive zamindar, in total contrast to Mathur. What Madhav lacks, though, is Matangini's energy and vitality: 'His clear placid complexion had turned a little dull either through want of exercise or too much comfort' (8). We will remember that Mathur's complexion has been described as 'dull and dark' (7) earlier. Thus, both men are dull, a quality which signifies *tamas* or lethargy, ignorance, sloth. Matangini, in contrast, is full of power and charm. The dimming of the lustre of her complexion is not a sign of dullness or torpor, but of anxiety and oppression. Clearly, the embodied female *shakti* or the energy that both men wish to possess, she is seen as the object of desire, the woman who can give value, meaning alongwith direction to the lives of these indolent men. Both Mathur and Madhav represent different kinds of social privilege or prestige. Bankim is implying that unless the privileged are yoked in the service of society, they lack direction or purpose. Their lives are wasted in idle self-indulgence, or worse, in wickedness and fraud. Yet, Bankim is quick to contrast the attitudes of the two cousins to Matangini. While Mathur regards her merely as a sexual object, a potential conquest, Madhav admonishes him against prattling about 'a respectable woman passing along the road' (10). Sexual mores are thus of great importance in the novel; the chaste, the respectable, the self-regulating are seen as virtuous, while those who are sexually predatory or transgressive are not forgiven. This is in keeping with Bankim's larger view of Dharma (see Haldar 1989, 55–58), but also creates a tension between the desired and the forbidden.

It is clear that Matangini is the cherished object of embodied desire; whoever wins her affection will be the real victor at the end of the novel. The struggle is for modern India, no less – to whom will it ultimately belong? The contenders are not just the *asuric* or demonic Mathur and the *daivic* or angelic Madhav, but also the man who is her husband, Rajmohan. The latter is described as 'the very image of Death' (Chatterjee [1864] 1996, 12) when he is first seen in the novel. By now, we already know that the marriage is a failure. It is, in fact, clear through the novel that the two do not seem to have any sexual relations, though Rajmohan, callous and coarse though he may be, is the very personification of sexual jealousy. A cruel, brutish man of enormous strength, but with a warped moral sense, Rajmohan is both villain and victim. In the third chapter he shouts to his wife, 'I'll kick you to death' (13). His utter lack of consideration for Matangini is one aspect of his wickedness of personality; the other is that he is willing to rob his own benefactor. Perhaps, it is that ingratitude, rather than his cruelty, that turns Matangini decisively away from him.

The complexity of his character arises, I would contend, out of his ambiguous class position. By caste, he belongs to the same group as Mathur and Madhav; he is actually a distant cousin of theirs. But unlike them, whose grandfather rose from being a servant to a master, Rajmohan is unable to do so. In fact, in betraying Madhav, perhaps, he too wishes to rise above himself though usurpation and force. Rajmohan is frequently angry and abusive with Matangini; there is a deep frustration in him in not being able to possess what by right is his. He is the unhappy husband who chafes bitterly at not being worthy of his wife's acceptance. But the real question is who or what does Rajmohan represent? We have seen that Mathur and Madhav respectively stand for the reactionary and the progressive bourgeois elites who are vying for the control of the emerging nation. If so, then what of Rajmohan? I argue that Rajmohan stands for the lumpenised and degraded petty bourgeoisie under colonialism, alienated from its own people and country. Though not quite of the proletariat, Rajmohan in his alienation from Matangini is symbolic of the ordinary folk being unable to 'man' the nation, so to speak. Beneath him are the hired robbers, musclemen and thugs, either enforcing or destabilising the established order, depending on whom they serve. And below them all, invisible, impoverished and brutalised, is the vast peasant underclass that is simply not in touch with and therefore cannot espouse the delicate and precious blossom of the new nation in the making. As in India's own case, the struggle for/ of the nation is often perceived as a struggle between the colonial and the national elites, with the national proletariat sidelined totally. Yet, for the struggle to bear fruit, the proletariat needs to line up behind the worthy elite in the latter's attempt to overthrow imperial rule.[7] In this novel, the elite is symbolically split into the worthy and the unworthy, while the proletariat is almost invisible, only to surface now and then in a criminalised, brutish and alienated form. Matangini is the spirit of the nation, a type of 'Mother India,' whom

Bankim deified later so eloquently and popularly in his song '*Bande Mataram*,' incorporated into *Anandamath* after its composition.

Bankim is at pains to provide the genealogy of the bourgeois leaders of this society. Bangshibadan Ghose, the progenitor of the clan to which Mathur and Madhav belong, is a menial servant to begin with. His rise signifies the destruction of the old feudal order of pre-colonial India and the rise of an intermediate class under colonial rule. The manner of Bangshibadan's elevation is typical of Bankim's narrative strategy. When the zamindar dies, his young wife, Karunamayee, takes the servant as her lover. Again, the woman becomes the embodiment of power and wealth; by attaining Karunamayee, Bangshibadan comes to possess the fortune, which is now in contention. Karunamayee, like Matangini after her, embodies the spirit of the nation in her attractive femininity and fecund womanhood. The split in the elite that I mentioned earlier is evident in the contrary dispositions of two of Bangshibadan's sons. Ramakanta, the elder son, is industrious and hardworking, but closed to English education and modernity. His son, Mathur, thus comes to represent a corrupt and dying tradition. The other son, Ramkanai, though indolent and extravagant, educates his son Madhav in Calcutta. What is implied is that the rightful heir to the 'e/ state' that is India ought to be someone who combines the industry of Ramakanta and the education of Madhav; only such a person can be the worthy partner of Matangini and 'husband' the modern nation. The third son, Rajgopal, dying childless, has bequeathed his property to Madhav, the worthier of his two nephews. It is this will, which legalises the bequest, that Mathur is after. If Matangini represents the future of India, Ramgopal's will represents its past. Who should inherit the legacy of the past and direct the future of the country – this is the question at the heart of the novel. Madhav's offer to help Rajmohan is yet another instance of the responsible elite trying to fulfill its duties to the underclass, but in this case, it is Rajmohan who rejects Madhav's offer. Matangini intervenes to ensure that the past does not entirely miscarry. She saves Madhav, but cannot consummate her love for him. The ideal combination of the past, present and future is not to be, at least not yet; the conditions are still not propitious. Yet though the experiment fails, it does highlight some choices before the nation.

In the above analysis I have deliberately not resorted to what might be termed a vulgar materialist reading. Such a reading, which reduces all the so called superstructural elements to the base of class and economic determinism does injustice, if not violence, to Bankim's strategy of representation. This is because Bankim uses both native categories like the theory of *gunas* derived from Samkhya with modern ones from his understanding of Indian realities as an English educated civil servant of the British colonial government. That is why, none of these characters are 'pure' types; rather, they embody complex, even contradictory tendencies and therefore invite multiple significations. Thus, for one, materialist notions of class need to be juxtaposed with idealistic categories such as *gunas* or ideal types to get a better understanding of Bankim's representational methodology. Even so, an allegorical reading such as I have attempted, can be shown to be consistent when applied to the book as a whole.

Tara, Mathur's faithful and long suffering first wife, must not be forgotten in this equation. She plays an important role in saving Matangini's life and honour. She is the other half of a feminine pair that counterparts the male duo of Mathur–Madhav. If Matangani is modern India, Tara is traditional India, representing the best of the residual culture, those vestiges that though soon to be eclipsed, will serve a constructive role in the building of the new world.

Thus, at the end of the novel, after many adventures, Madhav is saved, Mathur hangs himself and Matangini is banished. How simple, yet stark the resolution and how seemingly misogynistic. Matangini, whose boldness makes her risk her life to save her beloved Madhav is, however, not rewarded at the end of the book. She is sent back to her father's house and the novelist tells us that 'she died an early death' (Chatterjee [1864] 1996, 126). The energy of the new India that she represents cannot find fruition in this novel. Her union with Madhav is impossible, though both personally and ideologically they constitute the basis of the new India that is to come. It would seem that for Bankim, India's destiny is to be shaped by the new English-educated elite, but somehow this cannot be affected easily. There are insurmountable barriers to this project of refashioning India. Perhaps, the real hitch was the hidden but dominant and all pervasive colonial presence, which is merely hinted at in the book. India's modernisation was not smooth, but badly distorted. There is no easy or happy end in sight to Matangini's problems.

As Sarkar (2001) is at great pains to show, Bankim is uneasy with female desire and sexuality. In *Krishnacharitra* he takes the relatively minor incident of Arjuna's abduction of Krishna's sister Subhadra, both defending and interpreting it at considerable length to justify how, under certain circumstances, the *dharmic* or dutiful man might take control of the force of female sexuality for a higher cause. Matangini, even if she is the driver and engine of the plot, is a destabilising vector. For the higher good of society she must be set aside. Madhav's and Matangini's passion for each other, likewise, must remain unfulfilled, at least under the present circumstances. Instead, both Matangini's confinement and the attack on Madhav serve as the crises which divert this consummation to other ends. Simply put, the project of modern India needs to be shelved for the time being, its deferred realisation being the inevitable conclusion also of *Anandamath*, published nearly twenty years later. Bankim can still see no way out of the current impasse; the preconditions for the emergence of the new India of his dreams were simply not present even if such possibilities were evident *in potentia*.

What is interesting is that in this novel, the colonial power is seen as ambivalent at worst and benign at best. That Bankim is not naïve is shown in the fact that the character who symbolises British colonial authority is not English at all, but a 'shrewd and restlessly active Irishman.' Did Bankim understand that the Irish, who were themselves victims of colonialism, would be best suited to show colonial authority at its least abusive? At any rate, this Irishman, who is the Magistrate, ensures that justice is done, that Mathur cannot escape by bribing the police. British rule is thus seen as just - providential, if not paternalistic - an interlude when India can recover her strength, after centuries of oppression and suffering. Justice, equity, impartiality and peace – those virtues that both colonial authorities and their Indian collaborators often cited as the supposed features that legitimated the Raj, are, apparently, endorsed in this novel too as characteristic of British rule. What we therefore see is a complex picture of colonialism in which though the colonial authority is not directly criticised, the heroine, Matangini, cannot find the means to fulfill herself. Her love is thwarted, her aspirations crushed, her life threatened. What is more, she is imprisoned and almost raped. In the end, her survival against all odds is itself almost a miracle. But Matangini's life is not a success. She does not get what she deserves. Her courage, fearlessness, loyalty, in fact all these and her loveliness too, are wasted.

That Bankim personally confronted this dilemma is clear in an essay such as '*Bharatbarsher Svdhinata Ebang Paradhinata*' (India's Independence and Dependence):

> All work of governance is now in the hands of the Englishmen – we are unable to do anything on our own because we are dependent on others. Because of this we are not learning how to protect our country and how to govern our country – our national qualities are not getting any scope for their fulfilment. Hence it must be agreed that in this respect dependence is an impediment to progress. But we are learning European literature and science. If we were not dependent on a European nation, we would not have been fortunate enough to enjoy this bliss. So on the one had our dependence has been harmful to us and on the other hand we are making progress. (quoted in Haldar 1989, 100)

Bankim, then, found himself in an impossible situation, somewhat like Matangini. Just as Matangini and Madha – and other pairs of doomed lovers in Bankim – suffer from two forms of contradictory desire, so does Bankim, in his attitude to the Raj. It is this contradictory consciousness that Kaviraj has called 'unhappy.' On the one hand is the 'socially sanctified' form of desire within marriage, but, on the other hand, is the more powerful, 'socially unsanctified form of passion ... that threatens the mapping and the whole architecture of the social world' (Kaviraj 1995, 6). In Bankim's own thinking they correspond, respectively, to the politically sanctioned approval of British rule and the prohibited desire to be emancipated from it.

I have been suggesting that the tragedy of Matangini, a tragedy of unfulfilled potential, frustrated love and self-sacrificing heroism is also, allegorically, the tragedy of a newly emergent India. This India, whose possession is fiercely contested by forces of tradition, modernity and colonialism is, in the end, a broken if not defeated India. It is an India that is beset and oppressed from all sides, an India whose coming into its own is frustrated. Perhaps, at a more propitious time, the combination of forces required to guide its destiny might emerge; as far as the novel is concerned, this possibility is postponed. Matangini's transgressions are thus only partially successful. The dream of creating a new society from the remnants of a decaying older order is thus a failed experiment in this novel. Like Hester Prynne, Matangini will have to wait for another time and space before she or someone like her can live happily with her chosen mate. In the meanwhile, her struggle and sacrifice do leave a mark on society.

In *Rajmohan's Wife*, Bankim was trying not just discover the right formula to write a successful novel, but also the right formula to create a new India. The project of inscribing a new India continues in many other novels and novelists throughout the nineteenth and early 20th centuries. In Rabindranath Tagore's *Gora* (1909), for example, we find the seeds of a new society in the union of Gora and Suchorita on the one hand and of Binoy and Lolita on the other. With the guidance of Anandamoyi and Poresh babu, the younger generation is offered a fresh opportunity to refashion a new world. In *Rajmohan's Wife*, however, Matangini's efforts are not rewarded with success. Yet, her survival is in itself a kind of partial success. There is hope for India, but the experiment to recreate the nation will have to be conducted again, with different actors. It is not that Bankim did not write stories with happy unions between the heroes and heroines; but these tales lacked the power and dynamism of those novels, such as *Rajmohan's Wife, Durgeshnandini, Kapalakundala, Bishbriksha, Krishnakanter Will* and *Rajasingha*, where love triangles, unrequited passions, unbearably conflicting desires and unhappy unions dominate the plot.

Before I end, I would like to return to the symbolic significance of *Rajmohan's Wife* as the 'first' Indian English novel. As in the murky beginnings of any genre, the commencement of Indian English fiction too is shrouded in mystery. Kylash Chunder Dutt's *A Journal of 48 Hours of the Year 1945* (1835) and Shoshee Chunder Dutt's *The Republic of Orissa: Annals from the Pages of the Twentieth Century* (1845), the remaining contenders after the disqualification of Panchkouree Khan's *The Revelations of an Orderly*, are very difficult to find, appreciate, or relate to. They have become obscure, if historically significant, texts. Toru Dutt's *Bianca or A Young Spanish Maiden* (1878) published after *Rajmohan's Wife* is incomplete. Even *Rajmohan's Wife* as we know it today is not entirely the book that Bankim wrote, but is a reprint of a reconstruction that Brajendra Nath Banerji published in 1935. The first three chapters of the novel, which was originally serialised in the weekly, *Indian Field*, are unavailable. What Banerji obtained is the complete text of the novel *except* the first three chapters. Banerji used Bankim's Bangla translation of these missing chapters to translate them back into English. This, indeed, is part of the difficulty with the laboriously tedious and stylistically unsatisfactory passages that Ghosh quotes in his essay, without quite discovering at least part of the reason for their plodding turgidity. At any rate, the text that we have today is made up of three chapters that are an English translation of Bankim's Bangla translation of the English original, plus the remaining chapters as Bankim had written them originally in English.

This inaccessibility of the 'original' text is a part of the mystery of *Rajmohan's Wife*. Just as we shall never know *exactly* what Bankim really wrote in the first three chapters, we shall also never be able *fully* to grasp the significance of this originary text. The text is thus an emblem not just of a false start or of failed experiment at the creation of a new India, but also, in a sense, of an *unfinished* project, both artistically and ideologically. It is incomplete not only in that it is unavailable in its original form; it is also incomplete in the sense that its completion is promised elsewhere, in some other time or text. Its 'real' meaning can therefore only be conjectured at or reconstructed. This reconstitution of a lost or unavailable text is, however, not a fanciful or irresponsible exercise. For the serious student of Indian English literature, it is an attempt to reconnect with a period pregnant with possibilities, a moment of creation, when not just a genre but a nation was being invented. The seemingly multiple possibilities in that beginning need to be harnessed into the two or three practicable trajectories that emerged out of that initial churning. *Rajmohan's Wife*, when read allegorically, illustrates one such possibility for both the genre and the nation. Tantalisingly evasive, the text nevertheless leaves a valuable trace, which we may construe as an attempt or *essay* at both novel writing and nation building.

5.4 CONCLUSION

The importance of *Rajmohan's Wife* only increases when we realise that it is probably not just the first English novel in India, but in all of Asia. Its dramatic location at a critical juncture of linguistic, cultural, national and colonial history only adds to its fascination. In Bankim's slender work, not just a new India, but an emerging Asia seeks to find its voice in an alien tongue. In this effort, a spark shoots across the narrative sky comet-like in the flash-form of a new beautiful, spirited and romantic heroine, Matangini. There has been nothing like her in Asian fiction before. Created from an amalgam of classical and medieval Indian and modern European sources, representing a totally unprecedented imaginative leap into what might constitute a new female subjectivity, Matangini is a memorable character. In all of Indian English fiction, there are few women who have her capacity to move us or the narrative in which she is placed. She, moreover, embodies the hopes of an entire society struggling for selfhood and dignity. Her courage, independence and passion are not just personal traits, but those of a nation in the making. This subtle superimposition of the national upon the personal is Bankim's gift to his Indian English heirs. The trail of an epoch-making novel like *Midnight's Children* (1981) can thus be traced back to Bankim's more modest trial as far back as 1864.

Though we may no longer subscribe to the idea that certain master narratives dominate human history and imagination, we can still appreciate the interconnectedness of stories, their multiple and entangled paths, their complex emergences and tangled endings. That the story of *Rajmohan's Wife* is connected with other stories should by now be abundantly clear. It would be reductive and self-defeating to see it as an isolated and unsuccessful attempt at writing in English or as a part of the story of Bangla vs English as the medium of creative writing in India. *Rajmohan's Wife* gains in value and interest when we see it as a part of the story of modern India itself. This is a story that is still being written; in that sense it is a work in progress, which is exactly how I would like to see *Rajmohan's Wife* too. As a work in progress, rather than a false start, it negotiates one path for India's future growth and development. In this path, the English-educated elites of the country must lead India out of bondage and exploitation. While the Rajmohans and Mathurs must be defeated, Matangini must find her happiness with her natural mate, Madhav. However, the latter is not possible just yet; Matangini has therefore retreat to her paternal home. Like an idea ahead of its time, she must wait till she can gain what is her due. But not before she enjoys a brief but hard-earned rendezvous with her paramour and smoulders across the narrativescape of the novel with her disruptive power. Indeed, the *novelty* in Bankim's novel is precisely the irruption, the explosion that Rajmohan's wife – both the character and the story – causes in the narrative firmament of modern India. Like a gash or a slash, the novel breaks the iterative horizons of a somnambulant subcontinent, leaving a teasing trace that later sprouts many new fictive offshoots.

Rajmohan's Wife is a rather modest, even slight, effort compared to Bankim's mature masterpieces. Yet, I believe that its symbolic, metaphorical and allegorical importance ought to be recognised. It is how we read this text, the sorts of concerns that we can bring to bear on it that makes it possible for us to see the role it played in the shaping of modern Indian culture. The text, when read in the context of Bankim's own project and the larger project of imagining a nation, becomes luminous and productive in ways that are unavailable when we regard it either as a false start in the wrong language or an eminently forgettable, juvenile first novel.

WORKS CITED

Ahmad, Aijaz. 1992. *In Theory: Classes, Nations, Literatures.* London: Verso.

Aurobindo, Sri. (1894) 1972. 'Our Hope in the Future.' Reprint. Sri Aurobindo Birth Centenary Library. Vol. 3: 99–102. Pondicherry: Sri Aurobindo Ashram.

_____. (1907) 1972. 'Rishi Bankim Chandra.' Reprint. Sri Aurobindo Birth Centenary Library. Volume 17. Pondicherry: Sri Aurobindo Ashram.

Bandyopadhyay, Chittaranjan. 1983. *Anandamath: Utsa Sandhane.* Calcutta, Ananda Publishers.

Banerji, Sunil Kumar. 1968. *Bankim Chandra: A Study of His Craft.* Calcutta: Firma K. L. Mukhopadhyaya.

Bose, S. K. 1974. *Bankim Chandra Chatterji.* New Delhi: Govt. of India Publications Division.

Chakrabarty, Dipesh. 2000. 'Subaltern Studies and Postcolonial Historiography.' *Nepantla: Views from South.* 1.1: 9-32.

Chatterjee, Bankimchandra. 1969. *Bankim Rachanavali (English Works).* Edited by Jogesh Chandra Bagal. Calcutta: Sahitya Samsad.

_____.(1864) 1996. *Rajmohan's Wife: A Novel.* Edited by Meenakshi Mukherjee. New Delhi: Ravi Dayal.

_____. (1882) 2005. *Ānandamaṭha; or, The Sacred Brotherhood.* Translated, with an introduction and critical apparatus by Julius J. Lipner. New York: Oxford University Press.

Chaudhuri, Nirad C. 1987. *Thy Hand Great Anarch.* New York: Addison-Wesley.

Davis, Mike. 2000. *Late Victorian Holocausts.* London: Verso.

Fanon, Frantz. (1967) 1976. *The Wretched of the Earth.* Reprint. Translated by Constance Farrington. Harmondsworth: Penguin Books.

Ghosh, Amitav. 2005. *Incendiary Circumstances: A Chronicle of the Turmoil* of Our Times. Boston: Houghton Mifflin.

Gupta, Mahendranath. 1985. *The Gospel of Sri Ramakrishna.* Translated by Swami Nikhilananda. New York: Ramakrishna-Vivekananda Vedanta Center.

Haldar, M. K. 1989. *Foundations of Nationalism in India: (A Study of Bankimchandra Chatterjee).* Delhi: Ajanta Publications.

Jameson, Frederic. 1986. 'Third World Literature in the Era of Multinational Capital.' *Social Text* 15 (Fall): 65-88.

Kaviraj, Sudipto. 1995. *The Unhappy Consciousness: Bankimchandra Chattopadhyay and the Formation of Nationalist Discourse in India.* Delhi: Oxford University Press.

Lal, Malashri. 1995. *The Law of the Threshold: Women Writers in Indian English.* Shimla: Indian Institute of Advanced Studies.

Mishra, Ganeswar. 1990. *How Indian is the Indian Novel in English.* Bhubaneswar: Department of English Utkal University.

Mukherjee, Meenakshi, Ed. 2002. *Early Novels in India.* New Delhi: Sahitya Akademi.

Mund, Subhendu Kumar. 1997. *The Indian Novel in English: Its Birth and Development.* New Delhi: Prachi Prakashan.

Porter andrew N. 2003. *The Imperial Horizons of British Protestant Missions, 1880-1914.* Grand Rapids, MI: Wm. B. Eerdmans Publishing Co.

Raychauduri, Tapan. 1988. *Europe Reconsidered: Perceptions of the West in Nineteenth Century Bengal.* New Delhi: Oxford University Press.

Sarkar, Tanika. 1994. 'Imagining a Hindu Nation: Hindu and Muslim in Bankimchandra's Later Writings.' *Economic and Political Weekly* 29.39 (Sep 24): 2553-2561.

_____. 2001. *Hindu Wife, Hindu Nation: Community, Religion, and Cultural Nationalism.* London: E. Hurst.

6
SUBJECTS TO CHANGE: GENDER TROUBLE AND WOMEN'S 'AUTHORITY'

6.1 INTRODUCTION: THE 'WOMEN'S QUESTION' AND TEXTUALITY

Matangani, Bankim's heroine in *Rajmohan's Wife*, as we have already seen, is a very attractive figuration not just of the new Indian woman, but also an important driving force in the bigger project of nation-making. Married to an unworthy husband, she feels a transgressive passion for Madhav, who is her brother-in-law. To save him from her other brother-in-law's nefarious machinations and her own husband's treacherous part in them, she risks her life and honour. Her desserts at the end of her courageous efforts, however, are only banishment, followed by an early death. Though Bankim places a female protagonist at the centre of his very first fictional composition, he is not sure what to do with the strength, energy and erotic power that he endows her with. All his fictional career, he would struggle with this issue. Not just Bankim, but every single agent of transformation in that period, starting with Ram Mohan Roy, places the women's question at the very heart of the nation-making project. Partha Chatterjee begins his celebrated essay on this subject with the following observation: 'The women's question was a central issue in some of the most controversial debates over social reform in early and mid-nineteenth century Bengal – the period of the so-called "renaissance'" (Chatterjee 1989, 233).[1]

However, in order to understand women's subjectivities, it is essential also to look at the actual writings by women, which were burgeoning at the same time. This chapter considers precisely such topic by shifting the focus from male to female authors. In examining issues pertaining to women's authority I wish to highlight some of the writers of the late nineteenth century India who played a significant role not only in changing their own consciousness, but also in altering public opinion about the status of women in their society. These women writers were not only subject to change, but also change agents in their own right; in recounting their life-transforming journeys, this chapter celebrates both their struggles as well as their successes in the broader project of altering women's subjectivities.[2]

Simply speaking, anxious as they were over questions of identity, what did these women really want? And how did they go about getting it? As we think over these issues, we discover that the women themselves were not just being changed, but were changing, in unprecedented ways their lives, times and societies. In addition, we see how gender, caste and community relations came to be reconfigured in and through the writings of women as also in the literature about them. In the ensuing transformation of India that took place during this phase, the righting of gender inequalities was a key concern. Some even considered it the most important single issue and the one prerequisite for India's entry into modernity. Indeed, it is this absorption in women's issues that distinguishes the really significant protagonists from the less important ones.

From the early part of the nineteenth century up to the independence of India in 1947, a good many such books by Indian women were published, an analysis and interpretation of which sheds light not only on what might be called the Indo-British encounter, but also on colonialism, nationalism, conversion, gender relations, caste, class, language and identity–in other words, on the evolution of modern India itself. What makes these books so remarkable is that they map overlapping and contentious domains: they are not only about the emergence of a new kind of private subjectivity in a certain section of Indian women, but also about the surfacing of new kinds of social and political consciousness. Most of these books could not have been published without the active support and encouragement, the patronage even, of British or American benefactors. From the coloniser's point of view, such literature was useful in conveying the impression that the Raj was not just benign, but actively beneficial to the oppressed natives. That is to say, the British ruled not so much through coercion but consent. It is clear that one such mask of conquest was the whole discourse of 'Improvement,' which both the Liberals and Utilitarians employed to justify empire. The native elites also lent support to this imperial project by championing various kinds of social reform movements. Of course, the two were neither exactly the same nor were they comfortably compatible with each other. The Indian reform project often ran afoul with imperial authority, increasingly so, as the national struggle for liberation gathered force.

Women occupied a curious pride of place in both these discourses. The signifier 'woman' not only represented real people who by all accounts were an oppressed group, but also a highly politicised space that was sought to be appropriated by the various competing forces of the time. The women of the Raj, the memsahibs, were themselves both oppressed and oppressors, as has now been increasingly shown.[3] Similarly, Indian women were at once doubly oppressed, but also singularly privileged as the favoured site of contest for various social and cultural forces vying for ascendancy. 'The women's question,' thus, was at the heart of the very self-constitution of modern India. It is no wonder, then, that all major male writers of that time made women the central figures of their narratives, as indeed, did the social reformers before them. But in this struggle over 'woman,' what women themselves had to say was often ignored, forgotten, or marginalised. The best example of such systematic elision is the near erasure from the national consciousness of a truly radical and utterly formidable figure such as Pandita Ramabai. Until recent years, this Brahmin widow, who had studied the Vedas, married a man from a different caste, then converted to Christianity, worked with Hindu widows and other downtrodden women and also fought with her church, besides being critical of imperialism, was relegated to the back pages of history. Both imperialists and nationalists had found her too disquieting and subversive to handle. Over the years, she was forgotten, bypassed by those who decide what is Indian and what is not. Though some excellent studies on her have appeared in recent decades, she remains largely unremembered and marginalised.[4]

While there is perhaps no other figure as radical as Pandita Ramabai, the other women of that age who wrote about their lives and times, either in the fictional or the autobiographical form, are also of great interest for the kinds of positions they took and the experiences they recorded. With most of these women, we find a great deal of personal and public courage combined with some degree of compromise and conformity to the norms of their times. After studying their lives and works, it becomes apparent that the coming of India into modernity was not just engineered by outstanding men, but also engendered by a series of remarkable women. The contributions of these founding 'mothers,' however, is not fully understood or acknowledged even today. One reason for this is that they lacked, quite literally, the 'authority' of the men.

To extend my discussion of 'authority' in the Preface, in this case authority quite simply means the ability to become authors, to imagine, to create, to write, to speak, to be heard and thereby to exercise the power of the word over the minds and hearts of many. It was only towards the latter part of the century that women's authority, both textual and social, began to be registered. Yet, of all sections of Indian society, it is the women who were perhaps most deprived of letters. As Pandita Ramabai, quoting the Report of the Education Commission of 1883 and Census of 1880–1881 pointed out, of 99.7 million women in British India, 99.5 million were not able to read and write (Ramabai 1888, 102). The female literacy rate, in other words, was an abysmal and shocking 0.2%. Even those who constituted the 0.2%, according to Ramabai, "cannot all be reckoned as educated" since they had received only the most rudimentary kind of instruction, that too in the few mission schools or at the hands of private tutors (Ramabai 1888, 102-103). It is therefore impossible to overemphasise how important writing was to these women and how central to their emancipation. The cover of Meera Kosambi's reprint of Ramabai's works shows her in the customary white sari of a widow, seated by a potted plant, concentrating on her writing. The image of a woman writing in that period could not have been less revolutionary than that of an 'untouchable' dressed in a suit, tie and shoes, holding a book in his hand, as Dr Ambedkar has been depicted for over sixty years. From an inauspicious victim, the window as writer, then, becomes a powerful icon of change and hope.

Ramabai Ranade (not to be confused with Pandita Ramabai with whom she shares her first name) in her *Reminiscences* narrates how in her aristocratic and feudal Brahmin family reading and writing were 'unthinkable' for women (Ranade 1969, 37). When Ramabai's paternal aunt (*atya* or father's elder sister), who could read and recite some scriptures, became a widow, her elder uncle 'decided that teaching the girls in the family to read and write brought ill luck. When the women heard of this, they came to fear even the thought of reading or writing' (37). At the age of eleven, after Ramabai marries Mahadev Govind Ranade, a prominent social reformer and judge, her education begins with the inscription of 'Shriganeshayanamah' (salutations to Lord Ganesh): she says, "It was my first chance to handle a slate and a pencil and my first glimpse of the alphabet" (ibid.). It takes her two hours to write and recognise those seven letters (ibid.). Just before her marriage, there is a poignant incident concerning the presents that she has asked her father, Annasahib, to bring for her from his trip to Pune. Daji, her elder brother, calls her to say that he knows what she had asked her father to bring even though she had said nothing. The little Ramabai is astounded that her brother knows and wishes to find out how:

> 'Impossible! I said. "How can you know? Are you a god? Only my Ganapati knows. But he is mine and won't tell anyone."
> Daji said, "Oh go on! Your Ganapati! What does he know? I know you have asked for dolls of pearl and a saree.' (39)

Ganapati, the elephant-headed God, is one of the favourite deities of Maharashtrians. Here, Ramabai means that her God will keep her secrets and not divulge them carelessly to her brother or anyone else. On persisting, however, her brother tells her that he knows because he has received a letter from their father. Unable to understand what that means, Ramabai keeps repeating her question till Daji gives her 'a good slap': 'I gave up, but my question remained unanswered. How could one find out such things from a letter?' (ibid.). So alien is reading and writing to her that little Ramabai is quite unable to understand the simple fact that a person could write on a piece of paper, post it to someone in a different place and that the recipient could read and understand what the writer has set down. It is only later that Ramabai realises, as it were, that letters are even more powerful than deities – or, indeed, are like deities themselves, both conveying and concealing so much information and knowledge, equipped with the power to make or break.

Luckily for her, her husband and his family were very keen on Ramabai's education. She mentions how many of the women in her husband's family knew how to read and write. Yet, paradoxically, while the men encouraged her, despite her initial failures and frustrations, it is the women who formed a close-knit group to mock and tease her (ibid., 47). When that failed, they remonstrated,

> You see, even if the men folk like it, you should read just once in a while. Isn't this reading disrespectful towards the elders in the house? What do the men know? We have to spend our whole life among the women in the family. The men are there for such a short while. They may ask you to read once, twice, ten times. You can always avoid listening. They will give it up after a while, in sheer disgust. (47)

The force of learning is such that it threatens the power relations even among the women of the family, let alone between the men and the women. The women themselves become the guardians of their own ignorance, zealously preserving it and preventing neophytes such as Ramabai from breaking rank.

Unfortunately for them, Ranade even begins to teach his wife English. Now that the unthinkable has come to pass, the obstacles against Ramabai multiply because learning English is considered even more sacrilegious. The 'rising symbolic *and* cultural power as projected from the middle of the nineteenth century,' to use Shefali Chandra's phrase, put Ramabai squarely in middle of a maelstrom over the politics of cultural identity in India (Chandra 2007, 285). But in the end, through enormous persistence and patience, Ramabai succeeds: 'For the sake of my education, I had to put up with a lot of harassment, direct or indirect, from the women of our family. But I did not give up my studies.' (Ranade 1969, 50) That Ramabai goes on to become an important author in her own right is only poetic justice. Yet, this 'authority' is so hard fought and won that its afterlife is precious to us even today. By tracing, therefore, how these women came into authority, this chapter aims at recuperating their struggle and also celebrating it. Had it not been for them, the project of svaraj would never have progressed. How could the selfhood and autonomy of a whole people be attained if one half of them was kept in misery and oppression?

In addition to a shift in the subject matter from male texts to female 'authority,' the change of location in this chapter from the Bengal to the Bombay Presidency is also deliberate. Usually, it is the former which is most studied and discussed when it comes to India's modernisation. However, similar processes were at work in other parts of India too, especially in the Presidency capitals of Bombay and Madras, where the contact between the Indian subjects and their colonial rulers was strongest. If anything, the other provinces and states of India were actually ahead of Bengal in some aspects when it came to the process of modernisation. Maharashtra affords a unique example when it comes to the struggle for the rights of women. This chapter concentrates on some extraordinary women from this region. Three of those taken up for detailed analysis were writers and activists, besides being Brahmin converts to Christianity. Indeed, all protagonists in this chapter were also Maharashtrians, though somewhat dispersed, like Anandibai Joshi, the first Indian woman to get a medical degree from the USA, or Clarinda, the eponymous heroine of A. Madhaviah's novel, a Tanjore Brahmin lady of Marathi extraction.[5]

6.2 ANANDIBAI, TARABAI, RAMABAI

These three women were quite remarkable in their courage and fighting spirit. Two of them, Anandibai and Ramabai, actually crossed the dark waters to go to England and North America. The first, who became a doctor, was highly honoured by her community and city, even though she had met with the stiffest resistance in her quest to educate herself then qualify for the medical profession. Perhaps, one reason for this was that she never ceased to be a Hindu or really broke with her caste compatriots. Also, she died very young, before she reached the age of twenty-two, quickly entering the stuff of legends. Though she did not write her own story, she left a rich cache of letters that she had exchanged with Gopalrao, her husband, which became valuable sources for her life. Based on these letters, her life has been recounted many times. The first to write on her was Rachel L. Bodley, her American friend and senior medical doctor. Author of the Introduction to Ramabai's *The High-Caste Hindu Woman* (1888), Bodley wrote Anandibai's brief but illustrious story. A year after Anandibai's death in 1887, Caroline Healey Dall, an American feminist, wrote her life. In 1912, Kashibai Kanitkar wrote the first Marathi biography on Anandibai. By the time, nearly a hundred years later, that Shrikrishna Janardan Joshi wrote the best selling Marathi novel *Anandi Gopal* (1968), Anandibai really entered the Maharashtrian hall of fame.

Anandibai was most likely India's first woman doctor in modern times, certainly the first one to get a degree from the United States. Married when she was nine to Gopalrao Joshi, who was twenty years older and a widower, she was lucky to find in her husband a social reformer, determined to teach his little bride how to read and write. Eventually, outshining him, she got an MD from the Philadelphia Medical College after overcoming incredible obstacles.[6] It is quite an amazing story because she was not just ostracised by Hindu society, but spat upon and stoned by her co-religionists. On the other hand, there were all kinds of blandishments for the Joshis to convert to Christianity, including the offer of free passage to the United States as well as the waiving of fees for medical school. However, Anandi declared that she would not convert, not only because she did not need to change her religion, but also because the demand of the times was to have Hindu lady doctors, not just those who became Christian converts. When she did get her degree, she was not only congratulated by Queen Victoria, but became quite famous in India. She was appointed as the Physician in Charge of the female ward in the princely state of Kolhapur, but unfortunately, died soon after – at the age of twenty-two – as did many talented people in those days. Her ashes were sent back to the US, where her host and 'masi' (maternal aunt) Mrs Mary Carpenter kept them in the family cemetery in Poughkeepsie, New York.

Another remarkable reformer and early feminist from Maharashtra was Tarabai Shinde. In *Stri Purush Tulana*, (Comparison between Women and Men) written in Marathi in 1882, she struck at the very roots of both patriarchy and caste hierarchy. A member of the Satyashodhak Samaj, she was an associate of Jyotiba and Savitribai Phule, important non-Brahmin and anti-caste campaigners in Maharashtra. Shinde's pamphlet is often considered the first feminist text of India because it is a far-reaching critique of gender and caste inequality, tracing both to social attitudes sanctioned by scriptures. According to Susie Tharu and K. Lalita,

> *Stri Purush Tulana* is probably the first full fledged and extant feminist argument after the poetry of the Bhakti Period. But Tarabai's work is also significant because at a time when intellectuals and activists alike were primarily concerned with the hardships of a Hindu widow's life and other easily identifiable atrocities perpetrated on women, Tarabai Shinde, apparently working in isolation, was able to broaden the scope of analysis to include the ideological fabric of patriarchal society. Women

everywhere, she implies, are similarly oppressed. (Tharu and Lalita 1991, 222)

Tarabai's open attack on some Hindu scriptures, condemning them for being the source of the oppression of women and the lower castes, stirred a great controversy in those times. In fact, even today, the question of whether the master texts of Hinduism authorise gender and caste inequality or whether they can be interpreted to promote equality and justice is still debated.

Furthermore, it is not only the content of her pamphlet that was revolutionary. So was her manner of addressing the issue and her style. As Vidyut Bhagwat observes, Tarabai's 'exposure of male stereotypes and images of women appeared almost a century before Simone de Beauvoir's *The Second Sex*' (cited in Tharu and Lalita 1991: 223; also see Bhagwat, WS27). Besides, it is the directness and immediacy of her colloquial Marathi that inaugurates a new feminist polemic, identifiably pioneering a uniquely Indian tradition of feminine *ecriture* or 'women's writing,' quite in contrast to the pedantry and equivocation of the 'high' masculine style of the times:

> I'm sure there are very few men who are ruined by women but it would be difficult even to guess at the number of women ruined by men. You are far too clever for women. You are, in fact, nothing but scoundrels of the first order! You are so cunning that you will pass through a sugarcane field without letting those sharp leaves touch you, let alone scratch you. You organise big meetings every day, deliver impressive speeches, offer unwanted advice to all and sundry and do a hundred other such stupid things. You are nothing but learned asses! (Tharu and Lalita 1991, 235)

One can quite imagine the waves of shock and horror that would have swept through the hearts of respectable gentlemen when they read these words as also the chuckles of recognition and approbation that might have convulsed women readers of this text. In different ways, thus, Tarabai's forty-page pamphlet created a stir in Maharashtrian society, encouraging other women to speak out against the abuses of patriarchy. When speech was neither as free nor as safe in India as it is today – it is still not in several parts of the country, especially for women – Tarabai's courage and candour are nothing short of extraordinary.[7]

Pandita Ramabai (1858–1922) wrote her first and most famous book in English. Author of *The High-Caste Hindu Woman* (1888), published in Philadelphia under the name of Pundita Ramabai Dongre Medhavi, she, if anything, had an even more controversial and chequered career. She was born to Anant Shastri Dongre, a teacher of Sanskrit and Lakshmibai. The Dongres also belonged to the Chitpawan Brahmin community of Maharashtra, like the Ranades. Her father taught her Sanskrit and she proved her prowess in the language by earning the title 'Pandita.' At the age of twenty-two, however, she shocked orthodox Hindus by marrying a man from a different caste, Bepin Behari Medhavi, a Bengali Kayastha. She was ostracised and reviled for doing so. Worse, Medhavi died soon after, leaving her a widow, then the most despised situation for a Hindu woman. Rather than succumb to the crippling and ignominious role reserved for an upper-caste Hindu widow, she decided to go to England for further studies. Whether she converted to Christianity because this would facilitate her passage in addition to saving her from Hindu widowhood, is a moot point. Even Anandibai, as mentioned earlier, had been offered a scholarship if she and her husband agreed to embrace Christianity, something which both of them staunchly refused to do. Ramabai, in any case, did convert, joining the Church of England.

She travelled to England and later to America, championing the cause of the oppressed and abandoned widows of India. She also became a staunch advocate for women's education. She started the Mukti Mission in 1889 in Kedgaon, outside Pune and Sharada Sadan in 1890, to offer shelter and education to young widows. Never a conformist, she broke with the Church of England and became a Pentecostal evangelist (Miller n.d., 64). Many of her activities were funded by missionaries in the USA, England and other countries abroad. The Mukti Mission still continues, using the name, story and legacy of Ramabai to continue its proselytising propaganda.[8] In fact, during his travels in America, Swami Vivekananda himself ran into some of Ramabai's supporters, who had used her work to attack Hinduism and raise money to convert Indians to Christianity. Recent studies such as Kosambi's, however, show Ramabai as much more than simply a Christian evangelist or an early feminist. She had the capacity to critique and redress both native and colonial hegemonies. In her book on her travels in the USA, for instance, she did not hesitate to criticise the colonisers for exterminating the native Americans:

> If these same Europeans had discarded their firearms and weapons and defeated the Red Indians in wrestling or by fighting them with their own weapons, such as bows and arrows, quartz knives and bone-tipped lances, they would have proven themselves to be truly brave. But sad to say, those who called themselves pious and went forth to enlighten the ignorant, to rescue people from hell and lead them to heaven, ended up by utterly annihilating the poor innocent Indians through deceit, trickery, cruelty and false speech. (Ramabai, 2003, 71)

In another context and in reply to a letter from her white Christian mentor, Ramabai says 'I have with great effort freed myself from the yoke of the Indian priestly tribe, so I am not at present willing to place myself under another similar yoke.' (quoted in Tharu and Lalita 1991, 245) Towards the end of her life, the colonial Government conferred upon her their highest civilian honour, the 'Kaiser-e-Hind'; to the mainstream nationalist movement, however, she remained a controversial, perhaps adversarial figure.

What makes Ramabai's book *The High-Caste Hindu Woman* special is that it is the first account of the state of Indian women written from the inside. The book is organised in chapters that describe the condition of women in India from childhood (Chapter II), through married life (Chapter III), to widowhood (Chapter V), recounting the religious and social place of women (Chapter IV) while outlining the ill-effects of women's oppression on society (Chapter VI). The book ends with a recommendation for action and an appeal for funds to carry out a programme of reform.

Ramabai's account, contrary to claims that consider it a radical attack on Hindu traditions, is actually quite balanced. She quotes the passages that support women in the *shastras* (scriptures) and also goes to great lengths to show how the rite of sati (concremation) was promoted on the basis of a deliberate distortion in the translation of a Rig Vedic hymn, which in fact asks the widow to return to the world of the living:

> It was by falsifying a single syllable that the unscrupulous priests managed to change entirely the meaning of the whole verse. Those who know the Sanscrit characters can easily understand that the falsification very likely originated in the carelessness of the transcriber or copyist, but for all that, the priests who permitted the error are not excusable in the least. Instead of comparing the verse with its context, they translated it as their fancy dictated and thus under the pre-text of religion they have been the cause of destroying countless lives for more than two thousand years. (Ramabai 1888, 80)

Nevertheless, her overall conclusion about the then prevailing scriptural attitude to women is unmistakable:

> I can say honestly and truthfully, that I have never read any sacred book in Sanscrit literature without meeting this kind of hateful sentiment about women. True, they contain here and there a kind word about them, but such words seem to me a heartless mockery after having charged them, as a class, with crime and evil deeds. (56)

It is interesting, if not ironic, to notice that just four years earlier in *Stri Dharma Niti* (1883) Ramabai had praised Sita (Ramabai 2000, 84). In *The High-Caste Hindu Woman*, however, she is far more critical of Hindu sacred literature. The secular proverbs and customs she cites are scarcely any better when it comes to voicing their distrust and dislike of women (Ramabai, 1888, 57). The hold of Manu is shown to be still very strong on the general populace, even influencing the British courts to adjudicate in favour of men in court cases demanding the restitution of conjugal rights (62–63). She demonstrates the clear collusion between Hindu patriarchal interests and colonial governmentalities in keeping the women suppressed.

The chapter on widows is, expectedly, the most horrifying and pathetic. Based on the 1880–1881 census, it notes, there were nearly twenty-one million widows in India, of which 669,100 were below nineteen years of age (Ramabai, 1888, 109). Of the 250 million people of India, depending upon the same census (1), if the number of women was about 120 million and given that there were at leave five million fewer women than men (28), then about one sixth of them, or over a shocking 16%, were widows. From infanticide to sati, from constant suppression during her childhood to a usually oppressed wedded life, the status and position of Indian women, according to Ramabai, was appallingly bad and in urgent need of rectification. She ends this chapter with what we might call 'a widow's prayer,' written by a pupil of a *zenana* [woman] missionary:

> Oh Lord, hear my prayer! No one has turned an eye on the oppression that we poor women suffer, though with weeping and crying and desire, we have turned to all sides, hoping that some one would save us. No one has lifted up his eyelids to look upon us, nor inquire into our case. We have searched above and below, but Thou art the only One who wilt hear our complaint, Thou knowest our impotence, our degradation, our dishonor.
>
> Oh Lord, inquire into our case. For ages dark ignorance has brooded over our minds and spirits; like a cloud of dust it rises and wraps us round and we are like prisoners in an old and mouldering house, choked and buried in the dust of custom and we have no strength to go out. Bruised and beaten, we are like the dry husks of the sugar-cane when the sweet juice has been extracted. All-knowing God, hear our prayer! Forgive our sins and give us power of escape, that we may see something

of Thy world. O Father, when shall we be set free from this jail? For what sin have we been born to live in this prison? From Thy throne of judgement justice flows, but it does not reach us; in this, our life-long misery, only injustice comes near us.

Thou hearer of prayer, if we have sinned against Thee, forgive, but we are too ignorant to know what sin is. Must the punishment of sin fall on those who are too ignorant to know what it is? O great Lord, our name is written with drunkards, with lunatics, with imbeciles, with the very animals; as they are not responsible, we are not. Criminals, confined in the jails for life, are happier than we, for they know something of Thy world. They were not born in prison, but we have not for one day, no, not even in our dreams, seen Thy world; to us it is nothing but a name; and not having seen the world, we cannot know Thee, its maker. Those who have seen Thy works may learn to understand Thee, but for us, who are shut in, it is not possible to learn to know Thee. We see only the four walls of the house. Shall we call them the world, or India? We have been born in this jail, we have died here and are dying.

O Father of the world, hast Thou not created us? Or has perchance, some other god made us? Dost Thou care only for men? Hast Thou no thought for us women? Why hast Thou created us male and female? O Almighty, hast Thou not power to make us other than we are, that we too might have some share in the comforts of this life? The cry of the oppressed is heard even in the world. Then canst Thou look upon our victim hosts and shut Thy doors of justice? O God Almighty and Unapproachable, think upon Thy mercy, which is a vast sea and remember us. O Lord, save us, for we cannot bear our hard lot; many of us have killed ourselves and we are still killing ourselves. O God of mercy, our prayer to Thee is this, that the curse may be removed from the women of India. Create in the hearts of the men some sympathy, that our lives may no longer be passed in vain longing, that saved by Thy mercy, we may taste something of the joys of life. (87–88)

Though fashioned to appeal to religious sentiments of her American readers and donors, this prayer actually demonstrates the power of literacy and literature. What is more, there is a subtle subversive criticism implied here of the clearly patriarchal and slow-to-respond, if not indifferent, God to whom the prayer is addressed.

What is at work through Ramabai's text is the power of writing not just as composition but as rhetoric, engendering the kind of authority that women in nineteenth century India never had. Ramabai's tract provided enough ammunition for a century of feminist struggles in India, setting into motion an unstoppable chain reaction that would result not only in legal and constitutional remedies, but also in far-reaching educational and social reform. Before her were men like Ram Mohan Roy, whose campaign against sati, she acknowledges:

> The custom went on unmolested until the first quarter of the present century, when a man from among the Hindus, Raja Ram Mohun Roy, set his face against it and declared that it was not sanctioned by the Veda as the priests claimed. He wrote many books on this subject, showing the wickedness of the act and with the noble co-operation of a few friends, he succeeded at last in getting the government to abolish it. Lord William Bentinck, when Governor-General of India, had the moral courage to enact the famous law of 1829, prohibiting the Suttee rite within British domains and holding as criminals, subject to capital punishment, those who countenanced it. (Ramabai, 1888, 78-79)

But it was when women themselves assumed the responsibility of fighting for their rights that the real struggle for gender justice became established on a firm footing. In this great cause, Ramabai was a very important proponent. Her authority not only influenced her times, but continues to move, shock and inspire us today.

6.3 KRUPABAI AND SHEVANTIBAI

Krupabai Satthianadhan (1862–1894) is justly better known for her literary, rather than polemical writings; the two novels she published, *Kamala* (1894) and *Saguna* (1895) are not devoid of real artistic merit. In fact not only was she the first Indian woman to write a complete novel in English, but she was the only Indian woman to have written *two* novels in English in the nineteenth century. *Saguna* was originally serialised in *The Christian College Magazine* from 1887 to 1888. When the chapters began to appear, Krupabai was only twenty-five. The only prior work of fiction in English by an Indian woman, which had come out about ten years earlier, was the incomplete novel, *Bianca*, by Toru Dutt. Published serially in the *Bengal Magazine* from January to April 1878, it did attract some attention but is usually considered an imperfect effort. *Saguna*, on the other hand, is an autobiographical story of a young Indian Christian girl growing up in central India. The most important character in the novel is the heroine's older brother Bhaskar, incidentally, the name also of Krupabai's own brother. The subtitle of *Saguna*, 'A Story of Native Christian Life,' shows that it was an attempt at writing a realistic *bildungsroman*. *Saguna* is convinced of the superiority of the Christian religion, especially that version of it, which her adored, passionate and idealistic brother, Bhaskar, had initiated her into. Inspired by his faith, Bhaskar wants to do great things for his country and fires Saguna's imagination with his zeal, asking her to help in this grand and noble enterprise. Yet Saguna is not to be swept away by the wave of Westernisation that is engulfing the elites of India. She is well-grounded in her own culture and customs and is critical of those who imitate Western manners and mores blindly. Since her family has changed its faith but not its culture or patriotism, there is no identity crisis in her life.

Kamala, Krupabai's second novel, was also serialised in the *Madras College Magazine* in 1894, seven years after *Saguna*. In the meanwhile Krupabai had continued writing. Among her sketches and articles, a notable one is 'The Story of a Conversion' based on the life of her father-in-law, Rev W. T. Satthianadhan. Krupabai had moved to Madras at the age of sixteen to enter the Madras Medical College after she was too weak and ill to leave for England on a scholarship to study medicine. No doubt, her desire to study medicine and become a doctor was influenced by the life of that other remarkable Maharashtrian woman, Anandibai Joshi (1865-1887), who had become the first Indian woman to get a medical degree from the United States. Krupabai, despite being a very good student, however, could not complete her medical education. Her health failed, then she suffered a nervous breakdown. In 1881, she married Samuel Satthianadhan and started a school for zenana [girls] under the auspices of the Christian missionary society. She also began her writing career seriously. By the time she wrote *Kamala* she was a fairly well-known and established writer, at least in South India.

It is intriguing that Krupabai chose to write *The Story of a Hindu Life*, which was the subtitle of *Kamala*, after she had written *Saguna: The Story of a Native Christian Life*. What made her revert to a Hindu protagonist who was not only a Hindu, but also a Brahmin girl, first a child-wife and soon after, a widow? I believe that Padma Anagol, missing the true chronology of the two books, regards *Saguna* as the later text, thus showing a movement in the writer's oeuvre from benighted Hinduism to liberating Christianity:

> Saguna, the subject of Krupabai's second novel, is presented as a complete contrast to Kamala. In contrast to the 'dark' life led by Kamala, Saguna's life is described as bright, influenced by the 'new order of things,' which Krupabai says is sweeping all over India. (Anagol 2006, 33-34)

According to Anagol, Krupabai's purpose is to show that the only way out for the oppressed Indian woman was conversion. Saguna, unlike Kamala, goes to a mission school, where she can make friends with other girls like her and even choose which man she might marry.

It is true that *Kamala* tells the story of a typical colonial female subject fit for reform. Ramabai had already campaigned in the West about the pitiable state of Indian child-wives and widows, victims of superstition, tradition and social repression, economically dependent, defenceless and made all the more wretched for want of education. In *Saguna*, Krupabai seems to etch the antidote for this – the portrait of a young woman who enjoys the fruits of education as also the advantages of a liberal upbringing that only a girl nurtured in a native Christian household might experience. *Kamala*, as against this, illustrates apparently the other side. The protagonist, when she becomes a young widow, cannot break out of her traditional constraints and social restrictions. Even though she has a young admirer in Ramachander, who is willing to risk the opprobrium of marrying a widow, 'Her religion, crude as it was, had its victory' (Satthianathan [1885] 1998, 155–156). She chooses the life of a pious widow devoting herself to charity and good works, sacrificing any possibility of personal happiness and fulfilment.

Yet the story is neither mere propaganda for conversion as the solution to the problems of young Hindu widows, nor a social reform tract. While *Saguna* was presented to Queen Victoria, who expressed her appreciation for it, even wanting to read other books by the author (Satthianathan [1885] 1998, ix), there is no evidence of whether or not *Kamala* was also equally well-received by the Empress of India. Clearly, Satthianathan might have received greater incentives for continuing to write tracts that valorised conversion to Christianity as the solution to the Hindu women's problem. Yet, she chose to revert to the life of an upper-caste, Hindu woman, who becomes a widow. Unlike Anagol, I am not even sure if the 'solution' has already been implied or suggested in the contrasting life of the Indian Christian protagonist of the earlier novel. Indeed, there is no overt condemnation or criticism of Hindu society and traditions, even though Kamala's husband is a cad and her in-laws greedy and scheming. Instead, her sheltered upbringing, her saintly guardian and the lingering detail with which the daily life and customs of upper-caste Hindus is described, signify a sympathetic portrayal of a society in the throes of great change. Far from advocating conversion to Christianity and social reform under a superior if paternalistic colonial administration, I feel the novel leaves the solution to the protagonist's dilemma to the reader. Kamala chooses not to break free, though the possibilities of such a breakthrough are implied in the text. Could it be that Krupabai had foreseen how, though delayed, change was inevitable even in Hindu society and how, in the meanwhile, women such as Kamala would have to sacrifice themselves?

Interestingly, the final ambiguity of the novel is deepened by the fact that Kamala's sacrifice is shown to be not entirely in vain. According to its concluding gloss, 'Kamala spent all her money in unselfish works of charity; and her name lives even to this day almost worshipped by the simple folks of the place.' (Satthianadhan [1885] 1998, 156) Kamala does not go to hell for dying a heathen nor is she condemned by her author for not breaking free of the shackles of her religious and communal identity. Instead, her posthumous apotheosis is traditional, even Hindu, earned clearly by forsaking the more individualistic pleasures and personal fulfilments that the 'new' Indian woman of those times was beginning to taste. Even so, the novel does not deny Kamala a certain kind of release, a manner of eventual self-possession, her own brand of svaraj, perhaps. Kamala remains Brahmin, Hindu and a widow, but has not lived and died in vain. Through piety and self-sacrifice, she too has transcended the limits of the social and religious norms of her age.

Ultimately, Saguna and Kamala both desire fulfilment but seek it differently, one in the new possibilities that conversion to Christianity offered to natives, the other in the more restricted if less gratifying destiny within the Hindu fold. Yet key to both protagonists and their life-choices, is education. Indeed, these books signify a noticeable shift in the approach to the women's question, in that education and social reform were seen as key to women's empowerment in India, more so than conversion or change of faith. The latter was seen to facilitate the former and deemed important only in so far as it did so.[9] In fact, when Hindu women all over India began to step out of the bounds of tradition and enter educational institutions in large numbers, it was demonstrated that reform was possible without conversion. As Partha Chatterjee puts it,

> Formal education became not only acceptable, but in fact a requirement for the new *bhadramahila* (respectable woman),

when it was demonstrated that it was possible for a woman to acquire the cultural refinements afforded by modern education without jeopardising her place at home. (Chatterjee 1989, 246)

By the end of the nineteenth century a silent revolution on an unprecedented scale was already under way. The after-effects of this revolution still resonate in the remote backwaters of India where the empowerment of women through education has yet fully to take place.

As it happens, Shevantibai Nikambe (1865–1930?) published a novel round about the same time as Satthianadhan, devoted almost solely to the desire for education of her eponymous protagonist. *Ratanbai: A Sketch of a Bombay High Caste Hindu Woman* (1895) was recently reprinted twice, first by the Sahitya Akademi and then by the Oxford University Press.[10] These reprints afford us a chance to read and re-read this almost forgotten text by the makers/forebears of our modern literary culture.

Ratanbai is typical of its times in that it reflects a deep ambivalence to the cultural economy of colonialism. This, to all appearances, is a single-issue novel, written almost as a propaganda tract to promote the education of upper-caste Hindu women. That the author herself ran a school for such purposes would suggest that she was not only well qualified to write on this topic, but was also promoting her own interests, howsoever indirectly. Indeed, there is ample evidence to show that the book was actively encouraged, if not patronised, by the British colonial administration. For instance, it is not only dedicated to Queen Victoria, 'with profound gratitude and loyalty,' but in the Preface, Shevantibai praises Victoria's 'happy rule in my dear native land' which 'is brightening and enlightening the lives and homes of many Hindu women.' (Nikambe [1895] 2003, 5) Shevantibai is thus implying a direct link between the reign of a woman monarch and her (Hindu) women subjects. There is also the Preface by the wife of a former Governor of Bombay Presidency, Ada Harris, which harps on the need for Hindu women to be educated.

A just and productive assessment of the ideological bases of the novel requires a careful appraisal of the nature of the colonial encounter in India. It would be erroneous to assume that the British were entirely in favour of reform or that, in this case, the orthodox Hindu party was entirely opposed to it. If the latter were the case, indeed, how would one explain the fact that most reformers, including Nikambe herself, were high-caste Hindus? What this alerts us to, is the possibility of another angle to the whole story: perhaps, reform was actually an Indian project in which the British were involved, but only, in a secondary role. Such a view makes us question and re-evaluate the conventional post-colonial wisdom even on a matter as seemingly straightforward as the imposition of English education on India. Instead of seeing the latter as the brainchild of Macaulay that turned into the handmaiden of the Empire, we, more accurately, perhaps, perceive it as the fulfilment of an Indian demand in the garb of a British administrative order. Since English or modern education was something that Indians wanted but not for the same reasons or interests that the British wished to give it to us.

That is why if we look for resistance to colonial authority in the conventional way in Nikambe's novel, we just do not find it. In fact, to all appearances, there is no evidence of the coercive aspects of British rule in it. In such circumstances, if anything at all is to be discovered about the 'true' nature of colonialism in this novel, it would be by reading closely its delineation of the so-called private sphere, where the lives of Indians, especially their economic, caste and class relations are vividly described. It would then be possible to infer how impoverished and depressed the majority of the populace was and how this was a direct consequence not just of social inequality and internal oppression, but also of colonial rule and modernity themselves. That the book is unashamedly about the upper castes, the privileged classes, to which the British looked to prop up their regime, in fact, only underscores this point. But does this mean that the book advocates the education of upper-caste Hindu women only with a view to make them more useful and loyal subjects of empire?

That colonialism was 'enlightening' was precisely the ruse that permitted the contradiction between democratic rule at home and despotism in the colonies. It was this contradiction that, ironically, precluded any possibility of British rule acquiring true hegemony. The consent of the governed was neither openly sought nor fully obtained. Therefore what characterised the history of British rule in India was not so much persuasion on the one side and collaboration on the other, but coercion and resistance respectively. In *Ratanbai*, however, we see little of the latter aspect of British rule. Indeed, the only social interaction between Indians and the British comes off rather well, without the least racial slur or insult. This aspect of the text is illustrated in the party at Mrs B's that is described at great length. Here native subjects are not only socialised in the presence of their rulers, but the latter too are made to understand that upper-caste Hindu women will continue to treat their rulers as outcastes and therefore accept only uncooked 'clean' food, such as fruit, from them.

At the time the novel was written, conversion was also thought to be a valuable, though not mandatory step in the right direction. Shevantibai was herself a convert to Christianity, but in her book she does not advocate this openly. There is the more subtle reference at the end of the novel to 'the Book.' This 'beautifully bound and gilt-edged Book' (Nikambe [1895] 2003, 91) is seen as the real basis of the changed life of the protagonist and her husband. It is a book that both of them know and have accepted: 'we shall make it our guide in life.' (Ibid.) However, this turning of the young couple from being people of rituals, superstitions, myths and customs somewhat, to people of the Book is never highlighted, but only quietly suggested at the end. In this respect, Shevantibai's novel is actually quite different from some of the other conversion narratives of her time where this issue assumes centrality.

While conversion is not emphasised, the education of women is. That becomes, ostensibly, the single point of focus of the novel. If we were to ask the question, 'What does Ratanbai desire?' Then the answer that the book proposes most unequivocally, is, 'education.' It is this singularity and clarity of purpose that makes Ratanbai a rather unique character in the annals of Indian literature. Desires are often confused and contradictory, to say the least, indeed often in conflict with a character's true self-interest. Yet in this case, there is neither confusion, contradiction nor conflict, simply a focussed consistency and reinforcement. Indeed, the difference between desire and interest is collapsed in the novel. The result is a remarkable eroticisation of women's education, over all conflicting temptations, including marital happiness and material well-being:

> How often, with an aching heart, she would sit dreaming about school life! Her teacher, her companions, her singing lesson, her English lesson, the translation class, came before her and then the longing would come, 'Oh! Could I but go to school once again.' (Nikambe [1895] 2004, 43)

While such pining, aching desire for school is likely to have few parallels in literature or life, it was not without foundation in late nineteenth century India, especially among a certain section of women who sought to improve their conditions. As Pandita Ramabai put it in the very opening words of the 'Appeal' with which her famous book, *The High-Caste Hindu Woman* concludes:

In the preceding chapters I have tried to tell my readers briefly the sad story of my countrywomen and also to bring to their notice what are our chief needs. We, the women of India, are hungering and thirsting for knowledge; only education under God's grace, can give us the needful strength to rise up from our degraded condition (Ramabai 1888, 107). It is also not difficult to see, besides, how such passages echo the passion of a character like Jane Eyre, for instance, to 'improve' herself and her prospects.

Also noteworthy is how certain males are seen as primary proponents and supporters of this desire, while certain women are seen as antagonists and obstructers. In the novel, both Ratanbai's husband and father-in-law support her desire to be educated while her mother-in-law and consequently, her own mother, oppose it. The battle of the sexes therefore has both the men and women pitted against their own ostensible interests. This only goes to underscore the complexity of patriarchal social and gender relations during that period. Ratanbai not only wins in the end, but her husband is also shown to be remarkably free of the kind of 'education envy' that has been characteristic of later Indian males in various narrative and discursive registers. Prataprao fails in his BA examinations at the very same time as Ratanbai passes her annual school examinations at the top of her class. This proves catastrophic for Ratanbai; she is not even allowed to receive her first prize from the Governor's wife. Prataprao, however, intervenes to ensure that his wife's studies are not interrupted, while, like a good Hindu wife, she keeps prayers and vigils for his success.

If an advocacy of women's education is the primary purpose of the novel, *Ratanbai* has also a secondary but equally important feature. It is written almost as an ethnographic study of the mores of upper-caste Hindus of the Bombay Presidency. The first edition of the book has not only photographs of the author, but of 'A Shenvi Brahmin Girl (A Pupil in Mrs Nikambe's School),' 'A Konkanastha Brahmin Family,' and 'A Group of High Caste Young Hindu Wives (In Mrs Nikambe's School).' These illustrations not only validate the narrative in the eyes of her British readers, but also document the lives and times of a certain social group. This latter task is carried out systematically throughout the novel in detailed descriptions of dress, food, fasts, rituals, festivals, worship, pilgrimage, marriage, death, widowhood and so on. This provides a vivid picture of considerable sociological and historical value. Original Marathi and Sanskrit words are used throughout the text and are glossed by the author in footnotes to lend not just veracity but also specific detail to the descriptions. Kinship relations, much more complicated in Hindu extended families than in modern Western ones, are neither 'translated' nor condensed into simpler or generic English ones.

On another note, one of the most dramatic and poignant episodes in the book is the sudden widowhood of Tarabai, the wife of Dinanath, who is the younger brother of Ratanbai's father. The sudden death of her husband and the dramatic transformation that it brings in Tarabai's life is underscored by her first appearance since the event:

Out of the second carriage a most astonishing and pitiful figure stepped out and seated herself on the ground, weeping loudly. Then, bending her head, which was shaved but covered with her '*padar*' she knocked it against a huge stone and became desperate with grief.... The young widow again knocked her forehead against a stone in desperate grief. She would indeed have preferred to have followed her husband on the funeral pyre. Her life was a blank now. The light – the god of her life – was no more. 'What is the use of living!' thought she. She fell backwards and appealed to the god of death. 'Oh, death! carry me away,' exclaimed the poor, stricken creature; and with the last word she fainted away. For two hours there was utter confusion and no one would ask her to come in – not even the servant; and there she sat on the bare ground, crushed with grief, until she fainted away. The fainting and falling attracted the people of the house and the servant was ordered to bring some water, which was sprinkled on her face; and when she came to herself, she was led into the verandah, where she sat down – a sight of pity and misery. (Nikambe [1895] 2004, 26–27)

The subsequent pages describe not just Ratanbai's stunned response to this reversal of fortunes, but also Tarabai's own story, which shows how great the contrast was between a happy, successful and powerful wifehood against an utterly unhappy, hopeless and powerless widowhood. The tonsure of the head, the removal of the fine clothes and ornaments, the desexualising and dehumanising of Tarabai are portrayed without sentimentality or posturing, as is frequently the case in modern reconstructions. It is this starkness and matter-of-fact tone which makes the event so effective in the narrative. In contrast, the death of Anandabai, Ratanbai's mother, towards the end of the novel, though marked by great sorrow and mourning in the family, does not strip Ratanbai's father of all his power and authority as the male head of the household. Thus juxtaposed these two deaths serve to demonstrate the gender inequalities in Hindu society very effectively.

Having said that, *Ratanbai*, does not set out overtly to problematise or interrogate several aspects of the society that it describes, including the above-mentioned condition of widows. Rather, it takes great pains lovingly to describe many integral features and customs of upper-caste Maharashtrian life, such as *mangalagauri* (a ritual practiced especially by married women), the ceremonial taking of each others' names by a married couple, the *maher-sasar* (natal vs marital) politics and so on. Such descriptions, with their very imperative to record and therefore preserve for posterity a way of life, suggest, in fact, a clear understanding of the forces of history. Shevantibai was well aware that she was living through times of tremendous change in which the Hindu society she was describing was fast transforming before her very eyes. Her attempt to record, document and even celebrate this way of life was not a sign of her conservativeness, but instead a subtle acknowledgement that these ways were unsustainable under the onslaught of modernity. At the end of the novel, not just Ratanbai, but even the widowed Tarabai, are educated, while Prataprao, Ratanbai's husband, has gone to England for higher studies and is about to return to India 'via America, Japan and China' – a rather circuitous route, but one which suggests a new globally integrated family. Tarabai herself is no longer in widow's weeds, but in 'reformed' dress, with her hair grown back. She is said to look 'very sweet', and though still not wearing *kumkum* or ornaments, she reportedly dresses in a modern 'print jacket' and wears a shawl when outdoors. Thus, the five years which the narrative covers, records changes that can be considered nothing short of revolutionary for a society such as the book describes.

Altogether, however, the end of the novel forges an idealised synthesis between forces of tradition and modernity, reform and conservation, Christianity and upper-caste Hindu ways, imperialism and national identity, women's emancipation/education and the continuation of patriarchal norms – all under the aegis of Queen Victoria's benign rule. Though such a dream was practically impossible, its eloquent idealisation reveals the author's longing to reconcile the contradictions of her times in a way that was most appealing to her. In the final analysis, it must be admitted, the novels of Krupabai and

Shevantibai created a new consciousness. While not as radical or self-conscious about gender and caste inequalities as the works of Pandita Ramabai or Tarabai Shinde, these novels, because they are imaginative, fictional portrayals rather than polemical tracts, indeed, may even be the more persuasive and moving.

6.4. RAMABAI RANADE, *CLARINDA*, AND LAXMIBAI

After Shevantibai, it is perhaps fitting to turn to the 'quiet' feminist writer who followed her. Ramabai Ranade (1862–1924) was the second wife of the distinguished Judge, author and social reformer Mahadev Govind Ranade (1842–1901). Ranade was one of the links between the Bengal intelligentsia and their Maharashtrian counterparts. He founded the Prarthana Samaj, modelled on the Brahmo Samaj, a reformist Hindu organisation, besides participating in many social and political movements of his time. He was also the mentor of Gopal Krishna Gokhale who, in turn, was Gandhi's guide, if not political guru.

Ramabai was married to Ranade when she was just eleven. At first, taking a child bride seemed to go against Ranade's campaign opposing child marriages. But Ranade not only educated her, he also patiently groomed her to be a writer and social leader in her own right. She began to participate in the women's activities of the Prarthana Samaj through its women's wing, the Arya Mahila Sabha, which was founded in 1881. She helped start the High School for Indian Girls in Pune in 1884. This was a time when women were not even supposed to be seen in public, let alone attend school and 'If a woman was seen in any kind of footwear or carrying an umbrella she became an object of derision' (Ranade 1969, 221). The allusion is clearly to Anandibai Karve, another intrepid widow and social reformer, who as early as 1889, walked the streets of Bombay with shoes and umbrella. As she remarks in her autobiography, people 'often peeped out of windows and from balconies at my untraditional behaviour' (Karve 1963, 63). The umbrella, traditionally a symbol of royalty, implied dignity and the shoes, not just dignity, but also mobility; together, the two represent the coming of age of the new woman, who from being dependent and housebound, was now bidding to be independent and mobile.[11] Ramabai went on to become president of the Arya Mahila Sabha in 1893. She also founded the Hindu Ladies' Social and Literary Club in Bombay, which became the forum for Hindu society ladies to meet and participate in the well-being of their less fortunate sisters.

After the death of her husband in 1901, Ramabai gave herself to public work in Pune. Her most important contribution was to visit hospitals and prisons to improve the lives of patients and inmates. She also helped to found and presided over the first session of the All India Women's Conference (AIWC), an organisation with which many famous Indian women, including Sarojini Naidu, were to be associated. She collected her husband's writings and also published her *Reminiscences* in 1910 in Marathi under the title *Amchya Ayushatil Kahi Athavani* (some reminiscences from our lives). She was also a pioneer and leader of the suffragette movement in Maharashtra and during debates on whether women should vote, was often held up as an example of a woman who had earned the right to vote (Ranade 1969, 223).

Ramabai's book is unique in that it is also a biography of the changing times, showing how a shy and unlettered little girl went on to become a leader of Hindu society. Ramabai, to all appearances, was a traditional woman. Keeping to convention, she never once refers to her husband by his name, but only as '*svatah*' or himself. Her life, in that sense, is the opposite to that of her namesake, Pandita Ramabai, who was a rebel. Even though Ramabai Ranade herself experienced the worst trauma of Indian womanhood in those days when she lost her husband, she lived with dignity and contributed immensely to her society. Without breaking radically from her tradition or even her faith, she managed to embody the promise of a better life for Indian women. This was possible through, what we might call, the gains of moderation. Ranade, her husband, was himself a political moderate. Ramabai, we might argue, was a moderate feminist. Neither a victim nor a revolutionary, she quietly pushed for change and improvement in the conditions of women. She too supported and espoused the causes that Pandita Ramabai had advocated, including self-reliance, education and an increase in the number of female doctors and teachers.

Apart from being a social reformer, Ramabai also became a pioneer in women's autobiographical writing in the Marathi language. Life-writing, especially for women, was practically unknown in those days. She honed it to a fine art, providing a model for those who came after. Her book is characterised not only by a meticulous attention to detail, but also by a direct, homespun style. The main characters are not just lively but well-rounded. With detailed accounts of domestic life, her narrative weaves a complex web of family relationships, providing a vivid portrait of Brahmin society of that time. This accurate and persuasive picture from the inside serves to counterbalance the polemics of missionaries or reformers who often painted Hindu society as degenerate and brutally oppressive. Here we see that matters are not so straightforward but that power in the family is mediated through complex networks and hierarchies, so that no one can wield it absolutely or unaccountably.

This complexity in patriarchal structures among Brahmin households is evident in Ranade's very marriage to Ramabai. Occurring a month after the passing of his first wife, whom he loved deeply, this was a kind of compromise forced on him by family obligations. As Ramabai observes:

> I was married in December of 1873. There was not much of a bridal procession. Actually, after the Vedic ceremony was over, we walked home.
>
> My husband had not eaten anything at my mother's house. Even when he returned home, he spoke to no one. He went to his own room and locked himself in. He was in deep agony that day.
>
> It was just a month since he had lost his first wife, who had been like a comrade to him. That great grief was yet fresh in his mind. To add to that, he had to yield to his father's stern

> insistence and marry again entirely against his resolve. Two principles were sacred to him – never to go against the word of his father and never to disturb the peace and well-being of his family. For this, he gave up a view which he had accepted as correct over a long period of time, the principle of the justice of widow-remarriage. He gave up his valued friendships. He even flung away his self-respect and the esteem arising from it. For the sake of the parental word, he faced the ridicule and lasting calumny of society. (Ranade 1969, 32)

As the passage above indicates, there had been a campaign against Ranade for not marrying a widow himself after advocating this recourse to the problem of child-widows in India. The book is important for showing, equally, the extensive hold that the family had on the principal actors of the time, both men and women, as well as the support system that it proved for them. Ranade, the moderate, accedes to his father's 'command' instead of rebelling against it. Yet, in doing so, he mentors his young second wife into a leader of the women's movement and an important writer.

Ranade, who was thirty-one while Ramabai was eleven, was both her teacher and husband. Ramabai, in turn, performed her *stri dharma* or duty as woman and wife with exceptional diligence and success. Yet what the book reveals to us is just how much this dharma changed in her own lifetime, how modified and modernised it became, partly with the help of liberal and supportive men. What is more, we see in her narrative a continuity in the reciprocal and mutually beneficial gender relations which she saw in her own parents and carried on through her own life with her husband. The marriage that to all appearances was retrogressive, in other words, produced a remarkably progressive advocate for women's rights in the mature Ramabai.

The next book considered here was not written by a woman at all, though its central character was a woman whose life, would certainly qualify as one of the extraordinary tales of early British colonialism in India. *Clarinda: A Historical Novel* (1915) by A. Madhaviah presents an interesting comparison, in fact, with *Ratanbai*. It was written near a decade later, by a progressive Hindu Brahmin from Madras, to show male solidarity with and encouragement for the cause of women's empowerment and liberation.

Madhaviah, the author of *Clarinda*, was a pioneering novelist in both Tamil and English. His early writings began appearing in the *Madras Christian College Magazine* in the early 1890s. It was in this very journal that Krupabai Satthianadhan's two novels, *Saguna* and *Kamala* were also serialised, around the same time. The character of Clarinda is drawn from a real person, a high-caste and well-born Maratha Brahmin of the late eighteenth century Thanjavur. She lived with an English officer and became a Christian. Like Saguna, Kamala and Ratanbai, Clarinda's progress bears the burden of multiple interpretations and discourse trajectories.

As a historical novel which is based on meticulous research, *Clarinda* helps not only to excavate and resurrect the life of a woman remarkable by any standards for her independence and spirit, but also someone whose story illustrates the actualities of a unique instance of the Indo-British encounter. The decay of the native states and civil society, the dysfunctionality of the Indian family and of traditional mores, the oppression of a caste-ridden patriarchal system with the eventual triumph and 'superiority' of the modern Western influence – or, more succinctly, the pitting of a decadent Hindu social order against a progressive Western (here Christian) one – are some of the key themes of the book.

If read as a national allegory, we find the 'good' but defeated Hindu (represented by Pandit Rao, who becomes a hermit) in retreat before an advancing Western, Christian political and cultural formation. Clarinda's English husband, Lyttelton, not only rescues her from a forced sati, but also gives her a kind of happiness and selfhood that few Indian husbands of that period could afford to their wives. Their relationship, thus, represents a different form of conjugal sharing, one based on equality and reciprocity, than was available to most Indian couples of that period. The missionary records of the real Clarinda willy-nilly also reveal the prudishness and theological prejudices of those who baptised her, but this is not an aspect that interests Madhaviah much. As Lakshmi Holstrom points out in her Introduction, for Madhaviah, Clarinda is a personification of courage, passion and even of women's emancipation. It is Clarinda's agency in her seizure of control over her own life and destiny that fascinates Madhaviah.

The backdrop of the novel, painstakingly recreated by Madhaviah, shows the struggle for supremacy between the English and the French in South India. The eclipse of native states and the triumph of British paramountcy, which were already historical facts by the time the novel was written, are explained, even 'justified', through a sort of rationalising of history through back-projection. Against the larger historical and political canvas, is the more contrived and melodramatic sub-plot of family intrigues and a doomed love story.

The turning point of the novel is Madhav's rejection of Clarinda's very bold marriage proposal. Clarinda, saved from a forced immolation by Lyttelton, is recuperating from her burns and scars in his house, under his protection. Madhav, her lover, comes to see her, but not with an honourable motive. He has been set upon by his father to propose to Clarinda that she live with him as his mistress so that he can take charge of her considerable estates and inheritance to repair his own damaged fortunes. Clarinda, anticipating him says:

> If therefore you really love me still and are willing to devote your life to a task at once heroic and noble, break this unjust and cruel custom, even as the first step in our holy endeavour to better our society and marry me.... (Madhaviah [1915] 2005, 205)

That both Clarinda and her author Madhaviah are aware of just how revolutionary is this speech, becomes clearly evidenced by the heroine's own self-consciousness admission: 'No young woman, perhaps, ever before spoke in this manner to any young man.' (ibid.) Madhav, of course, recoils in horror: 'Whoever heard of a Brahmin widow remarrying!' (ibid.) and again, 'How can I marry you? It is preposterous; it is impossible and you know it.' (207) By the time the book was written, however, this was neither preposterous, nor unthinkable, nor indeed impossible. Madhaviah must pave the way for how such dramatic changes took place in upper-caste mores by showing that Clarinda has no option but to marry Lyttelton, which she now does out of choice and to convert to Christianity, which too she decides to do on her own.

The sati episode is not necessarily borne out by the historical facts, but seems to have been invented by Madhaviah to justify his heroine's decisions (Madhaviah [1915] 2005, xxxiii). Indeed, Madhaviah's treatment of it is quite romantic, based on 'the colonial trope of the white man as chivalrous and romantic hero saving the distressed and beautiful princess' (xxxiii) as in Jules Verne's *Around the World in 80 Days* (1873). Rajeswari Sunder Rajan defines the stereotype thus:

> the widow is young, beautiful and a princess; the dead husband old, ugly and a king; the other villains a blood thirsty mob and a cabal of scheming Brahmans; the rescue itself an act of chivalry, combining daring adventure with the humanitarian gesture. (Sunder Rajan 1993, 43)

What happens in *Clarinda*, then, is very similar to the stereotype. To show Clarinda choosing Lyttelton for the sake of sexual passion as also converting to Christianity because she found her own religion unpalatable might have been too subversive; Madhaviah, thus interjects the incidence of sati as a mitigating circumstance to show Clarinda's remarriage as motivated not by passion, but the desire to do good to society as well. Even so, what is interesting is that according to the logic of Madhaviah's narrative, Lyttelton, by saving Clarinda's life twice, first from a snake bite and then from an enforced sati, seems to have earned his claim over her – quite literally, the life that he has saved is now by right his own. Yet, he endowed his heroine with an agency and self-consciousness, which were perhaps possible only a hundred years after the actual Clarinda passed into the dusty pages of history. Here Madhaviah is advancing his own liberal social agenda.

Thus, romance and realism intermingle in interesting and

meaningful ways in the novel. If anything in the novel does seem forbidding to the contemporary reader, it is, arguably, the somewhat dated and stilted style. Yet the efflorescence of Indian English fiction of the 1930s is still two decades away, so Madhaviah's earlier efforts need to be put in a proper perspective. Most of Madhaviah's other books in both Tamil and English were written before *Clarinda* and dealt with similar themes, including the position of women, the question of the Hindu widow and the issue of conversion to Christianity. Of his English works, the semi-autobiographical *Thillai Govindan* (1903) is more famous. In fact, *Clarinda* has been so much out of circulation that it has been rarely cited and never studied seriously. It is hoped that the reprint, edited so ably by Holmstrom, will put an end to the neglect of what is clearly an important early text of Indian English fiction.

The list of illustrious Maharashtrian women, especially those who lived unconventional lives and wrote their own stories, does not end with Ramabai Ranade. The last notable example in this essentially nineteenth century tradition of reformist autobiographers was Lakshmibai Tilak (1868–1936), the wife of another Chitpavan Brahmin, Narayan Vamanrao Tilak, a poet and writer, who converted to Christianity. Her story, *Smriti Chitre*, written in Marathi, was published in four parts from 1934 to 1937. It was translated into English as early as 1950. Lakshmibai, too, is illiterate when she is married at eleven to Tilak. Again, we see a struggle to acquire an education, besides learning how to read and write. After her husband's conversion, she faces a spiritual and moral crisis. Should she, as a good Hindu wife, follow him? Or should she cling to her ancestral religion. Eventually, she does follow, as the title of the English translation of her book declares. Her story, like the others in this chapter, is one of attaining personal fulfilment and selfhood after crossing many barriers and overcoming various obstacles. What distinguishes *Smriti Chitre* is its persistently humorous tone, both a genuine stylistic device and a defence mechanism; as she says at one point, 'I'm very like a rubber ball, bouncing back, again and again.' (quoted in Acharekar 2007) However, what is intriguing to modern readers is why she never criticises her husband, the impulsive and sometimes irresponsible Vamanrao, on whose account she had to undergo so many hardships. She did fulfil, it would seem, the *stri dharma* of the Hindu wife after all. No wonder that Lakshmibai completed her husband's epic, *Khristayana*, a work of considerable length and ambition, of which Tilak had written only the first eleven cantos before he died, writing the remaining sixty-one cantos herself.

6.5 CONCLUSION: MASTERS OF CHANGE?

The stories of most of these women have been annexed to or appropriated by either the grand narrative of triumphant Christianity or of emerging feminism. As Dorothy F. Lane shows, in the case of the former, 'the Empire of Britain' and 'the Empire of Christ' were practically coextensive (Lane 2005, 252). On the other hand, many feminists such as Tharu and Lalita regard these stories as part of the saga of emerging Indian feminism. Actually, they were far more complex, intersecting with and resisting power structures that were both colonial and patriarchal, both Hindu and Christian, both Indian and Western. Not always did they succeed in defining their terrain effectively or attaining the kind of svaraj that would ensue from a radical self-transformation. More often, in leaving one oppressive structure, they would collaborate with another. In rejecting Hinduism, for instance, some of these writers found themselves joining forces with colonialist Christianity in an inferior partnership. Even so, to use Padma Anagol's expression, they were 'Discriminating Converts.' Eventually, however, it was nationalism which proved to be the dominant ideology of the times.

Unlike Chatterjee (1989, 1993) however, I do not see clear material-spiritual, home-outside dichotomies in the nationalist resolution of the crisis of women's subjectivity. There are only thresholds and flows, with messy and myriad boundary crossings.

As Gauri Viswanathan says,

> ...interweaving and disentangling are the metaphors that most accurately describe the conversion experience, which meshes two worlds, two cultures and two religions, only to unravel their various strands and cast upon each strand the estranged light of unfamiliarity. (Viswanathan 1998, 4)

Many individual experiments occurred, characterised by courage and passion, as all the while the incipient national consciousness waited, brooding on the sidelines. The converts' initial resistance to this force – because they considered British colonialism, which favoured Christian missions, as the best guarantor of women's rights – ultimately waned even as it marginalised them. Later generations of converts soon aligned themselves with the nationalist upsurge. Women like Ramabai Ranade, on the other hand, who did not leave the Hindu fold, managed to come to the fore as better role models for the masses. We must not forget, however, that many of the latter group succumbed to another, perhaps subtler, form of conversion. That is conversion to a secular, liberal, Westernisation such as Macaulay had preached through the instrumentality and civilising mission of the English language. At any rate, both forms of conversion resulted in the creation and exercise of Indian English authority, which in turn changed the consciousness not just of Indian women, but of India itself.

Subject to change as these women were, they were also changing the very terms in which they were understood. While most commentators tend to view the struggles over women's subjectivity as battles between conservatives and liberals, traditionalists and modernists, feminists and patriarchs, colonised and colonisers, Hinduism and Christianity, or even mother tongues and English. Actually the situation was perhaps rather more complex and involved. What is clear, however, is that 'gender trouble' was at the heart of these relationships. That is why we need to examine them afresh. To my mind, neither male malevolence and female victimisation, nor mutual benevolence between the sexes presents an accurate picture.

It is only when we move beyond such persuasive stereotypes that we begin to see different models and possibilities at work. From irascible polemics to strategic accommodation, women's writing from that time shows a variety of stances and approaches to the gender question. What most of these women did share, though, was a belief that education was the key to empowerment. Then writing, which was one way of exercising textual authority, was essential to transforming consciousness. This was because Indian modernity itself was being fashioned, in large measure, through writing. It was also through the enlarged possibility of the print medium that most retrograde and rearguard attacks on women's rights were also taking place. There was a great deal of confrontation and cooperation between the different factions – between women and men, between the colonisers and the colonised, between the Indian languages and English so that it would be a loss to reduce this complexity. Yet in this tangle, what stands out clearly is the solidarity among the women, the manner in which they formed communities and forged alliances. The power of writing erupted through their agency. It is these first steps that started the long and arduous journey to gender justice in modern India.

WORKS CITED

Acharekar, Janhavi. 2007. 'Remarkable Self-Portrait.' Review of *Smriti Chitre* (*Sketches from Memory*) by Laxmibai Tilak, translated by Louis Menezes *The Hindu*. August 5, 2007. <http://www.hindu.com/lr/2007/08/05/stories/2007080550110300.htm>. Accessed January 18, 2012.

Anagol, Padma. 2006. *The Emergence of Feminism in India, 1850–1920*. London: Ashgate

Barr, Pat. 1989. *The Memsahibs; The Women Of Victorian India*. London: Century.

Bhagwat, Vidyut. 1995. 'Marathi Literature as a Source for Contemporary Feminism.' *Economic and Political Weekly* 30 (17): WS24–WS29.

Chandra, Shefali. 2007. 'Gendering English: Sexuality, Gender and the Language of Desire in Western India, 1850–1940.' *Gender and History*.

19 (2): 284–304.

Chakravarti, Uma. 1998. *Rewriting History: The Life and Times of Pandita Ramabai*. New Delhi: Kali for Women.

Chatterjee, Partha. 1989. 'The Nationalist Resolution of the Women's Question.' In *Recasting Women: Essays in Colonial History*. Edited by Kumkum Sangari and Sudesh Vaid. New Delhi: Kali for Women.

_____.1993. *Nation and Its Fragments: Colonial and Postcolonial Histories*. Princeton, NJ: Princeton UP, 1993.

Debi, Rashsundari. (1868) 1991. *Amar Jiban*. Reprint. Translated by Enakshi Chatterjee and edited by Tanika Sarkar. New Delhi: Kali.

Joshi, Shrikrishna Janardan. 1992. *Anandi Gopal*. Translated and abridged by Asha Damle. Kolkata: Stree, 1992.

Kosambi, Meera. 2007. *Crossing Thresholds: Feminist Essays in Social History*. Ranikhet: Permanent Black.

Krishnaraj, Maithreyi. 2007. 'Reclaiming an Incipient Feminism.' Review of *Crossing Thresholds: Feminist Essays in Social History* by Meera Kosambi. *Economic and Political Weekly* 42 (21): 1916–1918.

Karve, Anandibai. 1963. 'Autobiography.' In *The New Brahmans: Five Maharashtrian Families*. Translated and edited by D. D. Karve. Berkeley: University of California Press.

Lane, Dorothy F. 2005. '"One Power, One Mind": Religious Diversity and British Dominion in India.' *Literature & Theology* 19 (3): 251–264.

Madhaviah, A. (1915) 2005. *Clarinda: A Historical Novel*. Reprint. Edited with an Introduction by Lakshmi Holmstrom. New Delhi: Sahitya Akademi.

_____. 1916. *Thillai Govindan*. London: T. Fisher Unwin.

McGowan, Abigail. 2006. 'An All-consuming Subject? Women and Consumption in Late-Nineteenth- and Early-Twentieth-Century Western India.' *Journal of Women's History* 18 (4): 31–54.

Miller, Basil. n.d. *Pandita Ramabai: India's Christian Pilgrim*. Pasedena, CA: World Wide Mission.

Nikambe, Shevantabai. (1895) 2003. *Ratanbai: A Sketch of a Bombay High Caste Hindu Young* Wife. Reprint. Edited by Eunice D'Souza. New Delhi: Sahitya Akademi.

_____. (1895) 2004. *Ratanbai: A High-Caste Child-Wife* by Shevantibai Nikambe. Reprint. Edited by Chandani Lokuge. Afterword by Makarand

Paranjape. New Delhi: Oxford UP

Ramabai, Pandita. 1888. *The High-Caste Hindu Woman*. Introduction by Rachel L. Bodley. Philadelphia: Jas. B. Rodgers Printing Company.

_____. (1889) 2003. *Returning the American Gaze: Pandita Ramabai's The Peoples of the United States*. Reprint. Translated and edited by Meera Kosambi. Delhi, Permanent Black, 2003.

_____. 2000. *Pandita Ramabai Through Her Own Words: Selected Works*. Translated, edited and compiled by Meera Kosambi. New Delhi; New York: Oxford University Press.

Ranade, Ramabai. 1969. *His Wife's Reminiscences*. Translation by Kusumavati Deshpande of *Amchya Ayushatil Kahi Athavani*. 2nd reprint. New Delhi: Publication Division, Government of India.

Satthianadhan, Krupabai. (1885) 1998. *Saguna: A Story of Native Christian Life*. Edited by Chandani Lokuge. New Delhi: Oxford UP.

_____. (1894) 1998. *Kamala: A Story of a Hindu Life*. Reprint. Edited by Chandani Lokuge. New Delhi: Oxford UP, 1998.

Shinde, Tarabai. (1882) 2000. *A Comparison Between Women and Men: Tarabai Shinde and the Critique of Gender Relations in Colonial India*. Reprint. Translated and edited by Rosalind O'Hanlon of *Stri Purush Tulana*. Delhi, Oxford University Press.

Sunder Rajan, Rajeswari. 1993. *Real and Imagined Women: Gender, Culture and Postcolonialism*. London: Routledge.

Tharu, Susie J. and K. Lalita, Eds. 1991. *Women Writing in India: 600 B.C. to the Present*. Volume 1. New York: Feminist Press at the City University of New York.

Tilak, Lakshmibai. 1998. *I Follow After*. Translated by Josephine Inkster of *Smriti Chitre*. Delhi: Oxford University Press

Viswanathan, Gauri. 1998. *Outside the Fold: Conversion, Modernity and Belief*. Princeton, NJ: Princeton University Press.

7
REPRESENTING SWAMI VIVEKANANDA

7.1 INTRODUCTION

A dramatic moment in Swami Vivekananda's life, indeed in the story of the Indo-Western encounter in modern times, was on 11 September 1893, when Vivekananda first addressed the Parliament of World Religions in Chicago. This is how he described it in a letter to his disciple Alasinga Perumal in Madras:

> There was a grand procession and we were all marshalled on to the platform. Imagine a hall below and a huge gallery above, packed with six or seven thousand men and women representing the best culture of the country and on the platform learned men of all the nations of the earth. And I, who never spoke in public in my life, to address this august assemblage!! It was opened in great form with music and ceremony and speeches; then the delegates were introduced one by one and they stepped up and spoke. Of course my heart was fluttering and my tongue nearly dried up; I was so nervous and could not venture to speak in the morning. Mazoomdar made a nice speech, Chakravarti a nicer one and they were much applauded. They were all prepared and came with ready-made speeches. I was a fool and had none, but bowed down to Devi Sarasvati and stepped up and Dr Barrows introduced me. I made a short speech. I addressed the assembly as 'Sisters and Brothers of America,' a deafening applause of

two minutes followed and then I proceeded; and when it was finished, I sat down, almost exhausted with emotion. The next day all the papers announced that my speech was the hit of the day and I became known to the whole of America. Truly has it been said by the great commentator Shridhara – '*mukam karoti vachalam*' – Who maketh the dumb a fluent speaker.' His name be praised! From that day I became a celebrity and the day I read my paper on Hinduism, the hall was packed as it had never been before. I quote to you from one of the papers: 'Ladies, ladies, ladies packing every place – filling every corner, they patiently waited and waited while the papers that separated them from Vivekananda were read,' etc. You would be astonished if I sent over to you the newspaper cuttings, but you already know that I am a hater of celebrity. Suffice it to say, that whenever I went on the platform, a deafening applause would be raised for me. Nearly all the papers paid high tributes to me and even the most bigoted had to admit that 'This man with his handsome face and magnetic presence and wonderful oratory is the most prominent figure in the Parliament,' etc., etc. Sufficient for you to know that never before did an Oriental make such an impression on American society. (Vivekananda 2003, Vol 5, 20 – 21)

The accuracy of description has been disputed by some (see Chattopadhyaya 1999), but the immense significance of Vivekananda's sojourn in the West cannot be denied. It not only created the groundwork for the reception of Indian spiritual traditions in the West but also, on Vivekananda's return to India as a victorious champion, the preconditions for a revitalised national culture.

The transformation of Vivekananda from an unknown monk to India's first national hero is described quite effectively by B. G. Gokhale in a perceptive paper called 'Swami Vivekananda and Indian Nationalism' published almost sixty years ago:

In 1892 he was a little known sannyasi when Bal Gangadhar Tilak, the 'Father of Indian Unrest,' met him on a Poona-bound train. Five years later he was hailed all over the country as a conquering hero. He 'thundered from Cape Comorin on the southern tip of India to the Himalayas' delivering his message of nationalism which 'came as a tonic to the depressed and demoralised Hindu mind.' For five years he played the role of an itinerant prophet of a renascent India that had discovered its lost soul and was getting ready not only to recapture its past glories but also to save the world. Admiring audiences avidly heard all he had to say and seemed to welcome eagerly his message, which became the basis of a revitalised Hinduism. (Gokhale 1964, 35)

Vivekananda played a remarkable role in the emergence of the national culture that we have been exploring. While there were many competing versions of this, ranging from Christian, Muslim, Dalit, to Marxist articulations, the national consensus seemed to evolve out of a plural and non-exclusive Hindu strand of which Vivekananda was a key thought leader.

Two issues will be raised in this chapter on one of modern India's most charismatic and influential prodigies.[1] The first has to do with how Vivekananda has been represented in the secondary literature on him. The second which, in a sense, arises out of the first, has to do with what constitutes a 'fact' in a spiritual biography. Confronting both these issues is necessary in order to have a clearer comprehension of the impact of Vivekananda on his world, both in the East and the West, as also on the larger project of fashioning a usable past, which is the chief preoccupation of this book. In order to examine the kinds of issues involved, a retelling of Vivekananda's life, as a contrasting allegory to Madhusudan's, may be desirable. If nothing else, it will show just how extraordinary was its trajectory. Yet, perhaps, more importantly, such a review will also demonstrate why the issues that are raised are meaningful and significant.

7.2 THE LIFE[2]

Swami Vivekananda was born in Calcutta on 12 January 1863, the eldest son of Bhuvaneswari Devi and Viswanath Datta. His mother named him Vireswara after the deity Vireshwara Shiva, to whom she had offered prayers for a son. The family, however, called him Narendranath or Naren for short. His father was an attorney in the Calcutta High Court. Viswanath was a successful lawyer and enjoyed an affluent lifestyle. He appreciated good food, poetry and travel. Well-versed in both Western and Indo-Muslim culture, he was known to recite from the Bible and from the Persian poet Hafiz. A modernist by temperament, his agnosticism and liberalism placed him in opposition to many of the social conventions of his times. He was also large-hearted and generous, supporting a large number of idle, even shiftless relatives. As was often the case in nineteenth-century Bengal, while the father was a liberal, the mother was a religious and orthodox Hindu. Especially attached to the *Ramayana* and the *Mahabharata*, she was known for her piety, dignity and compassion. After Narendra, she had two other sons; of her four daughters, two died young.

As a child, Naren was boisterous, even naughty. He was also generous to wandering monks and holy men who came to the door of the Datta household. Initially, he was sent to school for a short while, then educated at home. He learned quickly and had a very good memory. He soon mastered the Bengali alphabet, learned long passages from the *Ramayana* and *Mahabharata* by heart, even crammed the whole text of a Sanskrit grammar. He also showed a logical and independent mind, capable at times of defying authority and conventions. As a boy who was growing up, he once asked his father, 'How shall I conduct myself in the world?' His father replied, 'Never show surprise at anything' – advice that Naren took to heart.

At the age of eight, he entered Pandit Iswarchandra Vidyasagar's famous school, the Metropolitan Institution. He studied English, which after some initial resistance, he excelled in. He showed a restless and energetic temperament, taking interest in a variety of things, including theatre, football, gymnastics, fencing, rowing, wrestling and cooking. He also showed a talent for singing. He was a candid and courageous boy, a natural leader. He was known to say, 'Do not believe a thing because someone says so; find out the truth for yourself.' As an adolescent he took to reading voraciously and also began to smoke.

In 1879, at the age of sixteen, he joined Presidency College, the premier institution of modern learning in Bengal. After a year, however, he transferred to the General Assembly's Institution, later known as Scottish Church College. According to some biographers, it was from the Principal of this college, Mr Hastie that he first heard of Sri Ramakrishna. Apparently, Hastie told Naren that the experiences that Wordsworth had written about in The Excursion could be actually seen in Sri Ramakrishna at *Dakshineswar*.

Naren, like many other Anglicised Hindus of his time, became attracted to the Brahmo Samaj, a reformist sect started by Raja Ram Mohan Roy. He joined Keshub Chandra Sen's Band of Hope. The Brahmo version of Hinduism was shorn of what were considered its superstitions and errors, including idol worship, the subjugation of women and several forms of caste hierarchy. Naren, however, showed his critical temperament even as a Brahmo liberal. It is said that he once asked Devendranath Tagore, who was then leader of one of the two main factions of the Brahmo Samaj, 'Sir, have you seen God?' He did not receive a direct reply but was advised to practice meditation. Later, Naren put the same question to Sri Ramakrishna. To his surprise, the latter replied, 'Yes, I see him as clearly as I see you, only in a much more intense way.'

In November 1881, Ramachandra Datta, one of Naren's relatives and a devotee of Ramakrishna, took Naren to see the Master at the house of Surendranath Mitra. Impressed by his singing, Ramakrishna invited Naren to visit him at Dakshineswar. On his very first visit, Naren felt the strange and irresistible power of Ramakrishna's love for him. With tears streaming down his face, Ramakrishna told him, 'What took you so long to come? How unkind of you to keep me waiting so long!' Naren was naturally surprised, even a little dismayed by this unexpected display of emotion and affection. Ramakrishna fed him sweets with his own hand, making him promise that he would visit again. Before he left, Naren asked Ramakrishna whether he (Ramakrishna) had seen God and was thrilled to receive an affirmative reply. Ramakrishna said, 'Yes, I have. I see Him as clearly as I see you, only in a much intenser sense.' Later, the master told him, 'God can be seen, but who cares to see him? People shed torrents of tears for their wives and progeny, over their wealth and property, but who weeps for a vision of God? If you cry sincerely for God, you can surely see him.'

During his next visit, Ramakrishna placed his foot on Naren's body. Naren's senses swooned as he found the whole world, including himself, vanishing. He thought he was dying and cried out, 'Sir, what are you doing to me? I have parents, brothers and sisters at home. Restoring him to his "normal" consciousness, the master laughed, All right, everything will happen in due time.' Though astonished and moved, Naren persisted with his scepticism. He wondered whether he had been hypnotised or if he had hallucinated. However, his positivist bent of mind had to yield before the higher states of consciousness that Ramakrishna induced in him. On his third visit, Ramakrishna touched him again and Naren completely lost consciousness. Ramakrishna bestowed special favours on Vivekananda because he saw the latter as a very highly evolved sage, descended to the earth for the welfare of humanity.

Narendra's sharp and fiercely independent mind took several years to accept Ramakrishna as his guru. In fact, it is hard to pinpoint the exact date when he accepted Ramakrishna completely. Initially Narendra did not refrain even from criticising the object of Ramakrishna's devotion, the Divine Mother, enshrined in the Dakshineshwar temple as Kali. Yet, over the years, repeatedly, the young man's reasoning was unable to comprehend the mysteries of life or solve life's problems. It was only the guru's unwavering love and grace that gave him peace. Ramakrishna's own enthusiasm and love for Narendra was as constant as it was intense. As far as he was concerned, Narendra was his from the moment he set eyes on the latter. Vivekananda later remarked, 'What do worldly people know of love? The master alone loved us genuinely.'

When Narendra first met Ramakrishna he believed in the Brahmo doctrine of monotheism. The worship of several gods and goddesses, including Kali, was therefore unattractive to him. Even Advaitic ideas of the identity of the Self with the Divine were difficult to accept. Being a positivist, he would say, 'What can be more absurd that to say that this cup is God, this jug is God and we are God too?' It was only when Ramakrishna actually gave him the superconscious state of Samadhi that Narendra began to accept a realm of awareness that was supra-sensual. The senses, he began actually to experience under Ramakrishna's tutelage, were not the only sources of knowledge. He was forced to accept that there were not only many levels of consciousness, but that the whole universe was permeated with Brahman or Spirit, indeed, that matter was full of consciousness too.

Narendra's inner struggle to reach a truth more satisfying that what he had learned by reading Locke, Hume, Spencer and Mill was accompanied by an outer struggle for survival. What attracted him to Ramakrishna was that the latter seem to speak and act from an almost limitless source of *anubhav*, the actual experience of the ultimate reality, while the others, as confused and uncertain as he himself was, only seemed to spout second-hand and bookish knowledge. Ramakrishna did not force him to give up or change his beliefs, but instead only directed him to the higher truths behind appearances. For instance he said, 'Even if you do not believe in images and forms, you can at least believe in an Ultimate Reality, who is the regulator of this universe.' He taught Narendra how even to turn his scepticism to spiritual benefit by praying: 'O God, I do not know you. Be gracious to reveal to me your real nature.'

In 1884 about four years after he met Ramakrishna, just when he was to appear for his BA final examination, Narendra's father suddenly died. Given the nature of the Hindu joint family then, this was nothing short of a great calamity. Generous to a fault, Viswanath had lived beyond his means; he died leaving accumulated debts. Creditors stalked the Datta household. Narendra, as the eldest son, faced the brunt of this downturn of fortune. The sole breadwinner gone, the relatives immediately began litigation over what was left. The very relatives whom Viswanath had offered refuge, now tried to grab what was left of his property. Bhuvaneswari Devi was left a widow, her children reduced to terrible penury. Narendra's erstwhile friends deserted him. Though he was starving, they did not even invite him to a meal. He wore out the soles of his shoes walking the streets of Calcutta, searching for any gainful and honest job. Everywhere, he faced rejection and disappointment. The cruelty and reality of the world were starkly revealed to him.

Dejected and grief-stricken, he thought that all was lost. He had begun to doubt the beneficence of providence and even the existence of God. Even in these worst of times, however, he was absorbed by the intellectual problem of a sovereign and merciful God presiding over a creation filled with evil and suffering. His biographers record how, one evening, totally drenched in the rain, tired and hungry, sitting on the pavement, he had a vision in which he understood how to reconcile a compassionate God with the misery in creation.

Ramakrishna, by his own mysterious process, apparently knew the truth of Narendra's circumstances and also the latter's troubled state of mind. Narendra got a temporary job, which was sufficient barely to support his family for the time being. When he visited Ramakrishna at Dakshineswar, he requested the holy man to ask Goddess Kali to relieve his (Narendra's) distress. Ramakrishna asked him to go into the temple and ask for whatever he wanted: 'She is the sovereign of the universe and can fulfil all your wishes.' At nine in the evening, Narendra went to the temple. In a state of ecstasy, he entered the courtyard. He too was sure that whatever he asked would be granted. Yet instead of wealth and worldly success, all that he asked for was wisdom and discrimination. Feeling a great peace within, he returned to Ramakrishna, only to realise that he had forgotten to ask for pecuniary benefits. Ramakrishna sent him to Mother Kali again and yet again. Yet in the presence of the deity his earlier resolve to beg for material riches vanished. He realised that, perhaps this whole drama had been enacted at his guru's behest, this was only to strengthen his resolve to renounce worldly life. This was a turning point in Narendra's life. Later, Vivekananda would turn into an ardent devotee of Kali, the very goddess whose worship he scoffed as a young man.

Ramakrishna trained Vivekananda for the higher life for over five years. He lavished special attention and care on Naren's development, as if the latter were marked for a special destiny. Through ecstatic song and dance, through homely proverbs and stories, though careful observation and practice, through chanting and meditation and through a variety of other methods, Ramakrishna prepared Vivekananda. But the real chord that tied master and disciple was the unique, elevating, unworldly love of the former, a love that was truly spiritual and transforming. From Ramakrishna he learnt the ideal of renunciation, while the privations at home softened his heart for the poor and the downtrodden. In Ramakrishna Narendra saw the embodiment of the spirit of religion. He saw how his master had transcended all barriers, whether of caste and creed, status or gender. The master's formula, that all religions and sects are different and equally valid paths to the same Ultimate Reality made Narendra reject narrow-mindedness and fanaticism. Ramakrishna, in turn, thought very highly of Naren. Several of his remarks attest to this: 'Narendra belongs to a very high plane – the realm of the Absolute. He has a manly nature. So many devotees come here, but there is no one like him'; 'Every now and then I take stock of the devotees. I find that some are like lotuses with ten petals, some like lotuses with a hundred petals. But among lotuses Narendra is a thousand-petalled one; 'Other devotees may be like pots or pitchers; but Narendra is a huge water-barrel'; 'Others may be like pools or tanks; but Narendra is a huge reservoir like the Haldarpukur'; and so on.

Towards the middle of 1885, however, the great play of the master's life seemed to be drawing towards its last act. Ramakrishna had a throat ailment, which was later diagnosed as cancerous. His householder devotees shifted him to a large and comfortable garden house, the Kashipur Udyan Badi on the outskirts of Calcutta. Ramakrishna now began to train his young boys, many of whom were looking after him, in great earnest. A band of twelve young men, all of whom renounced worldly life and became monks, attained a very high degree of spiritual proficiency under his guidance. Of them, Narendra was the leader.

During his master's illness, Narendra's longing for a concrete realisation of the Divine reached its peak. He would meditate for hours, totally oblivious to the swarms of mosquitoes hovering about. He stayed up nights crying out to God. Ramakrishna considered it the right time to initiate Narendra and the other disciples into sannyasa (renunciation), thus laying the foundations of the monastic order that Vivekananda established later. All those around Ramakrishna realised his greatness seeing him bathed in inner joy and calm though his body was wasting away. Narendra asked Ramakrishna to pray to the Divine Mother about his illness. Ramakrishna said that he told Her that he could hardly swallow any food, but She replied, pointing to those around him, 'Aren't you eating through so many mouths?' The master repeatedly said that God alone had become the men, animals, gardens, houses, roads and so on – the executioner, the victim and the slaughter-post' were all nothing but God himself.

Narendra found in Ramakrishna a living proof and demonstration of the truth of the scriptures. Consciousness was all-pervasive; the body was transient; the spirit was deathless. Ramakrishna, who constantly told his followers that all of spiritual practice lay in the renunciation of *kamanikanchana* or 'women [or men] and gold,' that is lust and greed, sex and money, instilled the high ideals of self-sacrifice and renunciation into his young disciples. Narendra directly asked the master who he was and Ramakrishna replied, 'He who was Rama and Krishna is verily this (Ramakrishna),' thus proclaiming his identity with the Divine.

The Kashipur garden house where the master spent his last days became the crucible of the Ramakrishna movement. The master passed on his powers to his beloved disciple, whispering, 'Now I have given you all I possess. I am a penniless beggar, a fakir.' He assured Vivekananda, 'You will accomplish great things in the world. Your very bones will teach. On 15 August 1886, Ramakrishna called Narendra to his bedside, speaking to him for the last time. A few minutes past 1:00 AM on 16 August, he gave up his body. He was cremated on the banks of the Ganga nearby.

A new phase in Narendra's life began after Ramakrishna's death.

The young disciples of Ramakrishna were now left orphaned, so to speak. The householder disciples who had supported Ramakrishna and the boys, now showed a reluctance to continue to do so. Money, even food, was scarce. Surendranath Mitra, one of the master's disciples, stepped forward to help at this crucial juncture. He paid what to the impecunious boys was the "princely" rent of Rs. 10 per month for a dilapidated house in Baranagore. The young disciples began to live there, practicing spiritual austerities. On a short visit to Antapur, all the young men, at Vivekananda's urging, took the sacred vows of sannyas or renunciation, before a sacred fire. Standing before the *dhuni* (flame), Vivekananda urged them to become 'Christs,' to realise God and to serve their fellow humans. It turned out that the day was 24 December, Christmas Eve. Baranagore now became a monastery. There was a shrine room in the house, containing the sacred ashes of the master, to whom daily worship was offered. A monastic life, consisting of hard work, meditation, worship, study and devotional music began to flower here. From 1886–1892, Baranagore became the first home of the Ramakrishna Order. It was during this period that Rakhal became Brahmananda, Yogin Yogananda, Baburam Premanada, Niranjan Niranjananda, Sasi Ramakrishnananda, Hari Turiyananda, Latu Adbhutananda, Sarad Trigunatitananda, Tarak Sivananda, Kali Abhedananda, Gopal Senior Advaitananda, Subodh Subodhandna, Tulsi Nirmalananda and Hari Prasanna Vijnananda. These became the apostles of Ramakrishna, while Vivekananda was their leader.

There was, however, a yearning among many of these young men to assume the life of wandering ascetics. In 1888, trusting only in the Supreme Power, Narendra set out into the vast and as yet unknown continent of India, as a wandering holy man. Over the next three years, he took various names, among them Vividhisananda and Satchidananda. Ultimately, however, it was the Maharaja of Khetri, one of his patrons, who persuaded him to assume the name Vivekananda, which was much easier to pronounce. The name means one who delights in discrimination; it was apt to the logically incisive mind of Narendra.

Vivekananda wandered all over India, undertaking a course of rigorous study and self-education. He mastered Sanskrit grammar and several difficult classical texts and spiritual traditions. He also paid his respects to several well known holy men of that time. He went first to Varanasi in 1888, the ancient city considered holiest by millions of Hindus. Returning from a temple there, he was pursued by a troop of monkeys. Thinking they may harm him, he began to run. 'Face the brutes,' an old sannyasin told him. When he turned around, his fear gone, he found that the monkeys retreated.

On his second visit to Varanasi in the following year, he discussed the scriptures with Pramadadas Mitra, a great Sanskrit scholar. He also visited Ayodhya, celebrated in the Ramayana as the birthplace and capital of Rama's kingdom. He went to Lucknow, Agra, Vrindavan, then farther up to Hardwar. On the way, at Hathras, he initiated his first disciple, Sarat Chandra Gupta, who was the stationmaster. At Rishikesh, both Sarat and Vivekananda contracted malaria. Leaving Sarat behind in Hathras, Vivekananda returned to Baranagore.

In 1889, Vivekananda set out again, visiting Allahabad first. In January 1890 he met the famous fasting saint of Ghazipur, Pavahari Baba. It was said that the Baba lived only on air – 'pavahari' literary means 'air-eater.' Vivekananda, who had many doubts at this time, wanted them clarified by Pavahari Baba. He even considered being initiated by the latter, but a vision of Ramakrishna dissuaded him from going ahead. His faith in Ramakrishna restored, Vivekananda left Ghazipur.

Vivekananda spent two restless years in further wanderings. The financial condition of the fledgling math at Baranagore was precarious; Vivekananda felt that he had not only to attain the knowledge which his calling as a monk demanded, but also raise the means to make the Order viable. He visited Bhagalpur, Benaras, Ayodhya, Naini Tal, Almora, Badarikashrama, Karnaprayag, Kedarnath, Srinagar, Tehri, Mussoorie, Dehra Dun, Saharanpur and Allahabad. In 1891 he visited Rajasthan, stopping earlier in Delhi. In Rajasthan he visited Alwar, Ajmer, Jaipur, Mt Abu, before travelling south to Kathiawar and Gujarat. There he visited Ahmedabad, Junagadh, Porbandar and

Baroda, before moving to Central India. He visited Khandwa, then went farther south to Bombay, Pune, Kolhapur, Belgaum, Bangalore, Mysore and then to Malabar and Travancore and finally to the very tip of India, Kanyakumari. Then he travelled North East to Tamil Nadu, stopping at Ramnad, Pondicherry, Madras and Hyderabad.

During these travels, Vivekananda met a variety of Indians from various social strata, religions and castes. He rubbed shoulders with princes and potentates, with pandits and prime ministers. Yet he also met the common people, the toilers and the tillers, the humble folk of the land, who were reduced to poverty and wretchedness. He understood many of the ills that plagued our land, including immense inequality and oppression. Yet, behind all the sorrow and trauma of this land – now under foreign yoke – he felt the strong throb of its soul. Though assailed by many superstitions and enveloped in ignorance, the people of India, he saw, were still simple, straightforward and God-fearing. He felt that he must do something for them.

A turning point in these travels was his meditation at the last bit of Indian rock on which the Kanyakumari temple was situated. He felt a vision of a new India rising before his mind's eye and he felt destined to bring it to reality. He also realised that the princes and the ruling classes would not bring about this new India. It had to be the common people, who needed most to be transformed and inspired. That is why when he went to Madras from Kannyakumari he gathered around him a devoted group of young men to work for the cause of new India.

Somewhere along these travels, he had also formed the intention of going to the Parliament of Religions to be held in Chicago in 1893. In Madras he announced his intentions of doing so. His devotees, especially a band of young men led by Alasinga Perumal of Madras, began to collect funds for this trip. Later, he got more help from the Raja of Khetri. He saw a vision in which he was walking on water and also received the permission from Sarada Ma, Ramakrishna's consort, to go West with the master's message.

On 31 May 1893, Vivekananda set sail for the US. It would be a long voyage, taking him through Colombo, Penang, Singapore, Hong

Kong, Osaka, Kyoto, Tokyo, to Yokohama and thence, crossing the Pacific Ocean, to Vancouver in British Columbia, Canada. From there he travelled to Chicago, the venue of the Columbian Exposition and the World Parliament of Religions. During this trip, Vivekananda wrote letters home describing his experiences and observations of the various countries and peoples that he had encountered.

The story of Vivekananda's participation in the Parliament of Religions is the stuff of which legends are made. In the West for the first time, in a totally different culture, he found himself practically penniless and friendless, without even an invitation to the Parliament or a letter of introduction. When he visited the Columbian Exposition, of which the Parliament was a part, he was both bewildered and impressed by the immense material and technological progress of the West. How far behind was India! It was the end of July 1893; he found out that the Parliament had been postponed until September. In his strange clothes, he was teased and stared at. Hotels in Chicago were very expensive; the cheaper ones often mistook him for a ' negro' and denied him lodgings. He soon ran through his meagre means. He was tired and depressed, wondering whether he would have to beat an ignominious retreat. He was advised that it was cheaper to live in Boston. Enroute, in the train, his regal bearing and strange appearance attracted the curiosity of a wealthy lady, Miss Kate Sanborn. She invited Vivekananda to 'Breezy Meadows', her home in Boston.

As Miss Sanborn's guest, he met many people in and around Boston. For most of them, he was an item of curiosity, the 'first Easterner and Hindu' they had ever met. The image of India that these people had was an unflattering one, derived mostly from the Christian missionaries. Now Vivekananda realised that one of his primary responsibilities would be to show a different India to the West, one that actually had something to offer to the modern world. In Boston, he also met Professor J. H. Wright of Harvard University, who agreed to write a letter of introduction to the Parliament so that Vivekananda could be a delegate. Professor Wright even bought him a train ticket to Chicago.

The train to Chicago arrived late in the evening. Vivekananda had misplaced some of the addresses of the committee members in charge of the delegates. He spent the night in a freight wagon in the rail yard. The next morning, he walked towards the Lake Shore Drive, asking his way to the Parliament. Hungry, he asked for food, as an Indian sannyasi is wont to, at the doors of the wealthy mansions lining the street. Because he was unshaven and wore soiled clothes, he was thought to be a vagabond and he was rudely turned away. Finally, tired and famished, he sat on the sidewalk. A kindly lady – who saw him from the window of her house – knew him to be a delegate at the Parliament and sent for him. She was Mrs George W. Hale, who not only gave him succour and shelter, but presented him to Dr J. H. Barrows, the President of the Parliament. Vivekananda, once again, had proof that providence was watching over him. The Hales became Swamiji's staunch devotees.

The World's Parliament of Religions, which was inaugurated on 11 September 1893, was a grant event. Part of the Columban Exposition to commemorate the 400th anniversary of the discovery of America, the Parliament was perhaps meant to show the West's supremacy in matters of religion and spirit as the Exposition was meant to demonstrate the West's material and technological superiority. Yet, this was an unprecedented opportunity for people of various faiths and cultures to talk to each other. There were many delegates not only from all over the world, but also from the Indian subcontinent. Not just Christians, but Muslims, Hindus, Brahmos, Theosophists, Buddhists, Jains and Parsis were represented. Vivekananda seemed unprepared and out of place in this august assembly of notables and dignitaries. Yet, when he stood up to speak, uttering the simple greeting 'Sisters and Brothers of America,' it is said that he was greeted with a loud, standing applause. He continued:

> It fills my heart with joy unspeakable to rise in response to the warm and cordial welcome which you have given us. I thank you in the name of the most ancient order of monks in the world. I thank you in the name of the mother of religions ... I thank you

in the name of the millions and millions of Hindu people of all classes and sects. I am proud to belong to a religion which has taught the world both tolerance and universal acceptance I am proud to belong to a religion which has sheltered the persecuted and the refugees of all religions and all nations on earth. (Vivekananda 2003, Vol. 1, p.3)

While the other delegates had tried to emphasise the strength and uniqueness of their own creed, Vivekananda struck a different chord. He spoke of the tolerance and universality of India's spiritual traditions. He spoke out against narrow-mindedness and fanaticism. He seemed to speak not only on behalf of Hinduism but of all faiths of the world, the only one of the delegates to do so. Vivekananda had succeeded in conveying in a modern idiom the great teachings of his master to a totally unfamiliar Western audience. In his final address he clearly said:

The Christian is not to become a Hindu or a Buddhist, nor is a Hindu or a Buddhist to become a Christian. But each must assimilate the spirit of the others and yet preserve his individuality and grow according to his own law of growth. If the Parliament of Religions has shown anything to the world, it is this: It has proved to the world that holiness, purity and charity are not the exclusive possessions of any church in the world and that every system has produced men and women of the most exalted character. In the face of this evidence, if anybody dreams of the exclusive survival of his own religion and the destruction of the others, I pity him from the bottom of my heart.... (24)

Vivekananda's intervention in the Parliament may be considered prophetic not just for India's influence on the West but also for the future of dialogue between the West and the East. Though his impact in the Parliament has often been exaggerated, there is no doubt that his debut was outstanding and that he made a great impression. *The New York Herald* called him 'Undoubtedly the greatest figure in the Parliament of Religions,' and added, 'after hearing him, we feel foolish to send missionaries to this learned nation.'

After the Parliament, Vivekananda became somewhat of a celebrity. A lecture bureau engaged him to tour the country. He needed the money to free himself from some of his patrons and to fund his activities in India. He toured and spoke tirelessly, subjecting himself to a punishing schedule. Later, he freed himself from the bureau because it was exploiting him. After a while, some of the Christian churches began to attack him in the newspapers, calling him a charlatan, fraud and immoral person. Those who went back to India also carried tales. Vivekananda faced not only slander but considerable opposition in his mission in the US. Yet, he never gave up and hardly ever retaliated. He also made many friends and followers.

From 1893–1896, Vivekananda travelled widely in the US as a speaker and preacher. While the American Renaissance had already created a favourable climate for Indian ideas, especially in New England, it was Vivekananda who laid the foundations for Vedanta in the US and then in Britain. Besides Chicago and Boston, he spoke in Iowa City, Des Moines, Memphis, Indianapolis, Minneapolis, Detroit, Buffalo, Hartford, Boston, Cambridge, New York, Baltimore and Washington. He was a very effective speaker, but was frequently outspoken. He abhorred cant and hypocrisy and preached against them. He also experienced the social problems in the US first hand: sometimes, taken for a black, he was refused admission to establishments.[3] Seeing the freedom and opportunity given especially to women in America, he was all the more outraged at the ill treatment and oppression of Indian women. Vivekananda admired material progress and science. In his letters to India, he wrote enthusiastically about several aspects of American life, especially its democratic spirit, cleanliness, order, hygiene, efficiency and prosperity.

Towards the end of 1894, Vivekananda's work began to assume a new depth and seriousness. He had already established the Vedanta Society in New York as a non-sectarian organisation devoted to Vedanta. In early 1895, he took up lodgings in New York City and began to give intensive courses on the yogas. These would later be revised into his first major publications. *Raja Yoga*, for example, came out in June 1895. A translation and commentary on Patanjali's Yoga Sutras, it attracted the attention of William James and Leo Tolstoy. Exhausted with his unceasing labours, Vivekananda retired for seven weeks to Miss Dutcher's cottage at the Thousand Island Park on the St Lawrence River. He also initiated two American disciples, Marie Louise and Leon Landsberg into sannyas, administering to them the vows of poverty and chastity. During his stay here, Vivekananda had many spiritual and mystical experiences. He also wrote some poems, taught intensely and was at his most inspired.

In July 1895, Vivekananda sailed for Europe. He was invited by Henrietta Müller and E. T. Sturdy to England and by Francis H. Leggett to Paris. He arrived in Paris in August 1895. He wrote enthusiastic letters describing that city and his experiences there. Later, he would also learn some French. From Paris, he went to London, where he again began to work earnestly. His British reception was quieter and less critical. The British upper classes and the press liked him. He also met Margaret E. Noble, the Irishwoman, who, as Sister Nivedita, became one of his foremost disciples.

In December, Vivekananda returned to the US Once again, he started lecturing intensely. The talks he gave were published as *Karma-Yoga*. J. J. Godwin, a professional stenographer, now joined him. To him we owe accurate transcripts of Vivekananda's subsequent lectures in the US, Europe and India. In 1896, Vivekananda recommenced his lectures, speaking at the Madison Square Garden, New York city. These lectures were published as *Bhakti Yoga*. Thereafter, he spoke in Detroit and at Harvard University. He also reinforced the work of the Vedanta Society in New York. His aim was to rationalise and universalise the truths of the Vedanta, thereby supplying the need for a non-sectarian world practice of spirituality. A careful examination of the record shows that from 6 December 1895 to February 1896, he gave seventy classes, ten public lectures, gave interviews, participated in initiations, wrote letters, had an extensive correspondence and wrote and edited his own lectures (Chattopadhyay, 1999, 40).

In May 1896, Vivekananda went again to England to meet the

famous indologist, Max Müller at Oxford. He also found new disciples in Captain and Mrs Sevier. The Seviers paid for the establishment of the Advaita Ashram at Mayavati, in the foothills of the Himalayas. Vivekananda toured the Continent in August 1896. He visited Geneva, Mer-de-Glace, Montreux, Chillon, Chamounix, St Bernard, Lucerne, Rigi, Zermatt and Schaffhausen. He loved the Alps and even wanted to climb Mont Blanc. He then met Paul Deussen, Professor of Philosophy at Kiel and renowned Orientalist. With him, Vivekananda visited Heidelberg, Coblenz, Cologne and Berlin. He also travelled to Amsterdam before returning to London. In December 1896, he travelled overland through Dover, Calais, Mont Cenis, Milan, Pisa, Florence, heading to Naples, from where he set sail for India.

Vivekananda had not forgotten India during these years abroad. He was forming the plans of the Math and Mission that he would establish. His letters were filled with instructions on the daily routine of monks and plans for a bigger headquarters for the Order. He wanted everything to be organised and managed on modern, efficient lines. He wanted to create a generation of selfless men who would have the courage to serve their less fortunate Indian brothers and sisters. He asked of them the strength of a kshatriya, the warrior and the learning and luminosity of the brahmin, the scholar. But this combination was to be transformed into a different kind of shudra dharma or work of service to the masses.

With some of these thoughts in his mind, he arrived in January 1897 in Ceylon (Sri Lanka) via Aden. His fame had preceded him. In Colombo, a huge reception awaited him. Swami Niranjanananda had already been sent there to receive him, while Swami Sivananda waited for him in Madras. What happened in Colombo was only a foretaste of things to come. Wherever Vivekananda went, he was feted and thronged. Bands played music in his honour, priests chanted Vedic hymns, flowers were strewn in his pathways, flags were unfurled, buntings and festoons decorated the streets that he walked. Huge crowds turned up to see him. He was honoured by civic receptions. The foremost citizens of the land, including princes, potentates, the landed and industrial gentry he visited, touched his feet. His carriages were drawn by enthusiastic students and devotees. He met rousing welcomes and celebrations. He was, in a sense, India's first national figure. This is because what he had succeeded in doing was nothing less than the restoration of the pride and dignity of India in the eyes of the world.

From Colombo, Vivekananda travelled to Kandy, Anuradhapuram, Jaffna, Pamban, Rameswaram, Ramnad, Paramakkudi, Madurai, Trichinapally and Kumbakonam, before reaching Chennai. He gave several public talks in Chennai, where the adulation of the people knew no bounds. Vivekananda was seen not just as the champion for the Hindus, but of all Indians, especially of the downtrodden and underprivileged. A group of educated youths decided to dedicate their lives to furthering his cause, the cause that was no less than the uplifting of all of India, the regeneration of Bharat Mata and of the *sanatana parampara* (the perennial path). Vivekananda's speeches in Chennai are memorable in that they convey his deepest aspirations for India and also outline his method of achieving them. In his talks from Colombo to Chennai, Vivekananda had offered a complete vision for the revitalisation and transformation of Indian society. Some of these lectures are the most inspiring and insightful utterances of Vivekananda.

Vivekananda arrived in Calcutta, his home city in February 1897. Though his reception was joyous and warm, it lacked the electrifying excitement of what was offered to him in Chennai. Calcutta, then the second city of the British Empire and the capital of India, was still very deeply entrenched in Western cultural dominance. Vivekananda paid tributes to his master, Ramakrishna and expounded on the bases of Vedanta to his fellow Calcutta residents.

When his brother monks and disciples met Vivekananda on his return to India, they found him considerably altered. His vision had expanded beyond narrow notions of personal salvation. Now he had much larger dreams and ideas. He had invented a new kind of spiritual activism for India and a new kind of philosophic spirituality for the West. It was only his magnetic personality and charisma that could enrol his guru-bhais or brother disciples to his way of thinking.

Most of the latter wanted to "enjoy" a quiet and withdrawn spiritual life without too many hardships or conflicts. They did not think that they had renounced the world to become servants of the people or the builders of a new society. Vivekananda, on the other hand, seemed to be stirring up a revolution. He gave a new interpretation to Ramakrishna's famous words, 'Religion is not for empty stomachs.' He felt that the nostrum for India's decay lay in the cultivation of strength and material development. He argued that what was passed off as *sattva*, the quality of tranquillity and illumination, was nothing but *tamas*, sloth and ignorance. Thus camouflaged, cowardice and defeat pretended to be detachment and tranquillity. Personal liberation, he argued, was already guaranteed to those who had taken refuge in Ramakrishna; what they therefore had to devote themselves to was the service and upliftment of their wretched and suffering brethren. All of the latter were representatives of God, *daridra narayana* (poor as God) and therefore demanded such attention.

His brother disciples, who respected him and loved him, often felt driven to obey him, even though they might disagree. At his behest, Swami Ramakrishnananda, who had faithfully looked after the master's shrine for twelve years, left for Chennai to assume charge of the work there. Swami Akhanandananada went to alleviate the sufferings of the famine-stricken in Mushirabad. Swamis Abhedananda and Saradananda were sent to the US. Vivekananda himself set about to initiate many young men into the Order. 'Arise and awake,' he exhorted, 'arouse and awaken others, fulfil your mission in life and you will reach the highest goal.' He urged the well-born and privileged to give up pride of caste and class and to devote themselves instead to the welfare of the poor and the lowly. He advised men to treat women better and women to educate themselves. To give his ideas a practical shape he formed the Ramakrishna Mission Association, with himself as its General President and Brahmananda as the President of the Calcutta centre.

From May to December 1897, Vivekananda travelled all over North India, sometimes accompanied by his brother monks and later by the Seviers, Miss Müller and Goodwin. He went to Lucknow,

Almora and later to Bareilly, Ambala, Amritsar, Lahore, Dharamsala, Murre, Jammu, Srinagar (Kashmir), Lahore, Delhi, Alwar, Khetri, Kishengarh, Ajmer, Jodhpur, Indore and Khandwa, before returning to Calcutta. In Lahore, he met a Lecturer in Mathematics, Ram Tirtha Goswami, who fell under his spell and later became the well-known saint, Swami Rama Tirtha. On these journeys, Vivekananda renewed contacts with some of his old patrons and admirers, who had befriended and hosted him during his *parivrajika* (wandering) days. Wherever he went, inspiring people to rebuild India was his priority. He wished to reawaken a pride and self-respect in the ancient culture of the Hindus, without the least taint of fanaticism or intolerance. He encouraged intermarriage between castes and subcastes and even supported the return of converts to the Hindu fold. He also advocated a new ideal for Indians, which would combine the 'Vedantic brain and the Islamic body.'

In 1898, Vivekananda travelled to Darjeeling, Almora and Kashmir, where he paid his homage at the famous Amarnath shrine. The monastery was shifted from Alambazar (where it was moved in 1892 from Baranagore) to Belur, on the west bank of the Ganga. The site of the present Belur Math was also purchased, enabled by Miss Müller's generous donation. Another donation by Mrs Ole Bull helped to complete the construction of the shrine, which was consecrated on 9 December 1898. On 2 January 1899, the monastery was shifted to Belur Math. Swami Swarupananda, who later edited the journal *Prabuddha Bharata* and became the first president of the Advaita Ashrama, Mayavati, was initiated by Vivekananda into monastic life. Vivekananda's faithful disciple and stenographer, Goodwin, died. Advaita Ashrama was itself founded on 19 March 1899. The Bengali journal *Udbodhan* was also started in early 1899.

Margaret Noble had come to India in January 1898 and travelled with Vivekananda to Kashmir. Vivekananda called her 'England's gift to India.' She was initiated into celibacy and given the name 'Nivedita', which means 'consecrated'. Nivedita was sent to work with Sarada Ma as also trained in Indian culture and mores. This proved, however, to be a difficult and chequered relationship.

After his Amarnath *darshan* or vision of Shiva in the form of the snow linga, Vivekananda felt an intense need for solitude. His mind seemed to turn from the Vedantic Absolute to Kali, the Divine Mother whom Ramakrishna worshipped so ardently all his life. Garlanded with human skulls, her tongue dripping with blood and an unsheathed sword in her hand, she presents an image of terror. Standing on the chest of her prone husband, Shiva, Kali embodies the dynamic force of Godhead. She is the creative energy of the cosmos personified. Vivekananda perceived Kali as omnipotent. He was consumed by the consciousness of her presence and power. He had a vision of the Divine Mother, an apocalyptic scene of death and devastation. After this experience he wrote the poem, 'Kali the Mother.' He said, 'Only by the worship of the Terrible can the Terrible itself be overcome and immortality gained. Meditate on death! Meditate on death! Worship the Terrible, the Terrible, the Terrible! And the Mother Herself is Brahman! Even Her curse is a blessing. The heart must become a cremation ground – pride, selfishness and desire all burnt to ashes. Then and then alone, will the Mother come.'

On 30 September 1898, Vivekananda stayed alone for a week in the dilapidated temple of the Divine Mother at Kshirbhavani. Destroyed by Muslim invaders, the temple lay in ruins. Distressed, the Swami thought, 'How could the people have allowed this to happen? Had I been here, I would never have permitted this; I would have laid down my life to protect the Mother.' Just then he heard the voice of the Goddess: 'What if infidels should enter My temple and defile My image? What is that to you? Do you protect Me, or do *I* protect you?' Later, he had the thought that he should raise the money to restore the temple, but once again heard the Mother say, 'My child! If I so wish I can have innumerable temples and monastic centres. I can even this moment raise a seven-storied golden temple on this very spot.' These extraordinary experiences convinced him that all patriotism or religious fervour belonged to a lower plane of consciousness; everything that was and everything that happened were according to the Divine will and plan. All sovereignty and agency were vested only in the Divine; the human only seemed the doer, but was no more than a puppet. Vivekananda felt that his mission was more or less accomplished; he was free of the world, at least spiritually. 'I have ceased making any more plans,' he said, 'Let these things be as Mother wills.'

In June 1899, Vivekananda sailed a second time for the West. From Calcutta, his steamship 'Golconda,' went to Madras, then to Colombo, Aden, Naples, Marseilles, arriving in London at the end of July. Swami Turyananda and Nivedita had accompanied Vivekananda. Fifteen days later, they sailed for New York. Vivekananda visited the Leggetts in their country home, Ridgely Manor in the Catskill Mountains in upstate New York. Returning to New York City, he lectured there and then went west. Stopping at Chicago, he eventually reached Los Angeles on the West Coast. In California, Vivekananda visited Oakland, San Franscisco and Alameda. A centre was started in San Franscisco. Vivekananda received a gift of 160 acres of land near Mt Hamilton, California. After his successful visit, he returned to the East Coast, stopping in Chicago and Detroit. Back in New York City, he gave lectures at the Vedanta Society. Later, he visited Detroit for a week.

In July 1900, he set sail for Paris to participate in the Congress of the History of Religions. Here he not only gave talks but argued with French Catholics and German Orientalists. He met J. C. Bose, the great scientist, Patrick Geddes (an academic), Pere Hyacinth (a former monk), Hiram Maxim (an inventor), Sarah Bernhardt, Jules Bois (a writer) and Emma Calve. He also visited Brittany and Mt St Michel. Travelling through Vienna, Hungary, Serbia, Romania, Bulgaria, Istanbul and Athens, he reached Cairo. Here, he and his companions mistakenly wandered into the sex district, where they were jeered and accosted. But later, the prostitutes came out into the street, knelt before Vivekananda and kissed the hem of his robe. This recalls an earlier episode when after an initial reaction, he returned to listen to a courtesan's song in the palace of a Rajput prince during his wandering days. From Cairo, Vivekananda took a boat to Bombay.

From Bombay, taking a train to Calcutta, Vivekananda arrived at Belur Math on 9 December 1900. Mr Sevier had just passed away at Mayavati. On 11 December he wrote to Miss MacLeod: 'Thus two great Englishmen [the other was J. J. Goodwin] gave up their lives for us – us, the Hindus. This is martyrdom, if anything is.' Vivekananda himself went to Mayavati to see Mrs. Sevier. He returned to Belur Math in late January 1901. Two months later, in March 1901, he took his mother on a pilgrimage to East Bengal. The party reached Dhaka in March, where he delivered public lectures. He then went to Chandranath, Chittagong and to Kamakhya, near Guwahati in Assam. After returning to Belur, he spent many quiet months in the monastery in his large room.

In 1902 many important visitors met Vivekananda including Okakura Tenzin from Japan. With Okakura, Vivekananda went to Varanasi and then to Bodh Gaya. In Varanasi, the Maharaja offered him a handsome donation, which was used to start the Ramakrishna Home of Service. Vivekananda's health was getting worse. He had symptoms of dropsy and of diabetes, which he had inherited. His feet were swollen, he could hardly close his eyes to sleep. Increasingly, he began to free himself of responsibilities, concentrating more and more on meditation and prayer. Always passionate in his beliefs, he now refused even to comment on day-to-day questions. On 15 May 1902, he wrote to Miss Macleod, 'A great idea of quiet has come upon me. I am going to retire for good – no more work for me.'

In the last days of his life, everything he did was unhurried, calm and deliberate. Towards the end of June 1902, he asked for a Bengali almanac, which he studied intently. Three days before his passing, to told Premananda where he wished his body cremated. He fasted on *ekadashi*, the eleventh day of the lunar month; on that day, he himself served Sister Nivedita her meal. On 4 July 1902, which was a Friday, he spent many hours in meditation. He sang movingly, a devotional song to Kali, had a hearty lunch, taught Sanskrit grammar for three hours in the afternoon, had a walk with Premananda and had a long conversation with his companions. He said, 'India is immortal if she persists in her search for God. But if she goes in for politics and social conflict, she will die.' At seven in the evening, he retired to his room, asking not to be disturbed. He meditated for an hour, then asked a disciple to fan him as he lay down. After another hour, his hands trembled, he breathed deeply once and then gave up his body. It is widely believed that he chose the day and time of his own death. That is it was no accident that this happened to be the American independence day.

His death left his brother monks somewhat nonplussed. They did not even have the presence of mind to take one last photograph of their dear brother and leader.

7.3 REPRESENTATIONS

This extensive account is itself a certain kind of representation of Vivekananda's life. What are the values that have informed it? Before answering this question, it might be apposite to ask, what do we mean by 'representation' in the first place? I think the word may be sued in two main senses. The most obvious and therefore the primary meaning of 'represent' is to describe, to re-present something or someone. This meaning of represent, as in the Oxford English Dictionary, suggests presence or appearance because, etymologically, represent goes back to the Latin *esse* or presence. To re-present, then, is to describe or to offer a 'likeness' of something. There is a gap between the actual presence and the likeness or description. A representation, therefore, cannot be totally accurate. If presence is likened to the thing-in-itself, there will always be a gap between it and its representation, between the noumenon and the phenomenon. The 'likeness,' furthermore, may actually be a kind of 'unlikeness'; that is why, someone may exclaim that my idea of Vivekananda is quite different from theirs. But that is only to be expected because every act of description is also one of interpretation. And there are as many interpretations as there are interpreters. I think this is what Swami Tyagananda highlights when he says that 'discovery is a two-track process' in which, on the one hand, 'we discover places or things or people' but on the other hand, 'we discover our own selves' (Tyagananda 2005, 29).

The other meaning of 'represent' is to stand in for, as when we speak of the House of Representatives. So to represent Vivekananda is also to stand for (or against) him. For example, in his name, a whole range of institutions and practices are established: there are societies, centres, schools, colleges, even residential layouts and roads named after him. Of these, some are of a general sort and may not signify anything more than respect or reverence for Vivekananda, but others imply that they are the authentic owners or carriers of his legacy. It is the latter who, in effect, control the apparatus of perpetuating his memory. They are doing Swamiji's work, as it were, or claim to be doing it, which gives them these special rights over controlling what people think of him. On the other side are those who would seem to be doing not so much Swamiji's work but that of 'truth,' 'science,' or 'secular knowledge.' They call themselves historians, academics, intellectuals, critics, or scholars. Indeed, there is competition between these stake-holders who generate competing interpretations. There may be yet another faction, those who oppose Swamiji and what he stood for; such detractors may see in him an opponent to their own agenda, whether religious or secular. Sometimes, such differences even get consolidated into schools or traditions. Again, Swami Tyagananda referred to some groups as devotees versus sceptics, those who see Vivekananda as divine as opposed to those who see him as only too human. Tyagananda asks an important question: whether it is possible to take a new look at Vivekananda, one that would not only reconcile these 'schools' of representation, but actually rediscover Swamiji for the present age (Tyagananda, 2005, 31). It is precisely this challenge that this chapter takes up.

But for such an integrated approach to be possible, I would argue that we have to come to terms with the crux of these two meanings of the word 'represent.' Some critics (see Spivak 1988), referring to Karl Marx, encapsulate these two senses of the word as 'portrait' and 'proxy,' or to go back to the German terms, *darstellung* and *vertretung* respectively. Indeed, both ways of looking at Vivekananda are relevant to my own inquiry, which is sympathetic to Tyagananda's project of taking a new look at Vivekananda. This brings me to an important gesture at self-disclosure. My immediate purpose or *prasanga* to study Vivekananda was to edit a new, one-volume collection of his writings for a general audience.[4] Such a project was exciting because most of the anthologies of Swamiji's work are either by disciples and devotees or by those who are the flag-bearers of his legacy. Moreover, many of these selections were for specific purposes or topics, such as Vivekananda on Women, on Education, on Hinduism, on India and her problems, on Youth and so on. To try to do a selection independently was therefore a major challenge.

But any such project of (re)discovery can only happen through the available literature by and on him. In other words, all these anthologies, including the one I worked on, must rely on the only available edition of his *Complete Works* published in nine volumes by the Advaita Ashrama of the Ramakrishna Math. This is because scholars or anthologists do not have access to the actual sources, but have to rely on what is available through the official publications.

Let me present one example of the difficulty that this poses: the recently discovered letters of Swamiji to the Maharaja of Khetri, Ajit Singh. These letters, as we know, were found in the dusty files of the record room in Jhunjhunu, Rajasthan, which was then in the princely state of Khatri. Two of these letters were first published in the *Times of India* of 24 February, 1999. The first is dated 15 February [1893] and talks about Vivekananda's encounter with a psychic, Govinda Chetty, an astrologer who predicts many things to Vivekananda, but also asks the latter to bless some *vibhuti* (holy ash) and give that to him. The letters were written without punctuation and had many other peculiarities (Chattopadhyay 1999, 433). For instance, Vivekananda calls the Maharaja, not 'Your Highness' but 'your "High Up."' The year is not written in the letter, but we know from other sources that it is likely to be 1893. When *Prabuddha Bharata* reprinted the letters, they not only 'corrected' the spellings and punctuation, but they changed the ending in the second letter of 22 May [1893] from 'yours obediently' to 'Yours in the Lord' (ibid.).

Now one might argue that such changes are minor and insignificant, but from the point of view of accuracy, they would be hard to justify. Just how much to 'correct' is a major issue in textual scholarship. While spelling may be modernised, punctuation inserted or standardised, even such minimally invasive sorts of alterations will change the flavour and savour of a text. We may never, for instance, know if Vivekananda was a good speller or whether his English 'improved' with the years! There are bigger epistemological issues at stake here, but I will come to them later. Right now we need to remember that it is possible that there are many other existing errors and erroneous emendations in the *Complete Works*. Besides changes, there are also several omissions and deletions. I discovered these many years ago when I wrote a paper on Vivekananda's letters. There are curious paradoxes in what the editors and publishers of these letters did to them. For instance, in one letter, Vivekananda says to the addressee: destroy this letter after you've read it or don't show this letter to anyone. The letter is published with these words in it! This is an example of a certain kind of fidelity to the actual text of the letter even if it means a deliberate or inadvertent disobedience of the Swami's command. But there are innumerable instances in the published letters where ellipses suggest the omission of text. I was given to understand that matters of a private, controversial, or otherwise inappropriate nature were omitted because they were not considered suitable to general readers. Who took these decisions and for what reasons remains to be investigated. Unlike Jeffrey J. Kripal[5] I am not at all suggesting that there is a secret in the deleted portions waiting to be discovered or even that some kind of deliberate censorship was applied to the letters. All I am saying is that what we do have is different from what Vivekananda actually wrote. Here is where both aspects of representation that I mentioned become crucial. Not only has Swamiji been presented to us in a particular way, but those who stand for him have exercised their right or power over how we might see him.

Let us consider the different genres of texts that make up the *Complete Works*. There are transcripts of speeches, original writings and translations, summaries of talks, letters, poems, conversations, interviews, even newspaper reports. Clearly the last three cannot be considered the works of Swamiji himself – their authors are others who summarised, transcribed, reported, or quoted him. Clearly, then, there are different kinds of texts involved here. The issue is one of the ontological and epistemological status of the documents on the basis of which Vivekananda is represented. That is, how do we learn or how do we cognise Vivekananda? What is the validity of the various sources of such knowledge? What methods do we use to evaluate their validity or credence? Before we have a system or method of addressing, if not answering such questions, our claims and counter-claims on the message or thought or philosophy of Vivekananda will at best be tentative, if not altogether erroneous.

The *Complete Works* presents other difficulties. The arrangement is neither strictly chronological nor thematic. There is an order or a system of organisation, but this is never clarified. The letters themselves occur in different volumes and in different series, as do poems, speeches and other writings. Even if the order is chronological, there are different kinds of chronology: for example, the chronology of the works as Vivekananda himself wrote them and, in contradistinction, the chronology of the discovery or publication of the works. Thus, Volume 9 is entirely composed of works that were not known when the earlier editions of the earlier volumes were being published. Another serious problem with the contents is that the contexts or dates or even the exact occasions of the texts are not always indicated. For this we have to consult other sources, mainly the biographies of Vivekananda. But the problem is that the biographies themselves have been based, in large measure, on precisely these sources themselves. This difficulty gets compounded in the large number of anthologies of Vivekananda. In these, the Swami's works are wrenched out of their specific contexts so as to make them eternal pronouncements, totally unrelated to space, time, or causality. For instance, Vivekananda may have said something on a particular topic, say, women, in a letter to a disciple. He may have said something else in a speech. He may have said a third thing in an essay that he published. Some of these comments may actually contradict each other. But not only are such contradictions removed, but the quotations sit next to each other in the anthology without any reference to where or when they first were written or spoken. The complexity or interpretive challenge of Vivekananda's thought is thus flattened out; the ideas, taken out of their contexts, are turned into prophetic utterances. Many arguments or claims are based on these secondary or even tertiary selections and arrangements. Instead of the 'real' thing, we have a pre-packaged, pre-cooked, even pre-digested Vivekananda, made easy, simplified, at times, rendered even into an 'instant Vivekananda.'

My intention is not at all to criticise the *Complete Works* or the editors of the previous selections on Vivekananda. Those who have worked on such projects have often done so quite selflessly for years, rendering a great service to the reading public. Their books are products of their devotion and care. Lacking other sources, these are invaluable and without substitute for any serious scholar or student of Vivekananda. Yet, nevertheless, they leave scope for greater accuracy and improvement. The enterprise of Western scholarship is not only more competent, but much more open, at least in many cases. The result is a periodic updating and improvement in the methods and practices of textual scholarship. Textual scholarship, of course, is culturally embedded. In a culture such as India's, in which the most sacred texts, the Vedas, were never even written down to prevent them from being polluted and corrupted and where the classical texts and treatises were often composed in highly compressed, mnemonic verses, the expertise to deal with modern texts from a variety of sources is still limited. There is much that we have to learn and do to make the best use of our own resources and traditions. An enormous amount of dedicated textual work and scholarship is required before we can have a somewhat clear idea of even so recent a figure as Vivekananda. I might add that I also have nothing as such against various simplified versions of the master's ideas, including the justifiably popular 'Thus Spake' series which the Ramakrishna Math has been publishing. Each of these anthologies represent Vivekananda to different audiences.

The purpose of this account of some of the issues and problems that occur in any attempt to understand Vivekananda is to point out the prerequisites of a genuine and far-reaching re-evaluation. I believe that this can only happen after we have a better edition of Vivekananda's works and better biographical and textual sources at our disposal. In the meanwhile, the debates will centre on differing interpretations of already 'known' data. It is to this that I shall turn my attention next. In this regards, I would argue that one's positions reveal as much about one's own values and prejudices as they do some facet of Vivekananda's personality or life-work.

Here it is important to remember that most of the biographies of the Swami are written from the point of view of Vivekananda's importance to India and its people. Perhaps there is a need to write a new life to suit the globalised world that we inhabit today. I do hope that such a biography gets written, because that is indeed the need of the day. For, as many commentators have noticed, Swamiji's message to the West was quite different from that to the East. When he faced the West, he spoke of the glories of Vedanta, trying to re-cast it as the foundation of a new universal religion. But when he faced his own countrymen and women, he was far more critical and exhortatory. He wanted not only to transform Hinduism but also Indian people, uplifting them from the morass of oppression, depression, ignorance and darkness into which they had sunk. As he said repeatedly, what he saw in India was just *tamas* (darkness) and cowardice masquerading as *sattva* or high philosophy. More than anything else, he abhorred the weakness of Indians: their lack of courage, dignity and inactivity appalled him. The inertia, the atavism and the quietism of the masses, an outcome of centuries of deprivation, violence and incapacity produced an almost physiological reaction in him. But, Vedantin that he was, somewhere in the soul of this defeated, even crippled, civilisation, Vivekananda still saw a spark of life and hope. Like breathing life again into a comatose body, Vivekananda re-awakened and re-energised the *pranamaya kosa* or the vital body of India. This dynamic aspect of the Swami's work, perhaps, far exceeded all his other achievements. This is the dimension that is not immediately visible or available to those who approach his works from a purely intellectual or mental perspective.

These speeches, that Vivekananda gave on his return to India after his more than three-year sojourn in the US, are some of his most moving and powerful works. From Pamban, where he first landed after coming to the mainland from Sri Lanka, to Calcutta, where he made his way up in the space of a few weeks, Vivekananda had already presented not just a clear diagnosis of the ailment of India, but also the blueprint of its revival. Consequently my own representation of Vivekananda, emphasises his role as the creator of a new India, the visionary who gave a whole people the *mahamantra* of *svaraj*. I would even go so far as to argue that a major aspect of Vivekananda's impact on the West was indirectly through his vision of a new India. Vivekananda influenced the West directly by giving it the new philosophy of Vedanta but he also influenced it indirectly by giving Indians a new sociology of India.

7.4 SPIRITUAL VS HISTORICAL 'FACTS'

Let me now briefly return to a question that I had raised earlier: what constitutes and is recognisable as a 'fact' in spiritual life? Or how important is literal truth in the representation of a religious figure? For instance, how important is it to know if during his *parivrajika* days Vivekananda travelled on foot, begging from door to door, or if he travelled whenever possible by train, even first class? Did he stay anywhere and with anyone, or, were his preferred hosts people like himself, people he knew well – the Bengali *bhadralok*? Trivial in themselves, can such questions assume importance if certain larger claims are made about Vivekananda's life and character based on their answers? Or, let us consider another set of questions. How important is it to know if Vivekananda smoked or not? Whether he ate meat, even beef and drank wine? These questions are not new and were answered uncompromisingly by Vivekananda himself. Yet our tendency especially in India continues to sanctify and sanitise such aspects of a saint's life. To give another example, how often are we in India aware that Jawaharlal Nehru smoked quite heavily? We hardly see pictures of him with a cigarette in his hand. Or that Aurobindo himself smoked until the 1920s? Or, to take the issue one level higher, that J. Krishnamurti allegedly had a sexual relationship for many years with Rosalind Rajagopal, the wife of his one-time friend and close associate? Perhaps, such questions are ultimately irrelevant to the life and mission of the spiritual person being studied. But what they do affect, quite certainly, is our understanding, our concept of what constitutes a spiritual life. Unlike some critics, I would not say that the public has a right to know. Not all kinds of knowledge are suitable to all people. For instance, in most cases, children do not need to know about the sexual lives of their parents. However, I would also argue that if and when such knowledge becomes essential to a fuller grasp of spiritual phenomena, it can be made available to the *adhikari* or the qualified seeker. Indeed, personally, I deeply believe that when the *sadhak* or spiritual aspirant is ready, whatever knowledge is required will be given to him by the very intelligence that informs his spiritual pursuits. Indeed, I would contend that '*adhikara*,' the right to know, like the right to information, as principle applies to both *sadhaks* and non-*sadhaks*. The latter may not accept it, but those who do (like the keepers of the legacy of a guru) must follow its dictates, thus being careful about what to divulge to whom.

These questions, as I have tried to argue, are not necessarily about the 'character' of a saint or master, but are really about the character of spiritual life itself. My approach to them is that the spiritual life is not what some people consider it to be, sanitised, idealised and stripped of all elements of what we call the human, the passionate, the sensual. Rather, the spiritual life uses all the powers and capacities that are normally within an individual in such a manner that they are directed to the higher end of self-perfection and self-mastery. As Swami Ramdas puts it, 'Each individual has to draw upon all the latent resources of his or her existence in order to rise to the height of absolute freedom...' (Ramdas 2001, 3). In other words, a spiritual life is important not just for what it is, but for what it stands for, what it represents. In all, it represents the potential for divinity within that specific individual and within each human being. When we worship the guru or a saint, we worship our own capacity for perfection. The spiritual master shows us what we ourselves can be one day. So, the sole spiritual fact that matters is that of transformation, the mutation from the mundane level to a fuller manifestation of our latent potentialities. All the other details are of less importance. If that transformation or transcendence is denied, then there is little left of value in a spiritual life; it loses its special significance, becoming just another 'ordinary' human life.

On this basis, let us now look at another kind of 'fact' or 'fiction.' For instance, how important is it to discover whether Vivekananda actually swam to the rock now named after him and that he stayed there for three days and nights, meditating on the future of India? The origin of such claims is the first edition of Swamiji's *Life* (1913) by his Eastern and Western disciples. Let us re-read the relevant passage: 'He plunged into the ocean and in spite of numerous sharks, swam across to the temple, his mind eager as a child to see the Mother. And reaching the shrine he fell prostrate in ecstasy before the Image of the Goddess' (Eastern and Western Disciples, 1913, vol. 2, 101). Those who wrote this version had not visited Kanyakumari and were quite ignorant of the exact location either of the temple or of the rocks. The only mention of this event in Vivekananda's own writings occurs in a letter dated 19 March, 1894, to Ramakrishnananda from Chicago, written in Bengali:

> At Cape Comorin sitting in Mother Kanya Kumari's temple, sitting on the last bit of Indian rock – I hit upon a plan: We are so many Sannyasins wandering about and teaching the people metaphysics – it is all madness.

Vivekananda clearly states that he meditated sitting in the temple, not on the rock to which he supposedly swam. Chattopadhyaya comments: 'The story of his swimming the shark-infested waters was fabricated in the biographies.... Once started, however, it was impossible to get rid of the swimming episode. So modern biographies hold that he first worshipped the Devi and then went over to the rock' (Chattopadhayay 1999, 100–101). In the latest edition of the *Life* (1979), this is how the same incident is narrated: 'After worshipping the Mother in the temple, it was to this holy rock that the Swami wanted to go for meditation. But how could he go? He had not a single pice for the boatman. Without more ado he plunged into those shark-infested waters and swam across' (*Eastern and Western Disciples* 1979, 341).

Chattopadhyaya, to my mind, argues fairly convincingly that the probability of Vivekananda's swimming across is small. Not only is there no mention of it anywhere in Vivekananda's own letters or reminiscences, but the original claim in the 1913 *Life* seems to have been based on the erroneous location of the temple on the island, instead of the mainland. The distance from the tip to the island is two furlongs. The notion that he swam because he didn't have the money to hire a boatman also seems to be implausible because his trip to Kanyakumari was sponsored by a Bengali gentleman, Manmath Bhattacharya, who accompanied him. Chattopadhyaya points out that from 1889, Vivekananda suffered from rheumatism, so it was unlikely that he would have swum across. If so, then on what basis do the writers of the latest edition of the *Life* stick to the tale of swimming across? Apparently, they have three eye witness accounts. One of these witnesses even claimed to have swum across himself to take food to the Swami. Of course! Vivekananda not only swam across, but stayed there for three days and nights on a barren rock; it would stand to reason that he would need to be fed. Interestingly, it is nowhere mentioned whether or not Vivekananda also swam back from the rock. Chattopadhyaya, of course, dismisses these witnesses either as unreliable or the whole story of witnesses itself: 'All these stories of witnesses seeing him meditating for three nights and fasting seem concocted' (Chattopadhayay 1999, 100-101). On the other hand, as Niveditaji of the Vivekananda Centre once challenged me, 'Can you prove that he *did not* swim across? If not, there is certainly scope for the belief that *he did*.'

In one of the first books on Sri Ramakrishna, *Ramakrishna: His Life and Sayings,* F. Max Müller, addresses the same issue. He speaks of the 'Dialectic Process' and the 'Dialogic Process' as ways in which a new religion or sect 'springs up and grows' through the changes produced by 'repletion, conversation' and 'oral tradition':

> Even Hegel's Dialectic Process, the movement of the idea by itself, that leads irresistibly from positive to negative and to conciliation, has its origin in what I should prefer to call by a wider name the *Dialogic Process,* of the greatest importance in history, both ancient and modern. (Müller 1951, 25)

The latter, according to Müller, is the process by which a fact gets modified through repetition, transmission and exchange before (and after) it becomes history. Hence, 'We do not and cannot know of any historical event that has not previously passed through this Dialogic Process' (26). This accounts for all the 'contradictions' and 'miracles' which are otherwise not intelligible or natural. Taking this into account, we may discover a way of getting to the kernel of truth even if it is surrounded by many embellishments: 'many a story distorted by the childish love of the miraculous will regain its true moral character, many a face disguised by a misplaced apotheosis will look upon us again with his truly human, loving and divine eyes' (28). Müller, however, sometimes confuses us by using dialectic and dialogic interchangeably (see 29), in describing how oral traditions work. Interestingly, he claims that even Swami Vivekananda's responses to his queries were free of 'the irrepressible miraculising tendencies of devoted disciples' (30). In the end, he ends up choosing whatever he considers authentic after sifting (threshing) through what he has gathered.

But what Müller does not allow is that there are many kinds of truth and at times, legends, myths and fiction are more appealing and persuasive than facts. Indeed, one would need to invent a new category of fact to understand what actually happened in the case of a spiritual phenomenon. Let us call this the 'poetic' fact to differentiate it from the 'historical' fact. Let me offer one illustration. In the 1960s, perhaps, still unaware of the doubts cast on the swimming episode, Eknath Ranade campaigned all over India for funds to build the Vivekananda Rock Memorial on the island on which Vivekananda was supposed to have meditated but in actual fact he may never have even visited! Those who have visited that memorial know what a noble and heroic endeavour it was. With state support and donations from ordinary people, more than rupees one crore was raised for the project. Inaugurated in 1970, the Memorial also has an adjoining campus of about 100 acres. Anyone who goes to visit it cannot but be impressed by it. Whether or not Vivekananda actually went to this rock, the Memorial stands to commemorate his visit. Though based perhaps on an error, there is no denying either its materiality or its capacity to inspire lakhs of visitors annually.

So which version is true? Which is a fact? I would simply say both are true, but in different ways. We know that in the last twenty years, the truth claims of history have come to be severely challenged.[6] What passes for history is just another narrative, another sort of story. It is not much different from fiction in its use of words, metaphors and linguistic figuration. It is also informed by a textuality that attests to its constructedness. Histories, in fact, resemble novels and other kind of fictional narratives. They too have a beginning, a middle and an end; they have heroes and villains; they also have plots, characters, situations, settings, atmosphere; what is more they even have climaxes, reversals, denouements. On the other hand, as we all know only too well, myths, legends, novels and other kinds of fiction are perhaps more 'true' than facts. Even 'science' which has scrupulously constructed itself over the last five hundred years or so as to exclude any scope for error or inaccuracy, is itself not a fixed, unchanging essence.[7] To say that 'according to science' or 'science says,' then, is an absurdity, because we need to specify which type of science, of what period, according to whom and of what culture. The category of science is neither beyond time, space, context and subject as is that of fact. For example, classical physics is a totally different kind of science from quantum mechanics. So is the case with the 'fact.'

So, I would suggest that both the versions of Swamiji's experience at Kanyakumari are 'true.' One is probably the historical truth – that he meditated in the temple on the mainland in the Kanyakumari temple, as he himself wrote in his letter and that did he not swim across to the rock; the other, consequently, is a poetic fact or truth that many still believe and find inspiring. Does this mean that I consider that the two are unrelated? On the contrary, in modern times, it would be advantageous, in the long run, for the spiritual truth to have its roots in the soil of the physical or the factual truth. But from there, it may soar to any height that it aspires to. The two kinds of truth ought, ideally, to support and reinforce each other. That is why the issue of representation that I have been discussing is so crucial. That is why we need exacting, even 'scientific' methods and expectations from our scholars. And yet, if and when, as is bound to be the case, these truths clash, we must allow for both of them to be valid in their own way.

To sum up, I would argue that a spiritual fact is a combination of a historical fact and a poetic fact. Usually, the latter two may go hand in hand, but when they appear to clash, we can have plural narratives which the historian or the *sadhaka* may each approach in his or her own way. Within the spiritual path, the *bhakta* (devotee), the *jnani* (knower) and the *karma yogi* (selfless worker) approach reality in different ways. This must apply even to Vivekananda himself. To say that one approach is the best would not be a *sanatani* or svarajist position. To say that all are the same or equally true would not hold up to modern scrutiny. To be a modern *sanantani*, then, is to discover a new path to the truth that is Vivekananda, a path which is not only committed to finding the 'truth,' but one which allows, even invites, many different versions of it, all the while retaining the privilege of choosing not just individually, but for larger collectives, what is the most suitable, persuasive, pragmatic and therefore, true path. In the present case, I would say that I cannot be sure that Vivekananda actually swam across to the rock, but I am sure that I appreciate the Memorial which commemorates his visit to the southernmost tip of India. What Vivekananda's life stands for, what the Memorial stands for, cannot be controverted by his not actually have swum to the rock. The *bhatka* (devotee) and the historian, in other words, do not necessarily have to be at odds. A good *bhakta* can be a good historian and vice-versa.

7.5 IMPACT AND SIGNIFICANCE

From a bare outline of his life, extraordinary as it was, it is impossible to form a notion of just how great Vivekananda's influence or impact were. In a book that is otherwise unsparingly critical, Narasinga P. Sil marks the astonishing power of the sheer splendour of Vivekananda's personality. For instance, when Mrs Allan sees him for the first time, she says: '[He] seemed to me so big, as though he towered above ordinary mortals. The people on the street looked like pygmies and he had such a majestic presence that people stepped aside to let him pass by' (quoted in Sil 1997, 22). Or, to cite another example, Josephine MacLeod, one of Swamiji's most faithful and long-standing admirers, recorded: 'The thing that held me in Swamiji is his *unlimitedness*. I could never touch the bottom – or top – or sides. The amazing size of him!' (quoted in Sil 1997, 23). As Romain Rolland in his Prelude to *The Life of Vivekananda and the Universal Gospel*, puts it: 'his pre-eminent characteristic was kingliness. He was a born king and nobody ever came near him either in India or America without paying homage to his majesty' (Rolland 1947, 5).

In his painstaking and exhaustive compilation, *Vivekananda: A Comprehensive Study*, Swami Jyotirmayananda quotes other well-known personages, some of whose views on Vivekananda bear repetition:

> C. Rajagopalachari: 'Swami Vivekananda saved Hinduism and saved India. But for him we would have lost our religion and would not have gained our freedom. We, therefore, owe everything to Swami Vivekananda.' (Jyotirmayananda 1993, 678–9)
>
> Jawaharlal Nehru: 'He was not a politician in the ordinary sense of the word and yet he was, I think, one of the great founders... of the national modern movement of India....' (679)
>
> Annie Besant: 'A striking figure, clad in yellow and orange, shining like the sun of India in the midst of the heavy atmosphere of Chicago, a lion-head, piercing eyes, mobile lips,

movement swift and fast – such was my first impression of Swami Vivekananda.... Monk, they called him, not unwarrantably, but warrior-monk he was and the first impression was the warrior rather than of the monk.... Purposeful, virile, strong, he stood out, a man among men, able to hold his own.... "That man a heathen!" said one, as he came out of the great Hall "and we send missionaries to his people! It would be more fitting that they should send missionaries to us."' (689)

K. M. Panikkar: 'What gave Indian nationalism its dynamism and ultimately enabled it to weld at least the major part of India into one state was the creation of a sense of community among the Hindus to which the credit should to a very large extent go to Swami Vivekananda. This new Sankaracharya may well be claimed to be a unifier of Hindu ideology. Travelling all over India he not only aroused a sense of Hindu feeling but taught the doctrine of a universal Vedanata as the background of the new Hindu reformation.... It is Vivekananda who first gave to the Hindu movement its sense of nationalism and provided most of the movements with a common all-India outlook.' (279)

As some of these opinions affirm, Vivekananda's greatest achievements include the reconstruction of Hinduism, the change of its image in the West, the starting of a movement of social and cultural regeneration, all of which were directly linked to the birth of Indian nationalism, which was taking place at that time. The key to all these contributions was Vivekananda's modernisation of Hinduism. Indeed, the Hinduism that he spoke about and expounded at the Parliament of Religions and, later, all over America was a new version, partly of his own invention, of an ancient tradition. What he learned from Ramakrishna he tried to interpret in the language of modernity that he imbibed as a young English-educated Calcutta man. Instead of a pagan, superstitious, idolatrous and barbarous set of rituals, customs and practices, which is how Hinduism had been by-and-large perceived, not just by missionaries, but by a large section of the educated middle-classes of India, Vivekananda turned it into a rational, universal philosophy, freed from dogma and authority. He did this by making Vedanta the spine of new Hinduism, bhakti (faith) its heart and the yogas its sinews. For the West, what he brought was indeed original and promising. As Ninian Smart says: 'The universalist message of Swami Vivekananda and of his Master, Ramakrishna, genuinely represents a new departure in world religions – the attempt to make the highest form of Hinduism a world faith' (quoted in Jyotirmayananda 1993, 182). He thus re-interpreted Hinduism not only to the West but to India. Essentially, his message was two-fold: when he faced the West, he was a teacher and practitioner of Indian spirituality; when he faced his fellow countrymen and women, he was a social reformer. As Tapan Raichaudhuri observes, 'Vivekananda had a two-fold agenda which he had time to pursue for less than a decade: to preach an universalist spiritual faith based on the life of his master which he saw as the ultimate realisation of the Vedantic truth and secondly, to create a mass consciousness through service and education' (Raichaudhuri 1998, 16).

In a reading of his selected letters, I had argued that Vivekananda's reconstruction of Hinduism consisted essentially of four elements: a) non-sectarianism; b) anti-ritualism; c) religion in the service of humanity; d) Advaita as the future religion of thinking humanity (Paranjape 1991, 178–179). Such ideas and his ceaseless propagation of them resulted in the creation of what Basu, in her book-length study, calls 'dialogic Hinduism':

> It was dialogic in two senses: within the interior of the nation itself it sought to bridge the gulf between conservatives and the reformists and in the context of Europe it sought to accommodate many of the Enlightenment values of rationalism, the spirit of scientific enquiry and the tenets of universal literacy. (Basu 2002, 196)

Of course, Vivekananda's message to the West was not always welcomed or well-received. On the contrary, it was often conveyed in the most hostile of circumstances. After his initial success, Vivekananda was regularly attacked and reviled by various Christian churches. Letters were written to his hosts and well-wishers, tarnishing his character, attempting to stop him from speaking. Vivekananda, with his outspokenness, exposed the fanaticism and falsehood of his detractors. Despite his great reverence for Jesus Christ, on whom he delivered some memorable talks, he was unsparing of the double standards and narrow-mindedness of some missionaries. For instance, in a lecture given at Detroit on 21 February 1894, he said:

> One thing I would tell you and I do not mean any unkind criticism. You train and educate and clothe and pay men to do what? To come over to my country to curse and abuse all my forefathers, my religion and everything. They walk near a temple and say, 'You idolaters, you will go to hell.' But they dare not do that to the Mohammedans of India; the sword would be out. But the Hindu is too mild; he smiles and passes on and says, 'Let the fools talk.' That is the attitude. And then you who train men to abuse and criticise, if I just touch you with the least bit of criticism, with the kindest of purpose, you shrink and cry, 'Don't touch us; we are Americans. We criticise all the people in the world, curse them and abuse them, say anything; but do not touch us; we are sensitive plants....' (Vivekananda 2003, Vol. 8, 211–212)

No wonder, even two years later, when he returned to Detroit, on 3 March 1896, he was greeted thus by the *Detroit Evening News*:

> The Hindoo-Brahmin-Buddhist fad of an effete and rotten orientalism has run its course in the east and it has been found that there is nothing in it.... After all these eastern isms had had their say, there was a regular mania throughout the occident for the religions that had done little for the masses of their votaries but to make dirty, lazy beggars of them.... He [Vivekananda] told not a single truth that does not form a stone in the foundation of our own western faith, but whenever Kananda [sic] said a pretty and truthful thing which may be heard from at Christian

pulpits every day, he was applauded to the echo by the people who know so little about the religion of their own fathers that they actually thought that this brown-faced Hindoo was making a new revelation to them.... Kananda [sic] had come to be forgotten and his work had utterly perished with him. And he is back again! .... His very presence is no compliment to the religious stability of Detroit. (Burke 1983–1986, Vol. IV, 17–18)

The record shows that he faced much of this hostility with silence, indifference and rare counter-attacks. In one of his more effusive responses in a letter of 1 February 1985, he writes to Mary Hale, quoting Tulsidas, 'when a great soul appears there will be numbers to bark after him' (Vivekananda 2003, Vol. 5, 73).

Vivekananda was also quite scathing in his attack on the Indian society in his time. One of his most radical theses was that India had declined because of its neglect of women. 'We are horrible sinners,' he says in his letter of 19 March 1894 to Swami Ramakrishnananda, 'and our degradation is due to our calling women, 'despicable worms,' 'gateways to hell,' and so forth....' (Vivekananda 2003, Vol. 6, 253). In the same letter he goes on to say, 'Do you think our religion is worth the name? Ours is only Don't-touchism, only 'Touch me not,' 'Touch me not....' (ibid.) In his letter to Alasinga Perumal, he is even more categorical:

> So long as the millions live in hunger and ignorance, I hold every man a traitor who, having been educated at their expense, pays not the least heed to them! I call those men who strut about in their finery, having got all their money by grinding the poor, wretches, so long as they do not do anything for those two hundred millions who are now no better than hungry savages! (Vivekananda 2003, Vol. 5, 58)

From statements such as these, it would appear that Vivekananda had a complete programme for the regeneration of India. In his speech in Ramnad (included in this volume), he clearly spelt out the dangers before his fellow-Indians:

> There are two great obstacles on our path in India, the Scylla of old orthodoxy and the Charybdis of modern European civilisation. Of these two, I vote for the old orthodoxy and not for the Europeanised system; for the old orthodox man may be ignorant, he may be crude, but he is a man, he has a faith, he has strength, he stands on his own feet; while the Europeanised man has no backbone, he is a mass of heterogeneous ideas picked up at random from every source – and these ideas are unassimilated, undigested, unharmonised. He does not stand on his own feet and his head is turning round and round. (Vivekananda 2003, Vol. 3, 151)

Indeed, if Vivekananda had not died young, he may have come into more direct conflict with the British authorities. His aim of decolonising India would have met with severe repression from the British authorities. Even a century later, however, the great task of freeing Indian minds from a subservience to the West has, however, not yet been fully affected.

As the authors of his *Life* summarise, Vivekananda's agenda for India consisted of the following:

> (1) the need to raise the masses, give them opportunities for all-round development 'without injuring their religion'; (2) the need to remove untouchability; (3) the need for the well-to-do to assist the suffering millions; (4) the need to give women opportunities for proper education and self-improvement; (5) the need for the universal spread of the right kind of education; (6) the need to cultivate the material sciences; (7) the need for technological and industrial development; and, above all, (8) the need to give freedom to society for its onward movement. (Vivekananda 2003, Vol. 1, 530–531)

Such a comprehensive programme articulated so clearly and consistently, was Vivekananda's long-lasting contribution to the building of modern India. Before Gandhi, it was Vivekananda who integrally combined personal spiritual practice with a larger social responsibility, drawing the middle classes into the larger national struggle.

What made his 'neo-Hinduism' special was Vivekananda's insistence on making social service the vehicle of modernisation. As Basu observes:

> In the absence of social and economic justice, the only way of exhibiting the attributes of a rational society is through social service for the uplift of the underprivileged. ....[I]n a society under domination economic liberation can only come about through a form of rigorous social service, which he sought to advocate as the ultimate spiritual act. Rather than segregating the ancient society from the rest of the world, Vivekananda's nationalism sought to ensure that a form of the Enlightenment was ushered in through the modern use of the Hindu religion which could enter into a dialogue with Western rationalism. (Basu 2002, 201).

According to her, this is what distinguishes Vivekananda's dialogic Hinduism from 'Brahmo scholasticism' and the 'pastoralism of the revivalists' (196).

When we observe the various responses to imperialism and modernity, we see in Vivekananda a unique trajectory that neither rejects modernity nor accepts imperial domination. Unlike M. K. Gandhi, whose rejection of modern civilisation may be considered 'romantic,' or Jawaharlal Nehru's scientific-secularist acceptance of it, Vivekananda shows a qualified acceptance of modernity along with a rejection of both materialism and imperialism. In this, the person who follows him closest is Sri Aurobindo. It was Vivekananda who first tried to synthesise the yogas in modern times; his treatises on Raja Yoga, Karma Yoga, Bhakti Yoga and Jnana Yoga, were the early attempts in this direction. Aurobindo built on these in his own work, *The Synthesis of Yoga* where he refers to Vivekananda (Aurobindo 1972, 6). Aurobindo, in turn, acknowledged the influence of Vivekananda on him, admitting that Vivekananda had 'visited' him during Aurobindo's incarceration in the Alipur jail.

That there was something quite unique in Vivekananda is attested to even by people who met him for just a few minutes. For example, Vivienne Baumfield shows the influence of Vivekananda on Sir Jamsetji Tata, the doyen of Indian industry and the founder of the Tata group. Vivekananda met Tata on a ship and asked the latter to help create men devoted to the sciences both 'natural and humanistic' (Baumfield 1998, 207). Jamsetji, who acknowledged Vivekananda's inspiration, went on to found the Indian Institute of Science in Bangalore. According to Baumfield, the phrase 'Science and Sanskrit' encapsulates Vivekananda's desire to bring together 'the best aspects of both the traditional Hindu and Western systems of education' (194). Vivekananda's scientific thought has received much attention at the hands of authors like Swami Jitatmananda, who has argued that Vivekananda anticipates some of the insights of quantum mechanics and new physics.

One of the reasons that Vivekananda continues to appeal to so many diverse kinds of people is because he was so radical and unconventional. In his letter of 1 November 1896 to Mary Hale, for example, he said, 'I am a socialist not because I think it is a perfect system, but half a loaf is better than no bread. The other systems have been tried and found wanting. Let this one be tried.' (Vivekananda 2003, Vol. 6, 381) Some have used such statements to invent a new category of thought called 'Vedantic Socialism,' attributing it to Vivekananda. Indeed, there have been several attempts, many of them serious and of considerable length, to argue that Vivekananda was a socialist (see for example, Biswas, Das Gupta and Rao in Works Cited). The latest of these efforts is the booklet *Vivekananda's Message*, edited by A. B. Bardhan, a veteran of the Communist Party of India (CPI), who claims to rescue Swamiji from fundamentalists and right-wing Hindus (see Roy 2003, 9).

Vivekananda's social thought, gleaned from his numerous writings, has been the subject of considerable interest. For instance, in the aforementioned letter of 1 November 1896 he outlines his theory of what Sri Aurobindo later so eloquently called *The Human Cycle*. Vivekananda speaks of the progressive shift in the rulers of the world, from the initial Brahmin phase to the now incumbent (some would say prevalent) Shudra period. Ideas such as these were later developed more extensively by P. C. Sarkar (Sri Anandamurti) in his notion of the Progressive Utilisation Theory (Inayatullah 1999, 3-4).

I would even argue that Vivekananda was perhaps India's first modern global citizen. No doubt, there were others such as Raja Ram Mohan Roy before him who had a similar breadth of outlook and cosmopolitan tendencies. Indeed, Ram Mohan Roy lived the last months of his life in England. No one before him had lived and travelled so extensively in the West, especially in the United States. Vivekananda was thus bi-cultural in a very contemporary way – he could live with equal ease in two cultures and three continents. He is thus a crossover figure, much ahead of his times, but a precursor to many others who followed his tracks later.

Mary Louise Burke's meticulous and exhaustive account of his travels in the West give us a picture of man who was both worldly and deeply spiritual in a complex way. For instance, during his stay at Ridgely Manor, he tried to play golf and greatly enjoyed chocolate ice cream (Burke 1983-1986, Vol. IV, 120-127). Generally, he ate well, even smoked and drank, but always maintained his two vows of poverty and chastity. This is illustrated in Deussen's account as Vivekananda's 'roommate' during their travels from Bremen to London in September 1896. 'You seem to be a queer sort of saint,' Deussen said to him, 'You eat well, you drink well, you smoke all day and you deprive yourself of nothing.' He replied in Sanskrit: 'I observe my vows.' 'And what consists of your vows?' Vivekananda explained 'They require [of] me simply *Kama Kanchana Viraha*, to renounce sex and gold' (283-288). Some critics have used such accounts to exaggerate Vivekananda's inner and outer conflicts. Notably, Sil describes Vivekananda's life as 'the striving of an ambitious, idealistic, impulsive and imaginative militant monk who envisioned, rather naively, a global spiritualisation in the manner of a Napoleonic conquest' (Sil 1997, 25). In his attempt to demystify Vivekananda, he goes to the other extreme of considering his life's mission a failure:

> In the end his fantastic vision of Hindu India bearing the beacon of spiritual light to the world never materialised. The impossibility and impracticability of such a monumental undertaking finds a pathetic expression in his final confession of failure at the end of his diseased, tumultuous and troubled life.... (Sil 1997, 25-26)

He concludes that Vivekananda far from being 'the herald of a brave new world of spiritual humanism' was actually 'a tragic figure whose brief but tumultuous public life was spent contending with multiple tensions and conflicts....' (181).

Despite such attempts to 'historicise' and debunk Vivekananda, his enormous power and dynamism have continued to inspire generations of Indians and Westerners. Apart from the Math and Mission that he founded, several other organisations and institutions have been set up in his name, supposedly to promote the causes that he stood for. Of these, one of the most remarkable is the aforementioned Vivekananda Kendra at Kannyakumari founded by Eknath Ranade. Whether or not Vivekananda swam to the rock on which Ranade built the impressive Memorial, the story of the latter's construction is remarkable. The idea of a memorial was mooted in 1963 by the Vivekananda Rock Memorial Committee in celebration of Vivekananda's 100th birth anniversary. Ranade joined the Committee as its Organising Secretary. With untiring zeal and persistence, he secured the permission from the state and central governments, raising money through small donations of common people. Inaugurated in 1970, the Memorial has an adjoining campus of about 100 acres. Ranade also had in mind the building of a Vivekananda Kendra International, but died on 22 August 1982. Recently, S. Gurumurthy and others have fulfilled this dream too, by establishing such a centre in New Delhi. While Ranade's example may be exceptional, it is not unusual. All over India, there are schools, colleges, hospitals, roads and residential colonies named after Vivekananda. In face of such overwhelming popularity and capacity to inspire, the notion that he ended his 'career on a note of despondency and defeat...' and that 'He ended his life not in delusion ... but in disillusionment'

(Sil 1997, 177) is hard to believe or sustain. All in all, an assessment such as Amiya Sen's seems more balanced and plausible: 'instead of typifying Vivekananda either as an ascetic or activist, reformer or conservative, patriot or prophet, it would be more reasonable to accept that he was perhaps all of these' (Sen 2000, 98).

It is reliably learnt, particularly from verifiable oral testimony, that after his great success in India, Vivekananda was under surveillance by British authorities. In a personal conversation on 16 November 2003, Swami Prabhananda, the present Secretary of the Ramakrishna Mission, said that there is sufficient evidence to show that he was under surveillance of the British for several years. Had his work of nation-building continued along certain lines, there is no doubt that the colonial government would have tried to check or arrest him. Though his ideas were about India's spiritual resurgence, they pointed to, indeed required, its political independence too. In that sense, he was truly one of the founders of Indian nationalism. In a broader sense, the 'work' that he embarked upon had many strands inextricably interwoven together; to separate, say, the political from the spiritual is thus not entirely feasible.

Not just the more overtly religious nationalist line from Bankim to Tilak to Aurobindo, but even the moderate line from Ranade to Gokhale to Gandhi (as Gokhale 1964 shows), believed in India's destiny as a vanguard of spirituality. Both sides understood that Indian nationalism needed a religious, dharmic basis. Vivekananda was central to this whole conception. None of these men, however, were religious fanatics or haters of other communities. Though their idea of nationalism was decidedly Hindu in character and spirit, it was neither majoritarian nor sectarian. They wanted a plural and democratic polity, which paid special attention to the disadvantaged and downtrodden sections of society. In a sense, Tagore too, despite his reservations against nationalism as a violent, chauvinistic and imperialistic force, did wish for a *svadeshi samaj* (indigenous society) which was the outcome of the spirit of the people expressing itself. Muslim, Dalit, Marxist and ultra-secularist nationalisms in India, however, do not fit this pattern. Even today, the result is an unease over what sort of nation we inhabit and where it is headed.

Fulfilling his own prophecy, Vivekananda died before he reached the age of forty. The (ongoing) story of the imagining of modern India, of which he was a key agent, is one of the most fascinating narratives in the history of humanity. The life and works of Swami Vivekananda are central to this story and to those who wish to understand it. But a man like Vivekananda belongs not only to India but also to the whole world. As he himself proclaimed, 'I shall not cease to work. I shall inspire men everywhere, until the world shall know that it is one with God.' (Vivekananda 2003, Vol. 5, 414) More than 100 years later that promise continues to be kept.

WORKS CITED

Aurobindo, Sri. 1972. *The Synthesis of Yoga*. Volume 21. Pondicherry: Sri Aurobindo Birth Centenary Library, 1972.

Basu, Shamita. 2002. *Religious Revivalism as Nationalist Discourse: Swami Vivekananda and New Humanism in Nineteenth-Century Bengal*. New Delhi: Oxford University Press.

Baumfield, Vivienne. 1998. 'Science and Sanskrit: Vivekananda's Views on Education.' In *Swami Vivekananda and the Modernization of Hinduism* edited by William Radice. New Delhi: Oxford University Press.

Biswas, Arun Kumar. 1986. *Swami Vivekananda and the Indian Quest for Socialism*. Calcutta: Firma KLM.

Burke, Mary Louise. 1983-1986. *Swami Vivekananda in the West: New Discoveries*. 6 vols. Calcutta: Advaita Ashrama.

Chattopadhyaya, Rajagopal. 1999. *Swami Vivekananda in India: A Corrective Biography*. Delhi: Motilal Banarsidass.

Das Gupta, R. K. 1995. *Swami Vivekananda's Vedantic Socialism*. Calcutta: Advaita Ashrama.

Eastern and Western Disciples. (1913) 1979-1981. *The Life of Swami Vivekananda*. Calcutta: Advaita Ashrama.

Gokhale, B. G. 1964. 'Swami Vivekananda and Indian Nationalism.' *Journal of Bible and Religion* 32 (1): 35-42.

Inayatullah, Sohail. 1999. *Situating Sarkar: Tantra, Macrohistory and*

Alternative Futures. Maleny, Australia: Gurukula Press.
Isherwood, Christopher. 1965. *Ramakrishna and His Disciples*. Calcutta: Advaita Ashrama.
Jitatamananda, Swami. 1986. *Modern Physics and Vedanta*. Mumbai: Bharatiya Vidya Bhavan.
Jyotirmayananda, Swami. 1993. *Vivekananda: A Comprehensive Study*. Madras: Swami Jyotirmayananda.
Kripal, Jeffry J. 1998. *Kali's Child: The Mystical and the Erotic in the Life and Teachings of Ramakrishna*. Chicago: Chicago University Press.
Kuhn, Thomas S. 1962. *The Structure of Scientific Revolutions*. Chicago: The University of Chicago Press.
Müller, F. Max. (1898) 1951. *Ramakrishna: His Life and Sayings*. Mayavati: Advaita Ashrama.
Paranjape, Makarand. 1991. 'Vivekananda's Letters: An Introductory Reading.' In *Perspectives on Ramakrishna-Vivekananda Vedanta Tradition*. Edited by M. Sivaramakrishna and Sumita Roy. New Delhi: Sterling Publishers.
Popper, Karl. 2002. *The Logic of Scientific Discovery*. New York: Routledge.
Ramdas, Swami. (1997) 2001. *Glimpses of Divine Vision*. Kanhangad: Anandashram.
Rolland, Romain. 1947. *The Life of Vivekananda and the Universal Gospel*. Mayavati: Advaita Ashrama.
Rao, V.K.R.V. 1979. *Swami Vivekananda: The Prophet of Indian Socialism*. New Delhi: Ministry of Information and Broadcasting.
Raichaudhuri, Tapan. 1998. 'Swami Vivekananda's construction of Hinduism.' In *Swami Vivekananda and the Modernisation of Hinduism* edited by William Radice. New Delhi: Oxford University Press.
Roy, Bhaskar. 2003. 'The Left turns to Vivekananda.' *Times of India*, 31 March: 9.
Sen, Amiya P. 2000. *Swami Vivekananda*. New Delhi: Oxford University Press.
Sil, Narasingha P. 1997. *Swami Vivekananda: A Reassessment*. Selinsgrove: Susquehanna University Press.
Spivak, Gayatri Chakravorty. 1988. 'Can the Subaltern Speak?' In *Marxism and the Interpretation of Culture*. Edited by Cary Nelson and Lawrence Grossberg. Urbana: University of Illinois Press.
Tyagananda, Swami. 2005. 'Rediscovering Vivekananda in the East and

the West.'" In *The Cyclonic Swami: Vivekananda in the West.* Edited by Sukalyan Sengupta and Makarand Paranjape. New Delhi: Samvad India in association with Centre for Indic Studies, University of Massachusetts at Dartmouth.

Vivekananda, Swami. 2003. *The Complete Works of Swami Vivekananda.* 9 vols. Calcutta: Advaita Ashrama.

———. 2005. *The Penguin Swami Vivekananda Reader.* Edited by Makarand Paranjape. New Delhi: Penguin.

White, Hayden V. 1986. *Tropics of Discourse: Essays in Cultural Criticism.* Baltimore: Johns Hopkins University Press.

Zinn, Howard. 2010. *A People's History of the United States.* New York: Harper Perennial.

8
SAROJINI NAIDU: RECLAIMING A KINSHIP

8.1 INTRODUCTION

I began working on Sarojini Naidu purely by accident. It was only after I joined the University of Hyderabad in February 1986 as a Fellow in English that I formed a serious interest in her life and work. In those days, the Schools of Humanities and Social Sciences operated from 'The Golden Threshold' on Nampally Station Road, in the heart of the city. The large campus of the university at Gachi Bowli, on the outskirts of Hyderabad, where we relocated later, was not yet ready. 'The Golden Threshold' had been Sarojini's home. It was, of course, was also the title of Sarojini's first collection of poems, published in 1905. This once beautiful house, now much altered and spoiled by the needs of its new occupants, still retained traces of its old grace and charm.

The house itself had had a chequered history. It was donated to the nation by Padmaja Naidu, the last surviving heir of the Naidu family. Indira Gandhi, one of the executors of Padmaja's will and India's Prime Minister, gave it to the newly started Central University of Hyderabad. Prior to that a part of it had been leased out to the Neo Mysore Cafe, where they served vegetarian fare to customers. Even earlier, it had been let out to a training college in 1938 after the family shifted to Zaheer Manzil in Red Hills. Later, probably in

1942, the family moved again to Sukh Niwas in Ramkote. Behind the main house in the compound of the 'Golden Threshold,' was a large extension built by Govindarajulu for his son, Dr Jaisoorya Naidu, who was also a doctor, though a Homeopath. Unfortunately, the father and the son could not get along. 'Jaisoorya Clinic,' as it was called, was hardly used by the person it was named after, though he did practice from these premises after the death of his parents.

Jaisoorya, the eldest son and his German wife, died without heirs. The youngest son, Ranadheera, led a rather sad life; an alcoholic and wanderer, he died young, during his mother's own lifetime. The two sisters fared better. The younger, Leilamani, was a rather acerbic civil servant, who lived for several years in Government accommodation on Janpath (formerly Kingsway), New Delhi and died a spinster. The eldest, Padmaja Naidu, came closest to inheriting her mother's mantle. A confidant, some believe lover, of Jawaharlal Nehru, India's first Prime Minister, she served as the Governor of West Bengal, before retiring to a bungalow on the Prime Minister's estate at Teen Murti house, New Delhi. It was here that she passed away. She too did not marry or leave any heirs behind.

Strangely enough, as a younger teacher of English in India, I felt that people like me were now the real heirs of Sarojini Naidu, if not literally, then at least literarily. I felt this way because the offices of the English Department were in one of the bedrooms of the main house. Though much partitioned and divided into little cubicles, this suite of rooms with an attached bathroom, had obviously been well designed and must have once been rather elegant. It was the many hours that I spent here that provided me the somewhat irreverent answer to repeated questions about my rather unfashionable involvement with Sarojini Naidu: 'I once shared her bedroom, you know.'

More seriously, the house did have an effect on me. The non-functioning fountain, unkempt garden, stinking lavatories, crowds of students and continuous clamour of the traffic outside – none of these could fully efface its special charm. Especially in the evenings or on holidays, the mansion seemed to return to itself, resonating with memories of all the brilliant and important people who visited it. 'The Golden Threshold,' though not quite as much as Anand Bhavan, was definitely one of the famous houses of our national struggle for independence. Sarojini herself in a letter to Nehru boasted about 'the most truly cosmopolitan society in India which... haunts The Golden Threshold even unto four generations....' Why, even the mango tree in the backyard planted by Mahatma Gandhi attested the significance of the house. It was a different matter that the tree bore little fruit.

I also learned that there was a Sarojini Naidu Memorial Trust, which had copies of important archival material. This was the house in which Sarojini and her siblings had been born. It originally belonged to the great Aghorenath Chattopadhyay, educated at Edinburgh, founder of modern education in Hyderabad state, philosopher, savant and alchemist. He and his wife Varada Sundari Devi had, in their own way, done much for the national cause. This house was on Jawaharlal Nehru Road, which began just after Mahatma Gandhi Road ended at the General Post Office.

The city of Hyderabad itself had many memorials to Sarojini besides these two houses. There was the Sarojini Devi Eye hospital near Mehdipatnam and the Sarojini Devi Road in Secunderabad, besides the Sarojini Devi Vanita Mahavidylaya, a leading college for women and so on. With all these associations and resources, it was sad if not surprising that no significant work had been produced on her in this city for the last several years. The decision to make a difference gradually stole upon me. Suddenly, so many connections with her life and work began to emerge, almost wherever I looked. I began to sense a personal connection with 'Amma,' as I began to think of her.

The incongruity of our situation was striking, I realised. We were surrounded by history but did little to understand it. Here I was, a specialist in Indian English literature, actually sitting day after day in the house of an important poet and national leader, next door to a Trust set up in her memory, yet making little use at all of my opportunities. I remembered how well the houses of poets and writers, not to speak of other historical monuments, were maintained in England. In contrast, how callous and careless we were! What was the point of talking about 'decolonisation' or 'postcolonialism' in our classrooms when we were neglecting to study the very writer in whose house we worked? Whether or not I was especially interested in Sarojini Naidu, I thought I had to look at her life and work seriously. It was my way of engaging not only with my immediate environment, of trying to be directly relevant to my location as an English teacher in India, but also of repaying, in a small measure, what we owed to those made this country ours.

The Sarojini Naidu Memorial Trust contained copies of Sarojini's letters, besides a fairly good collection of the primary and secondary materials on her poetry. The letters had not yet been published. There were also several unpublished poems, including juvenilia. Though there were at least two good biographies, both were outdated and inadequate. So much new material had now become available, which these biographers had not taken note of. I quickly realised that so much more could be and needed to be done on Sarojini Naidu. I therefore began to spend some time on my own in the Trust, acquainting myself with its resources. I taught a special optional course on Sarojini, perhaps the only one in any university to do so. Later I got a Homi Bhabha Fellowship for Literature to work on Sarojini Naidu. It supported my two year stay in Delhi, where most of the original papers were located, either at the Nehru Memorial Library or at the National Archives. Before the Fellowship ended in 1993, I had published a new edition of Sarojini's poetry and prose, with some hitherto unknown or unpublished pieces.[1] I also began to collect and organise her letters for a separate volume, which was published in 1996 by Kali for Women, New Delhi.

Though the university which now enjoyed her multimillion rupee property did little to fund research on her, nor did the Trust named after her have resources to encourage research, I had the satisfaction of thinking that I had done my own bit towards repaying my ancestral debts.

8.2 THE LIFE

Sarojini Naidu (1879-1949), was perhaps the most prominent woman among the leaders of the mass movement which fought for the independence of India. As a nationalist leader, poet, activist for women's rights, orator and celebrity, she was certainly one of the most memorable and colourful Indian women of this century. She was not only the first Indian woman to become the President of the Indian National Congress, but also the first woman Governor of any state in independent India when she assumed charge of the largest and most important United Province (now Uttar Pradesh). As one of the principal aides and followers of Mahatma Gandhi she was constantly in the limelight and was probably the best-known Indian woman of her time. She also had an international presence as India's cultural ambassador and spokesperson of the freedom movement. In her life converge some of the dominant cultural, social and political currents of pre-independence India. Thus, both in her own right and as a representative of her times, Sarojini deserves to be remembered and studied.

She was born on 13 February 1879 in Hyderabad. Her parents were Dr Aghorenath Chattopadhyaya and Varada Sundari. She was the eldest of eight children. Aghorenath, besides being a DSc from Edinburgh and the founder of modern education in the Hyderabad State, was an extraordinary person. A social reformer and alchemist, spiritualist and savant, he was a pioneer in all kinds of radical movements including Swadeshi, women's education as also the indigenisation of modern science long before they became popular elsewhere. Twice deported from the Nizam's dominions for his unorthodox views, Aghorenath nevertheless commanded great respect for his uprightness, nobility and kindliness. Varada Sundari, who had been educated in a Brahmo home for women while her husband was abroad, was also a remarkable woman. Not just a skilled homemaker, she was abreast with the happenings of the world – besides being a talented singer and storyteller. The eight children they produced were vibrant individualists. Virendranath became a revolutionary. An internationally well-known figure in world communism who knew Lenin and Stalin, he lived abroad in exile because he was a wanted man in British India. Mrinalini, or Gunnu Auntie, was a renowned educationist who – after studying in Cambridge – was for many years the Principal of a leading girls' college in Lahore. She founded and edited a famous arts magazine called *Shama*. Harindranath, the youngest son, was a poet, dramatist, actor and Member of Parliament. Suhasini, the youngest daughter, married a trade union leader and was active in the freedom movement. All told, it was an interesting, talented and diverse family that occupied a home that was one of the centres of every kind of intellectual adventurism and freethinking in Hyderabad.

Sarojini grew up in such an atmosphere. Her unconventionality, curiosity and openness can perhaps be traced to the upbringing she received as a child. Soon, however, her innate precocity asserted itself and she overstepped what she had inherited. Somewhat of a prodigy, she passed the Madras Matriculation Examination at twelve; she composed a 1300-line poem when she had barely entered her teens; and she fell in love with a much older widower from a different caste when she was fourteen. Her father, sensing trouble, arranged to send her abroad on a scholarship given by the Nizam of Hyderabad. Though she spent three years in England, first in London and then at Girton College, Cambridge, she proved to be a poor scholar. Instead, she read and wrote poetry. Through Edmund Gosse, she met some of the most important poets of the 1890s. Before she returned to India, she travelled to the Continent.

On returning she contracted a marriage with the man she loved, Dr Govandarajulu Naidu. The ceremony was performed by Pandit Veerasalingam Pantulu under the provisions of the Special Marriages Act which enabled people from different castes, communities or religions to marry. It was one of the first such unions in Hyderabad state. Her husband was a medical doctor, employed by the Nizam's Medical Services. Sarojini settled down to an upper-middle class life of domestic duties and drudgeries. From 1901 to 1904 she gave birth to four children in quick succession – Jaisoorya, Padmaja, Leilamani and Ranadheera. Her duties as a wife, mother and hostess occupied most of her time. However, her restless spirit rebelled against such an ordinary existence. She began to publish her poems and her first collection, *The Golden Threshold*, appeared in 1905. This was followed by *The Bird of Time* (1911) and later, by *The Broken Wing* (1917). In the meanwhile, she had begun to receive invitations to address the several social organisations, especially those devoted to the welfare of youth and of women, which had proliferated all over India since the renaissance of the nineteenth century. Both she and her audiences quickly discovered her innate gift for oratory; soon she became a popular speaker, very much in demand.

Though she had started looking for mentors even earlier, it was through her friendship with Gopal Krishna Gokhale, whom she met frequently in London in 1912-1914, that she entered the mainstream of national political life. Gokhale extracted a pledge from her to dedicate herself and her gifts to the nation. This, arguably, was the turning point in her life. Soon afterwards, she met Gandhi, Nehru, Jinnah and all the important leaders of her time. After Gokhale's death, she became a devoted associate of Gandhi. Largely through his influence, she succeeded him as the President of the Indian National Congress in 1925. Prior to her, the only woman to have occupied this high post was Annie Besant. Under Gandhi's leadership, Sarojini participated whole-heartedly in the freedom struggle. She also travelled extensively both in India and abroad, not just as a spokesperson of the Congress but as an outstanding extempore orator and an internationally recognised poet. She was jailed four times by the British, participated in the Civil Disobedience, Non-cooperation, Salt Satyagraha, Quit India and other movements, was a member of the Congress Working Committee, nursed Gandhi during some of his fasts and in general, bore witness to some of the most important events of the first half of the twentieth century. After India achieved independence, she became the first Governor of India's most populous state, the United Provinces (now Uttar Pradesh).

She led a rich, varied, hectic and satisfying life, dying in 1949 at the age of seventy. Longevity was not the least of her achievements because she was plagued by ill-health nearly all her life and suffered a variety of ailments including heart disease, rheumatism, lumbago, malaria, nervous disorders, broken limbs, spinal injury, fevers, headaches and so on. Sarojini was aware of her own unusual zest for life which would triumph over all illnesses. In a letter to her publisher William Heinemann, written when she was thirty-six she says:

> You'll be sorry to hear that I am rather seriously ill.... Govind, my husband, is very anxious and very cross with me. But I cannot unless I am really dangerously ill, lie abed and 'cease activities.' He says I shall truly die young, but I don't believe it: I have far too much vital energy of the soul and can stand, without making a sign, any amount of pain – and besides, good God – how can I die – I who love life and all humanity? (Paranjape 1996, 70)

Sick or healthy, Sarojini made the most of what she got from life. She was a figure full of energy and laughter, someone who in spite of tremendous suffering retained a comic view of life. As she wrote to Ranadheera on 14 February 1943 soon after her sixty-fourth birthday, 'one is not so concerned with a long life as with a "merry one" – merry as the sum of worthwhile, rich, full, interesting and who can say that mine has not been and is not in that sense "merry" as well as long?' (Paranjape 1996, 308). The letter, incidentally, was written from the Yervada jail. In a letter written to Padmaja over ten years earlier, also from the Yervada jail, she declared: 'In the course of a long and most variegated life I have learned one superlative truth ... that the true measure of life and oneself lies not in the circumstances and events that fill its map but in one's approach and attitude and acceptance of those things' (278). She certainly lived by these words till the end of her days.

8.3 POETIC REPUTATION

Sarojini's works have long been hard to get or out of print. *Sarojini Naidu: Select Poems,* edited by H. G. Dalwey Turnbull, was published by Oxford University Press, Calcutta, in 1930. But, besides being outdated, it has never been reprinted. Today it is almost impossible to find a copy of this book. During her lifetime, Sarojini supervised the publication of *The Sceptred Flute,* which includes all the poems from her three major collections, *The Golden Threshold* (1905), *The Bird of Time* (1912) and *The Broken Wing* (1917). This served in lieu of an edition of her collected poems. It was first published by Dodd, Mead and Co., New York, in 1937. An Indian edition was issued by Kitabistan, Allahabad, in 1943 and reprinted several times up to 1979. However, today a copy even of the reprint is difficult to obtain; not just the edition, but the publishing house itself is defunct. Moreover, there are several of her poems which *The Sceptred Flute* does not contain, including two juvenile compositions and *The Feather of the Dawn,* a book of poems edited by her daughter Padmaja Naidu and published in 1961, twelve years after the poet's death. Thus, there has been neither a complete edition of her poems, nor a truly representative selection.

However such has been the continuing demand for her poetry, especially after it began to be prescribed in some universities, that there have been two unauthorised 'quickie' editions of her poems, one by A. N. and Satish Gupta and another by the indefatigable Raghukul Tilak (see Works Cited), a well known writer of bazaar notes. Such *kunjis* or 'keys' constitute a genre of their own; cheap, examination-oriented and though badly edited and produced, they are popular substitutes for texts among a majority of students of English literature in India. These 'guides' have performed a function similar to anthologies in keeping the poet alive in the minds of a new generation of students. Today, however, even these 'bazaar notes' are not easily available.

Sarojini's prose is even less in circulation; it is practically inaccessible. The fullest collection can be found in *Speeches and Writings of Sarojini Naidu,* published by the great nationalist publisher, G. A. Natesan in Madras; its third edition came out in 1925. But even this is woefully incomplete because Sarojini remained in the public realm for another twenty-four years, until she died in 1949, during which period she must have given hundreds of speeches. This edition, moreover, has been out of print for decades. Hence, her prose is practically unknown, so much so that the fact that she wrote some memorable prose is almost forgotten today.

In this chapter while not making any special claims for the value or significance of her writings, I do wish to offer a new way of reading them. To begin with, we must remember that Sarojini Naidu was an important figure in India's recent history and that her work therefore deserves to be available to present and future readers. As a politician, nationalist leader, poet, activist for women's rights, orator and celebrity, she was certainly one of the most memorable and colourful Indian women of the last century. She was not only the first Indian woman to become the President of the Indian National Congress, but also the first woman Governor of a state in independent India. As one of the principal aides and followers of Mahatma Gandhi, she was constantly in the limelight and probably the best-known Indian woman of her time. She also had an international presence as India's cultural ambassador and spokesperson of the freedom movement. In her life converge some of the dominant cultural, social and political currents of pre-independence India. Thus, both in her own right and as a representative of her times, Sarojini deserves to be remembered and studied.

Yet, her career exhibits an intriguing paradox. She was one of those great people whose greatness is most difficult to identify and substantiate. Historians of the freedom movement invariably assign to her a minor role in the formation of the Indian nation. Important as a lieutenant and acolyte of Gandhi, by herself and on her own terms, she becomes relatively less so. Certainly, she made no epoch-making original contribution to either the ideology or practice of the struggle against colonialism. Even within the Congress, such an evaluation of her was not uncommon. This was evident even in the manner in which she became the Governor of United Provinces. It was Bidhan Chandra Roy who was first offered the Governorship by Jawaharlal Nehru in July 1947. Roy was in the USA at that time. Sarojini agreed to officiate in his place. When Roy returned to India in November, he decided to accept the more challenging office of the Chief Minister of West Bengal and consequently resigned his Governorship. It was only after his resignation that she was 'confirmed' as the Governor of UP; otherwise, she was to have handed over charge by the end of October 1947. Through her entire public life, she never ran for any elected office; most likely, she had no grassroots support or base in any part of the country. It is easy, therefore, to see her contribution as merely that of a celebrity publicist and public relations officer of the Congress in general and Gandhi in particular.

Similarly, in the women's movement, Sarojini's contribution is more that of a supporter and populariser than an original thinker or activist. When one examines the documents of the All-India Women's Conference or the Indian suffragette movement, for instance, one notices that other like Margaret Cousins and Ramabai Ranade, not Sarojini were the prime movers. Sarojini was a non-controversial and famous *Indian* figurehead who could lend the cause legitimacy and acceptance. Similarly, in the realms of ideas and activism, Sarojini was no radical like Pandita Ramabai nor a great organiser like Annie Besant in the field of religion and politics.

Nowhere is this paradox more obvious than in her poetry. Sarojini's poetry occupies a very limited realm of lyricism and is deliberately ephemeral thematically. Her indisputable metrical felicity and technical mastery have not prevented some of her poems from sounding like childish jingles. Indeed, with the modernist turn in Indian English poetry in the 1950s, a whole generation of poets grew up despising her poetry. Among them are P. Lal, Nissim Ezekiel, R. Parthasarathy, Adil Jussawalla, A. K. Mehrotra and Keki Daruwalla. Some of them have also been influential anthologists, editors and patrons of Indian English poetry. To them Sarojini was a particularly soft target: not only did she represent a dead aesthetic, but her romanticism was of a particularly meretricious kind. Whereas Rabindranath Tagore or Sri Aurobindo were harder to demolish or dismiss, Sarojini was a pushover because she had no pretensions to the depth or intellectual range of the other two figures. But despite her sinking reputation among a whole generation of poets and poet-makers, she has remained one of the most popular, widely-anthologised and studied of Indian English poets. Indeed, there are more books, papers and articles on her poetry than on any Indian English poet except Sri Aurobindo.

It is possible to attempt to solve the riddle of the greatness of Sarojini by suggesting that she was a minor figure in a major mode. In other words, though whatever she did was not necessarily profound or significant in itself, it was nevertheless performed on a scale which was truly extraordinary and central to the formation of the Indian nation. She could sustain this seeming contradiction not only because of the special circumstances in which she lived and which made her qualities rare and sought-after, but because she was truly outstanding in one sphere. Her unusual energy contributed to an extraordinary public presence, which was both dynamic and catalytic. In other words, her unique greatness lay in aspects of her life and personality which are no longer accessible to us through her written words. The text of Sarojini's greatness was living, not written like that of great male leaders like Gandhi or Nehru.

One instance of this lost greatness needs special mention. Sarojini was one of the most eloquent and moving orators of her time. though most of what she spoke had emotional and sentimental appeal rather than 'solid' thought or argumentation. She was not really a great thinker, but an able one; it was, instead, the force of her personality that created the impact that she was remembered for. She was, perhaps, the most effective purveyor of the sublime – transforming public speaking into poetry. Moreover, Sarojini was an unorthodox and irrepressibly candid person, one who could poke fun at Gandhi himself, not to speak of his more solemn, homourless and puritanical coterie. Her letters to her children, especially to Padmaja, reveal her as a chatty correspondent, reveling in caricature and witty gossip.

Finally, her greatness is most evident in her unconventional life, of which we have already had a glimpse. She passed the Madras matriculation at twelve, composed 1000-line poems in English at thirteen, fell in love at fourteen, spent three years in England without getting a degree, returned to India before she was out of her teens to marry Dr M. Govindarajulu Naidu and went on to have four children by the time she was twenty-five. When she was twenty-six, her first major collection of poems, *The Golden Threshold,* was published. She also began to speak in public, stepping out of the roles of wife and mother. She became a national leader and a poet of international renown before she was thirty-five; she also left home and entered public life full time. By forty-six she was the President of the Indian National Congress and the foremost woman of her time. She was jailed four times along with other national leaders; she toured India extensively and abroad frequently; she served on the Congress Working Committee, the apex decision-making body of the party, for several years; she was one of the most sought after speakers in India. At sixty-eight, she became the Governor of the most populous Indian state, Uttar Pradesh. Throughout her eventful and busy life, she overcame extraordinary odds and pushed the realms of activity for Indian women farther than perhaps anyone had done before her. She achieved all this without being inordinately privileged by birth or upbringing.

Thus, while it is easy not to take seriously the adoring and cloying praise of her contemporaries and admirers, it is equally necessary not to swing to the other extreme in dismissing her out of hand. A critical examination of her life and works reveals not only that crucial aspects of her achievement may not be easily accessible to us, but that we need to look afresh at whatever of her life and work is available to us. A career such as Sarojini's not only calls into question how great she really was, but also forces us to re-examine our received, mostly patriarchal notions of 'greatness', which are often intellectually elitist.

8.4 WORKS

Sarojini's poetic career began when she was just eleven. Arthur Symons quotes her in his Introduction to *The Golden Threshold:*

> One day, when I was eleven, I was sighing over a sum in algebra: it *wouldn't* come right; but instead a whole poem came to me suddenly. I wrote it down.
>
> From that day my 'poetic career' began. At thirteen I wrote a long poem *a la* 'Lady of the Lake' – 1300 lines in six days. At thirteen I wrote a drama of 2000 lines...I wrote a novel, I wrote fat volumes of journals. I took myself very seriously in those days. (Naidu 1905, 9)

Of these early works, only the first, the long poem '*a la* Lady of the Lake,' survives. Perhaps, it was the presentation of this book to the Nizam which resulted in her being awarded a scholarship by him for higher studies in England.

I found a printed copy of this poem in the Padmaja Naidu papers, Nehru Memorial Library. The title page reads: '*Mehir Muneer. A Poem in Three Cantos by a Brahmin Girl.* Madras: Printed by Srinivasa, Varadachari and Co., 1893.' There are corrections made throughout the book in a handwriting that resembles Sarojini's, including the title page, where 'A Brahmin Girl' has been scored and 'A Hindu Lady' written in its place. A revised edition, though, was never brought out. It is interesting to see how Sarojini did not wish to be identified as the author of the poem and used, first, the more traditional disguise of 'Brahmin girl,' then struck it out and wrote over it, 'A Hindu Lady,' for a possible second, revised edition, which never came out. Despite the camouflage, she wished to highlight both her gender and her religion or community because these would make the poem all the more remarkable for its time.

This is Sarojini's earliest published poetic work and among the first she wrote. While Padmini Sengupta makes no mention of it, Tara Ali Baig, in *Sarojini Naidu*, mistakenly calls it a play:

> She also wrote a little Persian play called 'Meher [sic] Muneer' which her father got printed in a local journal. A few copies of this play written in English were sent to friends. Among them was the Nisam of Hyderabad who was so charmed that he made a typically princely gesture...in 1895 His Exalted Highness

endowed her with a scholarship granting her passage to England for £300 a year. (Baig 1974, 16)

It is clear that neither Sengupta nor Baig got to see the printed copy of *Mehir Muneer*. In its present form, the work is clearly a poem and not a play; whether it was originally written in Persian as a play is impossible to verify today. However, the fact that Sarojini herself referred to it, mentioning its precise number of lines, that the text showed up in the Padmaja Naidu Papers, that it has corrections in Sarojini's handwriting and that Baig says it earned her her endowment, proves that Sarojini was indeed its author. My theory is that it was written originally in English as a poem and that perhaps a Persian version was also printed and circulated. Though Sarojini had learned Persian and translated from it, I wonder if she knew it well enough to write an original literary work of considerable length in it at the age of thirteen. At any rate, an English poem by that name exists and Sarojini was almost certainly its author.

Artistically, the poem is interesting, but flawed. The verses and rhymes are mostly childish, though there are bursts of inspired writing through the work. The poem, moreover, lacks unity and coherence. The first canto, about the birth of Mehir Muneer, seems to drag on for too long and has little to do with the main plot concerning the romance between Mehir and Badar, which takes place in cantos II and III. The most interesting aspects of the poem are its depiction of adult love in pre-adult terms. Here we have all the passion and innocence of such love without its guilt-inducing sexuality. This is also a children's world in that there are no disciplining and repressive authority figures in it to obstruct Meher and Badar's first night together. Sarojini's creation of unreal and magical worlds is also noteworthy; not only is the poem set in an exotic locale, but the exoticism is further heightened in the enchanted forest world in canto II. About it possible source, Khan observes that 'its story was adapted from one of Sir Edwin Arnold's[2] stories ' (Khan 1983, 6)

Her next collection, '*Songs* by S. Chattopadhyaya,' was printed privately by her father Aghorenath Chattopadhyaya in Hyderabad in

1896, contains poems which she wrote from 1892–1896. The collection was, thus, published when she was in England. We know that she sent letters and poems to her would-be husband, Govindarajulu, from England. Some of these poems found their way into *Songs,* along with a number of older pieces. This collection is the weakest of all her books. In fact, I have not found a single poem in it which is worth quoting or studying except as juvenilia. Its publication was not supervised by her, though the printed copies of both *Mehir Muneer* and *Songs* show correction marks in her handwriting. Perhaps, she intended to republish both later, but then dropped the idea. The poems in these two juvenile collections are hardly ever discussed by critics. I believe that I made *Mehir Muneer* available for the first time to a general audience by reprinting it in *Sarojini Naidu: Selected Poetry and Prose.*

It was with *The Golden Threshold* in 1905 that Sarojini's career as a poet really took off. Arthur Symons was responsible for the publication of this book. The poems in it belong almost wholly to two periods: 1896 and 1904. Sarojini had sent Symons some new poems in 1904 and he had already seen her earlier work in 1896. Symons says, 'As they seemed to me to have an individual beauty of their own, I thought they ought to be published' (Naidu 1905, 9). Sarojini then wrote to Edmund Gosse asking for his advice and permission in publishing the collection. Sarojini's dedication of the book to 'Edmund Gosse who first showed me the way to the Golden Threshold' shows how deeply she was influenced by him. Ironically, when Gosse had seen many of these very poems in 1896, he had been disappointed as he tells us in his Introduction to *The Bird of Time.* Now, thanks to Symons they were being published anyway. There was, however, yet another difficulty which no biographer or critic to my knowledge has mentioned. William Heinemann was unwilling to risk his money on the book, though it was recommended by Gosse and Symons and would carry an Introduction by the latter. The poet had to actually pay the publisher a tidy sum of £14 to cover the printing costs. This is revealed in Sarojini's letters to Gosse at the National Archives. The book, of course, went on to be a huge success; the first edition was sold out by the end of 1905, a new edition was published and quickly snapped up in 1906.

The Golden Threshold is, arguably, Sarojini's finest collection. The title is significant, hinting at the kind of romanticism that Sarojini practiced. What is the collection a threshold to? Does it refer to a key theme in the collection, that of growing up, bidding goodbye to one's dreams and of maturing person and woman? Or is it a threshold to her poetic career, which she hopes will be golden? Or, yet again, is the collection a sort of threshold or passage to India itself for Western readers? As a nationalistic poet, she would want to introduce her readers not to an earthen or clayey India, but a magnificent, golden India, embellished by her imagination as well as carefully ornamented enough to be pleasingly delectable to her foreign readers. At any rate, the title foregrounds the problem of representation which is at the heart of Sarojini's poetic project. Izaat Yar Khan could not find the manuscript of *The Golden Threshold* at the National Library, Calcutta; he concludes that it is lost. But manuscripts of several individual poems are at the National Archives, New Delhi.

This collection contains many of Sarojini's best known and loved poems, including several of the 'folk songs.' Of these, 'Palanquin Bearers,' is certainly the best-known and most-anthologised. The poem has an intricate metrical composition. Each line has four feet. The first lines of each of the two stanzas have two trochees followed by two anapaests; the other lines have an iamb followed by three anapaests. The dominant foot is the anapaest, which gives the poem its springy effect.

> Lightly, O lightly, we bear her along,
> She sways like a flower in the wind of our song;
> She skims like a bird on the foam of a stream
> She floats like a laugh from the lips of a dream.
> Gaily, O gaily we glide and we sing,
> We bear her along like a pearl on a string. (Paranjape 2010, 58)

This poem can be central to a symptomatic re-reading of Sarojini's poetry in terms of what it leaves out – the toil, sweat and oppression of the palanquin bearers. Hence, it presents a 'pretty picture' of a dying feudal order under colonialism. The poem, moreover, is in a section called, 'Folk Songs.' Sarojini makes the 'folk' sing of their reality in terms which would please the gentry. The folk are shown in idealised and idyllic postures, in effect, celebrating and glorifying their own oppression.

The poem does represent accurately some features of the situation depicted, though. Palanquin bearers were, indeed, known to sing as they worked, their verses meant to lighten the burdens that they carried. But the labour was heavy and hard. The verses were often repetitive and meaningless. Sarojini, too, tries to bring a similar formulaic repetitiveness to the poem. Once the first stanza defines a workable structure, it can be reused with slight variations. The two stanzas, hence, do not present any real development of thought but do constitute a sort of balanced whole. Though the situation is authentic, what the bearers are made to say is not. There is therefore a tension between the structure and texture of the poem, quite characteristic of her other folk songs. The folk cannot break out of the idealised mould into which they are cast.

The last poem of *The Golden Threshold*, 'To a Buddha Seated on a Lotus' (Paranjape 2010, 73), ensures that the collection ends on a spiritual note, a pattern followed in her other books too. Though not impressive in itself, it is remembered in the West because it was one of the three included in *The Oxford Book of Mystic Verse* edited by D.H.S. Nicholson and A.H.E. Lee in 1917. To me, the poem falls short of a significant insight into the mystical experience because the speaker merely wonders how ordinary people may reach the elusive end of nirvana.

The *Golden Threshold* was reviewed favourably both in the Indian and, especially, in the British press. There were reviews in *The Times* (London), *The Manchester Guardian, The Review of Reviews, The Morning Post, Athenaeum, Daily Chronicle, Spectator* and *T.P.'s Weekly*. *The Golden Threshold* made Sarojini a celebrity in both India and England. Never before had a book of poems by an Indian caused such a stir abroad. *The Golden Threshold* remains Sarojini's best and most popular book. She never quite exceeded what she achieved in it.

Sarojini's second collection of poems, *The Bird of Time*, was published by William Heinemann in 1912 with an introduction by Edmund Gosse; it was also published simultaneously in New York by John Lane. This book, too, was reviewed widely in India and in England. Sarojini was an established poet by then. Her readers in England expected both beauty and oriental glamour from her and she did not disappoint them.

The title is from Omar Khayyam and the title poem encapsulates Sarojini's poetic philosophy. When asked 'What are the songs you sing?' (stanza one) and 'where did you learn/ The changing measures you sing?' the singing bird replies that she sings of both the joys and sorrows of life and that she learned her songs from both nature and culture. There is a deliberate cultivation here of the minor mode; Sarojini is happy to write seemingly insignificant and ephemeral lyrics like a bird chirps its songs. The artifice is comparable to Blake's deliberate simplicity in his 'Songs of Innocence,' though not as profound in intent.

The Broken Wing, her third collection, was published by Heinemann in 1917. In its opening and title poem, she poses the question 'Song-bird why dost *thou* bear a broken wing?' It was actually the question that Gokhale asked her as indicated in the epigraph. Gokhale detected a hidden sorrow beneath her jovial exterior. The question posed in the first half of the poem is not answered in the second, but deflected. The poet replies that she will soar up even on a broken wing. The fact of incapacitation is not denied, nor is it explained. The conversation between Sarojini and Gokhale took place in the spring of 1914. If we read this poem as an allegory for Sarojini's poetic career, then it contains a prophecy of its impending loss of divine inspiration. In the same vein, we may venture to answer the posed question: the wing is broken because the poetic fashion has changed. With the coming of modernism, there was a paradigm shift in the technique and subject of English poetry, a revolution which passed Sarojini by. She remained a singing bird in a gilded cage in an age which had no place for her.

One of the poems in this collection, 'The Gift of India,' was read out to the Hyderabad Ladies' War Relief Association in December 1915 (Sengupta 1966, 95), with printed copies circulated; it was also recited at the Congress session of 1916 (91) before it appeared in The Broken Wing. The subject of the poem is the martyrdom of those Indian soldiers who died overseas fighting for the British against the Axis forces in World War I. There was a common feeling at that time that Britain would show its gratitude to India for the latter's support. Sarojini's poem may be considered sentimental and superficial, substituting rhetoric for authentically felt experience. Yet it is nationalistic in that it urges Britain to remember the 'gift' of India. One of the reasons that Congress leaders finally decided not to support the British war effort during World War II was because the 'Gift of India' was ignored and that British promises for greater autonomy to India were not considered reliable.

The Broken Wing did not receive as much praise as her earlier books. Instead, by now, not only was the praise lukewarm, but there was also considerable criticism of her limitations as a poet. In Europe, the first wave of modernism was beginning to gather momentum. There were to be cataclysmic changes in poetic fashion. Sarojini was swept aside by this tide. She never published another collection in her lifetime. When Padmaja published *The Feather of the Dawn* in 1961, modernism was the ruling mode in Indian poetry. The book was panned by Nissim Ezekiel, among others. Sarojini had been consigned to oblivion.

The Feather of the Dawn was published by Asia Publishing House. The ms is at the National Library except for five poems, 'Gujarat,' 'The Glorissa Lily,' 'Mimicry,' 'Blind,' and 'Unity.' Some poems have been copied on the Taj Mahal Hotel letter paper and dated July 1927. Padmaja Naidu's note says that the poems were composed during July–August 1927. In another note she explains the significance of the title:

> The title of this book of poems is from a dance by the *Denishawn Dancers* based on the Hopi Indian legend that a feather blown

into the air at dawn, if caught by a breeze and carried out of sight, marks the opening of an auspicious day.

In her letter to her younger daughter, Leilamani Naidu, dated 13 August 1927, Sarojini says: 'Bebe [Padmaja Naidu] is so pleased and excited about my new poems. It seems so strange for the mood to have returned suddenly after all these years! I have half a volume, ready in these few weeks and some of the poems are I think very beautiful' (Paranjape 1996, 196). Yet Sarojini never published the collection during her lifetime. Was she aware that the tastes had changed and the book would no longer be received well?

Overall, the collection clearly shows a decline in poetic inspiration and quality. The enthusiasm of the earlier verses has flagged and the themes seem more tired. 'Songs of Radha,' the most interesting poems in the collection, attempt to bring the rich tradition of Krishna poetry into Indian English, but fail to do so. This makes it all the more clear that a simple appropriation of such traditions into English will not succeed without in some degree remaking and re-experiencing the spirit of the originals. This Sarojini has been unable to do. 'The Quest' is the most 'mystical' of Sarojini's poems because it seems to actualise the transcendence of duality in its last couplet: 'I am a part of thee as thou of me, a part. / Look for me in the mirror of thy heart (Paranjape 2010, 194) At last she seems to have glimpsed what lies beyond the separation and pining of the lover for her beloved.

If we were to examine the career graph of Sarojini, it is clear that her reputation was at its highest from 1905 to 1907 and then declined afterwards. In India she continued to have a following until her death. But in the 1950s when modernism took over Indian English poetry, her reputation as a poet dipped to its lowest. This contempt for her poetry persists in an entire generation of poets and critics who are now in their fifties and sixties. Yet, throughout, her poetry has remained popular; there is scarcely anybody with an English-medium education in India who doesn't know her 'Palanquin-Bearers'. Perhaps, the time is now ripe for a reinterpretation, if not revival, of her works.

8.5 REINTERPRETATION

The most effective way of reviving an interest in Sarojini's poetry is by shifting the critical focus from an evaluation of individual poems to the underlying ideology of her poetry. The question then is not how good or effective a poet she was or even what the major themes and techniques of her poetry were, but what the nature of her poetic project was and how it was shaped by the dominant ideological structures of her time. We can then begin to appreciate the inner tensions and conflicts in her poetry. Thus situated, Sarojini's poetry becomes a rich and complex text which reproduces the contradictions and debates of her age.

Sarojini's poetry mediates between the usually opposing but sometimes complimentary forces of the English poetic tradition and her Indian sensibility, between the politics of nationalism and the aesthetics of feudalism, between the overwhelming power of modernity and the nostalgia for a threatened tradition, between the security of a comfortable patriarchy and the liberating power of the women's movement. Thus, Sarojini's text displays both resistance to and cooptation by the dominant ideology of her time, which was colonialism. There is in it both a compromise and a collusion with prevailing power structures, whether literary or political. Unlike Tagore, Sarojini was unable to liberate her poetry from these contradictions. Her work remained mired in them; hence, the vague sense of betrayal and eventual hostility of the Indian literary establishment after the initial adoration.

It has been a commonplace assumption that Sarojini's poetry is imitative of British romantic poets. There is no doubt that her poetry bears the stamp of British lyricism, yet the exact nature of this influence has never been worked out. The result is a plethora of possible and suggested influences, often not confined to the romantic poets. Sarojini herself identifies Sir Walter Scott as the model for *Mehir Muneer*. Gosse, her literary mentor and first critic, mentions the influence of Shelley and Tennyson. Turnbull speaks of Swinburne among other possible influences. Later critics have located her sources in the poetry of the Pre-Raphaelites and of the 1890s. Such claims have never been backed up by exacting scholarship but merely aired as self-evident verities. I believe that the question of the influences on Sarojini's poetry must be worked out with more precision and accuracy.

As a beginning in that direction, I shall quote from a letter which Sarojini wrote to Govindarajulu on 14 January 1896:

> Shelley and Byron, Moore and Scott, Keats and Campbell and Wordsworth were a brilliant starry coterie, but even as brilliant as their coterie, though rather differently, are the new poets. Fancy the young, passionate, beautiful poets gathered together in a radiant galaxy. William Watson with his sublime, starry genius, Davidson with his wild, riotous, dazzling superabundant brilliance, Thompson with his rich, gorgeous, spiritual ecstasy of poetry, Yeats with his exquisite dreams and music, Norman Gale, redolent of springtime in the meadows and autumn in the orchard, Arthur Symons, the marvellous boy, with his passionate nature and fiery eyes, all gathered together in the friendly house of that dearest and lovingest of friends and rarest and most gifted of [geniuses] Edmund Gosse. Take too the older men, with their beautiful gifts – Swinburne, with his marvellous spirit, his voluptuous ecstasy of word music, take that grand old Socialist William Morris hammering with golden thunders. Take that lovely singer Edwin Arnold and that graceful writer, the laureate of the English, Alfred Austin – who says we have no rare geniuses and true poets in these days? Of course the younger men are the more gifted and William Watson is the greatest and noblest of them all.... (Paranjape 1996, 2–3)

The note of girlish excitement can easily be explained if we remember that the poet was not yet seventeen when she wrote this. It is ironic that nearly all the poets Sarojini hails as geniuses, except Yeats, are forgotten today. The problem is not so much that she had minor poets for her models; she had little choice in that regard. Moreover, bad models do not necessarily make bad original poetry; there are many instances of minor poets inspiring major ones. What is more important, arguably, is the final product, not so much the source or influence. The problem in evaluating the latter in Sarojini's poetry is that most of the poets she mentions in her letter were, before the advent of copyright free books on the internet, entirely unavailable in India. These poets will have to be read in the original and then compared with Sarojini to get a clearer picture of how sensibility was shaped in her formative years in England. At any rate, it won't do to underestimate the extent of Sarojini's familiarity with English poets and literary fashions.

Even more interesting, perhaps, is the role she played, though unwittingly, in the creation of literary modernism. It was Sarojini who aided Ezra Pound in his acquisition of the Fenollosa Papers in 1913.[3] As we well know, Pound derived many of his ideas about the centrality and function of the image in poetry from these papers. Sarojini probably helped to arrange the meeting between Mrs Fenollosa and Pound during which the former handed over the papers to the latter in her presence.

Such study of the impact of the prevailing literary climate on Sarojini's poetry will yield several insights. Just one example is a better understanding of the structure of her poetry. Most of her poems have a repetitive, formulaic structure. The stanzas are almost identical in form and rhyme scheme, only the images and words are changed. Such a structure, clearly pre-modernist, is found in the roundel, an English variation of the French rondel, a literary form popular in the poetry of the 1890s. Its key features, including a simple rhyme scheme and refrains, are found in many of Sarojini's poems. Similarly, we find in Sarojini's poetry the penchant for mood, music and dreamy ephemerality which is common in the 1890s' poets, who were reacting to the high seriousness and moral questioning of the Victorian poets.

After the issue of influences, another matter which has received the attention' of Sarojini's critics is problem of representation in her poetry. It is customary, in this context, to quote Gosse's advice to the poet:

> The verses which Sarojini had entrusted to me were skilful in form, correct in grammar and blameless in sentiment, but they had the disadvantage of being totally without individuality. They were Western in feeling and in imagery, this was but the note of the mocking-bird with a vengeance.
>
> I advised the consignment of all that she had written, in this falsely English vein, to the wastepaper basket. I implored her to consider that from a young Indian of extreme sensibility, who had mastered not merely the language but the prosody of the West, what we wished to receive was, not a rechauffe of Anglo-Saxon sentiment in an Anglo-Saxon setting, but some revelation of the heart of India, some sincere and penetrating analysis of native passion, of the principles of antique religion and of such mysterious intimations as stirred the soul of the East long before the West had begun to dream it had a soul. Moreover, I entreated Sarojini to write no more about skylarks, in a landscape of our Midland countries, with the village bells somewhere in the distance calling the parishioners to church, but to describe the flowers, the fruits, the trees, to set her poems firmly among the mountains, the gardens, the temples, to introduce to us the vivid populations of her own voluptuous and unfamiliar province; in other words, to be a genuine Indian poet of the Deccan, not a clever machine-made imitator of the English classics. (Naidu 1912, 4-5)

Ironically, the passage which was meant to illustrate the end of her imitativeness is often quoted to prove its continuance. Apparently, to stop being imitative at someone else's behest is as big a sin as being imitative in the first place!

In any case, most critics agree that this is a seminal passage out of which we must construct the relationship of Sarojini to the dominant cultural ideologies of her time. Gosse's advice provokes a number of questions, especially because Sarojini appears to have followed it faithfully. Gosse gives her the choice between being a 'machine-made imitator' and a 'genuine Indian poet of the Deccan.' However, she was never accorded the latter status though she did write about the 'vivid populations of her own voluptuous and unfamiliar province.' James Cousins, one of her earliest and best critics, accused her of illogic and excess as early as in 1918. Lotika Basu, whose book on Indian English poetry was published in 1933, went further, criticising her poetry for being inauthentic and unrealistic:

> In Mrs Naidu's treatment of Indian subjects she does not give a realistic picture of India; she merely continues the picture of India painted by Anglo-Indian and English writers, a land of bazaars, full of bright colours and perfumes and peopled with picturesque beggars, wandering minstrels and snake-charmers.
>
> She is more intent on drawing an interesting picture of India than on representing India as it is. It is this which makes her verses rather disappointing. Talented and with not a little of the gift of the true poet, it seems to us Mrs Naidu has failed in becoming a true interpreter of India to the West. (Basu 1933, 94–95)

Thus, ironically, Gosse seems to have damned her to a fate as bad as what he wished to save her from. The change of subject from English topics to an Indian reality was not of much help; what was more crucial was the underlying aesthetics of representation which Sarojini accepted. While Gosse could question her choice of subject, he could not question the very aesthetics to which both he and Sarojini subscribed. His advice, hence, masked a hidden agenda which, perhaps, caused more harm to Sarojini than anything else.

This hidden agenda is evident in the task which Gosse set for Sarojini. His expectation of her for 'some revelation of the heart of India, some sincere penetrating analysis of native passion, of the principles of antique religion and of such mysterious intimations as stirred the soul of the East' betrayed the deep longings of the post-Industrial West for, some area of experience untouched by modernity, unspoiled, pristine and authentic.[4] In brief, a longing for its Other. To escape the oppressive and overpowering advance of the machine age seemed to be the compelling challenge before Victorian poetry. The poetic medievalism of the Pre-Raphaelites was one way of meeting the same need as was the search for fresh locales and topics in Browning and Tennyson. In its search of its Other, a convenient place for Europe to look was in Its vast colonial spaces. Here, it could find, to its own reckoning, all the savagery, primitivism, irrationality and mysticism that it had suppressed within itself. But for the natives themselves, such a search for Europe's Other was, no doubt, a *cul de sac*. In other words, Gosse's commission was, perhaps, impossible to fulfill because there was no such mysterious soul of India; in fact, any such notion of it was itself merely projection or construction from the keen reality of its absence.

In setting her such a task, Gosse was, willy-nilly, also setting a trap for Sarojini. The trap was to give to the West the picture of India which the West wished to see. The subsequent criticism of her poetry only proves how superbly Sarojini fulfilled her assignment. Her India is more artificial, exotic and picturesque, but less mysterious, alien, or dishonest than any account by an Anglo-Indian poet. With good reason too, because she knew her India, better than a foreigner would. Thus, in exceeding her brief, Sarojini subtly but certainly complicated the apparently simple relationship of the colonised and the coloniser. It could be argued that her poetry illustrates both a collusion with as also resistance to the dominance of the metropolitan aesthetic. It shows not only an obvious collusion in her apparently transparent obedience to Gosse, but also resistance in the manner in which she appropriates and nativises the Orientalist project. As an Indian, she is reclaiming her right to represent herself and the experience of her fellow Indians. Even if the poetic programme and its aesthetics are borrowed, the control over the representation is in native hands.

But why was such a project so appealing to the poet herself? The reasons, I believe, are both complicated and interesting. First, we must remember Sarojini's position as an aspiring Indian poet writing in English in the 1890s. To put it simply, at that time there were no 'poets', no publishers and no readers in India. There was no tradition of writing poetry in English to speak of and thus no *place* for an Indian English poet in society. There had been, no doubt, individual poets like Henry Derozio or Toru Dutt before her who had achieved some renown. The latter, incidentally, was, like Sarojini, a prodigy and had been discovered by the same Edmund Gosse. So, the patronage of Gosse was something Sarojini could simply not resist. The significance that Sarojini attached to Gosse's encouragement can be inferred from this letter which she wrote to him in 1896:

> I do not dare to trust myself to thank you for what you said on Sunday. You cannot know what these words meant to me, how people always colour my life, how when I am in the very depth of self-disgust and despair – as I often am – they will give me new hope, a new courage – no, you cannot know! Poetry is the one thing I love so passionately, so intensely, so absolutely that it is my very life of life – and now you have told me that I am a poet – I am a poet! I keep repeating it to myself to try to realise it. Will you let me tell you a little about myself because I want you to know how you have been an influence on my life ever since I was eleven years old. (Paranjape 1996, 27–28)

She tells him how he had been her literary idol from the age of fourteen or fifteen, through the time she came to England. Finally, she gets to meet him in person:

> Well, in January I first saw you – the magical legend had become a reality. I was not disappointed. Indeed I shall never forget that day because with one great bound I seemed to wake into a new large life, the life I had always longed for and so long in vain. From that day I seemed to be an altered being. I seemed to have put off childish things and put on garments of new and beautiful hope and ambition and I have gone on growing and growing I feel it, seeing more clearly, feeling more intensely, thinking more deeply and loving more passionately, more unselfishly, that beautiful spirit of art that has now become dearer than my life's blood to me – and all this I owe to you....
> As you have been for so long so good an influence on my

life I wanted you to go on for ever! I will send you everything I write and you must tell me what you think. I want you to be more severe and exacting than ever, the better I do, because I do not want to outlast the years but the centuries. That is very conceited of me, but is it not worthwhile to aim at the stars though one never gets beyond the mountain top? I don't think I am going to ask you to excuse me for taking up so much of your time, because I cannot go on being grateful to you in silence...without your knowing how much cause I have to be grateful to you for. (Paranjape 1996, 27-28)

No doubt, Gosse would have been embarrassed by Sarojini's effusiveness; the situation, however, doesn't concern two individuals as much as two types in the colonial encounter. What better example can we find of the plight of the colonial subject, forever locked in a relationship of dependence and gratitude to the metropolis! Grateful first for being colonised, for having an alien language imposed on us; grateful again when our efforts in that language are evaluated by our masters; grateful finally for the privilege of having our books published in the metropolis and for a subsequent re-import to our colonised country.

But if the dynamics of colonialism explains the reverence which Sarojini felt for Gosse, it doesn't fully account for the attraction of the model of representation which he had recommended to her. Here we must consider the contradictions and compulsions of her situation in India. As a sensitive Indian living in the semi-feudal state of Hyderabad, part of the larger British Empire in India, Sarojini, like other Indian artists and intellectuals, had to deal with the question of cultural preservation and identity. The onslaught of the all-powerful modernity, sometimes aided, sometimes obstructed by the colonial administration, presented a contradictory and confusing picture. Under threat was the very selfhood of the subject. So threatened, Indians tried to revive and mark out those areas of experience which seemed to be untainted by colonialism and Western modernity. Indian religion and spirituality constituted one such bastion to which many of the key figures of the Indian renaissance, from Ram Mohan to Gandhi, rallied. It offered shelter from both colonialism and modernity.

If Indian tradition in the shape of religion was attractive to intellectuals, the artists tried to see it in threatened lifestyles and ways of living. Here was living proof that India, though 'backward' and underdeveloped, had managed to resist the machine age. What Sarojini tried to do was to offer an entry into this unspoiled India. Of course, it would have been too painful to portray it with all the horrors of its poverty, inequality, disease and suffering; if only these were glossed over, then a very attractive image of India would emerge, traditional, vivid, vibrant, colourful and joyous. Moreover, in a period of almost exponential social and technological change, she could see vanishing before her eyes a way of life which the West had already lost and now pined for. She felt compelled to capture it in poetry and song because she probably longed for it herself. All these factors contributed to her attempt at offering to Indians a picture of themselves which they might be proud of, something that might salvage some of their crippled self-respect as a colonised and humiliated people.

Of course, Sarojini's ruse was no solution; everyone knew that her India was too romantic, too pretty to represent the Indian reality as they knew it. Perhaps, that is why her formula failed. It was based on a self-comforting delusion, not on self-criticism and courage. In contrast, Gandhi made no attempt to mitigate or underplay the extent of India's dependence or bondage. Rather, he highlighted them to remind the people of what they had lost, of what they had given away to the British. He transformed a nation of defeated people into rebels by reminding them of their own responsibility for their capitulation. While Sarojini made the life of the palanquin-bearers appear more attractive than it was by taking the poetic license of rendering the palanquin weightless, Gandhi's method was to inspire the bearers to stop carrying the palanquin, to stop cooperating with those who oppressed them.

When viewed in such a light, the problem of representation

in Sarojini's poetry assumes the dimensions of a crisis. All her palanquin-bearers, wandering singers, Indian weavers, Coromandel fishers, snake-charmers, wandering beggars and so on, the 'folk' in her folk songs, become suspect. They are all made to deny the hardship and toil of their occupations, hide their dispossession and marginalisation and celebrate their lowly and oppressed state. They become picturesque, exotic figures in tableaux, frozen in various attitudes of quaintness. These folk are pretty; they are simple; they are guileless; they are sincere. They are, moreover, in harmony with nature; the social order in which they live is seen as an extension of the natural order. Whether this order is just or unjust, whether they can rebel against it or not – such questions never occur to them. In other words, they are as their social superiors would like them: obedient, docile and yet fascinating, interesting, picturesque. A symptomatic reading thus hints at the rich context and subtext of these poems. Such a historicist-materialistic approach would explain the absences in Sarojini's text as examples of the overwhelmingly harsh reality of colonialism which the poems seek to repress and banish.

It is not just the ordinary folk in her poems who are thus (mis)represented. The India of her poems is similarly an exotic place. Hyderabad, where many of her poems are set, is an area of mystery, romance and medieval chivalry. It is presented in an alluring medley of images of exquisite dancers, exotic bazaars, latticed balconies, veiled ladies, elephants, rare spices, silks, precious stones, decaying forts, timeless tombs and an intriguingly deep lake which is the image of the poet herself. The city is ruled by a benevolent poet-prince and his courtiers. There is no conflict in this city; the various classes and religious communities live peacefully, in perfect harmony. This is so because there is no competition in the city, no capitalism. It has a stable feudal social structure, where everyone is happy with his or her place. No wonder many poems show a repeated fascination with retrogressive social customs and practices including sati and purdah.

Not just the subject, but the language of her poetry reflects her aesthetic predilections. The more ornate, more Latinate, more exotic, more unusual word or phrase is always preferred over the simple, functional and ordinary. There is a heightening of sensuality in the imagery until every sense is stimulated to excess. Visually, the images tend away from clear daylight and sharp focus to hazy, dream-like, dim and blurred states of experience. It is as if the poet prefers not to see very clearly, prefers not to confront reality. One indication of this is the number of times the word 'dream' recurs in her poetry. Overall, there is a definite tendency towards hedonistic self-abandon and escape from reality.

To sum up, then, Sarojini's aesthetics is feudal, though her politics is democratic nationalism. Her better poems like 'The Purdah Nashin', 'Indian Dancers', or 'The Old Woman', are those which embody the feudal ideal. Whenever she attempted poems on nationalistic subjects, as In 'To India', or 'Kali the Mother', the result was laboured and uninteresting. It is hardly surprising that while as a national leader she lived mostly outside Hyderabad, she returned to her city for her poetic material and inspiration. Indeed, she always remained loyal to the Nizam ostensibly, never bringing her politics home, where her husband was an employee of the Nizam. Such was her compromise with the feudal order of the society into which she was born and brought up. The isolation, stability, oriental splendour and, one might add, unreality of Hyderabad appealed to her. It gave her the comfort to retreat into a dream world, to deny the onslaught of modernity and capitalism. It was a place without aggression or greed, full of old-world grace and charm, with an unhurried pace of life – a place she found stifling as a housewife and mother, which she escaped from when she entered public life, which was for all practical intents and purposes sterile, limited and narrow, but whose very decadence was appealing artistically. Hyderabad became her Byzantium. It re-emerged as a place of order, stability and sensory overabundance in her poetry.

Before leaving the topic of her aesthetics, I must stress on the ways in which it did try to authenticate an Indian sensibility. Just as careful research and scholarship are required in place of casual assertions of the influence of British poetry on Sarojini's work, so must a similar scrupulousness be exercised in identifying the 'native' sources of her poetry. The only serious attempt in this direction has been made by P. V. Rajyalakshmi in *The Lyric Spring*. She shows how Sarojini used traditions from Sanskrit and Urdu–Persian poetry in evolving her poetics. Thus, not only in her deliberate choice of Indian subject matter, but also in her poetic technique, she enlarged the possibilities of her medium.

Nowhere is her use of Indian poetic traditions more evident than in her love poetry. Her heroes and heroines are not so many individuals as they are types and attitudes. An examination of a medieval treatise on love poetry, such as Kesavadasa's *Rasika Priya*, reveals a whole catalogue of such situations and attitudes:

1. *Nabodha:* the shy maiden frightened of meeting her lover alone.
2. *Abhisarika:* 'hastening towards'; a love-sick maiden, venturing out of her father's house at night to keep a tryst with her lover.
3. *Vesaka Sajja:* 'dress equipped'; the heroine, fully apparelled, waiting in her chamber to receive her lover.
4. *Mugella:* 'charming'; young woman conscious of her charms.
5. *Smarandha:* 'love blind'; a woman blinded by her passion.
6. *Sambhoga:* 'united joy'; looking forward to or actually enjoying the embraces of her lover.
7. *Utka:* longing; a woman waiting with deep longing in a lonely place for her lover.
8. *Swadhina:* 'independent'; woman who is free to indulge her emotions and likings.
9. *Svadhina-patika:* woman who has her husband in subjection.
10. *Praushita-patika:* woman pining for her lover-husband who is away.
11. *Kalaha-antanta:* 'quarrel-separated'; a woman yearning but too proud to make up.
12. *Manini:* woman sulking and rejecting her lover.
13. *Vipra labdha:* 'hurt-desire'; deceived or jilted woman.
14. *Khandita:* a 'immoral' woman whose lover is playing truant or is impotent. (See Walker 1968, 433)

Several of these types can be found in Sarojini's poetry. A deeper study involving a comparison of original sources is required.

Similarly, a key aspect of classical Indian aesthetics was the emphasis on *alankara* or the 'beautiful form' in poetry. There were elaborate lists of various devices and figures of ornamentation as of rules to apply them correctly. In the light of *alamkara shastra,* we can identify Sarojini as primarily a poet of ornamentation and beautiful forms. Every line, every idea, every image is embellished elaborately in her poetry. A thorough examination of the various devices that she employs may reveal her indebtedness to Indian poetry and poetics to an extent greater than is acknowledged.

It has often been remarked that Sarojini's poetry is superficial, that it lacks philosophical content. The poetess herself contributed to such an impression by her deliberate emphasis on the fleeting, momentary. Nowhere else in Indian English poetry do we find such celebration of mutability and transience. The image of the singing bird, whether soaring up or fluttering on its broken wing, recurs in her poetry. In her letter to Symons quoted in his Introduction to *The Golden Threshold* she says:

> You know how high my idea of Art is; and to me my poor casual poems seem to be less than beautiful – I mean with that final enduring beauty that I desire. (Naidu 1905, 9–10)

In another letter she adds:

> I am not a poet really. I have the vision and the desire, but not the voice. If I could write just one poem full of beauty and the spirit of greatness, I should be exultingly silent for ever; but I sing just as the birds do and my songs are as ephemeral. (10)

Such remarks provide a more challenging task to feminist critics than merely an identification of the image of women in her poems. No doubt, Sarojini's construction of femininity and masculinity is amazingly essentialist; furthermore, the women that she portrays are often not just conventional and subordinate, but appear to endorse the patriarchy themselves in their words, images and attitudes. Yet, one could argue that there is something undeniably and uniquely feminist in her aesthetics. Sarojini's deliberate espousal of ephemerality and her cultivated anti-intellectualism aligns her to all those women whose voices and words were lost, who were outside the purview of the high-brow, male-dominated notion of great art. In a sense, her own mother herself was such a woman who composed Bengali lyrics when younger.

The best contrast to Sarojini within Indian English poetry is Sri Aurobindo, though modernist critics tend to club them together and also dismiss them with identically facile gestures. Sri Aurobindo was an intellectual and philosophical poet who tried to use his poetry as a vehicle for an incredibly well-thought-out ideological project. He wrote several books of poems, capping his achievement with *Savitri,* a poem of over 24,000 lines. Sarojini, in contrast, wrote very little – mostly in the lyric mode. While Sri Aurobindo, obviously, had so much to say through his poetry, Sarojini, ostensibly, had so little. Nor did she feel the need to write grand or profound poems meant to be classics.

This does not mean that she was superficial or had no philosophy to convey through her poetry. On the contrary, the very refusal to philosophise was itself a part of her philosophy. Nowhere is her celebration of the fleeting present more evident than in her Spring poems, the second most important group of poems in her oeuvre after her love songs. The spontaneous and cyclic renewal of vegetal life to Sarojini seemed to contain the answer to the riddle of life. Actually, transience was not the problem, but the solution for Sarojini. Once accepted, it makes us free. Transience, paradoxically, is the proof of immortality. Because even death is transient. This the recurrence of Spring proves again and again.

In Sarojini's view, life is a balance of opposites and diversities. There can be no laughter without sorrow, no love without death. But she would revel in the entire process, not just embrace the pleasure and eschew the pain. Unlike many of the male poets, salvation for Sarojini is here and now, in life on earth, not in renunciation or denial of the world of senses. The dissolution of the centre through a keen sensual experience is her idea of emancipation. In this she is not just romantic, but also a believer in the cult of sensibility. The capacity to feel, to experience, to be one with life is crucial to her. And she seeks a heightening of this capacity repeatedly, feverishly and compulsively – almost like an addict. Hence, the element of exaggeration and excess in her poetry. Her senses are her source of ecstasy and life is the stimulant; often, she forces both the stimulants and the senses beyond their capacities in her attempt to reach her 'high.'

Overall, Sarojini, like the aesthetes and symbolists, was an idealist; she did believe in the soul, but a soul which worked through the senses, not one which was transcendental and which could only be reached through a repression and denial of the senses. Thus, while her poetry downplays the intellectual aspects of the human personality and celebrates the life of emotion and sensuality, it is not totally devoid of a philosophical content and foundation.

As a writer of prose, Sarojini was never well known. Except for a few booklets, she never published a sustained piece of prose in her lifetime. Her collected speeches are uneven in quality and lacking in well-developed or original thinking. In fact, most of the thousands of speeches she delivered were extempore. There is therefore no record of them. Especially from 1925 (when the third edition of her speeches and writings was published) to 1947 (when she became Governor of U.P.), I have been almost unable to find any prose by her. 'Mah Rukh Begum,' 'Women's Education and the Unity of India,' and 'Remarks While Conferring Honorary Degrees at the Silver Jubilee Convocation of Lucknow University,' were published for the first time in my collection *Sarojini Naidu: Selected Poetry and Prose*.

The two prose pieces, 'Mah Rukh Begum: A Romance of Fate' and 'Nilambuja' are the most interesting not only because they are the only examples of her literary prose. Thus, they show a continuity with her poetry. The rest of her prose consists of political speeches and biographical sketches.

The manuscript of 'Mah Rukh Begum' dated 6 May, 1897 in the National Archives shows it to be, like 'Nilambuja,' an early work, which also remained unpublished till I included it in my anthology in 1993 for the first time. It is thus the earliest available example of Sarojini's prose. Written when she was in England and only eighteen, it is a remarkable work, written in a highly ornate and stylised poetic prose. The period and atmosphere are evoked with graphic particularity and effectiveness. It is, moreover, replete with symbolic import despite the hackneyed ending. The piece shows that Sarojini certainly had the makings of a fine writer of fiction.

The situation in the piece is typical of the dilemma in Sarojini's work and life. The rebellious adolescent, Mah Rukh Begum, is a kind of self-representation of the poet. She is poised between two worlds – one offers her security and identity, the other freedom and, in a sense, death. But the conflict between the two never comes to a head because Mah Rukh finds both security and freedom where she is, thus being saved from making a life-threatening choice. The man she falls in love with, turns out to be her husband in the arranged marriage into which circumstances force her.

Mah Rukh has the makings of a rebel, but her rebellion is forestalled by her getting what she wants within the system which she thinks of as oppressive. This is the significance of the sub-title, 'A Romance of Fate.' But, surely, this turn of events is purely fortuitous, though it does seem to endorse, in a roundabout manner, the closed and repressive society in which she lives. What if the man had happened to be someone else? The implication is that at its very best, the system into which Mah Rukh is born, will suffice.

In her own life, though, Sarojini had to rebel. Her marriage to M. Govindarajulu Naidu was an inter-caste marriage which had to be solemnised according to Brahmo rites under the provisions of the Special Marriage Act of 1872 in Madras; this involved both the groom and bride having to deny that they were of any religion – Hindu, Muslim, Christian, Sikh, or Jain. This was an act of rebellion on Sarojini's part, yet it was supported by the pillars of the social reform movement of her time. We must not also forget that her parents had a Brahmo background. Varada Sundari studied and resided at a Brahmo home for girls while her husband, Aghorenath, was working for his DSc at Edinburgh.

In Mah Rukh we see both Sarojini's attraction and repulsion for the feudal Hyderabadi society into which she was born. Like Mah Rukh, Sarojini had an ambivalent relationship to it. She was neither able to accept it completely, nor rebel against it.

One of the most important speeches that Sarojini gave was her Presidential Address, to Indian National Congress, delivered at the 40th annual session of the Indian National Congress on 26 December 1925, at Kanpur. Sarojini was the first Indian woman to become the President of the Congress and the second woman, after Annie Besant, to do so. This is, perhaps, her most important public statement because here she speaks her own mind more than reflecting the dominant ideas of her time. Sarojini emphasises and foregrounds her gender throughout the address. There is a deliberate attempt to use her difference as a woman strategically and rhetorically. While she invokes traditional and even retrogressive stereotypes of the role of women in Indian society, she is doing so, perhaps, out of a sense of trying to represent her constituency. Certainly, Sarojini herself was very far from being an ignorant, unskilled and subservient housewife and mother as she makes her position out to be. In her policy perspective for the Congress, she stresses the Gandhian programme of village reconstruction as a solution to the problems of poverty and colonialism. She then emphasises her two pet themes, education and Hindu-Muslim unity, before ending on a characteristically sublime note with a quotation from the Upanishads.

Like her poetry, Sarojini's speeches were primarily emotional. They do not usually embody original ideas or theories, but reflect current, politically correct notions. She was a nationalist and a Congressite, a follower first of Gokhale and then of Gandhi. Most of what she said were the opinions of the Congress Party. But there were some issues which were dear to her heart. These she went back to again and again. One was education, especially the education of women. For Sarojini education was much more than book learning. It was, in essence, the realisation of the equality and fraternity of all human beings which followed upon the extirpation of all prejudices and chauvinisms. She also believed in the cultural and political unity of India, in its great past and even more glorious future as an independent country. She believed that this would only be possible through a national uprising in which the consciousness of the masses was raised by an elite. And this could be done through educating that elite to fulfil the role that history had given it.

In this sense, she was a diehard liberal. All the causes that she espoused, including her life-long championing of Hindu–Muslim unity and of the rights of women, were premised upon this liberalism. In the first cause, history proved her to be naive. She made lofty appeals to the higher sentiments in her audiences and moved them as few other orators did. But she often ignored the real motives of people and seemed to have a dim grasp of how central the struggle for power and dominance was in politics. As far as her role in the women's movement is concerned, she similarly believed in the benevolence of the patriarchy in India. When abroad she often clarified that she was not a feminist because India did not need Western-style feminism. She believed that conflicts between the sexes could be resolved through cooperation and not through confrontation. This was not so much a liberal feminism as a belief in Sarvodaya or commonweal. She considered society to be a totality and did not believe in the salvation of any single group or faction by itself. Nor did she, who had preached against narrow sectarianism, wish to be identified with any one special interest group. She did not subscribe to the solipsism of the group just as she didn't to the solipsism of the individual.

The appeal of Sarojini's rhetoric lay in her ability to strike the sublime key. It was Gandhi who gave her the title 'Bharat Kokila,' or the Nightingale of India. This was as much because of her speeches as of her poetry. As Harindranath Chattopadhyaya, her brother, observed:

> Sarojini came to be called Bulbul-i-Hind, the Nightingale of India, not, I am convinced, because of her verse, but because of her extraordinary oratory which poured through her like music, silver shot with gold, cataracting from summits of sheer

inspiration. (Quoted in Izzat Yar Khan 1883, 17)

In his tribute to her in Parliament, Nehru observed how she 'infused artistry and poetry into the national struggle' (Baig 1974, 163). It is as a practitioner of the sublime that she is memorable as a prose writer. It was her gift to shift the attention from the nitty-gritty of politics to the solace of some eternal ideals and principles. Her prose is, thus, more poetic than some of her nationalistic poetry, which is prosaic. Throughout, her sense of humour remained unfazed. In her 'Remarks' during the Convocation Address of Allahabad University, delivered just a month before she died, she made several light-hearted comments on the eminent personalities, including the Prime Minister, who had been conferred honorary doctorates. This shows what an original personality she was, witty, vain, irreverent, boisterous and utterly engaging.

8.6 CONCLUSION

All told, Sarojini's writings and letters offer us a vivid portrait of her multi-faceted personality. They reveal a woman who had a disease-prone body but an indomitable spirit, who could stand great pain and suffering but yet come out of it unscarred. She could laugh at herself and at others, with great panache and presence of mind. The poetess loved company and got along with a wide variety of people, she was broadminded and open to new ideas. With a unique capacity to enjoy herself even under adverse circumstances, she displayed patience and fortitude, that could and often did offer solace and comfort to others around her. Aware of the important role she was playing in India's national life, was confident and self-assured. Sarojini was both a great wag and a wit, with the discipline to make her personal life subservient to her public obligations – essentially optimistic and forward looking. With an inner faith which gave her strength, she was utterly free from prejudice of any kind be it caste, race or gender, nation or religion. Not a feminist but worked for the cause of Indian women, who though bourgeois in sensibility, values, beliefs, was yet an anti-imperialist, who loved spring and the bounties of nature, she tried to be a loyal wife and conscientious mother. This truly remarkable women worked tirelessly for Hindu–Muslim unity, who until the last days of her life showed rare solicitude for others. In short, managed the ambivalences and contrary pulls of her character as also her times to make her life both worthwhile and memorable.

Ultimately, the source of her strength was a deep and abiding inner faith. In her letter of 2 September 1920 to Gandhi she explained

> Immediate or apparent failure leaves me undismayed or even [un]disturbed in my inmost self because I am so certain of ultimate and real success. For I believe all thoughts and endeavours that are born of intense conviction are the guarantee of their own abiding triumph. (Paranjape 1996, 152)

Such confidence was unusual and remarkable even in the optimistic times she lived in. That Sarojini had intimations of a higher consciousness is clear from several letters and poems, but the fullest and clearest description of a transcendental experience is found in her letter of 2 August 1932 to Padmaja. Written from jail, the letter is also a statement of her most intimate beliefs. Sarojini realises that it is 'the lovely lyric' Shravan, the month of festivals, the month of Janmashtami, Nag Panchami and Raksha Bandhan:

> The world outside will be engrossed in commemorations and ceremonials with pageantry, music, crowds and all the colour and tumult of mass adoration...And yet...I wonder, if all the millions of worshippers in the sombre and splendid temples, steeped and drowned in the symbolism and gorgeous rituals of prayer and praise can ever 'realise God' as the phrase goes...so intimately and deeply, with so keen and sweet a consciousness of communion as one prisoner in a high-walled prison garden standing in the magic hour between sunset and sunrise in a shining sea of lilies...lilies, lilies, lilies, foam-white, pearl-white as clouds and the breasts of swans, white as manna and milk and the miracle of silver filigree

beaten out on fairy anvils into chalices of incense and nectar. Truly, Beauty is the Face of God and the perfume of Beauty his breath...And who needs to go on a longer pilgrimage than to step down from a roofed and walled chamber into the green and fragrant place where the Beauty of all Beauty exalts the Soul of the Seeker and Love, the Singer, the Dreamer whose vision knows no barriers and horizons....(Unpublished manuscript in Nehru Memorial Library)

Not unexpectedly, this passage reaches its climax in an almost mystical celebration of flowers. But in the beauty of the lilies, Sarojini sees a fusion of God as Beauty and God as Love. Poet, lover, seeker, dreamer – all find their unity in this passage, creating a rare coherence. This was the core of Sarojini's life, this fusion of reality and imagination, beauty and truth, love and God. This vision of the fundamental unity of the most cherished values of her life gave direction and substance to her various endeavours. In this sense, Sarojini was a traditional and not a modern person. Her life coheres, despite terrific oppositions; it does not fall apart into fragments.

Moreover, there is, as Nehru once said, something magical about those times, the whole struggle for independence:

> What a strange period this has been in India's history and the story, with all its ups and downs and triumphs and defeats, has the quality of a ballad or a romance. Even our trivial lives were touched by a halo of romance, because we lived through this period and were actors in greater or lesser degree, in the great drama of India. (Mahadevan 1989, 4)

It is possible though vicariously, to be touched by this romance while working on Sarojini. Through her a way of reading was found, accessing the rest of the major figures of that era. It is convincing that Indian academics, if it is to be meaningful, must locate itself in the larger tradition of modern Indian intellectual life. This begins with India's response to the west in the early nineteenth century and reaches its apogee during the anti-imperial struggle in the first half of this century. The writings of Sarojini Naidu constitute one additional and not insignificant set of documents in this still ongoing and unfolding grand narrative.

WORKS CITED

Abbas, K.A. 1980. *Sarojini Naidu*. Bombay: Bharatiya Vidya Bhavan.
Anand, Mulk Raj. 1933. *The Golden Breath: Studies in Five Poets of New India*. London: John Murray.
Ayyar, Subramanya P.A. 1957. *Sarojini Devi*. Madras: Cultural Books.
Baig, Tara Ali. 1974. *Sarojini Naidu*. New Delhi: Publications Division.
Basu, Lotika. 1933. *Indian Writers of English Verse*. Calcutta: University of Calcutta.
Bhatnagar, Ram Ratan. 1954. *Sarojini Naidu: The Poet of a Nation*. Allahabad: Kitabistan.
Bhushan, V. N. 1945. *The Peacock Lute*. Bombay: Padma Publication.
Chattopadhyaya, Harindranath. 1948. *Life and Myself*. Bombay: Nalanda.
Chavan, Sunanda. 1984. *The Fair Voice: A Study of Indian Women Poets in English*. New Delhi: Sterling.
Cousins, James H. 1918. *The Renaissance of India*. Madras: Ganesh and Co.
Dustoor, P. E. 1961. *Sarojini Naidu and Her Poetry*. Mysore: Rao and Raghavan.
Gupta A. N. and Satish Gupta, eds. 1982. *Sarojini Naidu: Select Poems*. Bareilly: Prakash Book Depot.
Gupta, Rameshwar. 1975. *Sarojini: The Poetess*. Delhi: Doaba House.
Home, Amal. *Sarojini Naidu: The Poet, the Patriot, the Orator, the Woman; Reminiscences*. 1949. Calcutta: Privately published by the author.
Iyengar, K. R. Srinivasa. 1983. *Indian Writing in English*. 3rd edition. New Delhi: Sterling.
Jha, Amarnath. n.d. *Sarojini Naidu: A Personal Homage*. Allahabad: Indian Press.
Khan, Izzat Yar. 1983. *Sarojini Naidu: The Poet*. New Delhi: S. Chand and Co.
Kotoky, P. C. 1969. *Indo-English Poetry: A Study of Sri Aurobindo and Four Others*. Gauhati: Gauhati University.
Mahadevan, T. K., Ed. 1989. *Mahatma Gandhi: Reflections on His Personality and Teachings*. Bombay: Bharatiya Vidya Bhavan.

Murthy, K.V. Suryanarayana. 1987. *Kohinoor in the Crown: Critical Studies in Indian English Literature*. New Delhi: Sterling.

Nagarajan S. 1989. 'Sarojini Naidu and the Dilemma of English in India' In *Kavya Bharati* 1: 23-43.

Nageswara Rao, G. 1986. *Hidden Eternity: A Study of the Poetry of Sarojini Naidu*. Tirupati: S.V. University.

Naik, M.K. et al. Eds. 1977. *Critical Essays on Indian Writing in English*. Madras: Macmillan.

———. Ed. 1984. *Perspectives on Indian Poetry in English*. New Delhi: Abhinav Publishers.

Naidu, Sarojini. 1893. *Mehir Muneer: A Poem in Three Cantos by a Brahmin Girl*. Madras: Srinivasa Varadachari and Co.

———. 1896. *Songs* by Miss S. Chattopadhyaya. Hyderabad: for private circulation.

———. 1905. *The Golden Threshold*. Introduced by Arthur Symons. London: Heinemann.

———. 1912. The Bird of Time: Songs of Love, Death and the Spring. Introduced by Edmund Gosse. London: Heinemann.

———. 1915. Gokhale the Man. (Booklet). Hyderabad: A. V. Pillai and Sons.

———. 1917. The Broken Wing: Songs of Love, Death and the Spring, 1915-1916. London: Heinemann.

———. (1917) 1919. *The Soul of India*. (Booklet). 2nd edition. Madras: The Cambridge Press.

———. (1918) 1925. *Speeches and Writings of Sarojini Naidu*. 3rd edition. Edited by G. A. Natesan. Madras: Natesan.

———. 1921. *Ideals of Islam*. (Booklet). Dacca: Matri Bhandar.

———. 1925. *Presidential Address Delivered at the 40th National Congress*. (Booklet). Kanpur: Reception Committee of the Indian National Congress.

———. 1928. *The Sceptred Flute: Songs of India*. New York: Dodd, Mead and Co. Indian editions, Allahabad: Kitabistan, 1943, 1946, 1958, 1979.

———. 1930. *Select Poems*. Edited by H. G. Dalway Turnbull. Calcutta: Oxford University Press.

———. 1961. *The Feather of the Dawn*. Edited by Padmaja Naidu. Bombay: Asia Publishing House.

Nair, K.R. Ramachandran. 1987. *Three Indo-Anglian Poets: Henry Derozio,*

Toru Dutt and Sarojini Naidu. New Delhi: Sterling.
Narasimhaiah, C. D. 1969. *The Swan and the Eagle*. Shimla: Indian Institute of Advanced Studies.
Naravane, V. S. 1980. *Sarojini Naidu: An Introduction to Her Life, Work and Poetry.* New Delhi: Vikas.
Natesan, G. A. and Co. 1914. *Mrs. Sarojini Naidu: A Sketch of Her Life and an Appreciation of Her Books.* Madras: Natesan and Co.
National Archives. n. d. *Sarojini Naidu: Some Facets of Her Personality.* Booklet: New Delhi, National Archives.
Paranjape, Makarand, Ed. 1996. *Sarojini Naidu: Selected Letters, 1890s–1940s.* New Delhi: Kali for Women.
_____. Ed. 2010. *Sarojini Naidu: Selected Poetry and Prose.* 2nd edition. New Delhi: Rupa.
Raghavacharyulu, D.V.K., Ed. 1971. *The Two-fold Voice: Essays on Indian Writing in English.* Guntur: Navodaya.
Rajyalakshmi, P. V. 1977. *The Lyric Spring: A Study of the Poetry of Sarojini Naidu.* New Delhi: Abhinav Publishers.
Schiller, Frederick. 1975. 'On Naive and Sentimental Poetry.' http://www.schillerinstitute.org/transl/schiller_essays/naive_sentimental-1.html
Sengupta, Padmini. 1966. *Sarojini Naidu.* Bombay: Asia Publishing House.
_____. *Sarojini Naidu.* 1981. New Delhi: Sahitya Akademi.
Shahane V. S. and M. N. Sharma, Eds. 1980. *The Flute and the Drum.* Hyderabad: Osmania University.
Singh, Amritjit, Rajiva Verma and Irene Joshi, eds. 1981. *Indian Literature in English, 1827–1979: A Guide to Information Sources.* Detroit: Gale Research Company.
Tilak, Raghukul. 1981. *Sarojini Naidu: Select Poems.* New Delhi: Rama Brothers.
Verghese, C. Paul. 1971. *Problems of the Indian Creative Writer in English.* Bombay: Somaiya.
Vishwanatham, K. 1969. 'The Nightingale and the Naughty Gal.' *Banasthali Patrika* 12: 127–40.
Wilhelm, J J. 1990. *Ezra Pound in London and Paris: 1908–1925.* University Park: The Pennsylvania State University Press.

9
'HOME AND THE WORLD': COLONIALISM AND ALTERNATIVITY IN TAGORE'S INDIA

9.1 REWORLDING HOMES

In the nostalgic opening of his essay 'Imaginary Homelands,' Salman Rushdie gives us a way of thinking of home as a lost past. Looking at a photograph of his family home in the Bombay of 1946, before he was even born, he says that it reminds him that 'it's my present that is foreign and that the past is home, albeit a lost home in a lost city in the mists of lost time.' (Rushdie 1991, 9)[1] 'The house is rather peculiar – a three-storied gabled affair with tiled roofs and round towers in two corners, each wearing a pointy tiled hat' (ibid.). Indeed, when Rushdie does revisit his 'lost city,' he finds his father's name still in the telephone directory, the number unchanged: 'It was an eerie discovery' (ibid.), he says. And when he actually visits the house in the photograph, he is 'overwhelmed':

> The colours of my history had seeped out of my mind's eye; now my other two eyes were assaulted by colours, by the vividness of the of the red tiles, the yellow-edged green of cactus-leaves, the brilliance of bougainvillaea creeper. It is probably not too romantic to say that that was when my novel *Midnight's Children* was really born.... (ibid.)

The word 'eerie' in this ephiphanic moment of return, suggests that what has happened is an instance of the uncanny, when something is at once homely and foreign, strangely familiar. In Rushdie's case, a great creative upsurge results from the emotional release that accompanies the return of the repressed.

Obviously, the incident also brings to mind Sigmund Freud's famous essay 'The Uncanny' (Das Unheimliche) of 1919. As Freud says, 'In this case too, then, the *unheimlich* is what was once *heimisch,* familiar; the prefix *'un'* ['un-'] is the token of repression' (Freud 1919). For our purposes, what is interesting is that the original German word that Freud used to define the uncanny was 'unheimlich,' unhomely, the opposite of 'heimlich' or homely. As Homi Bhabha says, using exactly these words,

> In the House of Fiction you can hear, today, the deep stirring of the 'unhomely.' You must permit me this awkward word – the unhomely – because it captures something of the estranging sense of the relocation of the home and the world in an unhallowed place. To be unhomed is not to be homeless, nor can the 'unhomely' be easily accommodated in that familiar division of social life into private and the public spheres. (Bhabha 1992, 141)

Bhabha's remark is directly linked to Rushdie's assertion that the 'physical alienation' of him and other diasporic writers compels them to 'create fictions, not actual cities or villages, but invisible ones, imaginary homelands, Indias of the mind' (Rushdie 1991, 10). Writers like Rushdie and critics like Homi Bhabha have contributed to the idea that being a migrant is the chief characteristic of the post-condition. In *The Location of Culture,* Bhaba goes on to equate this condition with that of 'world literature' itself:

> The study of world literature might be the study of the way in which cultures recognise themselves through their projections of 'otherness.' Where the transmission of 'national' traditions was once the major theme of a world literature, perhaps we can now suggest that transnational histories of migrants, the

colonised, or political refugees – these border and frontier conditions – may be the terrains of World Literature. The centre of such a study would neither be the 'sovereignty' of national cultures, nor the 'universalism' of human culture, but a focus on those 'freak displacements' – such as Morrison and Gordimer display – that have been caused within cultural lives of postcolonial societies. If these were considered the paradigm cases of a world literature based on the trauma of history and the conflict of nations, then Walter Benjamin's homeless modern novelist would be the representative figure of an 'unhomely' world literature. (Bhabha 1994, 17)

It is this turning of the 'unhomed' into the paradigmatic condition of our times that I shall interrogate later.

At the beginning of 'The World and the Home,' the earlier and related essay that I quoted from, Bhabha is echoing, as I mentioned, Freud's sense of the 'uncanny,' where he reflects upon the uneasy sense of the unfamiliar within the familiar, the unhomely within the home. In that essay, Freud pays attention to the way the word homely, meaning 'belonging to the house, not strange, familiar, tame, intimate' (Freud 1919) is also defined by what seems to be its apparent opposite 'concealed, kept from sight...withheld from others' (ibid.). In this slippage between homely and unhomely, what is supposedly outside the home but actually inhabiting it all along and reappearing only with the return of the repressed is what really interests me.

In his reading of Heidegger, Mark Wigley argues that the familiar, the homely, the house are produced precisely by masking the unfamiliar, so that the house always veils a fundamental unfamiliarity. For Heidegger, the uncanny is the sense of '"not being at home in the home," an alienation from the house experienced within it' (Quoted in Wigley 1995, 110). Further, Heidegger argues that it is only by being positioned outside of home that the home and the structures on which it relies can be perceived; 'home,' he writes, 'is precisely the place where the essence of home is most concealed' (114). Such ideas of home seem quite contrary to what is normally considered its basic sense – that of home being not just a dwelling or residence, but also a shelter, a place where 'one's domestic affections are centered' (*Dictionary.com*). It is, in the ordinary sense, a place of comfort and security, a retreat from the world perhaps, a space for growing up and reaching maturity, of rest, restitution and recuperation. But when we reflect on how often home is also a trap, a prison, an oppressive space of confinement and restriction, of stasis and stultification, or, in a word, the site of repression from which we seek to escape to be free, to realise ourselves, then the whole complex and contradictory nature of home becomes obvious.

This is one reason why Partha Chatterjee's celebrated dichotomy between the inside and outside, home and the world, as a way of understanding the nationalist resolution of the women's question in India becomes difficult to accept. Chatterjee says:

> The discourse of nationalism shows that the material/spiritual distinction was condensed into an analogous, but ideologically far more powerful, dichotomy: that between the outer and the inner....Now apply the inner/outer distinction to the matter of concrete day-to-day living and you get a separation of the social space into *ghar* and *bahir*, the home and the world. The world is the external, the domain of the material; the home represents our inner spiritual self, our true identity. The world is a treacherous terrain of the pursuit of material interests, where practical considerations reign supreme. It is also typically the domain of the male. The home in its essence must remain unaffected by the profane activities of the material world – and woman is its representation. And so we get an identification of social roles by gender to correspond with the separation of the social space into *ghar* and *bahir*. (Chatterjee 1989, 239)

Developing these ideas in his subsequent book *The Nation and Its Fragments*, Chatterjee argues:

> The colonial situation and the ideological response of nationalism to the critique of Indian tradition, introduced an entirely new

> substance to these terms and effected their transformation. The material/ spiritual dichotomy, to which the terms world and home corresponded, had acquired...a very special significance in the nationalist mind. The world was where the European power had challenged the non-European peoples and, by virtue of its superior material culture, had subjugated them. But the nationalists asserted, it had failed to colonise the inner, essential identity of the East, which lay in its distinctive and superior spiritual culture. Here the East was undominated and master of its own fate...But in the entire phase of the national struggle, the crucial need was to protect, preserve and strengthen the inner core of the national culture, its spiritual essence. No encroachments by the coloniser must be allowed in that inner sanctum. In the world, imitation of and adaptation to Western norms was a necessity; at home, they were tantamount to annihilation of one's very identity...Once we match this new meaning of the home/world dichotomy to the identification of social roles by gender, we get the ideological framework within which nationalism answered the woman's question... the nationalist paradigm...supplied an ideological principle of selection. It was not a dismissal of modernity but an attempt to make modernity consistent with the nationalist project. (Chatterjee 1993, 121)

But as our long preceding discussion shows, home has become an unfamiliar place and is often 'lost,' while what is strange and alien seems radically familiar to us. The home, moreover, as a site of repression, is actually unable to keep the threatening, contaminated space of the outside from penetrating deep within its innermost spaces. These spaces, in turn, seep or leak outside the home in deeply uncomfortable ways. While historians such as Ayesha Jalal may find Chatterjee's dichotomy 'both analytically and empirically unsustainable' (Jalal 2001, 263), I have tried to show that it is psychologically unconvincing and culturally unsustainable. The best example of this is the Rabindranath Tagore novel *Ghare Baire* from which the terms seem to have suggested themselves in the first place and which is the subject of this chapter.

If we turn from the home to the world, the latter suggests the earth and all its inhabitants, the totality of the different countries and peoples living on the planet, even the universe as a whole; more specifically it means humankind, people, or a 'sphere of activity,' or the state of the world (*American Heritage Dictionary*). Both home and world, though, suggest spaces – in that sense, the home is also a world and the world is, or ought to be, our home. Like the idea of home, the idea of the world has also received much attention in post-colonial discourse. If Bhabha has commented on the former, it is Gayatri Chakravorty Spivak, who invoking Martin Heidegger, refashions the idea of 'worlding.' She argues that if we were to remember that 'imperialism, understood as England's social mission, was a crucial part of the cultural representation of England to the English' and the 'role of literature in the production of cultural representation' was crucial (Spivak 1985, 243),

> ...we would produce a narrative, in literary history, of the 'worlding' of what is now called 'the Third World.' To consider the Third World as distant cultures, exploited but with rich intact literary heritages waiting to be recovered, interpreted and curricularised in English translation fosters the emergence of 'the Third World' as a signifier that allows us to forget that 'worlding,' even as it expands the empire of the literary discipline. (ibid.)2

In other words, the world is not a given, but is 'worlded' in a certain way by forces such as imperialism so that this very fashioning is often forgotten when we consider the texts of the colonised. It could be argued that those who are 'unhomed' like Rushdie, Bhabha and Spivak, produce with the power of the metropolitan discourses, their own type of worlding. In this worlding, however, it is home and the various things it stands for that become unhoused, scattered, dispersed, marginalised.

But in speaking of the home and the world, it would be impossible, at least for a contemporary Indian, not to think of Rabindranath

Tagore's classic *Ghare Baire,* or its English translation by Surendranath Tagore, *The Home and the World.* Indeed, the title of Bhabha's essay is an (un)self-conscious inversion of Tagore's and Chatterjee's categories are also richly allusive of it. While Chatterjee does not refer to Tagore's text at all, Bhabha, though he mentions it, does not reflect on his play on its title, nor does he analyse the text in detail. After all, unlike most of the other authors he considers, Tagore was securely, if sometimes not entirely comfortably, located in not only in the 'home of his language,' Bangla, but in Bengal and India itself. Consequently, he does not represent the 'transnational histories of migrants, the colonised, or political refugee – these border and frontier conditions' (Bhabha 1994, 17) that Bhabha valorises. Yet, neither does Tagore narrate 'sovereign' national cultures that Bhabha defines as contrasting the 'freak displacements' that he considers central to the 'cultural lives of postcolonial societies' (ibid.). Yet, it can be suggested that in a novel like *Ghare Baire,* Tagore does portray 'the trauma of history and the conflict of nations' (Bhabha 1992, 146). Could it be, then, that Bhabha's categories do not quite hold, that novelists well-housed in their own native cultures and societies can also produce 'paradigmatic' literature about the modern condition? The relationship between home and the world, in other words, is so intertwined that privileging one over the other only creates a distortion and disequilibrium of the sort that Spivak had warned us against. The implications of which are the 'worlding' of the unhomed in a kind of 'first world' of modernity and the privileging of the interstitial or in-between spaces between home and host countries such as only diasporas are supposed to occupy. Or as Rosemary Marangoly George at very beginning of *The Politics of Home* phrases it,

> As imagined in fiction, 'home' is a desire that is fulfilled or denied in varying measure to the subjects (both the fictional characters and the readers) constructed by the narrative. As such, 'home' moves along several axes and yet it is usually represented as fixed, rooted, stable – the very antithesis of travel. (George 1989, 1)

And she comes to such a conclusion after reading world writers in English, not those who might be conventionally placed in national literatures. Fiction blurs the space between the home and the world, resisting the construction of the home as a purely private place or the national as solely a public arena. The 'unhomed' writers that Rushdie and Bhabha celebrate are, in some ways, very much at home both in the West, where they usually find themselves, as well as their native countries, where they return for their fictional succour and are often treated as celebrities, besides being studied more diligently and widely than in the West.

Through this discussion of Bhabha and Spivak, we return 'home' to the primacy of the national in the period under study. It is national culture rather than the liminal space of dispersal that canonical writers in this book are preoccupied with. Of course, to them the question of displaced peoples all over the world was tied up closely to the logic of imperialism itself, which caused such upheavals. To these writers, home and the world were not oppositional or dichotomous. Rather they were closely involved with one another. Especially a writer like Tagore, who though the most widely travelled of all the leading Indian writers of his time, was very much at home in the world. Even today, the cultural contact between India and the other nations of the modern world in countries as far-flung as Argentina and Japan is traced to Tagore's first visit to their shores. In the re-worlding that decolonisation would effect, Tagore, who always returned home, played an important role as a forerunner. Tagore's nationalism did not contradict his universalism; though deeply rooted in his own culture, the world was his home.

9.2 COLONIALISM AND CONSCIOUSNESS

Before turning to Tagore's text, a very quick clarification would point to the obvious difference between the original and the English version. While *ghare* may well be rendered as '(at) home,' how could we justify *baire* being translated as 'world'? *Baire*, more properly, suggests 'outside,' rather than the world. The contrast in the original, then, is more between the inside and the outside of a home, between the private and the public, than between the home and the world. The word *baire*, thus, implies that a person is outside the home, perhaps at large in the world, but may well return. As in: 'She's away but is likely to be back at some time.' It is this possibility of return that Tagore's original retains and which is lost in translation that makes the crucial difference between the two. In either case, the category on which the contrast between the *ghare* and the *baire* or the home and what lies outside it, hinges is *ghar* or home. Accompanying that word are of course its very rich and connotative possibilities, some of which it might be useful to unpack further.

Does 'home' refer to one specific home or to something larger? Does it refer, for instance, to a region, such as Calcutta, when we say that Calcutta is our home? Or does home refer to Bengal? Or to India itself? Or to any place where we feel at home, however far away we might actually be from home? As Sankara says, 'Svadesho bhuvanam trayam' – all the three worlds are my home.[3] But what about a home in which we do not feel at home, where we feel alienated and out of place? A home in which we experience dislocation and even death? This also begs the question of what we mean by 'outside?' Is being outside the same is being settled elsewhere, being an exile or expatriate or a diasporic person? Does it mean that one is permanently displaced or away for the time being, travelling outside one's normal habitation for a while? But what if someone is always away, or as Dom Moraes once considered himself, is *Never at Home* (which is actually the title of his autobiography)?

Our home may actually be something rather small, like our bodies, though we may feel peculiarly uncomfortable with/in them. Is the home, our home exclusively or a place we share with others? Our home may be a very small part of the real world, confined in fact, just to one building, or even more restrictively, to our physical bodies. On the other hand, our home, our real self may be very inclusive, embracing many others. As Whitman announced in 'Song of Myself': 'I am vast; I contain multitudes.' Or it could be an even wider, ever-expanding space, *akhanda brahmanda mandala*, as the seers of the

Upanishads proclaimed, an infinite arrangement of galaxies.

It is obvious from these ruminations that both home and the world have many levels of meaning from the ontological, metaphysical, psychological, sociological, to the cosmological, from the merely literal to the richly metaphorical, from the poetic to the ideological. What is more, none of these meanings can be set aside entirely, no matter how restrictive we choose to be. Questions of colonialism, culture and change, such as we have been addressing, are therefore implicated in larger universes of meaning and signification which we can deny only at our own peril. These questions are ultimately questions of consciousness. Curiously enough, this is one point on which we might actually have a convergence between diametrically opposed ideologies such as Marxism and practical Vedanta. To change the world also means to change our consciousness of it as also of our roles, our very selves in it. What happened in Bengal in the nineteenth century was precisely about changing the consciousness not just of some characters but of this country itself. At the very heart of this clash of cultures, the collision between British imperialism and Indian society, were questions of autonomy, self-hood, or to use a Gandhian word, svaraj. It is even possible to go so far as to say that the whole project of imagining or forging a nation was but a subset of this larger question of autonomy or svaraj.

Power and resistance to power, which might be seen as the dominant tropes of the encounter between the colonisers and the colonised, embody, in the final analysis, a struggle for autonomy, for selfhood and for svaraj. These exertions over the meaning of a new individuality and a new collectivity were really about imagining into being the condition for the creation of a economic, political, social, cultural order in which the humanity, dignity, equality and autonomy of the individual could be maintained. That is why it seems important that the kind of phenomenology of this period that we are attempting gets the vocabulary and the idioms of these struggles right. Words like svaraj have a resonance and dimension, which is irreducible to any other synonym or substitute. While we need to be critical in the usage of such words, it is also enabling to define the terms of discourse and to frame them in a culturally responsible and rooted manner.

And here the issue of translation is at the very core of our concerns. To deal with literary and cultural encounters in colonial and post-colonial India, then, is to confront the question of translation. That is because we have to grapple with two or more languages of being, two or more ways of seeing the world, two or more systems of cognition. To erase this multiplicity and difference is to deny the complexity of this encounter, to reduce it to this or that usually political motive. It is to do violence to our own past and present, not to speak of irreparable damage to our future. What is needed, therefore, is to be cognisant of two or more modes of being and reference, without collapsing the one into the other. This requires a kind of critical perspectivism that has a sort of double or multiple vision, the capacity simultaneously to have a dual focus.

If so, what is the relationship between the *ghar* and the *bahir*, the inner and the outer, the private and the public, the personal and the political, psycho-spiritual and the socio-economic, the native and the colonial, the Indian and the Western – in a word, between the home and the world? It is clear that there is no obvious conflict or dichotomy between the two, that they are not mutually exclusive. Instead, there seems to be continuous interrelationship between the two. The personal is the political, as is all too familiar to us by now. The quest for conjugal happiness in *Ghare Baire* is thus directly linked to the struggle for a new India. Why is this point of such great importance? That is because the world in which the novel is set, is out of joint and to set it right requires the kind of reorientation which will also transform the most personal of relationships. This is what we believe Tagore suggests to us.

Yet we must see these two poles as not being related dialectically as much as dialogically. In dialectics, one side cancels or supersedes the other before it is in turn cancelled or superseded. Such a mechanism of endless opposition does not produce the kind of breakthrough in which both can not only co-exist but get transformed. It would be preferable to see the interpenetration of opposites in a manner, which is dialogic so that what is produced is not antithesis versus thesis but a sort of third space. This third space is not Bhabha's interstitial space between the nation and nationlessness – a sort of grey area that the diaspora is supposed to occupy. Rather, it is the possibility inherent in the here and now of every situation of conflict or competition, a finger of hope pointing to what is neither oppressed or oppressive, neither victimiser nor victim, neither dominant nor subordinate, but something else, something autonomous without being either subservient or repressive. This is the space of non-violent action, of autonomy and of svaraj.

The encounter between the colonisers and the colonised is marked not just by the exercise of power and of various kinds of resistance to power, but also by the struggle for autonomy and selfhood, the aspiration for svaraj and dignity. Always, such a struggle is not just about changing material conditions and structures of being, but also about the creation of a new consciousness. Also the very act of engaging in such a process or even talking about it is only possible through some type or the other of translation or multilingualism, in which more than one set of terms or discourse styles will have to be adopted. Finally, a successful marking of issues and insights will produce a sort of third space that is neither coloniser nor colonised, neither oppressor nor oppressed, neither victimiser nor victim, but something else that defies such dichotomies and liberates us from them.

9.3 SOME NINETEENTH CENTURY TYPES

Having suggested what is the crucial tropes or recurrent motifs of the encounters between the colonisers and the colonised in the previous chapters, let us revisit them briefly here in a slightly modified form. Reductive or over-simplistic though such an exercise might be, it will still serve to refresh the positions already discussed in the previous chapters.

To start with, let us reconsider Ram Mohan Roy, the emblematic figure who appears at the very beginnings of the Bengal renaissance and the creation of Indian modernity. Placed at the very beginning of the most crucial phase of the Indo-British encounter, his life and work offers a telling narrative of the progress of colonialism in India. What we find in Roy are greater possibilities of autonomy and svaraj than in a later figure like Michael Madhusudan Dutt. That is because imperialism is not yet fully established and instutionalised in Ram Mohan's time. Those who wish to see a unilinear progression of imperialistic dominance and hegemony will therefore be disappointed. Just as the conservatives who ruled Britain had a greater respect for native cultures of India than the liberals who followed them, the beginnings of British paramountcy in India actually afforded greater spaces for native agency than the later decades of empire. What makes Bengal so interesting is that if offers the entire colonial spectrum in graphic clarity.

Yet to revert to Ram Mohan Roy, his letter of 1823 to Lord Amherst would characterise a substantiation of a certain position in the Indo-British encounter. He requests the British government to 'promote a more liberal and enlightened system of instruction, embracing Mathematics, Natural Philosophy, Chemistry and Anatomy with other useful sciences' (Roy, 1990, 98) after denying the usefulness of Sanskrit learning in all its available branches at that time. It could be called the insufficiency thesis. Ram Mohan Roy's basic argument is that traditional knowledge in India, whether it is Vyakaran (grammar), Vedanta (a branch of classical philosophy), Mimamsa (another branch of Indian philosophy) or Nyaya (logic) is inadequate. In fact, he demolishes and even mocks these 'sciences' one by one, showing how ridiculous they are in the light of contemporary Western learning. What is therefore required for India's progress, he contends, is the infusion of Western knowledge, which can only be done through English. Of course, it is crucial to distinguish Ram Mohan Roy's position from that of Macaulay's. Ram Mohan Roy by no means indulges in a blanket dismissal of all the intellectual traditions of India as did Macaulay. Yet, the tone of his description of traditional learning in India is satirical bordering on the contemptuous. He does discredit this knowledge as being inconsequential to the point of being farcical and ludicrous. But unlike Macaulay, he does not believe that the solution lies in absorbing European literature. Rather, he asks for Chemistry, Astronomy and other practical arts and sciences, following the recommendations of Calvinist missionaries like William Carey. Ram Mohan wants a revolution in India not too different from what happened in Europe. He is therefore an indigenous champion of an Enlightenment that cannot, when we examine world history, be considered the sole preserve of Europeans.

This insufficiency thesis finds its most vocal supporters in what came to be called the Young Bengal group. Though its members were rather different and distinctive, we have already picked on Michael Madhusudan Dutt as a good representative. While Ram Mohun Roy resisted conversion to Christianity, but rationalised and modernised Hinduism, Madhusudan went over completely, even losing his patrimony and community in the bargain. His return to Bengal and Bengali after an unsuccessful foray into complete Anglicisation has often been seen as the classic embodiment of the recurrent pattern of the loss and recovery of the self under colonialism. Whether the loss was total in the first place is debatable as is the question of the nature and extent of the recovery. What is more certain, however, is that there is no simple passage possible between the world of the colonised to the world of the colonisers. Is Madhusudan's rewriting of the *Ramayana* more than merely a critique of tradition? By making the 'manly' Meghnad the hero who is outwitted and defeated by the more effeminate and devious Rama and Lakshmana, is Madhusudan doing more than just inverting the power structure of the traditional epic? Are Rama and Lakshmana like the British in India, who came to trade but stayed to rule? While these questions remain unanswered, it is clear that by-and-large Madhusudan considered Hindu society to be morally bankrupt and culturally decadent. A new creation could take place only with a substantial rupture with the past. The rotten trunk of the old Hindu civilisation would have to be cut off before something new and better could grow.

Sri Ramakrishna, the great spiritual master and guru of Swami Vivekananda, an unlettered but vastly gifted religious leader, endowed with a definite sense of a grander purpose, may be seen as exemplifying the opposite position of the spiritual, if not the cultural and intellectual, self-sufficiency of India. From a rustic and non-literary background, he nevertheless shows a great erudition in the older tradition of oral wisdom. That this was actually a classical tradition, not just a subaltern one is clear, when we see the number and quality of his preceptors, starting with the Bhairavi Brahmani, his Tantric guru and ending with his formal Vedantic guru, the sannyasi, Totapuri. The order of sannyasins that he inspired was thus an offshoot of the much older tradition of intellectual leadership instituted by Sankara. That he could tame, domesticate and transform a modern positivist like Narendranath Dutta in the 'volcanic,' if cosmopolitan Swami Vivekananda, can be read as the allegory of the synergy, if not triumph of tradition over modernity. We can be reasonably certain that one of the causes of the decline of the Brahmo Samaj was its reintegration into a modernised and reconstructed Hinduism that Sri Ramakrishna was instrumental in inspiring. Not just Vivekananda, but Keshub Chandra Sen and a whole generation of Western educated 'progressive' young men came under Ramakrishna's influence. Not just the viability but the inventiveness of Indian traditions was demonstrated. Ramakrishna reinvented Hinduism in terms of the *sarva dharma samabhava* (equality towards all religions), that Gandhi later made the fulcrum of a new nationalist consciousness.

Between these two poles of insufficiency and self-sufficiency are a host of interesting and challenging figures. Bankim, on the one hand, who is seen nowadays as the progenitor of a certain kind of Hindu communalism, but who was more properly a moderniser and anti-colonialist, not to speak of the father of modern Bengali prose. Not just Bankim, but Vivekananda, Sri Aurobindo and Subhas Chandra Bose all represent a certain masculinist type of resistance to colonialism. Aurobindo's project, ultimately, went much beyond revolutionary anti-imperialism to a kind of transformative futurism or spiritual evolutionism that would result in a mutation in human consciousness and a radical metamorphosis in terrestrial life. Bose's authoritarian militarism as Nehru's secularist Fabianism were also experiments that follow between these two poles of insufficiency and self-sufficiency. Neither Bose's militarism, which still has its adherents, nor Nehruvian secularism, which was the state ideology for decades, have not been entirely able to dislodge Gandhian spiritualist-humanism as a key element of the mentality of the nationalist bourgeoisie. But perhaps the most interesting of the intermediate figures is Tagore.

In Tagore's work and thought we see an attempt to attain a balance and mediate between these positions. In his texts, cultures are seen neither as sufficient or as insufficient in themselves but always in a process of negotiation and evolution. The static, the rigid, the fixed, the mechanical come under his critical scanner and disapproval. In his lectures on nationalism, for instance, Tagore attacks the mechanistic and aggressive urge to power that he saw as the European nation's characteristic and defining feature. Of course, we must also keep in mind that what Tagore means by nationalism in these lectures is actually that extension of the national that expresses itself as the imperial. In other words, though the lectures criticise nationalism, their real subject is imperialism.

Tagore was one of the several makers of modern India. Like Gandhi, Nehru and Maulana Azad, Tagore wanted the Indian experiment in nation-building to be somewhat different from the European one. The nation that he envisaged would steer clear of the narrow and exclusivist prejudices of states defined by a single identity, whether of language, religion, or ethnicity. At the same time, the universalism that he promoted did not imply either a capitulation to Western culture nor the erasure of the local, regional, or the national. An authentic cultural position did not mean a fanatical rejection of the Other nor an ingratiating submission to it. Neither collaboration nor conflict was the sole recourse of a vibrant and self-confident culture, but rather a continuous engagement with the particulars of a given situation. Coercion, consent and resistance did not exist in different compartments for Tagore, but were deeply intertwined.

9.4 RE-READING TAGORE

From such a perspective, if we examine his writings, we see a careful and critical mediation between political extremes at work in his most significant novel *Gora* (1907-1908). Through his eponymous protagonist, Tagore rejects both the extremes of Hindu fanaticism and comprador elitism. The first part of the book shows the inadequacy of the former, while British imperialism comes under attack later, somewhat indirectly. It is only when Gora goes to the countryside that he finds the brutal face of British rule. The oppression of the peasants and the economic pauperisation of the villages opens his eyes to the structural realities of imperialism behind the rather polite façade of paternalistic collaboration offered to the native bourgeoisie. From being a 'good' subject, Gora become as 'bad' subject and finds himself in jail. When he returns, he is disgusted to discover that he has become a 'national' hero. The very middle class which refuses to move a muscle to help the poor has now transferred the guilt of its apathy into adulation for him. Gora's long disappearance from the text serves to give the other characters the space to resolve their complicated personal and social relationships. Gora, in turn discovers what have been his own fatal flaws – first the neglect of and ignorance about the peasantry, but equally so, the suppression and disregard of the other half of India, its women. It is now that Suchorita's face appears in his mind's eye, merging with that of his mother, Anandamoyi, who is of course Mother India herself. He clearly understands that a new India can only be created by including and recognising its women. This will have to be a collaborative and cooperative project, harnessing the agencies and energies of both the sexes, not a hyper-masculinist imposition of the will of a strong man on the passive and compliant masses.

Tagore uses two couples to work out his vision of a new India. Binoy and Lalita serve not only as foils to Gora and Suchorita, but are perhaps the mainstay of the book. Binoy, not Gora is the real hero, because Binoy is closer to the average person. Gora's extremism invites the disapproval of the narrative voice. In *Gora* Tagore tells us that what appears to be most Hindu is actually least so. It is a foreign element masquerading as the authentic internal one. The West that we internalise is the real enemy, more dangerous than the West out there. Tamed of its semitic zeal, such an element may coexist with the others in a larger rainbow of many cultures that is India. But when it strives to dominate, taking over the whole spectrum of political and cultural possibilities, it must be tamed and neutralised. This only Suchorita's feminine sexual energy can do. Without her, Gora's cultural nationalism would turn pathological and destructive, not only to his own household, but to the nation in the making.

Gora ends with the major characters preparing for a long journey outside Calcutta. Their actions have raised a storm which must be allowed to subside before they can return. The seeds of a new society are to be nursed in another soil before they can be transplanted back. Tagore explores three formulae of nationalism in *Gora*. Hindu nationalism, based as it is upon an unrepentant and unreformed tradition is rejected, as is the slavish and imitative collaboration with the British raj that is represented by both Varadasundari and Pani Babu. The latter is an especially inapt, not to speak of inept, prospective groom for Suchorita because he would stifle and obliterate her soul, not for some higher cause but for the sake of his own already bloated ego. Such idolatry is intolerable to Tagore. Gora's own formula for what constitutes a true Indian is not cumulative. It is not the Punjab plus Sind plus Gujarat plus Maratha and so on that we celebrate in our national anthem penned by none other than Tagore himself; instead, it is arrived via negative, neti neti,[4] neither Punjab, nor Sind, nor Bangla, nor Brahmin, nor Dalit and so on. What is left, of course, is a sort of basic common denominator of humanity, shorn of all caste marks or identity tags. The real Indian is simply the essential man or woman. Paresh Babu, Anandamoyi and the two young couples qualify as the inheritors of an authentic Indian tradition as well as the progenitors of the new Indian nation. Together they form the basis of a new society that is yet to emerge fully as the novel ends.

Gora is an earlier text than *Ghare Baire* (1915-1916) but it anticipates it. Gora becomes Sandeep in *Ghare Baire* while Binoy is transformed into Nikhil. More importantly, from being Gora's *shakti* or supporting power, Suchorita is changed into Bimala, who is at the centre of *Ghare Baire* and Nikhil's wife. Instead of two couples, we have a triangle. While the device of two couples in *Gora* reduplicates the ideal of masculine-feminine bonding and partnership out of which the new India will be born, the love triangle in *Ghare Baire* ends in a catastrophe. Two men, representing different forces of history compete for her. She is Bengal – or even India – herself. Nikhil, virtuous, generous, decent and devoted, is also effete, condescending and somewhat apathetic. He lacks both the virility and the vitality of Sandeep. Sandeep too, because he is mendacious and unscrupulous, is unworthy of her. He represents the new emerging leadership of India drawn from the middle classes, while Nikhil stands for the dying, feudal aristocracy, which is losing its power. Bimala is 'seduced' by the emerging forces of history, which seem irresistible. She is deceived by the mask of idealism and national service that Sandeep wears, unable to fathom behind it his hunger for power and megalomania. Sandeep is exposed to be a selfish demagogue, a trickster ultimately, who unleashes vast and destructive forces. The novel and the film end rather differently. While the former is somewhat open-ended, leaving the final outcome of the catastrophe ambiguous, Ray's film is tighter showing the almost inevitable death of Nikhil. Ray begins the film at the end of the book, thus intensifying, as Andrew Robinson says, its 'sense of predestination': 'From its outset we know that Nikhil and the woman he loves are doomed' (Robinson 1987, 269). Interestingly, this is the reverse of how Ray treats *Nashtanir*; in his *Charulata,* he shows a more hopeful end than in Tagore's novella. My feeling is that Ray's moral code is more stringent than Tagore's; while Amal's innocence saves Charu, Sandeep's corruption dooms Bimala, who must share in it for consciously giving herself to it against the codes of her wifely *dharma*.

Bimala's education has been painful, to say the least. It has entailed not just leaving the secure comfort of her home, but stepping beyond the threshold of what is proper. Her return is marked by a realisation that is dearly bought. As Heidegger would say about the unhomely,

> This experience now becomes a way of learning how to freely use what is one's own....The journeying into the unhomely must go 'almost' to the threshold [grenze] of being annihilated in the fire, in order for the locality of the homely to bestow that which gladdens and saves. (Cited in Risser 1999, 344)

The novel ends without giving us the benefit of seeing how Bimala uses her newly acquired knowledge to gladden and save.

While *Ghare Baire* has been read as Tagore's critique of the swadeshi movement, it shows a more general suspicion of and distaste for politics, with its depiction of the amoral and often violent pursuit of power. It is also a commentary on the dynamics and tensions between the inner, more enclosed worlds of the domestic sphere and the rough-and-tumble of life on the outside. In the end, the latter invade the former and overrun them. Yet, the political implications of the love triangle show a clear indictment of colonialism. What, after all, is wrong with the marriage of Nikhil and Bimala? While the former is determined to educate his wife and give her the freedom to grow both intellectually and emotionally, this seems actually to be a ruse to evade the crucial problem of a lack of sexual passion or gratification in the marriage. We can interpret this to mean, in contradistinction to Partha Chatterjee, that the political invades the personal long before Sandeep, with his fiery brand of nationalism physically enters his sheltered household. Under colonialism, the colonised male invariably suffers a symbolic castration and emasculation. The comfort, even luxury of the life of a Zamindar's wife is still, as Bimala realises, bordering on the insipid or sterile. Even an average feudal marriage in 'colonised' times cannot be entirely satisfying or fruitful. The inequality institutionalised in the political sphere blights the marital bed of the protagonists. The novel, like many others set in those times such as *Devdas* or *Sahib, Bibi, Golam*, depicts the impossibility of a mutually satisfying and joyous relationship during colonial rule.[5] It is as if colonialism thwarts and frustrates eros and spurs thanatos. Sandeep, if only he had been noble, faithful and sincere, might actually have been the best partner for Bimala. However, neither Tagore nor his times would condone adultery. The love triangle ends in calamity.

Today, after he has been canonised and idolised so incontrovertibly, it is difficult to imagine just how much Tagore was reviled and abused in his lifetime. For this novel itself he was both praised by Yeats and scorned by Lukacs (see Datta 2002). His Indian readers considered the novel unpatriotic and anti-national. In one of his last essays on Tagore, Nirad C. Choudhury (1987) describes the poet's life as a lonely struggle against personal loss, economic difficulty and public scorn. He was not spared even when he died; his funeral turned into a fiasco, with unruly mobs disrupting the solemnity of the occasion. Certainly, *Ghare Baire* too invoked decades of criticism and abuse from varieties of readers and critics. Tagore was accused of having written a book promoting immorality and adultery. Yet, it is believed that it is only in this kind of intrepid and sometimes unpleasant mediation with various aspects of our complex realities that the quest for autonomy, whether personal or social, can be sought.

The seeds of the destruction that we have seen in *Ghare Baire* are already present in a compressed form in *Nastanir* (1901), translated as *The Broken Nest*. An added reason to review this text is because, like *Ghare Baire,* it was made into an equally exquisite film, *Charulata* (1964), by Satyajit Ray.

'He was not so much offended by the loss of the money, but this sudden revelation of treachery made him feel as if he had stepped from his room into a void.' (Tagore 1997, 68) – this is what happens to Bhupati, the protagonist, on discovering that his brother-in-law and manager, Umapati, has not only been cheating him, but is so brazen about it. Umapati has been caught misappropriating funds and misusing Bhupati's name to run up debts. This betrayal is immediately juxtaposed with Bhupati's relationship with Charu, his wife: 'Bhupati could not tell Charu everything' (67); there is already a gulf between them. 'That was the day Bhupati had come inopportunely to the inner rooms of the house. At that moment his heart longed to feel that faith had a definite place in the world' (68). But Charu is sitting in the dark, brooding over her own misunderstanding with Amal, Bhupati's cousin: 'her sorrows had extinguished the evening lamp' (ibid.). The third person in this triangle, Amal, is also the victim of misunderstanding. He thinks that Umapati and his wife Manda have left because Charu has complained to Bhupati about Amal's improper behaviour with Manda: 'In a way, Manda's farewell was a deportation order for Amal as well....Now his duty was very plain – he should not stay even one more minute.... For such a long time, with unwavering confidence, Bhupati had kept him in his house' (69). Bhupati, on the other hand, is grappling with other matters: 'What with ungrateful relatives, besieging creditors, jumbled account books and an empty cashbox, Bhupati was then at his wit's ends. There was no one to share his prosaic sorrows – he was preparing to stand alone and fight against heartache and debt.' (ibid.).

Tagore shows us three fully-drawn, complex characters, each isolated by his or her own misconstruction; each loves the two others, but is unable to operationalise his or her feelings purposefully. This is, no doubt, at first appearance a domestic, even personal crisis. But a careful reading of the novel shows that it has much larger ramifications. Bhupati's home, with its confusions and politics, reflects the state of late nineteenth century *bhadralok* society, with its own internal contradictions and tensions. Bhupati, as the owner of an English newspaper, wishes to be the mover and shaker of public opinion. He is driven, even seduced, by the bigger project of nation building, which has captured the imagination of the best and brightest minds of his time. It is the erotic possibilities of this project that ostensibly keep him away from his real wife of flesh and blood, Charu. Charu is lonely and pines for him in the inner chambers of the house, like a bird in a gilded cage, the image that Ray shows us at the beginning of his cinematic adaptation. The newspaper is Bhupati's bride-substitute and Charu's rival, as overtly stated more than once in the text. The other man in the film, the more active and energetic Amal soon presents himself as a rival to Bhupati in Charu's imagination. But Amal, not entirely unlike Bhupati, is also interested in a bigger project than Charu. He has literary ambitions; Charu is merely his first reader and muse. Both men, for different reasons, spurn the woman of flesh and blood in favour of an ideal, which serves as the substitute object of their passion. Charu, in the end, is left with nothing. Her foray into literature, for which she has a genuine talent, has only been to secure Amal's affections. She does not admit to her attraction towards him openly, but discovers its devastating after-effects only after Amal, realising how close he has come to betraying Bhupati, leaves for London, after accepting a proposal for an arranged marriage. Bhupati, misunderstanding Charu's dalliance thinks that the way to her heart is through literature. Unsuccessful even at this ruse, he turns away, once again to journalism, this time going to Mysore, preparing to leave Charu behind. His greatest disillusionment has been the discovery of Charu's love for Amal and this domestic betrayal breaks his spirit as well as destroying the nest that is their home, as the title suggests.

The crisis in this novel, then, is both public and private, both in the realms of public engagement as well as private ethics. Bhupati's impracticality, though at first harmless, becomes more damaging as the novel unfolds. So does his infatuation to become the shaper of public opinion, a role that he is inadequate to assume. His failure in the public sphere costs him the breakdown of his marriage. Charu's inability to attract Bhupati, her turning to Amal for sustenance and her inability to restrain her emotions to what is really available to her causes a parallel breakdown, resulting in her losing her husband's affection and, perhaps, his company as well. Both Bhupati and Charu, then, are failures. They are unable to balance the contrary claims of desire and duty or *kama* and *dharma*; the result is both a civic and domestic tragedy. The emerging Indian nation cannot be built by impractical dreamers, nor by failed lovers/spouses; in both the public as well as private domain success demands not just a certain self-awareness but enormous competence. Those who delude themselves are unable to build either nations or happy homes. The only character of the three who escapes this catastrophe of the rapidly disintegrating nest is Amal. In a way, it is his innocence that both causes the crisis in the home and saves him in the end.

While he has shamelessly exploited his sister-in-law's affections, he has never intended any harm to domestic life. Charu has inspired him to become a writer but when her role in his life threatens his duty to his elder brother, he withdraws from the situation. True, he leaves Charu without support, floundering, but he has at least saved himself from moral opprobrium; he has, after all, not betrayed Bhupati. Bhupati, betrayed by both the world and his wife may take partial cheer in that his younger cousin has not joined the ranks of those sinning against him.

In Ray's version, all is not lost in the end; there is the possibility of Bhupati and Charu actually reaching out to each other across the gulf of misunderstanding that has separated them. This is prepared for by Charu's earlier rising to the occasion to inspire Bhupati to rally himself after his defeat by the unscrupulous forces of the world. It is she who offers to help him start his newspaper again. Why does Ray give a somewhat more hopeful conclusion to the story? To my mind it is because his version is produced in independent India. The success of the national project seems to offer the kind of hope that was impossible during colonialism to people like Bhupati and Charu. Yet, Ray does not hesitate to suggest, in the scene in which Charu looks at Amal through her binoculars, that the more suitable father of Charu's child is Amal, rather than Bhupati. It is Amal, not Bhupati or Charu who will carry the burden of both nation and home-making into the future because he alone of the three has both the practical competence and the moral rectitude to undertake such a project. Amal, then, emerges as the solution, however partial, to the crisis of the *bhadrasamaj* in *Nashtanir*. In his clean break with Charu, the moral order is restored. Sandeep, in the later novel, is much more degenerate and unscrupulous version of Amal; a much heavier price is therefore demanded before the moral equilibrium may be righted and it is not clear whether that ever happens, in spite of Nikhil's sacrifice.

While proposing these three paradigms of our interaction with the colonising West, there is no wish to valourise any particular approach as more or less effective. Each paradigm is, moreover, much more ambivalent that it appears at first. This is because the whole field of culture is complex and involved. Neither Indian attitudes to British rule, nor British attitudes to India can be encapsulated into any easy formulae. Yet, there are these broad patterns that recur repeatedly, which we have tried to identify. Our discussion cannot be complete, however, without invoking a person who does not figure as prominently in the Bengali imagination as he does in the national. We refer, of course, to Mohandas Karamchand Gandhi. Along with Ashis Nandy and others, we believe that in Gandhi all the currents of India's quest for modernity and nationhood intersect most graphically. While it is written elsewhere about Gandhi's approach to these questions, one might just say that what he embodies is the curious paradox of an upholder of tradition also being its greatest critic and a critic of modernity who is also the most radically modern person of his times. Gandhi's modernity was, to put it somewhat curiously, already *post*modern. He wanted to create a modernity that was not so much anti-modern, but drastically *non*modern. Of course, he failed, but before that he had thoroughly reengineered Indian traditions so profoundly and irrevocably that not only is there no going back, but the way forward is also unalterably civic and secular. Gandhi tried to reworld the home in ways that would at once make us at home in the world and also make the world a non-threatening, homely place.

9.5 DOMINANT/SUBALTERN ALTERNATIVITY

To conclude let us briefly confront what admittedly may seem like a deep conservatism informing this argument. Why are all the protagonists of my narrative Hindu, upper-caste men? Where are the subaltern voices, one might rightfully ask? Why have we not dealt with religious and ethnic minorities, Dalits and other subalterns? Today when the marketing of margins has become almost *de rigueur*, what I have attempted is certainly risky if not unfashionable. However, it is hoped this is a critical conservatism, not an unthinking one. Without attempting an elaborate defence, suffice it to simply say that it is only in the light of a certain kind of 'progress' over 150 years that we might today ask questions such as these, highlighting the subaltern question. The subaltern does, did always speak, but who is her voice? Today we might pause to hear it because of the sort of society that these creators of modern India fashioned. Today, they themselves may be considered marginal because the centre has been completely overrun by its former margins. There is no space left there for anything 'mainstream.' Those who study the dominant, middle-class culture of India are thus a rare species. To reread these 'middle class' opinion leaders, therefore, is unusual, if not subversive of the dominant trend or established ideas of marginality. Rather than don the carapace of marginality, claim to speak on behalf of some oppressed group or the other, it might be more productive to see how progressive in their own times these makers of modern were. That they were mostly concerned with upper-caste, Hindu India must be admitted, though, again, here Gandhi is an exception, which is precisely why he is so threatening to a certain brand of Dalit politics.

Gandhi comes closest to an upper-caste leader assuming the mantle of leading the lower castes out of their oppression. He therefore negates a certain kind of oppositional and exclusivist identity politics which is the mainstay of a special brand of Dalit self-assertion. While we might sympathise with such a self-assertion, we must be prepared to engage with it critically. The crucial question in this regard is whom has it most benefited? There is no denying that a certain vocal, educated and upwardly mobile section of the Dalits have wrested greater benefits by adopting such a confrontationist posture, the vast majority of the really oppressed underclass whom they claim to represent is still waiting to be rescued or reap the benefits of state policies. Caste jealousy against the dominant, even privileged Dalits is wreaked upon them by their more unfortunate and helpless brethren. What the vanguard has gained is arguably at the expense of the majority; worse, these bitterly fought gains have resulted in an incalculable loss of sympathy, producing greater divisions and alienation in the body politic. Whether it is a question of Dalits, minorities, or women, Gandhi is the most consistently proactive and responsible among the protagonists of modern India.

While this question needs further debate, simply the very fact that subaltern voices and criticism has become the mainstay of public culture proves the success, rather than the failure of the nationalist project. Such devolution of cultural power was built into the very mechanism of our anti-colonial struggle. Greater democracy and freedom is thus the natural fruition of the very conception of the Indian nation rather than its unmaking as our post-nationalists are wont to argue.

The dominant culture of modern India whose contours we have tried to sketch was, admittedly, concerned primarily with the terms of India's relationship with British imperialism in specific and Western modernity in general. Once this relationship was defined so as to ensure a certain modicum of dignity and autonomy for India in the comity of nations of the world, other intra-national readjustments were bound to follow. The builders of modern India were trying to right a relationship of structural inequality with the West. Once this was achieved, they were sure that gender, class, caste and religious equalities could also be achieved as an irreversible consequence of an anti-imperialistic nationalism. That is why, when we turn from the narratives of dominant culture to that of, say, the women, we find a distinct shift in the emphasis. The role, status, position and subjectivity of women within the Hindu patriarchy is the central concern of the women writers, rather than questions of colonialism proper. Similarly, Dalit and other subaltern texts are primarily concerned with justice and equality within Indian society, even if this means going outside the Hindu fold or collaborating with British rule. However, it may be argued that these sub-national concerns are inextricably interlinked with the bigger questions that I have alluded to of autonomy, selfhood and svaraj in the context of British imperialism. There is no former without the latter.

Dominant cultures need to be studied not just for their absences and erasures as is the prevalent practice today, but also for their presences and additions. From Ram Mohan Roy to Mahatma Gandhi, the dominant intellectual and cultural tradition of Hindu India has tried to forge not so much a counter-modernity, but an alternative modernity that while it was distinctly Indian, also had universal aspiration. This 'distinctness' was neither uniform nor identical in these thinkers, but hardly any one of them would have endorsed the idea that Indian modernity would be merely a replication of the Western prototype. Thus they were not so much in favour of synthesising the East and the West, the home and the world, the inner and the outer, the traditional and the modern, the spiritual and the scientific, the female and the male and so on, but constantly mediating and negotiating between the two to produce something other than them. This other was not a hybrid, not some kind of mongrel in-betweeness, but a third *kind* of world, without the pejorative associations of that term. A crucial methodological instrument in this process was translation, but as an actual practice and as a metaphor for a larger way of apprehending our reality. Translation was a way of reworlding the home and of domesticating the world. That is why in our contemporary postcolonial practice, I consider translation to be crucial, not just in our reading of translated texts, but also in our preserving the double vision that comes from having more than one register of thought.

The makers of modern India tried to rewrite the monolinguality of modernity and imperialism in our own multiple tongues and voices. The cacophony that ensued had the capacity of transforming modernity itself, rendering it polyphonic and chaotic. From the universe of rationality, the attempt was made to create a multiverse of wisdom. In the process, various paradigms of coping with the dominant West were tried out – of these, the insufficiency and the self-sufficiency thesis are significant. But even more significant was a position that refused to argue from either of these positions, but included them both. Tagore and Gandhi, in their own rather different ways, can be cited as examples of this method. But what they share with their other contemporaries and predecessors like Ram Mohan Roy, Bankim, Ramakrishna, Vivekananda, Aurobindo, Bose and others is a deep and abiding concern for the autonomy, self-hood and svaraj. The habitus of this new society is provisionally the nation state, but also civil society and community life based on equality, justice and plurality. Gandhi's *ram rajya*, it would be fair to argue, is a deeply religious version of the secular welfare state, not merely the latter idea garbed in religious terminology so as to capture the imagination of the so-called ignorant masses in a vocabulary comprehensible to them. Furthermore, it is also probably Gandhi's vision of a new, radically modern state. This intermingling of an apparently unworldliness with a this-worldliness becomes the habitus of a new home for an India that has broken its colonial shackles and is ready to assert her own sense of selfhood and dignity once again. Because it is only upon the restoration of our selfhood and dignity that we can say that we are at home in this world, not beggars, slaves, or aliens in it.

WORKS CITED

Arora, Poonam. 1995. 'Devdas, Indian Cinema's Emasculated Hero: Sado-Masochism and Colonialism' *Journal of South Asian Literature*. 30 (1/2): 253–76.

Bhabha, Homi. 1992. 'The World and the Home' *Social Text*. Third World and Post-Colonial Issues, 31/32: 141–153.

_____. 1994. *The Location of Culture*. London: Routledge.

Chaudhuri, Nirad. 1987. *Thy Hand, Great Anarch! India: 1921–1952*. London: Chatto and Windus.

Chatterjee, Partha. 1989. 'The Nationalist Resolution of the Women's Question.' In *Recasting Women: Essays in Colonial History*. Edited by Kumkum Sangari and Sudesh Vaid. New Delhi: Kali for Women.

_____. 1993. *The Nation and Its Fragments: Colonial and Postcolonial Histories*. Princeton: Princeton University Press.

Datta, P. K., Ed. 2002. *Rabindranath Tagore's The Home and the World: A Critical Companion*. New Delhi: Permanent Black.

Dutt, Michael Madhusudan. 1993. *Madhusudan Rachnabali*. Edited by Kshetra Gupta. 12th edition. Calcutta: Sahitya Sansad.

Freud, Sigmund. 1919. 'The Uncanny' (Das Unheimliche). Translated by Alix Strachey. 1 February 2001. Web. Accessed 2 February 2012 http://people.emich.edu/acoykenda/uncanny1.htm.

Gandhi, Mohandas Karamchand. (1909) 1998. *Hind Swaraj*. Ahmedabad: Navjivan, 1998.

Gates, Jr., Henry Louis. 1991. 'Critical Fanonism.' *Critical Inquiry* 17: 457-70.

George, Marangoly Rosemary. 1999. *The Politics of Home: Postcolonial Relocations and Twentieth Century Fiction*. Berkeley: University of California Press.

'Home.' *Dictionary.com Unabridged (v 1.1)*. Random House. Dictionary.com http://dictionary.reference.com/browse/home

Jalal, Ayesha. 2001. *Self and Sovereignty: Individual and Community in South Asian Islam Since 1850*. New York: Routledge, 2001.

Macaulay, Thomas Babington. 1990. 'Minute on Indian Education of February 1835.' In *Tradition, Modernity & Swaraj*. 1.1: 99-107.

O'Connor, Erin. 2003. 'Preface for a Post-Postcolonial Criticism.' *Victorian Studies* 45.2: 217-246.

Paranjape, Makarand. 2003. 'Home and Away: Colonialism and AlterNativity in India.' *New Literatures Review* 40:116-130.

Parry, Benita. 1987. 'Problems in Current Theories of Colonial Discourse.' *Oxford Literary Review* 9: 27-58.

Ray, Satyajit 1983. Director. *Ghare Baire*. Feature film.

Risser, James. 1999. *Heidegger Toward the Turn: Essays on the Work of the 1930s*. Albany, NY: SUNY Press.

Robinson, Andrew. 1989. *Satyajit Ray: The Inner Eye*. London: Andre Deutsch.

Roy, Ram Mohan. 1990. 'Address to Lord Amherst, 11th December 1823. In *Tradition, Modernity & Swaraj*. 1.1: 96-98.

Rushdie, Salman. 1991. *Imaginary Homelands: Essays and Criticism, 1981-1991*. New Delhi: Viking.

Said, Edward. 1983. *The World, the Text and the Critic*. Cambridge: Harvard University Press.

Spivak, Gayatri Chakravorty. 1999. *A Critique of Postcolonial Reason: Toward a History of the Vanishing Present*. Cambridge and London: Harvard University Press.

_____. 1985. 'Three Women's Texts and a Critique of Imperialism.' *Critical Inquiry*. 12.1 (Autumn): 243-261.

Tagore, Rabindranath. (1915) 1985. *Ghare Baire*. In *Rabindra Rachanabali*. Volume 8. Calcutta: Visvabharati. Translated by Surendranath Tagore as

The Home and the World. 1919. New Delhi: Penguin.

_____. (1986) 1997. *Gora*. In *Rabindra Rachanabali*. Vol. 7. Calcutta: Visvabharati. Translated by Sujit Mukherjee. New Delhi: Sahitya Akedemi.

_____. (1917) 1985. *Nationalism*. London: Macmillan.

_____. (1971) 1977. *The Broken Nest*. Translation of *Nashtanir* by Mary M. Lago and Supriya Bari. Madras: Macmillan.

Whitman, Walt. 1855. 'Song of Myself'. *DayPoems*. 31 January 2001. Web. Accessed 2 February 2012. < http://www.daypoems.net/plainpoems/1900.html>

Wigley, Mark. 1995. *The Architecture of Deconstruction: Derrida's Haunt*. Cambridge, MA:MIT Press.

'World.' 2004. *The American Heritage Dictionary of the English Language*. 4th edition. Boston: Houghton Mifflin Company. <Dictionary.com http://dictionary.reference.com/browse/world>

10
SRI AUROBINDO AND THE RENAISSANCE IN INDIA[1]

10.1 THE ORIENTALIST PREDICAMENT

We have tried to see how in the Indo-British encounter in the nineteenth century a great many attitudes, approaches and positions become evident on both sides. While the exact nature and outcome of this encounter are still topics of debate, what is generally considered indisputable is that a new consciousness comes into being. The vanguard who spearheaded this consciousness was a new intelligentsia derived from precisely those classes which were an outcome of colonialism. The paradox of history is that though they owed their existence to colonialism, they also grew to resist it. This paradoxical character of the Indian ruling elites continues to this day, professing to resist transnational neo-imperialism even as they are co-opted by it, still leading to a cultural confusion and a crisis of identity which, it would seem, each generation must confront all over again and attempt to resolve. The very nature of this encounter, then, is of a perpetual crisis, both threat and opportunity, in present times as it was in the past. Those involved in the shaping of India's destiny cannot but become embroiled in it.

The Palestinian born Christian Arab and progenitor of the current wave of post-colonial studies, Edward Said, himself was a product of such a crisis. We only have to the read extensively discussed

Orientalism (1978) in a slightly different way to realise this. When it is read symptomatically, it becomes not an actual, historical account, which of course it is to some extent, but an anguished polemic arising from the author's own personal investment and reaction to being 'Orientalised.' Unfortunately, much of post-colonialist scholarship has been an outcome of a more literalist reading of Said, resulting not only in a limited understanding of actual historical processes, but also in fundamental errors and distortions. Some of these might have been mitigated if not averted, at least insofar as our notions of colonial India were concerned, had one of the early but masterly responses to this book been taken seriously. David Kopf's review of the book, which appeared in *The Journal of Asian Studies* in 1980, is also a testament of his own personal investment in the discipline that used to be called Orientalism until Said gave it a bad name if not a new meaning. Kopf argues that Said is mistaken at least on two counts. First of all, Said is historically inaccurate. His 'monolithic treatment of Orientalism' fails to see the complexity, variety and internal contradictions of the British attitudes to India. The 'representatives of the colonial elite also develop their own ambivalence about and polarised response to, subordinate Oriental cultures' (Kopf 1980, 496). Thus their scholarship was not merely a handmaiden of power, even when it was funded by or allied to imperial agendas, as Said in his application of Foucault to colonial knowledge-production concludes.[2] It was actually possible, in other words, that colonisers for a complex set of reasons might at a particular historical juncture, wish to and actually accomplish what is in the real and long-term interests of the colonised. In India's case, then, there were indeed many positive outcomes of this encounter even if they do not warrant dubbing the whole colonial interlude as beneficent or providential.[3]

More importantly, regardless of what the coloniser intended, the colonised derived their own lessons from this encounter. Not only did they anticipate much of Said's strictures against the ills of colonial rule, they also responded vigorously to them: 'there are vast differences in approach and in program between Said and the renaissant Indian intelligentsia' (Kopf 1980, 497). The outcomes of the latter were, perhaps, much more far-reaching, significant and long-lasting than anything the colonisers might have ever imagined. No wonder that even today, we have been expending so much of ourselves in teasing them out much as Said did in *Orientalism:* 'In many ways my study of Orientalism has been an attempt to inventory the traces upon me, the Oriental subject of the culture whose domination has been so powerful a factor in the life of all Orientals' (Said 1978, 25).

To return to Kopf's review, however, it is crucial to see how the colonised elite react to the coloniser's attempts to reconstruct them:

> Historical Orientalism had a concrete reality, was complex, internally diverse, changed over time and was never monolithic. It was quite independent of Said's 'discourse'; its focus and expression varied with time and with place. It was certainly not a unified set of propositions, universally accepted by all Westerners involved in Oriental administration and scholarship, whose progressive refinement was inseparable from the Western powers' gradual acquisition of much of the world's real estate. (Kopf 1980, 499)

Paradoxically, Kopf's collapsing Indian 'Occidentalism' into these two positions goes against the grain of his own criticism of Said's notion of Orientalism:

> In the process of responding to the power differential that separates the world of their origins from the world of their professions, the members of an intelligentsia become polarised into two camps – xenophile and xenophobe, herodian and zealot, Westerniser and nativist. (Kopf 1980, 495–496)

While much of this book has resisted such a binary or easy categorisation of the Indian responses to British colonialism, Kopf's dichotomy is of great heuristic value even today in explaining the kind of fractures that the Indian psyche still suffers from. It is also useful in discussing Sri Aurobindo's own attitude to the so-called

Indian renaissance. The central problematic of this renaissance was 'how an Indian modernistic movement could possibly be nurtured by, or flourish under, Western colonialism....How could India achieve any lasting benefits from a foreign ruler who deprived it of political and economic autonomy?' (ibid.) Kopf goes on to answer his own question thus: 'I discovered, much to my amazement, the contrary proposition that the Bengal Renaissance and Indian national awakening would have been inconceivable without the British colonial experience.'(ibid.).

Kopf's belief is based on his observation of similar movements elsewhere, which also emerge as a reaction to political, economic and cultural oppression:

> Now, after having studied comparable movements in Asia, Africa and the United States, I am convinced that the social process of renaissance constitutes a new sense of identity among representatives of an exploited ethnic group, religious community, culture, or sex; and that the new consciousness emerges as a salvationist ideology among the intelligentsia of the penalised group, who act as brokers or intermediaries to representatives of the dominant or colonialist power.
>
> It is almost a truism to declare that the great majority of nations in the world today owe their existence to liberation struggles against foreign tyranny and oppression. (ibid.)

Obviously, this does not mean that exploitation and oppression themselves are desirable or prerequisite to a renaissance; many groups may actually be destroyed or ground under to the point of extinction.[4] Yet it is also true that some of these groups do develop the capacity to raise their consciousness to the point that they find a way to survive and plan better futures for themselves. According to Kopf:

> consciousness raising is precisely what the Bengal Renaissance and other renaissances are fundamentally about. The educated few become aware of their disadvantage in the context of Western dominance or of the dominance of whites or males,

invent ideological blueprints to revitalise their communities and form associations and institutions to rid their cultures of abuses and shortcomings. (501)

The year following Kopf's review, Jan Nederveen Pieterse wrote an extended, 400 page account arguing a similar thesis in *Empire and Emancipation: Power and Liberation on a World Scale*. In fact, he went a step farther, pointing out how movements for emancipation themselves turned imperialistic when they became too successful. What could be a better example of a former colony turning into an empire than the United States with its internal colonisation of the native Americans, blacks, Hispanics and other minorities, its external colonies such as Puerto Rico or the Philippines and its world-wide imperialistic domination? Even India, oppressed for so many centuries, having become a nation after so much struggle and suffering, had to learn the hard way after its misadventures in Sri Lanka, the price of sub-imperial muscle-flexing.

Yet when Sri Aurobindo (1972-1950) wrote 'The Renaissance in India,' the battle for svaraj was far from won. Indeed, Aurobindo himself was in the thick of it, having been at the forefront of the national struggle for a brief period from 1907-1910, before he withdrew from active politics to devote himself to yoga in Pondicherry.[5] There, from his retreat, he wrote most of his major works, serialising them from 1914-1921 in his journal, *Arya*. It was also in the pages of *Arya* in 1918 that 'The Renaissance in India' appeared. From Ram Mohan to Aurobindo, as we have seen in these pages, is a fairly long journey, both temporally and ideologically. When we reach Aurobindo, we see what is India's mature and well-considered response to colonialism. But to see just how far India has come, it may be useful to look back over some of the milestones – in this case – from the past. There is scarcely a better pretext to do so than Aurobindo's carefully worked out retrospective of that period of India's history that came to be known as the Bengal, or in a more extended sense, the Indian renaissance.

10.2 A SEMIOLOGY OF GRAVESTONES

One way of arriving at Aurobindo's 'The Renaissance in India' is by re-invoking the names of some men, British and Indian who, separated from us by almost two hundred years, died before reaching their prime. What these men had in common was that they were all participants, even makers, of what we call the renaissance in India. It might be instructive to compare their lives with some of the famous makers of modern India who came after. And one, somewhat unusual, way to do so is by looking at the memorials erected to them by posterity. To that extent, what I propose to do may be called a semiology of tombstones: considering how each is connected to the others may produce a meaningful narrative of the progress of ideas in India. What do their graves tell us? What kind of story may we glean from revisiting them? In narrativising these memorials, can we reconstruct the broad contours of the Indo-British encounter? These are some of the questions that I hope to ask before I go on to discuss Aurobindo's essay 'The Renaissance in India.'

To understand India's road to modernity, it is imperative to visit Kolkata. In many ways, this is still India's first city, even if it takes some time and effort to discover why. Each trip reveals a little more about how we all came to be this way, how India became a nation. One way to pay respects to the past of this city is to stop at its oldest cemeteries.

Among the famous memorials that crowd the old colonial cemetery on Park Street are the graves of at least two very famous figures associated with the Indian renaissance. While looking for them, walking through rows of cenotaphs and memorials to the dead, one cannot but begin to get a feel of what might have happened in India two or three hundred years ago. The actual experience of visiting this cemetery and walking through these old graves is quite different from reading books about colonialism; here there is direct contact with history, a visceral sense of the past rising up from the ill-kempt and decayed stones to talk to one of what has been. The cemetery, then, is like a house of history.[6] This particular one dates back to 1767, to the very beginnings of British power in India, just ten years from the decisive Battle of Plassey, which the British won, virtually wresting control of Bengal from Siraj-ud-Doula, the Nawab. The earliest identifiable grave dates back to 1768. The cemetery was closed in 1895. It thus coincides almost perfectly with the period in the preceding chapters.

Not long before its last memorial was erected, this cemetery was 'immortalised' by one of the greatest colonial writers, Rudyard Kipling, in *City of Dreadful Night* (1891):

> The tombs are small houses. It is as though we walked down the streets of a town, so tall are they and so closely do they stand – a town shrivelled by fire and scarred by frost and siege. Men must have been afraid of their friends rising up before the due time that they weighted them with such cruel mounds of masonry. (Kipling [1891] 2009)

The necropolis is recognisably imperial, commemorating the men who conquered and ruled India and died here, with their loved ones. The dominant style is neo-classical, with Grecian columns, pyramids, statues, fading rhymes etched on stones.

The first thing that is immediately noticeable as one scans the gravestones is the numbers of those who died young, especially women. Several of the latter died in childbirth, but most of the dead were claimed by tropical diseases. The last were legion: dysentery, cholera, typhoid, tuberculosis, malaria, filariasis, leprosy, syphilis, rabies, alcoholism and so on. There are also graves of several little babies and infants, snatched away before their prime. So many died young, unable to bear the strain of the weather and the inhospitable conditions in India. Yet, they kept coming – and stayed to rule for nearly 150 years. Their graves are a silent marker of what happened to the British in this country.

As one walks through the cemetery, one sees many graves that are in a state of disrepair. Perhaps those who lie in them have no living descendents or they live far away from India; none at any rate is at hand to tend to their remains. In some vaults, whole families are buried. The living who erected these monuments to their deceased and beloved relatives often wrote simple verses praising their fidelity, sacrifice, nobility, bravery, or some special trait or mark of character to remember them by. Many of the inscriptions record the pious hope that at the time of the resurrection the souls of all those loved ones will be saved. Though buried in sub-tropical India, they expect to find themselves in the same heaven as their compatriots from distant shores.

Walking along the rows of graves without a guide, it is hard to locate those one needs to see. An idea channelises the efforts: look for graves which are well-maintained because unlike the others, these belong to the famous. Suddenly one is face-to-face with a tall, triangular memorial, clean and whitewashed; approaching it is a thrill: it contains the mortal remains of Sir William Jones (1746-1794), the founder of the Asiatic Society, Chief Justice of the Calcutta High Court and one of the pioneering Orientalists of the time. Jones was thirty-seven when he arrived in Calcutta in 1783. During the rest of his life of roughly nine years, he not only translated *Shakuntala* (1789), but also *Hitopadesa* (1786), *Institutes of Hindu Law or the Ordinances of Menu* (1794) and *Gita Govinda* (1799). He also wrote nine odes to Indian gods and goddesses, the first example of the use of the English language for purely Indian themes. Jones's enthusiasm for things Indian was not qualified or arrested by his Christianity. In one of his letters (to Earl Spencer) he wrote, 'I am no Hindu; but I hold the doctrine of the Hindus concerning a future state to be incomparably more rational, more pious and more likely to deter men from vice, than the horrid opinions inculcated by Christians on punishment *without end*.' (Jones 1970, vol. II, 766) Jones died young, relatively speaking, but what is more, like the Baptist missionary William Carey, he died in India. When a man gives the best portion of his life to another country, whether as a colonial administrator or as a scholar, we cannot but think of him as our own. Buried in India, Jones, belongs to us 'forever,' especially since he did not hold any special brief for Christian ideas of hell and heaven. Sure enough, his fortunes in his own home country have dwindled considerably.

Both as a writer and as a scholar, he is well-nigh forgotten in Britain. But can we in India afford to forget the man who first translated *Abhijnanasakuntalam* into English?

The other grave to be looked for in this cemetery is that of the young 'East Indian' poet, Henry Vivian Louis Derozio (1809–1931). Born of an Indo-Portuguese father, who had shortened his surname from De Rozario and a mother whose parentage is not established, this first of Indian English poets died before reaching the age of twenty-two. He was a teacher at Hindu College, but was removed by the Board of the College for preaching atheism, a charge that he vehemently denied. By the time he expired, he had already published two volumes of poems and several well-regarded essays in various newspapers and periodicals. What is more, he owned and edited a newspaper himself, called *The East Indian*. The only known portrait of this young prodigy hangs in the library of Presidency College. The painting is frayed, decaying, but is still a proud possession of the College. There is also a hall named after Derozio, with his bust, though covered with pigeon droppings, gracing the entrance. It is ironic that the very college that expelled him now vaunts its association with him. In sonnets such as 'To India – My Native Land' Derozio, though Westernised and English-educated, expressed for the first time in India proto-nationalist sentiments in the English language.

Not too far is the other famous cemetery on Lower Circular Road. Though many famous people including C. F. Andrews and John Drinkwater Bethune are also buried here, for the purposes of this book, the famous grave here is that of the first 'modern' Bengali poet, Michael Madhusudan Dutt (1824–1873). Madhusudan loved England and the English language as a young man. At the age of seventeen he wrote a small poem whose first line declares, 'I sigh for Albion's distant shore' (Chaudhuri 2002, 94). Writing to his friend Gour Bysak, he declared, 'Perhaps, you think I am very cruel, because I want to leave my parents. Ah! my dear! I know that and I feel for it. But 'to follow Poetry' (says A. Pope) 'one must leave father and mother" (95). He dreamed of making his mark as an English poet. He left home, converted to Christianity and was disowned by his father. Eventually, he did go to England but if it had it not been for Vidyasagar's charity, he and his family may actually have starved to death in cold and distant Europe. Before leaving India, he wrote a series of wonderful literary works, not in English but in his native Bangla. These works won him fame and celebrity. On his return, his law practice made him rich for a time but he lived extravagantly, even recklessly. He died almost a pauper. This is a summary rehearsal of the story we have already recounted earlier in this book.

Why are these three men mentioned who lie buried in some of the oldest cemeteries of Calcutta? This is because they were all participants of what was at one time called the Bengal Renaissance, even the Indian renaissance. Examining their lives, works and even their graves will convince us that what they represented was something unique and unprecedented in Indian culture. Whether we can call it a renaissance or not is debatable, but it was quite different in content, style and substance from what was available in Indian earlier. What is more, they represent a certain movement in ideas which is germane to the discussion

10.3 THE RENAISSANCE IN INDIA?

Can what happened in Bengal in the early nineteenth century be called a renaissance?[7] This question is important, even crucial to our project. *The Renaissance in India* was the title of James H. Cousins' book (1918) and of Aurobindo's series of essays in *Arya* published later in the same year. A concurrent and overlapping term was the Bengal renaissance, also used to describe the broad and fundamental manner in which Indian society changed with the colonial impact. This is how Kopf defines it:

> 'Renaissance' has referred to, among other things, Bengal's contribution to a modernised India, the earliest modernisation of a vernacular language and literature, the emergence of a historical consciousness, the search for a new identity in the modern world and the reconstruction of Hindu tradition to

suit modern needs. 'Renaissance' has also been identified with social reform and religious reformation, cultural and political nationalism, asceticism and the spirit of capitalism and with such intellectual currents as rationalism, scientism and secularism. (Kopf 1980, 500)

This term had become quite popular in India by the latter half of the nineteenth century. According to David Kopf, the word 'renaissance' was first used by Ram Mohan Roy:

> Though it is by no means certain when the term renaissance was first used in nineteenth-century Calcutta, Ram Mohan Roy referred to recent events in Bengal as being analogous to the European renaissance and reformation. Ram Mohan allegedly told Alexander Duff, the missionary, that 'I began to think that something similar to the European renaissance might have taken place here in India.' (Kopf 1969, 3)

What is interesting about this account is that its source is a book published in 1879, G. Smith's *Life of Alexander Duff* (vol. I: 118). Nowhere in Ram Mohan's original writings does the word seem to be used. In other words, it is likely that this idea of a renaissance is of colonial British attribution. Even so, the natives soon adopted it as Kopf goes on to show:

> In 1894, the Hindu nationalist and philosopher, Aurobindo Ghose (1872–1950), wrote a series of essays on Bankim Chandra Chatterji in which he continually used renaissance to depict the age of the great Bengali novelist and of his entire generation of intellectual and creative giants. (ibid.)

I shall turn later to these essays of Aurobindo, where we first glimpse his assessment of the Indian renaissance, later.

But, for the moment, let us continue with Kopf's assessment. Though Kopf admits that 'the type of acculturation' that he is studying 'results from an extreme power differential between a Western society that is technologically and militarily superior and a non-Western society that is not' (Kopf 1969, 4), he is still unable to question the fundamental premise of renaissance which his account revives and reifies. This Kopf himself acknowledges in his Preface:

> As a rule, the Indian renaissance of the nineteenth century is treated within the context of cultural continuity and change under British colonialism. Therefore, the historiography of that renaissance is divided between the advocates of British 'impact' and the advocates of Indian 'response.' If British influence is considered paramount, then the writer stresses change and regards the renaissance as a form of Westernisation or modernisation. If, on the other hand, Indian response is stressed, then the focus is on the Indian heritage and the renaissance is viewed as a reinterpretation of tradition. Not infrequently, scholars have looked upon the phenomenon as a synthesis between 'East and West.' (Kopf 1969, vii)

But in his three-fold model of impact, response and synthesis, clearly Hegelian in its origin and orientation, Kopf nowhere questions whether there was a renaissance in the first place and if what happened could indeed be called by that name. Yes, there was the British impact and the Indian response, both of these multi-dimensional and varied; perhaps, there was hybridity too, if not synthesis. Again, words such as modernisation and nationalism have been used to describe the outcome of the encounter. But it is still unclear whether renaissance is the right term for these phenomena.

Perhaps, it may be more plausible to conclude that this idea of a renaissance in Bengal and then in India in the nineteenth century was more or less a colonial idea, which many Indians later accepted without serious questioning. As Professor Kapil Kapoor, a senior colleague, said to me in a conversation, 'There was no renaissance to speak of, but if you persist in calling it that, remember it was a slave's renaissance, quite different from what happened to the free people of Europe.' This makes us wonder if there a political agenda behind the idea of the renaissance in India? Just because many Indians came to adopt the word as a self-description does not automatically imply that it was real or justified; by the same token, even if the coinage was of colonial vintage and quite motivated, what actually happened cannot be denied or devalued.

We get a clue to the politics of such naming when we consider some of the most enthusiastic celebrations of it. There are two that vie for the first place, each by very eminent personages. The first is by the great historian Jadunath Sarkar, quoted on the very first page of his book by Kopf:

> The greatest gift of the English, after universal peace and the modernisation of society and indeed the direct result of these two forces – is the Renaissance which marked our 19th century. Modern India owes everything to it. (Kopf 1969, 1)

This comment was made in 1928. In 1943, Sarkar was even more categorical:

> It was truly a Renaissance, wider, deeper and more revolutionary than that of Europe after the fall of Constantinople...under the impact of British civilisation [Bengal] became the path-finder and light-bringer to the rest of India. In this new Bengal originated every good and great thing of the modern world that passed on to the other provinces of India. From Bengal went forth the English-educated teachers and the Europe-inspired thought that helped to modernise Bihar and Orissa, Hindustan and Deccan. New literary types, reform of the language, social reconstruction, political aspirations, religious movements and even changes in manners that originated in Bengal, passed like ripples from a central eddy, across provincial barriers, to the farthest corners of India. (Sarkar 1943, 498)

Joya Chatterjee analyses Sarkar's remarks in considerable detail, arguing that they were an outcome of the demonisation of the Muslim past of Bengal as a dark age and the communalisation of Bengali historiography (Chatterjee 1994, 150–190).

The other remarks, by Nirad Chaudhuri, as quoted by Kopf, are more in favour of Orientalism:

> Historically, European oriental research rendered a service to Indian and Asiatic nationalities which no native could ever have given.... The resuscitation of their past fired the imagination of the Hindus and made them conscious of a heritage of their very own which they could pit not only against the Muslims but also against that of the more virile English. Psychologically, the Indian people crossed the line which divides primitive peoples from civilised peoples. (Kopf 1969, 12)

Chaudhuri's unregenerate anglophilia is well known. His *Autobiography of an Unknown Indian* was dedicated 'To the memory of the British Empire in India which conferred subjecthood on us but withheld citisenship; to which yet every one of us threw out the challenge: 'Civis Britannicus Sum' because all that was good and living within us was made, shaped and quickened by the same British Rule' (Chaudhuri 1951). What is also important is that the notion that Indians knew nothing of their history and past before European Orientalists gave it to them is, strictly speaking, not true. Even during the Moghul period, many key Sanskrit texts including the Ramayana, Mahabharata and the Upanishads were translated into Persian. In fact, several groups, which had no access to Sanskrit, managed to learn about their own culture through such translations. This proves that they were in circulation, even if intermittently. The translations of the Orientalists, moreover, would have been impossible without the help of Indian pundits, who supplied them the texts and helped the former interpret them. What was more significant is that the mode of circulation and transmission of these texts changed under colonialism; from being passed on strictly through oral and restricted transmission, they now became widely available through the print medium to all castes and classes who could read them, whether in Sanskrit, English, or vernacular translations.

The very enthusiasm with which the term 'renaissance' was embraced by colonial subjects makes us suspect its provenance. Could it be that the idea of the renaissance was advanced because it disguised the colonisers' designs and flattered the colonised? Or that it projected both the anglicisers and the anglicised in a better light than they perhaps ought to be seen? Instead of calling themselves subjects, servants, imitators, or collaborators, they gave themselves the exalted title of being renaissance men and women.

Instead of Ram Mohan's reported remarks to Duff, perhaps a more likely source of the idea of a renaissance was Macaulay's notorious Minute. Though he did not actually use the word renaissance, his phrase 'great revival' fairly sums up what was implied (Macaulay 1990, 102). It was Macaulay who argued that the West could transform India the way in which the Classical languages had changed Western Europe and the Western European languages themselves had civilised Russia: 'What the Greek and Latin were to the contemporaries of More and Ascham, our tongue is to the people of India' (ibid.). He went on to add: 'The languages of Western Europe civilised Russia. I cannot doubt that they will do for the Hindoo what they have done for the Tartar' (103). Macaulay not only put an end to the older kind of Orientalism, he also provided the newly formed subjects of English reasons to feel good about their subjection. The idea of the Indian renaissance, it would seem, thus came from the discursive practices of the liberal-missionary colonial turn in the 1830s.

What we see at work here is a complex confrontation and interweaving of two narratives: that of the Orientalists and that of the Liberal administrators. The latter, incidentally, were Liberals only because their politics back home in Britain was Whig, not Tory; they were proponents of the free market, of new ideas such as utilitarianism and positivism. Macaulay, for instance, laid considerable emphasis on the economic imperatives in his Minute, arguing that English education was more profitable, whereas Sanskrit and Arabic had to be subsidised by the state: 'we are forced to pay our Arabic and Sanscrit students, while those who learn English are willing to pay us' (Macaulay 1990, 103). He urged the Committee on Public Instruction, therefore, to heed to market forces. Yet, it is important to remember that the liberals, as far as India was concerned, were rather intolerant and dismissive of its culture. Not only did Macaulay claim that 'a single shelf of a good European library was worth the whole native literature of India and Arabia' (101), but also asserted that

> all the historical information which has been collected from all the books written in the Sanscrit language is less valuable than what may be found in the most paltry abridgments used by the preparatory schools in England. In every branch of physical or moral philosophy, the relative position of the two nations is nearly the same. (ibid.)

The groundwork for such views had already been laid by James Mill's *History of British India* (1818), which was a sustained secular and scholastic iteration of contemptuous prior dismissals of Indian culture, religion and history by evangelists such as Charles Grant and William Wilberforce.[8] Together, both ideologies merged to demonstrate the obvious and decided inferiority of Indian civilisation and thus to justify British rule in India. The Liberals and the missionaries supplied the most uncompromising and harsh critiques of Indian society and culture. Incidentally, as Said (1979) himself elaborates, Karl Marx also contributed to the idea that British rule was the prerequisite to break up the atavistic, feudal *ancien regime* and to propel India into the teleology of history.[9] It would seem that the idea of the Indian renaissance drew support from all these dominant colonial discourses, the Orientalist, the Liberal, the missionary and to a lesser extent, the Marxist. Inspired and directed by them, their Indian collaborators took up the idea too partly because it showed them in a better light. From such a standpoint 'renaissance' becomes yet another mask of colonialism, a mask, ultimately of one's own conquest and subjugation. At another level, it is merely the continuation of the sexual imagery that goes from invasion, subjection, possession and so on, to its logical outcome of a new birth.

Furthermore, if renaissance means rebirth, we must remember that this is a recurring process in India. After all, this is a civilisation that believes in reincarnation, not just of individuals, but also, by extension, of cultures. We thus have had several rebirths, several renewals – this is the Vyasa parampara that Professor Kapoor (2004) has expounded with passionate originality. If so, could the Bengal renaissance of the nineteenth century be one among the many historical and mythic renaissances or reawakenings that India went through in its 5000 year history? It is only the exceptionalism of modernity that considers it unique.

It should be evident from the foregoing discussion that that we must re-examine, even problematise this idea of the renaissance instead of taking it at face value. To do so is to look at it in a slightly different light, not so much in terms of what Western knowledge did to us, but what the discovery of ancient India did to Europe. We will realise that the latter is sometimes underplayed in conventional histories of the Western culture so much so that a respected historian even considers that Britain was merely a catalyst, remaining unchanged in this encounter (Raychaudhuri 1999). One of the few books that attempts to do justice to what happened to Europe during the colonial encounter is *The Oriental Renaissance* by Raymond Schawb. This book, translated from the French and published in English argues that the Europeans had two, not one renaissances. The first was the well-known one that extended from the fifteenth to the seventeenth centuries approximately and was triggered by the discovery of Classical texts and knowledge systems. Behind this, of course, was the Arab renaissance and Europe's contact with that renaissance through the Crusades, Moors and Turks. But Schawb argues that there was another renaissance, which has not been properly assessed and acknowledged. This he calls the 'Oriental Renaissance.'

Indeed, the impact on Europe of the discovery of the 'Orient' was stupendous. In India, Sir William Jones, postulated the common origin of the Indo-European languages. Arguably, European Enlightenment was influenced by this 'invention' of the classical past of India and of the far East. One could even argue that the non-dogmatism of the Enlightenment came out of the discovery of Eastern classics, which were characterised by both plurality and rationality. There is a similar argument that it was the European encounter with Latin American indigenous societies, like that of the Incas, which gave Europe the idea of socialism. This is evident in the way Latin America figures in a book such as Voltaire's *Candide*. We might also refer to Montaigne's famous essay 'Of Cannibals,' and the idea of the 'commonwealth' in *The Tempest* for other examples of non-European origins of major European ideas. The impact of the discovery of India, of course, was felt as far off as in the US, with Emerson, Thoreau and other members of the Boston 'Brahmin' community.

But if renaissance is an inappropriate term, what do we call the massive re organisation of Indian society that did take place in the nineteenth century and onwards? Perhaps a better word for what happened is reform, not renaissance. But even the word reform has its problems. Swami Vivekananda (1863–1902), for instance, was critical of it. In his address to the people of Madras he minces no words:

> To the reformers I will point out that I am a greater reformer than any one of them. They want to reform only little bits. I want root-and-branch reform. Where we differ is in the method. Theirs is the method of destruction, mine is that of construction. I do not believe in reform; I believe in growth. (Vivekananda, 1994, vol. 3, 213)

Such quotations serve to highlight a crucial debate in Indian attitudes to the Western impact. Earlier, in the chapter on Tagore, I had suggested that there were a variety of responses to this Western impact ranging from a position which begins with the insufficiency of Indian civilisation to one that proclaims its total self-sufficiency. Of course, these positions were as strategic as they were actual; that is, they signified different ways of coping with the superior power of the West. Gradually, however, those who wanted to build a new society on the rejection and destruction of the old gave way to those who sought continuity and change simultaneously. Here, it has been argued that in all these debates what was constant was the desire and articulation of some form of svaraj or autonomy for India. At whatever point they might begin these men and women wanted to fashion an Indian self that would not be subordinate to that of the West. What our recent history has shown is a repeated marginalisation and rejection of those who were unable to imagine or strive for such an autonomy but were content with the status of mere subordination.

That is why Vivekananda holds Indians responsible for their own downfall, as Gandhi later did in *Hind Swaraj*. Vivekananda is unwilling to blame others:

> Materialism, or Mohammedanism, or Christianity, or any other *ism* in the world could never have succeeded but that you allowed them But yet there is time to change our ways. Give up all those old discussions, old fights about things which are meaningless, which are nonsensical in their very nature...We are neither Vedantists, most of us now, nor Puranics, nor Tantrics. We are just 'Don't touchists.' Our religion is in the kitchen. Our God is the cooking-pot and our religion is, 'Don't touch me, I am holy.' If this goes on for another century, every one of us will be in a lunatic asylum. (Vivekananda, 1994, vol. 3, 167)

This emphasis on the self as both the cause of a society's decline and the source of its regeneration is typical of a culture as radically *self*-centric as India. But it is also clear from such accounts that this self-centrism was also critical, not merely defensive. Every single thought-leader declined to advance the view that everything was perfect with Indian society or its traditions. But these thinkers also held that Westernisation was not the answer to all our problems either. It is this third way which is the most difficult but also the most valuable. And it is this third way that Aurobindo also points to.

10.4 'THE RENAISSANCE IN INDIA' BY AUROBINDO

Let us now come to the subject of this chapter, Sri Aurobindo and his analysis of the renaissance in India.

Aurobindo's early thoughts on the renaissance appear in his laudatory series of essays on Bankim, published in seven instalments in *Indu Prakash*, a Bombay-based, bilingual Marathi-English weekly newspaper, between 16 July 1894 and 27 August 1894 (Aurobindo 2003, 766). In the second of these essays, originally appearing on 23 July 1894, Aurobindo located Bankim's formation as the outcome of a society 'the most extraordinary perhaps that India has yet seen – a society electric with thought and loaded to the brim with passion' (94). This is how he went on to describe it:

> Bengal was at that time the theatre of a great intellectual awakening. A sort of miniature Renascence was in process. An ardent and imaginative race, long bound down in the fetters of a single tradition, had had suddenly put into its hands the key to a new world thronged with the beautiful or profound creations of Art and Learning. From this meeting of a foreign Art and civilisation with a temperament differing from the temperament which created them, there issued, as there usually does issue from such meetings, an original Art and an original civilisation. Originality does not lie in rejecting outside influences but in accepting them as a new mould into which our own individuality may run. This is what happened and may yet happen in Bengal. (ibid.)

What is striking is the enthusiasm, even poetic eloquence, with which Aurobindo describes the renaissance in 1894, when he served the Maharaja of Baroda in various administrative departments and still signed his name as 'Arvind A. Ghosh' (746; 750; 754). It may be useful to discuss these early views at length so as to compare them with his more considered reflections nearly twenty-five years later.

Though so positive about the renaissance, he was also quick to note that the new social and political ideas that arose were 'on a somewhat servilely English model' (Aurobindo 2003, 95). The most significant impact was registered 'into the channel of literature' for the Bengali's 'peculiar sphere is language' (ibid.). What was more significant, perhaps, was that 'like its European prototype, though not to so startling an extent,' the Bengal renaissance was marked 'by a thawing of old moral custom':

> The calm, docile, pious, dutiful Hindu ideal was pushed aside with impatient energy and the Bengali, released from the iron restraint which had lain like a frost on his warm blood and

sensuous feeling, escaped joyously into the open air of an almost Pagan freedom. The ancient Hindu cherished a profound sense of the nothingness and vanity of life; the young Bengali felt vividly its joy, warmth and sensuousness. This is usually the moral note of a Renascence, a burning desire for Life, Life in her warm human beauty arrayed gloriously like a bride. It was the note of the sixteenth century, it is the note of the astonishing return to Greek Paganism, which is now beginning in England and France; and it was in a slighter and less intellectual way the note of the new age in Bengal. (ibid.)

This is a remarkable assessment, especially because this period was characterised by so much reform giving rise to the institutionalised, middle-class morality. The loosening of the moral law that Aurobindo speaks of certainly applies to the breaking down of caste and gender barriers, the creation of a new individuality and unprecedented freedom of thought and knowledge. But instead of the Hindus, who were old pagans, turning into new pagans, they actually got somewhat Christianised and Semiticised, either through outright conversion, as we have already seen, or through reform movements such as the Brahmo Samaj or the Arya Samaj. Finally, Aurobindo stresses the celebration of life, a new appetite for this world rather than the negative asceticism of traditional Indian spirituality, as one of the gifts of the new age.

The later, more mature series on 'The Renaissance in India' consists of four essays by Aurobindo that were first published in *Arya* from August to November 1918. On the very first page, Aurobindo refers to James H. Cousins, without mentioning his book, *The Renaissance in India,* by name. Actually, Cousins' book was also published in 1918. Aurobindo's four-part series, thus, was written in response and appreciation.[10] Cousins was an Irish poet and Theosophist who came to India in 1915 at the behest of Annie Besant. He had just taken over as the Principal of the Theosophical College at Madanapalle in 1918. In the eleventh chapter in his book Cousins discusses Indian art, sculpture, painting, poetry and religion with the view to promote in India the kind of 'redemptive revivalism' that had inspired the Irish not just to assert their spiritual roots in opposition to British materialism, but also to bid for self-determination and independence. Cousins declares in his Preface that he wishes 'to communicate a larger and deeper comprehension of the spiritual, mental and emotional forces that are moulding the India of [the] near future' (Cousins 2005, Preface). Like Andrews (1912) before him, Cousins is at pains to correct the misrepresentations of India in English writings, thus anticipating the Saidian critique of Western writing on India. Cousins is also keen to show that India not only has a cultural and spiritual unity, but that in at least three moments in her past, under the Maurya, Gupta and Mughal empires, she had achieved political unity too. After refuting such misunderstandings and distortions of Indian culture, much of the rest of the book is devoted to discussions of specific Indian artistic and literary works.

Cousins' book is also valuable as another meaningful attempt at establishing an Indo-Irish connection, which would work in contradistinction to the Indo-British one. Cousins compares the Irish and the Indian situations, speculating on how a cultural nationalism itself was a cosmopolitan phenomenon, capable of proving the ideological basis for emerging states. According to him the spiritual sources of nationalism were more important than the material; the artist, by affirming the former, would help lay the basis for a national education and culture, thus preparing the way for the latter. For Cousins, thus, there was a basic complimentarity in the decolonising movements in Ireland and India. Common to both are a return to the spiritual roots of a politics of anti-colonialism, a process in which artists and poets had a key role to play. Moreover, Cousins himself questioned the term renaissance claiming that Indian culture, though in a state of decline, had not lost its memory of the past altogether; so when its continuity was not entirely lost, how could the present revival be called a rebirth?

When compared to the earlier references to the renaissance, the first thing we notice in this series by Aurobindo is the tempering of his earlier enthusiasm. In fact, at the very start of 'The Renaissance in India,' Aurobindo poses the question, like Cousins, about the appropriateness or lack thereof of the term 'renaissance' for what happened in India:

> There is a first question, whether at all there is really a Renaissance in India. That depends a good deal on what we mean by the word; it depends also on the future, for the thing itself is only in its infancy and it is too early to say to what it may lead. (Aurobindo 1997, 3)

Aurobindo immediately compares what happens in India with the European renaissance:

> The word carries the mind back to the turning-point of European culture to which it was first applied; that was not so much a reawakening as an overturn and reversal, a seizure of Christianised, Teutonised, feudalised Europe by the old Graeco-Latin spirit and form with all the complex and momentous results which came from it. (ibid.)

He points out crucial differences between to two as also the greater similarity with the Irish situation:

> That is certainly not a type of renaissance that is at all possible in India. There is a closer resemblance to the recent Celtic movement in Ireland, the attempt of a reawakened national spirit to find a new impulse of self-expression which shall give the spiritual force for a great reshaping and re-building.... (ibid.)

In discussing Cousins' point that the continuity of Indian tradition had never been totally broken, Aurobindo says that this was true only for 'Indian spirituality which has always maintained itself even in the decline of the national vitality' (5). What is more, according to him,

> it was certainly that which saved India always at every critical moment of her destiny and it has been the starting-point too of her renascence. Any other nation under the same pressure would have long ago perished soul and body. (ibid.)

That is why, carrying the metaphor of body and spirit forward, he argues that the true shape of the Indian renaissance would be a new body, cured of old defects, but still able to express its native genius, which was spiritual:

> The shaping for itself of a new body, of new philosophical, artistic, literary, cultural, political, social forms by the same soul rejuvenescent will, I should think, be the type of the Indian renascence, – forms not contradictory of the truths of life which the old expressed, but rather expressive of those truths restated, cured of defect, completed. (ibid.)

Furthermore, he refutes some common European misconceptions on the nature of Indian civilisation, misconceptions that have been echoed by Westernised Indians too (Aurobindo 1997, 6-7). The chief of these was that India was merely metaphysical and totally inept when it came to the material realities:

> She was alive to the greatness of material laws and forces; she had a keen eye for the importance of the physical sciences; she knew how to organise the arts of ordinary life. (6).

He then proceeds to outline three characteristics of ancient Indian society. He says that 'spirituality is indeed the master-key of the Indian mind' (ibid.); that ancient India is marked by 'her stupendous vitality, her inexhaustible power of life and joy of life, her almost unimaginably prolific creativeness' (7); and, finally, that the 'third power of the ancient Indian spirit was a strong intellectuality' (8). Yet, he does acknowledge a fall, 'an evening of decline' (14). There were, he contends, 'three movements of retrogression' (ibid.): first, a 'shrinking of that superabundant vital energy and a fading of the joy of life and the joy of creation'; secondly, 'a rapid cessation of the old free intellectual activity'; and, finally, the diminution of the power of Indian spirituality (ibid.). It was under such conditions of decline that the European powers swept over India to wrest control over it (ibid.). Under the impact of English colonialism, much that was old and moribund was destroyed; the nation itself might have perished under such adversities. But luckily, there was some life left still, which responded with renewed vigour:

> It revived the dormant intellectual and critical impulse; it rehabilitated life and awakened the desire of new creation; it put the reviving Indian spirit face to face with novel conditions and ideals and the urgent necessity of understanding, assimilating and conquering them. (15)

It is clear that the earlier enthusiasm for the renaissance is now substituted by the urgency of what needs actually to be done in the future:

> The recovery of the old spiritual knowledge and experience in all its splendour, depth and fullness is its first, most essential work; the flowing of this spirituality into new forms of philosophy, literature, art, science and critical knowledge is the second; an original dealing with modern problems in the light of the Indian spirit and the endeavour to formulate a greater synthesis of a spiritualised society is the third and most difficult. Its success on these three lines will be the measure of its help to the future of humanity. (ibid.)

Aurobindo is not the only thinker who extends the value and implications of the Indian reawakening to the global, even species stage; James Cousins had also ended his book of the same title with a similar hope and prophecy (Cousins 2005). Aurobindo, like the Theosophists, believed that the rise of India, the rediscovery of her ancient genius, her capacity to excel in the modern world and her putting forth a new realisation would have a crucial role to play in the very future of humanity.

Aurobindo concludes the first essay by asserting that the true work of the Indian renaissance is not political, economic, intellectual, or even cultural, but it is a unique spiritual mission that India must fulfil:

> The work of the renaissance in India must be to make this spirit, this higher view of life, this sense of deeper potentiality once

> more a creative, perhaps a dominant power in the world. ... Only in a few directions is there some clear light of self-knowledge. It is when a greater light prevails and becomes general that we shall be able to speak, not only in prospect but in fact, of the renaissance of India. (Aurobindo 1997, 16)

The renaissance in India is no longer a settled fact, something taken for granted as having already occurred. Instead, it remains half-hidden, in the womb of futurity, waiting to take birth, to come into being, to manifest itself. Aurobindo has thus given the term a totally new meaning and orientation.

In the second essay, Aurobindo sums up what he said earlier by considering the renaissance to consist of 'a complex breaking, reshaping and new building, with the final result yet distant in prospect' (17). He identifies three 'impulses' that arise from the 'impact of European life and culture' (ibid.). These are a revival of 'the dormant intellectual and critical impulse'; the rehabilitation of life and an awakened 'desire for new creation'; and a revival of the Indian spirit by the turning of the national mind to its past (ibid.). In a word a true renaissance would happen only with 'the ancient goddess, the Shakti [power] of India mastering and taking possession of the modern influence, no longer possessed or overcome by it' (ibid.). But what did the Western impact exactly do to India? It reawakened 'a free activity of the intellect'; 'it threw definitely into ferment of modern ideas the old culture'; and 'it made us turn our look upon all that our past contains with new eyes' (20). In the process there was some consolidation of the new consciousness in the work of Bankim and Tagore, even a reaction and assertion of the value of India's culture in Vivekananda (21–22), but only a 'new creation (22) would end the identity crisis of modern India, which was still half-Indian and half-European.'

In the third essay, Aurobindo offers an outline of the possibilities of a new creation. He predicts that the 'spiritual motive' will be the dominant force in India (23). By spirituality, he does not mean either metaphysics or asceticism, but a constructive, life-affirming and vigorous transformation of life, which would be the culmination of over a hundred years of spiritual experimentation from Ram Mohan to Ramakrishna to his own times, 'the reassertion of a spiritual living as a foundation for a new life of the nation' (26). He next considers literature, painting and politics, showing how mixed the results have been, except for some outstanding works by Bankim, Tagore and the Bengal school of painting, which has been able to revive the inner spirit of Indian expression (28–31). It is only when India is politically free that the true shape of things to come will be revealed:

> It is probable that only with the beginning of a freer national life will the powers of the renaissance take effective hold of the social mind and action of the awakened people. (31)

Aurobindo, thus, considers decolonisation as a prerequisite for a true renaissance in India. Till then, 'by the force of inertia of thought and will and the remaining attachment of a long association,' the present chaos and flux would continue, with the new 'still powerless to be born' (34).

In the fourth and last essay in the series, Aurobindo once again stresses that the best course of action for India lies in being herself, recovering her native genius, which is a reassertion of its ancient spiritual ideal. But because he has emphasised the latter so much, he takes great pains to disabuse the reader as to its true nature. It is not a religiosity or descent into irrationality:

> Again, we may be met also by the suspicion that in holding up this ideal rule before India we are pointing her to the metaphysical and away from the dynamic and pragmatic or inculcating some obscurantist reactionary principle of mystical or irrational religiosity and diverting her from the paths of reason and modernity which she must follow if she is to be an efficient and a well-organised nation able to survive in the shocks of the modem world. (Aurobindo 1997, 32)

It is neither a retreat from the world into asceticism, nor the fanatical adherence to any one religion (33). Instead, 'spirituality is much wider than any particular religion' (ibid.). In addition, spirituality includes the mind and the body: 'a human spirituality must not belittle the mind, life or body or hold them of small account'(34). He adds that there was never ' a national ideal of poverty in India as some would have us believe'(ibid.).

Yet, the spiritual ideal was quite different from the mental or the physical: 'The spiritual view holds that the mind, life, body are man's means and not his aims and even that they are not his last and highest means' (ibid.). The real goal is 'to prepare a basis for spiritual realisation and the growing of the human being into his divine nature' (36). In this both philosophy and science can only be helpers and instruments; politics, economics and sociology too, only the means of arranging the life of human beings in larger groups and collectives. The spiritual ideal includes and exceeds all these so that it can provide

> first, a framework of life within which man can seek for and grow into his real self and divinity, secondly, an increasing embodiment of the divine law of being in life, thirdly, a collective advance towards the light, power, peace, unity, harmony of the diviner nature of humanity which the race is trying to evolve. (36-37)

But many in India themselves do not believe in this ideal, influenced as they are by European ideas. Europe, on the other hand, without quite abandoning its materialist bias, is opening itself to Eastern influences (37).

India must find her own path because she 'can best develop herself and serve humanity by being herself and following the law of her own nature' (38). This means neither a rejection of all that comes from the West, nor a sort of retreat into too much religion; indeed ' true spirituality,' according to Aurobindo, 'rejects no new light.' (ibid.). The fall of India was a reality and so should be the recovery: 'The fall, the failure does matter and to lie in the dust is no sound position for man or nation.' (ibid.) He does not agree the reason for this could have been that 'too much religion ruined India,

(39), unless by religion is meant 'things external such as creeds, rites, an external piety.' (ibid.) But if by religion is meant a spiritual ideal that seeks 'to know and live in the highest self, the divine, the all-embracing unity and to raise life in all its parts to the divinest possible values' (ibid.). then there was not 'too much of religion, but rather too little of it' (ibid.). It is only in the knowledge and conscious application of the ideal that the future of both India and the world lies. Whether she can rise up to this task or not is a question that he leaves open: 'Whether she will rise or not to the height of her opportunity in the renaissance which is coming upon her, is the question of her destiny' (40).

Aurobindo wrote these essays in 1918; reading them over ninety years later makes us marvel at his vision and self-assurance. What distinguishes his essay from all the writing on the Indian renaissance before and after is that he goes much farther than his predecessors or successors. While they are content to consider the renaissance purely in terms of its material and mental aspects, only Aurobindo redefines it so as to encompass the deeper, spiritual meaning of the term. When Cousins speaks of the spiritual mainsprings of both the Celtic and Indian awakenings, he is more concerned, as Joseph Lennon in *Irish Orientalism* shows, with how the Irish used both their own mythic past and oriental spirituality as a counter to the regime of a capitalist rationality imposed by colonialist modernity. In Aurobindo's case, the entire basis of the discussion was different. Rather than seeing the spiritual as a way to inflect the material, he saw the material as the means to the spiritual.[11] To him, the Indian renaissance was not merely about decolonising the present through a rediscovery of the past but about the possibility of perfecting the human condition itself through an integral and harmonious development of all that was potential to it. Aurobindo's sights were thus set way beyond the more immediate exigencies of counter-colonialism or imagining a new nation. Concerned as he was with these processes, they were meaningful to him only as part of the grander narrative of the evolution of the human spirit. His revelation may be considered extremely utopian, but unlike similar millenarian projects, it is grounded in a very sure grasp of the material conditions of his times. The teleology of the Indian renaissance was part of a vaster plan in which India would have to play a key role.

If we were to evaluate the recent cultural history of India in the light of these essays, we will clearly see that the course of post-independence India has stressed the regaining of material, even military might, not necessarily the reaffirmation of India's spiritual ideal. So, to that extent, Aurobindo has been proved both right and wrong. Right in that the spiritual is realised not in the denial of the material but actually in the robust plenitude of the material subordinated to the spiritual ideal. We see in present-day India a great effort to attain such material prosperity. But whether the spiritual idea of India remains intact is a question that is not easily answered. To all appearances, India has gone the way of the rest of the world, worshipping mammon. Overwhelmingly, our religion, too, is consumerism. To say that spirituality is the master key to the Indian psyche these days may seem more the exception than the rule. Yet, culture operates at many levels. What may appear predominant at the surface may not be as fundamental deeper down. Perhaps, the deeper structures of the Indian mentality are still grounded in the quest for individual and collective self-realisation.

Certainly, in the light of Aurobindo's ideas, we might infer that the one true gift of the renaissance was the modern Indian nation. As Kopf says,

> Indeed…renaissance and nationalism are so closely related in India that it is often difficult to distinguish one from the other. For example, do we characterise the new sense of community (in Hindu India) based on language, religion, customs, manners, literature and history as renaissance or as nationalism? Is renaissance simply a misnomer for the pre-politicised stage of cultural nationalism? (Kopf 1969, vii–viii)

Despite all its drawbacks and failings, this nation seems to be the best means that we have to preserve our culture and to express our own destiny. This nation has not only survived the ravages of the partition, but every conceivable threat, both internal and external, to its very existence. But having met and overcome these challenges, it seems to be poised to take our civilisation to new heights. This is not an inconsiderable achievement. Can India embody the best of its unique cultural heritage and also become a modern nation? This is the question that we must wait for the future to answer.

To my mind, the most important contribution of Aurobindo to the discussion on the Indian renaissance is, as is often the case with his work, in what is yet to be realised. Aurobindo says that the rise of India is necessary for the future of humanity itself. The third and most difficult task for the Indian renaissance has been the new creation that will come from a unique fusion of ancient Indian spirituality and modernity. This fusion will be instrumental in spiritualising the world and in bringing about what many have called a global transformation. In our present times of the clash of civilisations, such an idea may seem too perfectionist or impractical, but, ultimately, the very survival of the planet depends on a hope and belief that something of this sort is not only possible but inevitable.

10.5 CONCLUSION

I started by referring to my visit to the graves of some of the famous men of the Bengal, nay Indian renaissance, of the nineteenth century. I should end by invoking them once again: Sir William Jones, Henry Derozio, Michael Madhusudan Dutt, but to this list let me now add the names of the even more illustrious Swami Vivekananda and Sri Aurobindo. If we place them in chronological order, we notice a peculiar progression from the British to the Indian and from Indian to the international. Jones was English, Derozio Eurasian, Dutt converted to Christianity, Vivekananda reversed this trend, converting some Westerners to Vedanta and finally Aurobindo brought about what might be called a new creation in that he fused the ancient Indian with the modern Western.

From the European Christian Park Street and the racially mixed Christian Lower Circular Road cemeteries, we shall have to move farther inland to pay our homage at the *samadhis* of Hindu Swami Vivekananda and post-Hindu Aurobindo. Swami Vivekananda's mortal remains are enshrined in a simple but elegant two-storey temple at the Belur Math, on the banks of the Hooghly. The Math itself is a modern structure, built in the last days of the British Empire. It is an eclectic mix of Rajputana and Eastern, with neo-Classical, colonial architectural styles. Across the river, we can see the more traditional temple complex of the Dakshineshwar Kalibari, which Rani Rasmoni built in the second half of the nineteenth century and where Sri Ramakrishna came as the temple priest. Sri Ramakrishna's *lilaprasanga* (episodes of his lifeplay), as his great biographer, Swami Saradananda characterises his life, was played out mostly inside the compound of that temple. The Belur Math was inspired by Swami Vivekananda, his foremost disciple, who also founded the order named after him, the Ramakrishna Mission. The Mission was a wholly new and modern phenomenon, but one which was inspired by the deepest springs and stirrings of tradition and which had its roots in the soil of spiritual India. Swami Vivekananda's samadhi has many visitors, who bow before his image and visit his room upstairs. The shrine is immaculately clean and there is daily worship conducted there by the designated priests of the Ramakrishna Order.

Sri Aurobindo's *samadhi* is even farther away, in Pondicherry, in South India. One can reach it from Madras by taxi. Inside a fairly well-appointed though not ostentatious set of French villas, you come across a raised platform which houses his remains. This is always covered with flowers and beautifully decorated. Above it, to keep off the bird droppings, is an embroidered canopy slung from the branches of the beautiful 'service tree,' whose roots must go pretty close to the casket in which he was buried beneath. The courtyard of the house has many trees and is surrounded by the buildings which housed Sri Aurobindo, the Mother and their closest attendants. In one of these, Sri Aurobindo lived most of the last twenty-five years of his life, confined to a few rooms on the first floor. He never left those premises and showed himself only rarely to people on *darshan* days. What he was trying to accomplish was nothing short of a transformation of human consciousness. He believed that just as the mind 'descended' on earth some 2.5 million years ago or so with the rise of Homo Sapiens as a species, a higher faculty than the mental would also be the natural, biological characteristic of a higher species than the human. This evolution from the human to the superhuman was, to him, not so much pre-ordained, as ardently desired, by nature. The question really was whether we wished to participate in this unfolding or to resist it. His partner in this endeavour, the Mother, who outlived him by almost twenty-five years, is also interred next to him in that twin *samadhi*. The shrine is the hub of all the activities in a very modern ashram. It is, indeed, a living space, integrated into the daily routines of thousands of *ashramites* and visitors. As such, of all the graves we have visited, it is the most active one. An endless stream of people visits this *samadhi* each day, to bow or kneel before it, to offer it flowers, to meditate around it. Those who believe feel very palpably the force of Sri Aurobindo and the Mother emanating from it.

From William Jones to Sri Aurobindo is a long way. In the nearly 200 years that elapsed from the birth of the former to the death of the latter, India itself changed irrevocably. When Jones died, the challenge before India was nothing short of a cultural death or subjection, such was the pressure of the material and mental subordination under colonialism. But by the time Sri Aurobindo left his body in 1950, many of these challenges had been met and exceeded. India reengineered itself on an unprecedented scale, even becoming a modern nation in the process. That this nation is a functioning democracy that feeds about 20% of the world's population is only one aspect of its achievement. That it has survived culturally and spiritually, in addition to prospering materially and scientifically is even more remarkable. Whether we appreciate it or not, there was a widespread turmoil and alteration of Indian society in the nineteenth century that paved the way to this transition. Whether or not it was a renaissance is questionable, yet it did open up the avenues to the progress of Indian society. India itself has moved ahead to recapture the means to study and disseminate its own culture. From colonialism to nationalism and beyond – such is the trajectory of our ongoing journey. The future beckons to us, inviting us to be the protagonists of our own narratives. This is certainly one of the legacies of the Indian renaissance.

WORKS CITED

Andrews, Charles Freer. 1912. *The Renaissance in India: Its Missionary Aspect.* London: Church Missionary Society.

Aurobindo, Sri. (1920) 1997. *The Renaissance in India and Other Essays on Indian Culture. The Collected Works of Sri Aurobindo.* Volume 20. Pondicherry: Sri Aurobindo Ashram.

———. 2003. *Early Cultural Writings. The Collected Works of Sri Aurobindo.* Volume 1. Pondicherry: Sri Aurobindo Ashram.

Bandyopadhyay, Sekhar. 2005. *The Namasudra Movement.* New Delhi: Critical Quest.

Chatterjee, Joya. 1994. *Bengal Divided: Hindu Communalism and Partition, 1932-1947.* Cambridge: Cambridge University Press.

Chaudhuri, Nirad C. 1951. *The Autobiography of an Unknown Indian.* London: Macmillan.

———. (1979) 1997. *Hinduism: A Religion to Live By.* New Delhi: Oxford India Paperbacks.

Chaudhuri, Rosinka. 2002. *Gentlemen Poets in Colonial Bengal: Emergent Nationalism and the Orientalist Project.* Kolkata: Seagull.

Chaudhuri, Sukanta. 2004. 'Renaissance and Renaissances: Europe and Bengal.' Centre of South Asian Studies Occasional Paper no. 1. Cambridge: University of Cambridge.

Cousins, James. (1918) 2005. *The Renaissance in India.* Edited by Dilip Chatterjee. Kolkata: Standard Book Agency.

Derozio, Henry. (1923) 1980. *Poems of Henry Louis Vivian Derozio, A Forgotten Anglo-Indian Poet.* Edited by Francis Bradley-Birt. 2nd edition. New Delhi: Oxford University Press.

Dhar, Pulak Naranyan. 1987. 'Bengal Renaissance: A Study in Social Contradictions.' *Social Scientist.* 15.1: 26–45.

Dutt, Michael Madhusudan. 1993. *Madhusudan Rachanabali.* Edited by

Kshetra Gupta. 12th edition. Calcutta: Sahitya Sansad.

Foucault, Michel and Colin Gordon. 1990. *Power/Knowledge: Selected Interviews and Other Writings; 1972-1977*. New York [u.a.]: Harvester Wheatsheaf.

Gandhi, M. K. (1909) 1994. *Hind Swaraj*. Ahmedabad: Navjivan.

Hardt, Michael and Antonio Negri. 2000. *Empire*. Cambridge, Mass: Harvard University Press.

Heehs, Peter. 2008. *The Lives of Sri Aurobindo*. New York: Columbia University Press.

Jones, William. 1970. *The Letters of William Jones*. 2 vols. Ed. Garland Cannon. Oxford: Clarendon Press.

_____.1993. *Sir William Jones: A Reader*. Edited by Satya S. Pachauri. New Delhi:
Oxford University Press.

Kapoor, Kapil. 2004. 'Loss, Recovery and Renewal of Texts in Indian Traditions.' *Evam*. 3.1&2: 12-37.

Kipling, Rudyard. (1891) 2009. *The City of Dreadful Night*. Web. ebooks@Adelaide. Accessed 4 February 2012. <http://ebooks.adelaide.edu.au/k/kipling/rudyard/city/chapter8.html>

Kopf, David. 1969. *British Orientalism and the Bengal Renaissance: The Dynamics of Indian Modernisation, 1773-1835*. Berkeley: University of California Press.

_____. 1980. 'Hermeneutics versus History.' Review of *Orientalism* by Edward W. Said. *The Journal of Asian Studies*. 39.3: 495-506.

Lennon, Joseph. 2004. *Irish Orientalism: A Literary and Intellectual History*. Syracuse, NY: U of Syracuse Press.

Macaulay, T. B. (1835) 1990. 'Minute on Indian Education.' *Svaraj, Tradition & Modernity*. 1.1: 99-107.

_____. 2003. 'Sri Aurobindo's "The Renaissance in India"' in *Critical Practice*, 10.2: 74-86.

Pieterse, Jan Nederveen. 1990. *Empire and Emancipation: Power and Liberation on a World Scale*. London: Pluto Press.

Raychaudhuri, Tapan. 1999. *Perceptions, Emotions, Sensibilities: Essays on India's Colonial and Post-Colonial Experiences*. Delhi: Oxford University Press.

Roy, Arundhati. 1997. *The God of Small Things*. London: Flamingo.
Said, Edward W. 1978. *Orientalism*. New York: Viking.
Sarkar, Jadunath, Ed. 1943. *The History of Bengal*. Part II. Dacca: The University of Dacca.
Sarkar, Susobhan. 1979. *On the Bengal Renaissance*. Calcutta: Papyrus.
Smith, G. G. 1879. *Life of Alexander Duff*. New York: A. C. Armstrong and Son.
Stokes, Eric. 1959. *The English Utilitarians and India*. Oxford: The Clarendon Press.
Vivekananda, Swami. (1989) 1994. *The Collected Works of Swami Vivekananda*. Calcutta: Advaita Ashrama.

11
THE 'PERSISTENT' MAHATMA – REREADING GANDHI POST-HINDUTVA

> *I know that friends get confused when I say I am a Sanatanist Hindu and they fail to find in me things they associate with a man usually labeled as such. But that is because, in spite of my being a staunch Hindu, I find room in my faith for Christian and Islamic and Zoroastrian teaching and, therefore, my Hinduism seems to some to be a conglomeration and some have even dubbed me an eclectic. Well, to call a man eclectic is to say that he has no faith, but mine is a broad faith which does not oppose Christians – not even a Plymouth Brother – not even the most fanatical Mussalman. It is a faith based on the broadest possible toleration. I refuse to abuse a man for his fanatical deeds because I try to see them from his point of view. It is that broad faith that sustains me. It is a somewhat embarrassing position, I know – but to others, not to me!*
>
> – M. K. GANDHI (*Gandhi 1927*, 425; *Gandhi 1999*, VOL. 35, 254-55)[1]

11.1 REMEMBERING SANATANA DHARMA

The last chapter of this book is reserved for the greatest of modern Indians, Mohandas Karamchand Gandhi (1869-1948). Most of this book has been devoted to writers, but each of them was much more than a writer. This is equally true of Gandhi who besides being so much else, was also an important writer, one of the most prolific of our times. His collected volumes extend to 100 large-sise volumes, totalling over 50,000 pages. Of these, the space occupied by his books is relatively small, though he did write original and influential works. It is his speeches, letters and journalistic writings that make up the bulk of his work. Gandhi's journalism was very much a part of his activism. For about forty years of his life, he edited and published newspapers and periodicals, which became the vehicles of his ideas. His first foray into journalism was *The Indian Opinion,* which Gandhi took over in 1903 when he was in South Africa. After his return to India, Gandhi ran, for several years, two periodicals, *Young India* and *Navajivan*. Later, he added a third, *Harijan,* which he continued to publish regularly for several years, despite the heavy burden of his political work. Gandhi wrote in many languages and though he campaigned against English, especially the danger it posed in displacing native languages, he wrote well and widely enough in it to exercise considerable authority.

This chapter is about the afterlife of the Mahatma, his marginalisation in contemporary India and the relationship of his legacy to 'Hindutva,' Hindu cultural nationalism that became a leading force in Indian politics in the 1980s. I call this chapter the 'Sanatani,' that is, literally, the 'eternal' Mahatma because it tries to bring out the peculiar quality of 'persistence' in his career, even after his death. This chapter asks what or who this Mahatma is and what aspect of his life is actually enduring.

Ii is suggested at the start of the book that the cultural plurality of India underwent a drastic alteration after independence. Gandhi was assassinated on 30 January 1948 by Nathuram Godse, a Hindu nationalist, who believed that Gandhi was harming his co-religionists and weakening India. The men who ruled India after Gandhi's death were Nehru-ites. Many of them were Westernised, English-speaking and foreign-educated Indians, whose knowledge of their own traditions, whether classical or vernacular, was somewhat limited; at any rate, they knew the modern, Western world better. Most of these men had already been a part of the British bureaucracy. There was a great deal of continuity between the colonial and the post-colonial administration. The moral, spiritual force that had been at the heart of India's struggle for freedom lost its centrality in Indian national life, replaced by a certain kind of worldliness, which however decent or well-intentioned, was neither uplifting nor exemplary. Indeed, over the years, it not only bred a certain complacency and arrogance in the ruling classes, but also, eventually, corruption and hypocrisy. Nehru may have remained somewhat of a Gandhian, but his own underlings were all Nehru-ites. However, from the margins of history, the ghost of Gandhi continued to haunt the nation. Every single movement for greater justice, democracy, environmental protection, or the rights of the common people of India drew its inspiration and sustenance from Gandhi's legacy.

Yet Gandhi posed a challenge not only to the Nehruvian secularists who ruled India for most of its years as an independent country, but also to the Hindu nationalists, who led the coalition government at the centre from 1998-2004 and continue to rule certain states in the country. Nehru-ites were Hindus only culturally; they were neither practising Hindus nor, for large part, spiritually inclined. The Hindu nationalists, on the other hand, are political Hindus, not necessarily spiritual either. These latter are still unclear about what to do with Gandhi, whether to own him up as Deen Dayal Upadhyaya and Nanaji Deshmukh, two prominent figures in the Hindu political right tried to, or reject him as an enemy as Godse and his ideological successors still do.

Gandhi, of course, was culturally, spiritually and even politically a Hindu in ways that are uncomfortable to both Nehru-ites and Hindu nationalists. It is that part of his legacy that I wish to examine in this concluding chapter. But in order to do so, it would be useful to try to define what Sanatana Dharma is – what is it that actually makes it Sanatana or perennial. Intended as an extended act of Sanatani understanding of the life and legacy of Mahatma Gandhi, this essay is also a political project. It tries to explore new ways of being Indian and Hindu, especially in so far as this relates simultaneously to being a citizen of contemporary India and a member of a wider world of free people. My central question is to ask if it is possible to politically Hindu in a way that is not Nehruvian-secularist nor Hindu-communalist? – for both these seem to be denials of the very essence of Sanatana Dharma. Or have we lost that space, that location, that ability altogether? Can one be a Hindu in a politically moderate, democratic, pluralistic way – be a modern, civic Hindu, that is – or has that possibility shrunk or eroded beyond recovery? Is the only way to be a good citizen of India to be a non-practising Hindu?

It is necessary to stress at the outset that such a perspective is offered as a contribution to an alter*native* (trans)nationalism that is both contestatory, emancipatory and at the same time painfully engaged with the dominant. The latter is, ultimately, none other than yet another somewhat horrific and anxiously rapacious manifestation of the former, which is why it must be opposed and resisted. The purpose of this engagement, then, is to refresh the perennial possibilities of an alter-globalisation because they embody a deep species aspiration, which each one of us shares, for a better world. Sadly, however, neither dominance nor dissent, are able to deliver such a world to us. In fact, dissent is often a sanctioned, if not sanctified, part of the dominant.[2] Gandhian s*atyagraha* is radical and far-reaching precisely because it dares not so much to break up or break out of the dominant or even to destroy it as Osama Bin Laden would, but rather more ambitiously, tries to transform it into becoming the co-author of Ram Rajya, Gandhi's name for the ideal polity for the multiverse which we inhabit.

Coming closer to my topic, I wish to focus on a special kind of *limitation* in Gandhi's thought. Simply put, this limitation was his refusal to engage with modernity on its own terms. Whether this limitation was also a source of his unique strength is debatable, but that it was deliberate and thoughtful is somewhat more likely. What I plan to do is to use a similarly *limited* agency to recuperate Gandhi, who, I argue, himself risks being marginalised in India's current self-fashioning. I propose to do this by offering what I call a Sanatani re-reading of Gandhi. If this chapter sounds familiar in an uncanny way, I shall be happy because I regard it not as a new adventure, but an act of remembering what it is to be a Sanatani in contemporary times. All are invited to share in this remembering.

11.2 THE IRRELEVANCE OF GANDHI

It is regrettable, if not totally unexpected, that no one seems to be talking about Gandhi in India.[3] The official custodians of his legacy, the Gandhian institutions, are declining. Denied of state patronage, they have not managed to keep up with the times. Their employees, who get neither government scales nor wages comparable to their counterparts in the non-governmental sector, are an unhappy lot. Forcing people to live 'simply' by paying them too little or to wear khadi have not done much to perpetuate Gandhi's legacy. Worse, there is a deeper despair that prevails in these organisations because of what might be termed the failure of a dream. Gandhian ideas no longer seem to be relevant; there seems to be no one either to practice or preach them. The old Gandhians, or should I say Gandhians of the old school, that is those who exemplified both the Gandhian lifestyle and ideology, are dead or dying by the year. They have no real successors. Gandhism, like many traditional world views, needs exemplars, not ideologues, to sustain it. Today there are neither exemplars nor even ideologues to perpetuate it. Neo-Gandhians – intellectuals, activists, ecologists, counter-culturists inspired by Gandhi – who spoke against modernity, industrialisation, consumerism, big dams, the economy of scale, right and left wing violence – have also been marginalised. With the apparent triumph of LPG (Liberalisation, Privatisation, Globalisation), no one listens to them either. In India, then, Gandhi has become an empty signifier.

This emptying is visible in the polity by the gradual desertion of those who might have been thought of as Gandhi's stakeholders, those whose rights and causes he championed so tirelessly. Some of these desertions and rejections happened even during his own life. For instance, one of Gandhi's most passionate projects, Hindu-Muslim unity, lay in shambles with the creation of two nations, India and Pakistan. The latter was the progeny of an ideology, popularly called the 'two nation theory,' that directly opposed most of what Gandhi stood for. The Muslim League propaganda, that Gandhi was a leader only of the Hindus was effective, at least to the extent that it found support in that section of Muslim elite who demanded and succeeded in creating an Islamic republic. That this rejection saddened and even crushed Gandhi cannot be doubted.

Another group whose interests Gandhi had fought for had also begun to turn against him in his own lifetime. These were the untouchables, whom he renamed Harijans, God's people. Under the leadership of Babasaheb Bhimrao Ambedkar, some of them broke away both from him and, subsequently, from the Hindu fold itself. Yet, large masses of the oppressed and depressed classes and castes did look to Gandhi as their friend and champion. This changed first in the south, where under the banner of Dravidianism, Tamil nationalism, anti-caste rationalism and anti-North Indianism, the DMK or the Dravida Munetra Kazhagam came to power. Something similar happened in North India, but several decades later, with the rise of BSP or the Bahujan Samaj Party and its rule of India's largest state, Uttar Pradesh. The word Harijan is seldom used, so vehemently is it rejected by those who call themselves Dalits or the downtrodden these days. Dalitism can be most palpably anti-Gandhian as is instantiated in the repeated attacks on Gandhi not only by leaders such as Kanshi Ram and Mayavati, but by a wide variety of Dalit intellectuals.[4]

Like the Dalits, women, whose rights Gandhi supported and whose entry into the national freedom struggle he encouraged, have also, it would appear, given up Gandhi. With the emergence of Western-style feminism in English/urban India, Gandhi is no longer seen as a proponent of women's empowerment. Instead, he is regarded as an enthusiast of Hindu patriarchy who believed that a woman's primary duty was to look after home and hearth. Women Gandhians are seldom well-regarded, certainly not in recent feminist writings. They, in turn, have not cared or tried to respond to such charges. Gandhi's contribution to women's empowerment is now a sort of fading memory; everyone thinks so but cannot say exactly how or why Gandhi was pro-women. Those who read his work a little more carefully are embarrassed by his repeated insistence on chastity or sexual abstinence. Similarly, they cannot say that his insistence that women made better satyagrahis because of their inherent capacity to bear suffering patiently is a compliment or a curse. It seems certainly more convenient to join those criticising Gandhi for his antiquated notions of women's subjectivity and role in society.

Gandhian Socialists, a peculiarly Svadeshi or indigenous type of left, with stalwarts like Rammanohar Lohia, Asaf Ali, Achyut Patwardhan, Narendra Dev and Jayaprakash Narayan are all dead. Their ideological mantle has fallen on lesser men, most of whom cannot even be mentioned in the same breath. These contemporary Socialists, who are scattered across several parties which have the word Janata in them, know or say little about Gandhi – Laloo Prasad and Mulayam Singh, are but two examples. The more confirmed or crimson communists – whether they call themselves Marxists, Naxalites, Maoists – not to speak of other revolutionary left-wingers – had little use of Gandhi to begin with. Now that the masses are not longer with Gandhi, they can afford to be openly contemptuous of the bourgeois reactionary who they say prevented the real devolution of power to the people or the real revolution in which the proletariat would have seized power once and for all as in the former Soviet Union or China.

But the most shocking and sudden eclipse of Gandhi from the popular imagination has come from an unexpected, Hindu source. Has Gandhi whom the Muslim communalists derided as the leader of the Hindus, been at last rejected by Hindus themselves? It would seem that there is some truth in this. With the rise of the BJP and its strident rhetoric of Hindutva after the 1980s, the last and most loyal followers of Gandhi, those 'ordinary' Hindus to whom he was and will always remain a Mahatma, also seem to have forgotten him. Nathuram Godse, the man who with the utmost deliberation and 'rational' justification assassinated Gandhi, who was considered by most Hindus to be an unHindu fanatic, instead, finds himself resurrected in those same Hindus who considered him most unlike themselves. Now voicing their sympathy with a political party whose platform is Hindutva, a political creed which at its best is majoritarian and at its worst Hindu supremacist, have these 'ordinary' Hindus repudiated Gandhi? The re-election of the Congress-led United Progressive Alliance (UPA) government to power in 2004 and 2009, too, is little consolation to Gandhians because the only deceased Gandhi that they seek to promote is Rajiv, now sought to be projected as the unifying national symbol of an upwardly mobile, globalising India. And the only living Gandhi that is the object of the nation's adoration, whom Forbes magazine rated as the world's third most powerful woman and whose renouncing of power has been hailed as one of the most noble acts of sacrifice in human history is, of course, an Italian Indian called Sonia. Needless to say, neither Rajiv nor Sonia seem to have even the remotest connection to Mohandas, I mean not just genetically, but ideologically. Sadly, then, Gandhi is today no longer even the leader of the Congress, let alone of the Hindus.

What does this gradual emptying or hollowing of the Gandhian signifier in India mean? Does it prove that Gandhi is well and truly irrelevant to India or is he simply waiting to be rediscovered in another unexpected way?

11.3 RECUPERATING GANDHI: A SANATANI ESSAY

If we regard Gandhi as an intellectual, at which description he himself would have baulked, we see in him a remarkable awareness that the clash of ideologies, systems and, yes, even civilisations, occurs at the level of categories. It is not just concepts, ideas, or ideologies that differ, but at their root lie deeper structures of thought, contrasting definitions of how to regard wo(man), God and society. To read *Hind Swaraj* yet again is at once to come across a refusal of the self to be defined in terms set by the other. The 'Other' in this text is primarily imperialistic, western modernity, a specific version of which was the British Empire. But there is also a more familiar, neighbourly Other, the violent, modern Indian, who had internalised the values of the adversary and wished to combat the latter with his own weapons. A freedom won through violent means, for Gandhi, is no better than the violent imperial state that he sought to replace. British rule without the British was no better than British rule by the British. Gandhi's trenchant treatment of Westernised Indians, including doctors, lawyers and English – educated elites, reminds us that we Indians have been equally responsible for blocking Svaraj. Gandhi did not want us to succumb to the conceptual framework or apparatus of the dominant even if he was unafraid of engaging with it. Not to fear the West is of course quite different from being a part of it. That is why he sought to define it in terms of his own civilisational framework. He used the traditional vocabulary of Kali Yuga, the iron age, to describe the way modernity allowed the machine to enslave and dehumanise us: 'The tendency of the Indian civilisation is to elevate the moral being, that of the Western civilisation is to propagate immorality. The latter is godless, the former is based on a belief in God.' (Gandhi, [1909] 1994, 63) Modern civilisation, he argued, does not improve us, does not encourage virtue, but instead leads us to vice, moral dissipation and the multiplication of wants.

While Gandhi's critique may be modern in one sense, even post-modern in another, it would not be easy to fit him either into the pre-modern or the modern or the post-modern. In fact, I think such attempts are misplaced in that they seek to read Gandhi from the narrative framework of the dominant. I have argued elsewhere that after its contact with the West, India learned the vocabulary and the discourse of modernity without necessarily arriving at the condition of modernity. Indian responses to modernity are hence, neither anti-modern or pro-modern as many people have argued, though such elements can easily be found. I have argued that India is a radically *non*-modern space, which nonetheless displays *elements* of the pre- the modern and the post-modern. But these elements cannot be confused with its matrix, which remains *non*-modern. In other words, India's narrative has a dynamics, which can neither be absorbed nor annexed by the dominant narratives of the West. Even Marx could not incorporate India into his universal master-narrative and had to invent a special category to explain India's centuries-long stupor of stagnation, which he called the Asiatic mode of production, to contrast it with the more historically amenable European feudalism. Without setting up a binary between India and the West, I would simply say that these have different narrative trajectories. I stress not polarity but distinction, not opposition merely but variation. My strategy, therefore, is not to read Gandhi in Western terms, but to read the West in Gandhian terms. This way, I sidestep the perennial tradition-modernity dialectic that is endemic or shall I say epidemic to academic discourse on India. It is as misplaced, then, to propose India's tradition in opposition to the West's modernity, thereby to locate Gandhi in the traditional, just as it to suggest that Gandhi's anti-modernity was actually an avant garde *post*-modernity, rather ahead of its times.

Instead I propose a different way of understanding India's narrative.

I would like to use the word 'Sanatani' to describe this narrative. This was a word that Gandhi himself often used to describe himself. Gandhi, by his own admission, was a Sanatani Hindu. Witness his famous remark to Ranchodlal Patwari in the letter of 9 June 1915: 'I will sacrifice this life itself to uphold the sanatana dharma as I understand it.' (Gandhi 1999, Vol. 15, 9) This he said at a time when a Sanatani Hindu was thought of as conservative and traditionalist, quite in contrast, to consider the example of North India, to the Arya Samaji, who was seen as a reformist. Yet Gandhi redefined what it meant to be a Sanatani Hindu. He upturned the entire belief system of the Hindus, especially those that pertained to social observances. He was, in that sense, the most reformist or modernising of all recent Hindus. His pronouncements and actions on untouchability, the rights of women and Hindu-Muslim relations, for instance, would put him in direct conflict with most so-called Sanatani Hindus of his time. His lengthy correspondence, not to mention his fast unto death, over the denial of temple-entry to untouchables in Travancore state, amply demonstrates his resolve to purge Hinduism of both social ills and irrationalities. In the end, Gandhi succeeded in redefining Hinduism in ways that no other national leader before or since has.

A Sanatani reclamation of Gandhi, therefore, is the need of the hour. My use of the category 'Sanatani,' though related to Gandhi's use of it, should not be equated either with right-wing exclusive Hindu attempts to appropriate the legacy of the Mahatma nor with notions of traditionalist Hinduism. Indeed, I could go farther to assert that Sanatana Dharma is not even the exclusive ideology or practice of a specific religious tradition or belief system, though I think that the Hindu self-characterisation of Sanatana needs to be taken seriously. By Sanatani I mean a certain way of regarding the self, society and the cosmos. Let me quickly spell out some of the features of this Sanatani *Parampara* or Sanatani narrative, as I see them. First, it has no point of origin and no closure. Secondly, it is pluralistic, without being relativistic; that is it accepts the unity of truth, but allows for a diversity of expressions and descriptions. Thirdly, it has no one central text, prophet, founder, or church. It is always a field of difference and debate, though not necessarily of conflict or opposition. Fourthly, its central tendency is to sacralise the world and all the objects contained in it. To such an extent is this drive manifest that it turns even secularism into a spiritual tradition and sanctifies instrumental rationality, which is itself the means of de-sacralising the world. It is this tendency that saves it not only from rapaciously preying on other human groups, but on non-human life.

The Sanatani is not anthropocentric, logocentric, or even theocentric, but radically *self*-centric, where the self is, ultimately, non-separate, radically relational and co-extensive with the cosmos. The Sananati, as its name suggests, is not fixated on time, but on the untimely and the timeless; though it allows for complex notions of linearity, evolution and teleology, its main focus is neither on the past or the future, but on the present. The Sanatani also has a complex sense of causality called Karma and an equally complex sense of axiology called Dharma. When both karma and dharma are individual, collective and cosmic, there can be no simple idea of doership or agency. Naturally, the ultimate reality cannot be restricted to the merely perceptible. Unlike the modern mind – this moves from inequality to equality – the Sanatani proceeds from identity of substance to variety, differentiation then hierarchy. Instead of equality of opportunity it stresses variety of aspiration. I could list many other features and characteristics, but will end with what I call the categorical imperative of the Sanatani, namely its *non*-exclusivity. The non-exclusive must not be considered identical with the inclusive. The opposite of inclusive is exclusive; to that extent the two will always be tied together. Those who claim to include will always exclude something or the other. The non-exclusive, on the other hand, has no opposite, because theoretically it does not exclude even the exclusive. Yet to remain non-exclusive, it cannot permit the exclusive to overrun it totally. That is how the exclusive remains as a non-dominant element in the non-exclusive. In other words, the Sanatani will have some exclusive elements, but the latter will not be allowed to dominate.

Am I trying to deterritorialise Sanatanism or to universalise it? The answer would be both yes and no. Yes, in that I think Sanatanism, like non-dualism, need not, cannot, be construed in ethnic or essentialist terms as confined to or uniquely expressive of any particular region of the world. As abstractions, the qualities that I identify as Sanatani are not necessarily geo-cultural or country-specific. Yet, I would argue that while Sanatani tendencies, characteristics or elements exist, to varying degrees, in all societies it is in India where they cohere to form a zeitgeist that has endured over centuries. I do not suggest that Sanatani=Indian/Hindu; rather that Indian/Hindu *should*=Sanatani. Not merely I, but I believe the cultural consensus in India, itself seeks to valorise the Sanatani in Indian traditions, without necessarily devaluing the non-Sanatani ones. What is more, in my schema, it would be possible to have Indian Sanatanism, British Sanatanism, US Sanatanism, just as we have Indian democracy, British democracy and US democracy and so on.

India's intellectual and cultural history, if seen in Sanatani terms, often shows it coming into contact or conflict with alternative perspectives. These latter I shall term co-Sanatani, non-Sanatani and anti-Sanatani. The co-Sanatani shares basic assumptions and premises with the Sanatani: for example, Jainism, Buddhism, Sikhism. There have been perennial exchanges, debates and crossovers between the Sanatani and the co-Sanatani. Then there is the non-Sanatani, which refers to those world views which are radically different from the Sanatani. The Abrahamic faiths may be cited as examples. All these have a point of origin and closure, are monotheistic and dogmatic and ultimately based on a community that is formed by a special covenant with God, who is the sovereign of the universe and the ultimate arbitrator. This does not mean that these faith traditions have totally devoid or lacking in Sanatani elements. In fact, it is clearly seen that the Sanatani elements in these traditions are encouraged or reinforced when they flourish in India. Secular modernity, communism, capitalism, imperialism, to name another, more recent set of ideologies, are also non-Sanatani.

How do the Sanatani and the non-Sanatani interact? There is every possibility of a peaceful coexistence, conversion, or limited syncretism between the Sanatani and the non-Sanatani. However in certain circumstances, the non-Sanatani can also turn into the anti-Sanatani. When that happens, the Sanatani is called upon to produce a response. These responses are often multi-dimensional, more or less vigorous or successful. Like all resilient traditions, the Sanatani may be considered to be endowed with self-correcting and self-renewing mechanisms. So its growth and development in history needs to be seen not so much as unbroken and continuous but as marked by losses and recoveries, ruptures and sutures. This moment of recovery, restoration and recuperation may be termed the 'neo' or *navya*-Sanatani.[5] The '*navya*' – is not a negative, pejorative, or reactionary; it cannot be dismissed as fundamentalist or revivalist. The '*navya*' to be genuinely so must be both new and old at the same time. It has to show a new way of being Sanatani, thereby rendering it simultaneously both unprecedented and recognisably the same as what is already known. One might borrow an idea from Kashmir Saivism to explain this familiar newness: *pratyabhijna* –the sort of self-recognition that is in fact predicated upon the self being already realised, but somehow forgotten by none other than itself in anticipation of the *camatkara* (miraculous wonder) of remembering as in Acharya Utpaladeva's *Isvaraprtyabijankarika*.

There is an epochal dimension to these acts of recovery and suturing, of recognition and remembering. The tradition produces its own cultural heroes and heroines to do the job. The process of mending is also one of minding, like searching for and splicing together the scattered threads of a fabric that has been torn or rent. Similarly, a tradition that has undergone a traumatic, even catastrophic blow finds ways of healing by rediscovering lost continuities and building new bridges from the past to the future. The present, so potent with possibilities, is not some essence from the past or the passing current that leads to an uncertain future, but a gift, a bequest, a joyous flow that liberates the beleaguered self of its false identification. As Gandhi said, the moment Indians know fearlessness, virtue and dignity, they are already free; no prison or imperial government can bind them then. It is only the free who can demand or attain freedom. Freedom is the prerequisite for and not the consequence of satyagraha. The praxis of the latter involves the invention of new methods and materials with which to effect the restoration of the flow of the *parampara*. *Sruti*, or non-contingent incarnates as human agency to heal the wounds in Smriti or the collective cultural memory. Unlike the Hebraic, which emphasises remembering, the Sanatani encourages re-membering, often paradoxically through radical forgetting: one must forget the holocaust of the Hindus, their defeat and humiliation, their oppression and trauma, their scattering, conversion, enslavement, transportation and so on, so that one may be free of either hatred or shame. The forgetting is not amnesiac or careless; it is, instead, mindful, deliberate and cathartic. It involves the knowledge of the truth, but the refusal to retaliate or seek revenge. It is only the power of deliberate *ahimsa* or non-injury that can serve as the solvent to dissolve past wrongs. In other words, the realisation of present power is not contingent upon the denial of past tribulations, nor is it forever unavailable to a conquered people; the memory of being crushed can be overcome by the immediacy of Svaraj. Forget that you are crushed, but rise up anew to an altogether different kind of battle, fought with altogether different kinds of weapons. Gandhi taught us how thus to turn our disadvantages to our advantages.

To my mind, Gandhi's *ahimsa* should be understood not so much as refusal to injure others, which it certainly was, but an active, even forceful and aggressive loving that brings about a transformation in the Other. Gandhi sought to turn the anti-Sanatani into the co-Sanatani; indeed, he refused to believe that Muslims and Christians were intrinsically anti-Sanatani, even if they might be doctrinally or historically so. Instead, he tried to recapture the other history of peaceful co-existence and common ancestry to suggest a uniquely Indian, even Sanatani, Islam and Christianity. His approach to the question of Hindu-Muslim unity was for Hindus to yield the utmost without compromising on essentials, even as they remained 'good' Hindus. In his speech at Nellore on 7 April, 1921 he said:

> As a *Sanatana* Dharma Hindu, feeling for my own faith, hoping that if the Faith was on its trial, I would be found in the front rank to give my life for its sake as a *Sanatani* Hindu, I wish first of all to address myself to my Hindu brethren and would say: 'If you would live in amity and friendship with the Mohammedan countrymen, the only way you can do so is never on any account to put a strain upon their religious fervour and always yield to them even though you may consider that their demands are unreasonable and unjust. But there is a condition attached to that submission even to unreasonable demands and that condition is that their demands do not encroach upon the vital part of your religious tenets. (Gandhi 1999, Vol. 23:11)

He goes on to list temple worship and cow protection as non-negotiable items to secure which a Hindu may even give up his life, but not, for instance, playing music before a mosque, which the Hindu should not insist on. Today's secularists want Hindus to be non-Hindus or un-Hindu in order to prove the extent of their willingness to accommodate *others*. Clearly, this is neither feasible, nor is it Gandhi's way. What Gandhi did see as clearly anti-Sanatani was Western modernity, or rather a specific manifestation of it in the form of racist and exploitative imperialism. 'Hard' secularism, which is itself the progeny of dogmatic Christianity, is ill-qualified to arbitrate between people of different religious persuasions in India. Instead, it is such non-compromising secularism, a scientific version of which is championed by someone like Richard Dawkins, that itself needs to be weighed on a Sanatani scale to measure its efficacy.

Gandhi poses a tough challenge to Hindutva. Should Hindutva 'kill' Gandhi, as Nathuram did, kill, that is all forms and avatars of Gandhism as they resurface from time to time? Or should Hindutva absorb, digest, assimilate Gandhi? The former is too formidable a task, one that is perhaps doomed to fail, not once but over and over again. Gandhi, the Mahatma, is not so easy to kill precisely because there is something Sanatani (persistent) about him. Pitted against such a legacy, it is Hindutva which risks weakening or perishing. If Hindutva, on the other hand, wishes to absorb Gandhi, which is the far more advisable alternative, it can only do so by changing itself fundamentally. Gandhi brings out this almost insurmountable internal contradiction within Hindutva. The only way that Hindutva can remain or become Sanatani is by repudiating its own Semiticisation or regarding the latter only as a temporary, rather, emergency response, while reaffirming its basic Sanatani orientation.

11.4 STILL SEARCHING FOR SVARAJ? GANDHI AND A NEW GLOBAL ORDER

In the context of the rise of religious fanaticism and intolerance the world over, it is above all a Sanatani Gandhi who can best serve our purposes today – this is what I have been trying to argue. Such a Sanatani Gandhi can rise only if he is not hijacked or subordinated to Nehruvian secularism, which is blatantly non-Sanatani, nor overtaken by reactive Hindutva which is also non-Sanatani, despite whatever official claims it might make. Like a true Sanatani, Gandhi spiritualised politics, tying up India's freedom with his own quest for liberation and self-perfection. Both the secularist, minoritarian Congress and the Hindu majoritarian BJP have de-spiritualised the

Indian polity, thereby divorcing power from piety, *rajkarana* from *rajdharma*. A Sanatani Gandhi can stand for a new political initiative in India, one that veers India away from the divisive and conflictual politics of vote banks and false populism, to a collective effort for cooperation and collaboration. A Sanatani Gandhi will restore the dignity and selfhood of common Hindus without forcing them either to secularise or to turn Hindutvavadis. A Sanatani Gandhi can demonstrate that one can be a Hindu in India without being anti-Muslim or anti-Christian. A Sanatani Gandhi shows how we can love India and its culture without being chauvinistic, self-righteous, or bigoted cultural nationalists. At least in the context of India, non-Sanatani, Western-oriented, post-modernist, or other readings of Gandhi cannot achieve this.

A Sanatani reconsideration of Gandhi is available not only in his writings on ashram vows and observances, but in Chapter XVIII of *Hind Swaraj* on 'Passive Resistance' where he spells out the prerequisites of a truth-warrior or a *satyagrahi*. These include chastity, poverty, truth, fearlessness (Gandhi 1994, 84), reminiscent of Patanjali's *yamas, ahimsa, satya, brahmacharya, asteya, aparigraha* (non-injury, truthfulness, chastity, non-stealing and non-hoarding). To observe these would be to qualify oneself to be a practicing yogi. In that sense, Gandhi wanted all his political workers to be satyagrahis or yogis first and foremost. These and his other 'religious' writings cannot be erased from the archive just as Sanatani cannot be erased out of Gandhi.

However, instead of a long an elaborate reconsideration, there is a far simpler and more effective way to recuperate the Sanatani Gandhi. It is simply to place *svaraj*[6] before us as a sort of discursive talisman. Do what I write and practice contribute to my svaraj and the svaraj of others like me? This is, to me a fundamental question. I would hazard to assert that much of the work of our champion dissenters does not actually contribute to svaraj in this broader sense. Unfortunately, the word itself has been translated as 'Home Rule' in the English translation, but on the last page of his text, Gandhi clarifies that 'Real home-rule is self-rule or self-control.' (Gandhi

1994, 104) This takes us back to the original, Upanishadic meaning of the word, which suggests not just self-mastery but liberation from suffering. What Gandhi does, however, is to make swaraj the bridge between the personal and the political, the individual and the social. Gandhian anarchism is not really a form of anti- or non-governmentality, but more a project of self-regulation and governance. A community made up of self-regulating individuals, living in dignity and according full respect to each other would be a good definition of Svaraj.

To me, Svaraj is also the interface between intra-national struggles and inter-national ones. Individuals, groups of individuals, communities, sub-nationalities, nations, even groups of nations can struggle for svaraj. The range of meanings that svaraj encompasses include anti-imperialism, self-determination, independence, autonomy, non-alignment, non-interventionism, right down to very specific acts of self-correction and self-culture. Svaraj implies not only freedom from oppression, but also the *refusal* to oppress. That is why it can serve as a link and common ground between both the rich and the poor, the powerful and the powerless, the strong and the weak. It allows for an alternative to the present rule of the world, which is rule or be ruled. US imperialism cannot be replaced by Soviet, Chinese, or some other kind of imperialism, but only by a non-imperialism, which is yet convincingly to be exemplified among the powerful nations. Can India rise to the challenge of becoming powerful, but not imperialistic? This would need nothing short of a new definition of power, which is nothing short of a new institutionalising of the state apparatus. This, in turn, can only happen when there is a new kind of rationality, which means, really, a new level of consciousness. Curiously, this is where the Gandhian and the Aurobindonian project seem to intersect. All this seems like a really tall order for a disturbed and refractory planet, plagued by strife and misery. But then there seems to be no way out, no way ahead. Such wisdom is not utopian so much as minimal and imperative to the survival of the species. It is the prerequisite, not the final desideratum of decent terrestrial life. If humankind must move ahead to such a pass, India will have to play its part. In that part, Gandhi's uniquely innovative Sanatanism will have proved to be crucial.

In Gandhi we may also find the resolution of the old Orientalist vs Anglicist controversy. Gandhi, as a Sanatani, placed himself squarely in the native traditions of the land. In *Hind Swaraj* he considered Indian civilisation as second to none, as naturally nourishing to its denizens as mother's milk. To give it up for imported powder milk or formula, however fashionable, would not do. But Gandhi was not against English either. He advocated its use for several purposes including international communication and widening our intellectual horizons. He was certainly not in favour of scrapping English, but would have liked it to be put in its proper place, so to speak, in the hierarchy and spectrum of native Indian languages. Like the vernacularists, Gandhi wrote extensively in Gujarati and Hindi, addressing his correspondents and audiences in these languages. But he was also a master stylist of the English language, especially known for his wit, brevity and clarity of expression. Gandhi was also familiar with Sanskrit; he not only read the Bhagawad Gita in the original but wrote a commentary on it. Gandhi, thus, translates the bitter fight between Westernisers and indigenists, showing us how to belong to our own land while living in the larger world as global citizens. Here he presents an interesting contrast with Nehru who famously remarked in his *Autobiography*:

> I have become a queer mixture of the East and the West, out of place everywhere, at home nowhere. Perhaps my thoughts and approach to life are more akin to what is called Western, but India clings to me, as she does to all her children, in innumerable ways; and behind me lie, somewhere in the subconscious, racial memories of a hundred, or whatever the number may be, generations of Brahmans. I cannot get rid of either that past inheritance or my recent acquisitions. They are both part of me and, though they help me in both the East and the West, they also create in me a feeling of spiritual loneliness not only in public activities but in life itself. I am a stranger and alien in the

West. I cannot be of it. But in my own country also, sometimes, I have an exile's feeling. (Nehru 1936, 597–598)

Unlike Nehru, Gandhi was deeply grounded in Indian traditions and quite unapologetically so. Nehru's attempts to romanticise his deracination would, from a certain perspective, almost seem like a self-indulgence, if not weakness. Like Tagore, Gandhi was cosmopolitan even if he was a nationalist; like Aurobindo, he was deeply steeped in Indian spiritual traditions, not merely the classical but the medieval too. Like Nehru, he wrote easily and stylishly in English, but unlike the former, he was fluent in many Indian languages too. Like many Indian literary masters of that period, he also translated key foreign language texts in Indian languages such as his native Gujarati. All these factors make him the cultural hero who shows us how creatively and constructively we may be Indians in our own times.

I end, as I began this book on 'Making India,' with Gandhi. There is a special reason for this. The kind of authority that I have been trying to analyse is best instantiated in him precisely because, at his exemplary best, Gandhi both furthers and deconstructs this authority. His exercise of such authority is both textual and extra-textual; it is a moral and spiritual force which though expressed or mediated through his texts, also transcends them, as it transcends the authority of his own body, which is both text and instrument of his lifework. Gandhi said famously 'my life is my message' – to that extent, his body is his text, which even after its death, continues to exist in both iconic and symbolic ways. Gandhi's body, like his texts is trans-lingual. The *Collected Works* of Gandhi, though originally written in different languages such as Gujarati, Hindi and English, are now all of them available in English translation. Thus 'translated,' Gandhi through both his texts and his body, continues to exercise his moral and spiritual power in India and abroad. It would require another book to tell the story of the persistent Mahatma, but this may be considered as a modest beginning towards that project.

WORKS CITED

Chossudovsky, Michel. 2010. 'Manufacturing Dissent': The Anti-globalisation Movement is Funded by the Corporate Elites". *Prison Planet*. Web. Accessed 17 February 2012. <http://www.prisonplanet.com/manufacturing-dissent-the-anti-globalisation-movement-is-funded-by-the-corporate-elites.html>

Gandhi, M. K. (1909) 1994. *Hind Swaraj*. Ahmedabad: Navjivan Publishing House.

_____. 1927. Young India. Volume 9. Ahmedabad: Navajivan Publishing House.

_____. 1999. *The Collected Works of Mahatma Gandhi*. Electronic book. 98 vols. New Delhi: Publications Division Government of India.

Ingalls, Daniel Henry Holmes. (1951) 1988. *Materials For the Study of Navya-Nyaya Logic*. Columbia, MO: South Asia Books.

Mountain, Thomas C. 2006. 'Why do India's Dalits Hate Gandhi?' *Countercurrents*. Accessed 28 January 2012. < http://www.countercurrents.org/dalit-mountain200306.htm>

Nehru, Jawaharlal. 1936. *An Autobiography*. London: John Lane.

Paranjape, Makarand. 2003. *Decolonisation and Development: Hind Svaraj Revisioned*. New Delhi: Sage Publications.

_____. 2008. 'The Sanatani Mahatma: Rereading Gandhi Post-Hindutva.' In *The Philosophy of Mahatma Gandhi for the 21st Century*. Edited by Douglas Allen. Lanham, MD: Lexington Books.

Utpaladeva. 2003. *Isvara Pratyabhijna Karika of Utpaladeva: Verses on the Recognition of the Lord*. Translated by Bansi Pandit. Edited by Lise Vail. Delhi: Motilal Banarsidass.

CONCLUSION:
USABLE PASTS, POSSIBLE FUTURES

The preceding chapters offer one account of how India became modern as also of how usable even to today's purposes this process was. I have tried to show how important literature and literary texts were to this process. It was as if literary texts, even when they were accessible only to a relatively small section of the population, created the mentality of a nation, especially among the middle classes.[1] Arguably, it was this mentality that was the necessary precondition to the much larger spread and reach of Gandhian ideas later, which broad-based the freedom struggle, not only making it a mass movement of unforeseen dimension but also the spearhead of Indian democracy. Indians writing in English, working in tandem with their vernacular counterparts, played a crucial role, giving rise to what I have called 'Indian English authority.' These texts continue to exert a powerful influence on the present by constituting what may be termed the 'usable pasts' of the nation.

Not surprisingly, the most spectacular and enduring achievement of India's coming into modernity was probably the creation of the Indian nation. Why was a nation so necessary? Because only a nation could safeguard and protect the civilisation that was India, saving it not only from hostile attacks from outside, but also answering to the aspirations of its people who had suffered so much under various forms of colonialism and subjection. The nation embodied the deep urge among Indians for svaraj or self-rule. But nation-formation also became inevitable because pre-colonial Indian communities and configurations could not last into the post-colonial age. A new state along the lines of a modern nation thus became the necessary alternative to the colonial system which Indians resisted and ultimately overthrew.

Arguably, the colonial conquest of India was itself possible because of a lack of a nation in India. The Moghul empire was not a nation; it was not even a monarchy in the European sense, but a peculiarly South Asian empire-state, with flexible relations with various kinds of subordinate entities within its region of influence. These sub-regional powers had grown restive; some, like the Marathas and Sikhs had begun to wield considerably authority and were more-or -less independent. The Moghul state, moreover, had already started disintegrating before it could become a modern entity. The rise of British imperialism in India was facilitated by a power vacuum left by the collapse of the Moghul power.

The East India Company, which operated in India on the basis of a Moghul imperial *firman* (order) itself charged the last emperor, the unfortunate Bahadur Shah Zafar, with treason, banishing him to Rangoon in Burma. He had been thrust into the position of the leader of an unsuccessful revolt against the Company in 1857. The last vestiges of his power stripped, his sons executed practically before his eyes, he was forced into exile with his favourite queen, Zeenat Mahal. Bahadur Shah was sainted upon his death according to popular sufi traditions. His grave in Yangon is maintained by grants from the Government of India, but there is no interest in bringing his remains back to India.

The last Moghul emperor, memorialised as a poignant and tragic figure, cannot serve as one of the makers of modern India. The Indian nation, as I argued in *Altered Destinations* is unprecedented (Paranjape 2009, 27); there is nothing in its pre-colonial past upon which it can draw for ideological or structural sustenance. Yes, as Rajat Kanta Ray (2002) argues, there is a sentimental basis for the nation in pre-colonial India, but it is hard to find traces of the idea of a sovereign nation state prior to the struggle against British colonialism in India. Despite all its flaws and drawbacks, what came out of this struggle cannot be dismissed. The Indian nation is the bulwark of plural, democratic and egalitarian possibilities that the people of the land longed for and cherished for centuries. If this nation has survived, even strengthened, against almost impossible odds, the reasons are to be found in the lives and works of those who conceived and brought it into being. These were remarkable individuals who through their active participation in the social and political life of their times created a public sphere where notions of the nation were engendered, augmented and finally effectuated.

The central argument of this book is that such a national culture and consciousness was engendered in India over a period of approximately 150 years from 1800 to 1950. Furthermore, one of the chief engines of this process were the English writings of several key thinkers and leaders, some of whom have been discussed in this book. The body of their works constitutes not just the 'usable past' of our nation, but is also the source of a sort of charismatic authority that is exerted in the form of their 'afterlives.' The Indian 'consensus' that I have tried to sketch was based not only on deep churning and far-reaching struggles with the colonial structures of knowledge and power, but also entailed a thorough engagement with Indian pasts. Though the makers of Indian modernity presented a wide range of views, almost all of them agreed that India had much to learn from the West and much to change in her traditions. Yet, nearly all of them also agreed that Indian modernity could not be a copy of the West. What was needed was a continuous negotiation so as to create a third kind of space, one that resisted Western domination without becoming entirely reactive or retrogressive.

The value and validity of reason in fabricating such a culture was understood, even endorsed; yet, there was a strenuous attempt to retain the holism and 'spiritual' value-orientation perceived to be essential elements of Indian civilisation. Reason, in other words, was put in the service of personal liberty and human rights, but in much less an individualistic way than in Europe. Somehow, the fruition of the individual lay, according to these thinkers, in the securing of the sort of collectivity that the national space implied. India's freedom from colonial rule and the creation of a new nation state were seen as the best ways to ensure personal liberties.

In a sense, these chapters may also be seen as attempts to chart the aesthetic and cultural bases of Indian liberalism. For despite threats and denunciations from both the left and the right, ultimately it is the success of the Indian liberal project that is daily in evidence in contemporary India. Indian liberalism was not only a cry against the tyranny of tradition, but also against colonial domination. While it strove to remove the obstacles to individual growth and fulfilment in all spheres, its main targets were social and political freedom. Yet, as suggested earlier, Indian liberalism was more concerned with the collective, with the national, than with the local or individual. The reason for this was that our leaders recognised that without a stable, democratic structure of self-government, no individual aspiration could be fulfilled. That is why the struggle for svaraj or autonomy became synonymous with the quest for national sovereignty. Indeed, Indian modernity may itself be seen as the quest for svaraj and struggle against various form of authority: the authority of the state, whether colonial or national; the authority of religious institutions and traditional practices; and the authority of exploitative economic relations.

The career of Indian liberalism bears deeper study and analysis. Most of the secondary literature on the subject has, however, concentrated on the impact of British ideas on India, not on the creativity and dynamism of the Indian response.[2] What is more urgently needed is a history of Indian liberalism, not of the British impact on India. A beginning has been suggested by D. V. Gundappa who argued that Indian traditions endorsed a sort of dharmic liberalism in which liberty and authority were 'correlates':

> Liberty belongs mainly to the self-regarding and authority mainly to the world-regarding attitude. Both alike are parts of the schooling which the soul needs for achieving its higher destiny; citizenship, which comprises both, is thus a discipline of Dharma. Modern liberalism is...the renascence of certain

elements of it, rather than an exotic plant imported anew into his garden. Roots of the philosophy of liberty and authority, individual development and social order, lay in the depths of antiquity, beneath the debris of a thousand years of alien conquest and domination; and a sap in them quickened at the touch of the new enlightenment introduced by Britain. (Gundappa 1987)

That there were liberal tendencies in Indian civilisation is well known. Examples of such thinking abound, for instance in the Santiparva of the Mahabharata, which is a disquisition on kingship and statecraft. Apart from the strongly libertarian thrust of Indian soteriology, whose applications to social and political life are possible, a strong sense of reciprocity between individuals and communities and a highly decentralised form of government characterised most epochs of Indian history.

Gundappa acknowledges that Gandhi was the key thinker in promoting this dharmic view of Indian liberalism, something that Professor Anthony J. Parel shows so convincingly in *Gandhi's Philosophy and the Quest for Harmony* (2006). One might even say that the somewhat effete and derivative nature of Indian liberalism as espoused by the likes of Surendranath Banerjee, Madhav Govind Ranade and Gopal Krishna Gokhale suddenly acquired a radical edge with Gandhi's transformation of it through his *satyagraha* or political action based on the insistence on truth. It was Gandhi who reconciled the schism between the two factions of Indian liberalism, the moderates and the extremists, who had split the Indian national Congress in its Surat session in 1907. Gandhi was, in a sense, an extremist, demanding *purna svaraj* or total freedom like the 'Garam Dal' (the hot faction) but also a moderate, like those in the 'Naram Dal' (the soft faction) in advocating non-violent resistance and non-cooperation as the means of achieving his ends. Of course, unlike the moderates, Gandhi's methods were 'unconstitutional' in that he urged Indians to break the colonial laws, which were unjust in the first place.

When a new India was being imagined in the nineteenth century,

Indian pasts were redeployed in the projection of a future in which Western knowledge-systems could be adapted to the Indian situation chiefly to produce material well-being through new social, political and economic institutions. This had to be done without entirely disregarding or utterly disparaging Indian traditions, which had proved inadequate to face the onslaught of colonialism and Western education. In a subtle or overt way, the supremacy of Western modernity was recognised without a total disavowal of Indian culture or traditions. While India's enchantment with Western modernity still continues, there is a fairly clear understanding that this does not entail a total rejection of things Indian or a repudiation of our mores and habits. What is more the Orientalists and their Indian partners produced a large body of work to show that there was much to be learned from ancient and medieval India. Even though British liberals like Mill or Macaulay dismissed this knowledge as worthless or inconsequential, it formed the basis of a radical self-reappraisal for most Indians.

The process of adapting Western ideas and institutions to Indian conditions resulted in a peculiar hybridity in the sensibilities of the key figures in this book, evident in their writings. A new mode of expression, which we may call Indo-Western for lack of a better term, developed, whose unique characteristics feature in the works of all the figures examined here. The various texts they wrote embodied this new syncretic aesthetics, showing us a way to be modern by breaking down the binaries between not just India and the West, but also between our pasts and our present. That it was also replete with political possibilities is obvious in the actual practices of the modern Indian state, which is itself an Indo-Western hybrid.

Not all sections and communities in India came into modernity in the same way or at the same time. My account has been confined to that of what might loosely be termed the *savarna* groups. The word traditionally means those with letters (*varna* = letters), but it also refers to the upper-castes who, willy nilly, were probably the only literate ones in times bygone. The conflation of literacy and higher caste status was, thus, not accidental but sociological. This book has been so concerned with writing, with literature, with Indian English authority that it has been more or less co-terminus with the efforts of upper caste Hindu groups. These groups were at the forefront, as I have indicated earlier, not only of Indian English, but also of vernacular Indian authority. Their covenant with modernity follows a certain trajectory, which I have tried to rehearse here.

There were, obviously, other groups who had a different relationship with both modernity and the construction of the Indian nation. The untouchables and lower castes, for instance, did not always see the British as oppressors or usurpers. These groups, in fact, faced an internal oppression at the hands of upper caste Hindu and Muslim elites and were, in that sense, doubly colonised and marginalised. However, they also found some succour and relief from upper-caste domination from the colonial masters, who encouraged and used them to counter upper-caste resistance and anti-colonialism. The imperial policy of divide and rule entailed a different set of relations with all subdued people, often pitting one against the other to maintain the hegemony of the rulers. Anti-caste movements naturally, derived support, tacit or overt from colonial authority. It is now fairly well-documented that caste as we know it today was a colonial creation.[3] This is not to say that there was no caste prior to the British conquest of India, but that it dynamics were quite different. Indeed, the institution of caste is better seen as dynamic than static, reinventing itself according to the exigencies of the times. For instance, from an insistence on commensality, endogamy and hierarchy, caste today serves more as an instrument of political mobilisation and upward mobility.

An outstanding example of a lower-caste protagonist of modernity was Babasaheb Bhim Rao Ambedkar. Ambedkar's modernism was founded on the supremacy of Enlightenment rationality, whose authority he invoked against not only religious superstition, but also against social oppression. Ambedkar, in the latter years of his life, broke from his ancestral Hindu faith to embrace Buddhism, which he reinterpreted as an instance of a native rationalistic and egalitarian religious tradition. In this, he too shows only a partial acceptance of Western modernity. He too tried to nativise the sources of his rational belief-system and basis of social relations. Much has been written on Ambedkar's faceoff with Gandhi and the latter's approach to modernity. Though Ambedkar differed quite strenuously with other upper caste makers of modern India, he too joined the nation-making project, not only as independent India's first law minister, but also as the chairman of the committee which drafted the Indian constitution.[4]

If upper caste leaders were locked into a clash with colonial authority, their lower caste counterparts were engaged in an effort to make these leaders and their vision of the new India more accountable to the deprived sections of their own community. These two struggles may be classified as anti-colonial and sub-nationalist respectively, embodying two dimensions of one larger movement that brought India into modernity. While apparently sharply at variance or even in conflict, they balanced each other by establishing the rights of all communities in the land to enjoy the newly formed nation.

It is this fact that the millions of statues of Ambedakar dotted all over India symbolise. Ambedkar in a blue suit, holding a book in one hand and pointing onward with the other not only represents the importance of reading, writing and learning in the upliftment of the masses, but also their aspiration to enjoy modernity. The suit, tie and shoes are emblems of this dignity which only modernity can confer upon the depressed classes. No amount of reform in tradition, as Gandhi advocated, is considered either reliable or desirable. It is only by leaving the space of the traditional India, the benighted Indian village, that these classes hope to find redemption. Ambedkar, pointing to the future, beckons these groups to brighter tomorrows in a new India. He assures them that the nation belongs to them too, that they have rights over it as much as the other groups. They too are entitled to 'enjoy' the nation. The fruits of modernity and nationality are not the sole preserves of the privileged classes. What may at first appear a long-drawn and continuing conflict between the advantaged and the deprived castes or communities is actually a part of the unfolding dialectic of democratic India.

But unlike the tussle between the different caste groups, the religious conflict in India led to the two-nation theory and, eventually, to the cataclysmic event of the partition. While Ambedkar became a pillar of the Indian nation, despite being such a critic of the Congress and of Gandhi, Mohammad Ali Jinnah, another modernist, led the movement that created Pakistan. Actually, Jinnah's modernism was purely pragmatic, premised on the sole aim of creating an Islamic nation, carved out of the Muslim-majority areas of colonial India. To this end, he collaborated with all sorts of special interests, even those that were neither modern nor liberal in their outlook. Eventually, the modernism of Pakistan led to authoritarian regimes controlled by the army or modern fanatical or extremist Islamic groups as exemplified by the Taliban. Between these two illiberal forces, a fragile democracy gasped for air and light from time to time. In other words, Muslim leaders in India rarely participated in the broader liberal project that both upper and lower caste Hindus tried to promote. In contrast, besides Hindus, privileged members of the Parsi and Christian communities also joined in the creation of Indian modernity and nationalism.

For a fuller rendering of how India became modern these other narratives would need to be added to our account. While this is outside the scope of this project, it should be fairly obvious that the lives and works of the figures I have chosen contributed to the creation of a national consensus in India which was liberal and modern. While their lower caste antagonists questioned the egalitarian claims of this liberal modernity, they did not entirely opt out of it either. Instead, by constantly pressing their demands, they secured constitutional sanctions and safeguards for their interests.

The Muslim separatists, on the other hand, never fully participated in such a project from its inception and, in the end, opted out to fashion their own separate destiny. In this process, at least the Pakistani Muslims tried to move closer to their Middle Eastern brethren in their attempt to create a distinct non-South Asian identity for themselves, but only met with partial success. The Muslims that remained in India, after many trials, have decided to join the larger Indian liberal and modern narrative, even if in a somewhat backward and subordinate position to begin with, their religious difference and economic deprivation making them susceptible to both political and religious demagogues.[5]

If Indian liberalism favoured private enterprise, it was by no means always supportive of *laissez faire* capitalism. A chief reason for this was Gandhi's own brand of socialism in which he regarded the rich merely as trustees, not owners of the wealth that they created. Its true owners, according to him, were the common people. The Indian welfare state was influenced by this concern for the poorest of the poor, the *daridra narayan* or the Lord in the form of the wretched of the earth. No wonder when the communists won any degree of popular support in India it was only when they participated in parliamentary democracy in the federal or central government. They are thus very much a part of India's liberal political spectrum. The Maoists, Naxalities and others groups who advocate an armed insurrection against the state have not yet won popular support though they continue to highlight the discontent of the dispossessed.

Though I have used the word 'liberalism' here, I do think that the motive for such an extraordinary coming together of diverse elements was not purely economic. Here, we might suggest a useful contrast with the much more recent European Union. There is not as yet a palpable love for the union of Europe; it is by-and-large a purely economic arrangement. The richer nations lament that they must contribute so much to the poorer ones even if their prosperity is founded on exports to these very countries. The poorer nations, so much in debt and suffering from the burden of forced structural adjustments, suffer from considerable heartburn at the easier life of their more affluent neighbours. Indian liberal nationalism, on the other hand, bred not just an expedient or convenient federation, but a sense of shared culture and solidarity of sentiment. Even though the movement was led in greater measure by the educated classes, the masses also willingly joined in.

The upper caste, largely Hindu, English-educated elites who make up this book wrote in English in addition to their native Indian languages. Through their literary endeavours they helped produce the mentality that made up modern India. That this mentality consisted of both ideas and emotions is obvious. Literature became the unique instrument which touched both these aspects of the Indian people. By exerting an enduring influence and authority on both their heads and hearts, these thought-makers and change-agents established that the Indian national culture would be plural, liberal and largely egalitarian in its orientation. Thus the unique phenomenon called modern Indian democracy came into being. Its roots were in the sacralisation of the idea of India as they were also in the official policy not only of secularism but of affirmative action to uplift the depressed castes. That they worked through literature made them special because writing itself, especially in English, came to carry an almost charismatic authority. The afterlives of these figures continue to exert a considerable influence over the direction that India takes today.

Much of traditional Indian art was preoccupied with narrating the stories of great heroes. I have tried to retell the stories of these makers of modern India in a similar fashion. I see this task as one more attempt to recover that part of our past which has unconsciously gone into the shaping of what we are today, a past which 'mere' history does not give us, but which we must seek through a mythopoetic re-enactment. My purpose is neither to write hagiographies nor to pass judgement on the lives and works of these figures, but to accept their narratives as one version of the story of the making of modern India. The reawakening of India, as its quest for svaraj, is far from over; indeed, it seems just now well-begun. The biggest challenges ahead are the institutionalisation of good governance, the eradication of poverty and the safeguarding of national interests from external threats. If these are accomplished, Indian democracy, powered by continued economic growth, will have much to contribute to the world.

WORKS CITED

Anderson, Benedict. (1983) 2006. *Imagined Communities: Reflections on the Origin and Spread of Nationalism.* London: Verso.

Dirks, Nicholas. 2001. *Castes of Mind: Colonialism and the Making of Modern India*. Pinceton University Press.

Gundappa D. V. 1987. 'Liberalism in India.' *Freedom First* (July).

Mehta, Uday Singh. 1999. *Liberalism and Empire: A Study in Nineteenth-Century British Liberal Thought*. Chicago: University of Chicago Press.

Moore, R. J. 1966. *Liberalism and Indian Politics, 1872–1922*. London: Edwin Arnold.

Nagaraj, D. R. (1993) 2010. *The Flaming Feet and Other Essays: The Dalit Movement in India*. Ed. Prithvi Datta and Chandra Shobhi. New Delhi: Permanent Black.

Paranjape, Makarand R. *Altered Destinations: Self, Society and Nation in India*. London: Anthem Books, 2009.

Parel, Anthony J. 2006. *Gandhi's Philosophy and the Quest for Harmony*. Cambridge: Cambridge University Press.

Ray, Rajat Kanta. 2002. *The Felt Community: Commonalty and Mentality Before the Emergence of Indian Nationalism*. New Delhi: Oxford University Press.

Robb, Peter. 2007. *Liberalism, Modernity and the Nation: Empire, Identity and India*. New York: Oxford University Press.

Rodrigues, Valerian. 2011. 'In Search of an Anchor: Muslim Thought in Modern India' *Economic & Political Weekly*. 46.49 (December 3): 43–58.

_____. 2011. 'Reading Texts and Traditions: The Ambedkar-Gandhi Debate.' *Economic and Political Weekly*. 46.2 (January 8): 57–66.

ENDNOTES

CHAPTER 1

1. Aijaz Ahmad (2005) in '*The Making of India*' offers interesting comments not on the verbal nuances of 'making' in this context, but also the different factors including the *bhakti* movements and the anti-colonial struggle that contributed to it.
2. The nation has often been narrativised in terms of conflict, not consensus, between actual personages – Gandhi vs Ambedkar, Gandhi vs Jinnah, Gandhi vs Nehru, or Nehru vs Bose; or between ideological positions – feminist vs patriarchal, national-bourgeoisie vs Marxist, dominant vs subaltern, upper caste vs dalit, and so on. However, the two, conflict and consensus are not opposites, but dialogically related, one emerging from or leading to the other, both continuously evolving and changing. In this context, see K. J. Shah's 'Dissent, Protest and Reform: Some Conceptual Clarifications.'
3. Professor Braj B. Kachru's extensive work on the Indianisation of English (1983) is notable in this regard. However, as Probal Dasgupta (1993) observes in his rather original and somewhat contrary exposition published ten years later, regardless of how nativised English is in India, its 'Otherness' never goes away.
4. I have argued this consistently; see for instance, 'Indian Anglophony'; and *Indian English and Vernacular India*.
5. For a distinction between power and authority see Norman Uphoff's 'Distinguishing Power, Authority and Legitimacy: Taking Max Weber at His Word by Using Resources-Exchange Analysis.'
6. The late Professor K. J. Shah claimed that tradition consisted of *anubhav* or direct experience, action (*achar*) that follows and *vichar* (thought) that can articulate the consistency of both. Even if not in this order,

these elements recur in most key texts. See for instance his essay, 'Of Artha and the Arthasastra.' Shah's daughter, Dr Veeravalli Srinivasan, wrote her PhD in philosophy (University of Delhi, 2000) on this very topic of 'Exemplar vs Ideologue.'

CHAPTER 2

1. In a sense, this is how Rabindranath Tagore saw him. Gandhi, in contrast, did not consider Ram Mohan Roy's role as that significant. Comparing him with Chaitanya, Gandhi felt that Ram Mohan Roy's modernity was not as consequential as it was made out to be. See footnote 12 for a more detailed analysis.
2. My early work on Ram Mohan was presented at the Conference on the Nineteenth Century, organised by Alok Bhalla, 10–12 December, 1987.
3. *Svaraj*, which henceforward will not be italicised, at its simplest means 'self-rule.' But to Gandhi, who wrote his classic denunciation of colonialism and modernity, *Hind Swaraj* (1909), it was nothing short of a total plan to transform both self and society. I have written extensively about the idea of svaraj not only in *Decolonization and Development: Hind Svaraj Revisioned* but also in *Altered Destinations: Self, Society, and Nation in India*.
4. The University of Chicago library lists almost 100 works on him in English and Bangla; the total number is probably more. In some of the Bangla works he is called 'Mahatma'(great soul) and 'Rishi' (great seer).
5. The secondary literature on Ram Mohan Roy is extensive. Kotnala (1975), for instance, lists 73 books in his 'Select Bibliography,' 219–222. For the biographical and factual details in the paper I have relied on Carpenter, Chatterjee, Collet, Crawford, Joshi, Kotnala, Majumdar, Nag, Sen, and Tagore (see Works Cited). S. Cromwell Crawford's *Ram Mohan Roy: His Era and Ethics* (1984) has been particularly helpful in the writing of the first section of this paper. Since then, only a couple of significant titles have been published including Noel A. Salmond's and Lynn Zastoupil's.
6. Saraswati is also the goddess of knowledge and wisdom; the symbolism is thus unmistakable.
7. For an account of Young Bengal, including some of its key representatives

see Chapter V, 'Radical Intellectualism' (Poddar 1970, 113–145).

8   See, for instance, his Preface to Ramabai Ranade's biography of her husband translated as *Ranade: His Wife's Reminiscences* (1963, 9–11).

9   Franz Fanon, for instance, has spoken eloquently about the adverse psychological effects of colonialism in *The Wretched of the Earth* (1975); see for instance, Ch. 5, 'Colonial War and Mental Disorders' 200–250.

10 For the close resemblance between histories and stories, see Hayden White's *Tropics of Discourse* (1978): 'the techniques or strategies that [historians and imaginative writers] use in the composition of their discourses can be shown to be substantially the same, however different they may appear on a purely surface, or dictional, level' (121) or Wallace Martin's *Recent Theories of Narrative* (1986): 'at present we have no standards or even suggestions for determining how the connections between events in fictional narratives might differ from those in history' (73). On how stories shape the way we see the world, we might cite Native American Thomas King's *The Truth About Stories* (2003).

11 See David Kopf 1969 and Kalyan Chatterjee 1976.

12 If the remarkable but not well-studied history of Anglo-Scottish Calvinism is to be traced, then Carey was probably influenced by the American Puritan revivalist, preacher, and theologian, Jonathan Edwards (1703–1758), who made it his life's mission to take Christianity to the 'Indians' in North America; Carey extended that mission to the 'real' Indians in India. Edwards' revivalism, an attempt to temper the fervour, some might say the fanaticism, of Calvinism with Enlightenment ideals, was extremely influential during his times.

13 See for instance Raymond Schwab's *The Oriental Renaissance: Europe's Rediscovery of India and the East 1600–1880* (1984) which is one of the many books that documents how important the 'discovery' of Sanskrit knowledge systems was to Europe's own development. It is fairly clear, for instance, that the discipline of philology, which later gave rise to modern linguistics, was born out the comparative linguistics that pioneers like Sir William Jones initiated in India in the late 18th century.

14 It was, in other words, not merely a 'mask of conquest' as Viswanathan (1989) in her well-known Saidian account contends.

15 Gandhi gave a talk at Cuttack, Orissa, on 24 March 1921, a report of which is available in volume 22 of the *Collected Works of Mahatma*

Gandhi (1999). During the Question and Answer session that followed, he criticised English education for enslaving Indians: 'The present system enslaves us without allowing a discriminating use of English literature' (1999, Volume 22, 462). He clarified, 'I don't want to destroy the English language but read English as an Indian nationalist would do' (ibid.). He also called Ram Mohan Roy a 'pigmy' in comparison to 'Chaitanya, Sankar, Kabir and Nanak' (ibid.). Earlier he called himself a pigmy too: 'I am a miserable pigmy' (ibid.). A year later, Gandhi received a letter asking him to clarify his views on English education. Writing in *Young India* of 27 April 1921, Gandhi repeated his criticism of English education: 'It was conceived and born in error, for the English rulers honestly believed the indigenous system to be worse than useless' (1999, Volume 23: 93). He also added that 'Chaitanya, Kabir, Nanak, Guru Govindsingh [sic], Shivaji, and Pratap were greater men than Ram Mohan Rai and Tilak' (ibid.). The issue, however, refused to die. On 10 May 1921, Tagore wrote to his friend and supporter C. F. Andrews that Gandhi was mistaken (Das 1996, 972). Andrews published an essay in the May issue of *The Modern Review* called 'Raja Rammohun Roy and English Education' (ibid.). Tagore once again took up the issue in his article 'The Cult of the Charkha' in the September 1925 issue of *Modern Review*: 'The difference in our standpoints and temperaments has made the Mahatma look upon Rammohun Roy as a pygmy – while I revere him as a giant' (rpt. in Das 1996, 538–548). Gandhi's response was published as 'The Poet and the Charkha' (*Young India,* November 5, 1925). He said, as quoted in the *Collected Works,* 'One thing, and one thing only, has hurt me, the Poet's belief, again picked up from table talk, that I look upon Ram Mohan Roy as a 'pigmy'. Well, I have never anywhere described that great reformer as a pigmy, much less regarded him as such. He is to me as much a giant as he is to the Poet. I do not remember any occasion save one when I had to use Ram Mohan Roy's name. That was on the Cuttack sands now four years ago. What I do remember having said was that it was possible to attain highest culture without Western education. And when someone mentioned Ram Mohan Roy, I remember having said that he was a pigmy compared to the unknown authors, say, of the Upanishads. This is altogether different from looking upon Ram Mohan Roy as a pigmy' (1999, Volume 33, 200–201).

16 See http://en.wikipedia.org/wiki/Ram_Mohan_Roy; accessed on 22 Nov 2007.

17 His English secretary during his stay in Britain, Sandford Arnot, says, 'The Raja was acquainted more or less with ten languages: Sanskrit, Arabic, Persian, Hindustani, Bengali, English, Hebrew, Greek, Latin and French. The first two he knew he knew critically as a scholar, the third, fourth, fifth and sixth he spoke and wrote fluently; in the eighth, perhaps, his studies did not extend much beyond the originals of the Christian Scriptures; and in the latter two, his knowledge was apparently more limited' (quoted in Poddar 1970, 48).

CHAPTER 3

1 There is some confusion over the degree of his racial admixture; in 'Politics of Naming: Derozio in Two Formative Moments of Literary and Political Discourse, Calcutta, 1825–31,' Rosinka Chaudhuri says: 'Derozio's claim as a native of India was all the more laudable, the subtext of this passage seems to suggest, because his father was Portuguese and his mother an English woman from Hampshire named Sophia Johnson – if there was any Indian blood in him at all, that might have been in a hidden corner on his father's side' (879). But E.W. Madge, whom Chaudhuri quotes, clearly states that Henry's grandfather, Michael Derozio, was listed as a 'Native Protestant' in the St John's Baptismal Register of 1789 (3). 'Native' in this context is a racial term used in contradistinction to 'European.' About his mother there is still greater confusion. Thomas Edwards, his first biographer, who with great effort meticulously researched and recorded the known information on Derozio's life, says 'One other relation it is needful to mention. Henry's aunt, his mother's sister, married a European gentleman, an Indigo Planter, at Bhaugulpore. Mr Arthur Johnson, Derozio's uncle, was born at Ringwood in Hampshire in the year 1782' (3). According to Edwards, Sophia was Henry's mother's sister. There is no mention of his mother; her name and ancestry remain unspecified. A misreading of Edwards might have lead to the repeated error of thinking that Henry's mother was an Englishwoman from Hampshire whose maiden surname was Johnson.

2 Consecrated in 1787, St John's was the leading Protestant house of worship of the British in West Bengal until the founding of St Paul's Cathedral in 1847. The grounds contain many monuments including the grave of Job Charnock, the founder of Calcutta. It was built by Lt

James Agg of the Bengal Engineers, who modelled it on St Martin-in-the-Fields in London.
3   An earlier version of this chapter appeared as '"East Indian Cosmopolitanism": *The Fakeer of Jungheera* and the Birth of Indian Modernity' in *Interventions: International Journal of Postcolonial Studies*. 13.4 (October–December 2011).
4   All further quotations from *The Fakeer of Jungheera*, unless otherwise stated, are from Chaudhuri (2008).
5   The editor in question was Francis Bradley-Brit who in 1923 brought out a selection of the poet's works for Oxford University Press. Sometimes, the dash is replaced by a comma, 'To India, My Native Land,' but the sonnet remains Derozio's best known and most widely circulated composition.
6   In April 2008, in an auditorium named after him in Presidency College, formerly Hindu College, Kolkata, where Derozio himself taught and was expelled, but now is enshrined in a bust.
7   As I have argued at length in *Indian English and Vernacular India* (2010).
8   See Chaudhuri's aforementioned 'The Politics of Naming' for a more detailed account of the term 'East Indian.'

CHAPTER 4

1   'Sankhyadarsan,' *Bankim Rachanavali* 226 cited in Chatterjee 1986, 57.
2   Nandy 1983, 99.
3   See for instance Louise Bennet's 'Colonialism in Reverse'.
4   For an inspired account of this contradiction, especially as it relates to the problem of writing history itself, see Dipesh Chakrabarty's *Provincializing Europe: Postcolonial Thought and Historical Difference* (2000).
5   This position is, of course, very contestable; see, for instance, Frank Donoghue, *The Last Professors: The Corporate University and the Fate of the Humanities*.
6   I use 'Datta' to refer to the recovered Madhusudan. As he himself wrote from his much impoverished state in Europe in 1866 to his benefactor, Ishwarchandra Vidyasagar: 'You might drop the vulgar form "Dutt,"'(Gupta 1980, 618).
7   When I first started working on this narrative, there were very few

sources on Madhusudan's life in English. Subsequently, Ghulam Murshid's Bengali biography appeared, as did its English translation. However, I find that the new material has only confirmed the basic 'plot' that I had read in Madhusudan's life. Indeed, the Bangla title, *Ashara Chalane Bhuli* (Duped by Hope's Trickery) of Murshid's biography suggests a similar story of delusion and rediscovery.

8   Consider the 'discovery' and the world-wide fame attending to previously unknown authors like Arundhati Roy or Arvind Adiga on their being conferred the Booker Prize.

9   These letters of Madhusudan were only to be found in the *Madhusudan Rachanavali*, along with his other English writings till Ghulam Murshid brought out *The Heart of a Rebel Poet: Letters of Michael Madhusudan Dutt* in 2004.

10 See Clinton B. Seely's detailed discussion of this point in Datta 2005, 21.

CHAPTER 5

1   Sri Ramakrishna is playfully punning on the author's name, Bankim, which also means slightly bent. An earlier version of this essay appeared in Mukherjee 2002, 143–160.

2   According to Davis 2000, the mortality figures were much higher.

3   Incidentally Sarkar's earlier 1994 essay 'Imagining a Hindu Nation: Hindu and Muslim in Bankimchandra's Later Writings' offers a more complex and nuanced narrative, thus showing a scholar's own position shifts in changed circumstances or with a hardening of her political stance. Also see Porter 2003 for a useful discussion of such encounters between Christian missionaries and native subjects.

4   First published in *Kunapipi; A Journal of Post-Colonial Writing* in 1997, then in *Kenyon Review* in 1998, the essay was also published in *Pushcart Prize Annual* in 1999, in a Bengali version in the Puja issue of *Desh* in 1998 as *'Kathashilper Mayay Gatha Ei Basundhara'* before being reprinted in *Incendiary Circumstances: A Chronicle of the Turmoil of Our Times* (2005, 103–119).

5   The Ravi Dayal reprint of the book was reissued in 2009 by Penguin India.

6   See the Google Books free e-book: <http://books.google.com.sg/books?id=PVUEAAAAQAAJ&printsec=frontcover&

dq=The+Revelations+of+an+Orderly&source=bl&ots=GuX1Zp-Y4p&sig=gMgK_4Lgz-3iqi49KSwrsN12Tvg&hl=en&ei=0ouuTZ-yC8qrrAeZ99T3CQ&sa=X&oi=book_result&ct=result&resnum=9&ved=0CFAQ6AEwCA#v=onepage&q&f=false>; accessed 20 April 2011.

7   This view of the underclass is arguably rather limited if not inaccurate as the Subaltern Studies scholars have tried to show at great length. What is required, as Dipesh Chakrabarty suggests in 'Subaltern Studies and Postcolonial Histriography,' is a broader definition of 'political.'

CHAPTER 6

1   Similar questions are also raised in *Nation and Its Fragments: Colonial and Postcolonial Histories* (1993), where some of this material reappears.
2   The title of this chapter is inspired by the phrase 'subject to change,' with its multiple meanings. Though used several times as a book title earlier, it alludes to Susie Tharu's book about the discipline of English Studies in India. More than anything else, it is feminist studies that has pushed disciplinary and hermeneutical boundaries in recent times, something that this chapter wishes to foreground in its reading of forgotten Indian English texts by women of the late nineteenth century. 'Reconsidering women,' in the subtitle is meant to be in dialogue with 'De/Siring Women: Re-addressing Gender Relations in Indian Novels,' a PhD Dissertation by Sharon Pillai, (Centre for English Studies, Jawaharlal Nehru University, 2007). Pillai uses desiring in at least three senses of the word – what women desire, what is desired of them, and how they 'de-sire,' or re-engender themselves out of patriarchal determinations – all of which are relevant to my readings of these texts. I am also grateful to Sharon for reading and commenting on an earlier draft of this chapter.
3   See for instance Pat Barr's *The Memsahibs; The Women Of Victorian India* (1989).
4   This despite the interest in her work in the last few decades with books such as Uma Chakravarti's and Meera Kosambi's studies and editions of Pandita Ramabai.
5   Besides these, a number of other women writers, activists, and reformers were active in Maharashtra. They include Anandibai Karve and her sister Parvatibai Athavale, both widowed when they were young; Soonderbai Powar, an associate of Pandita Ramabai; Dr. Rakhamabai, who refused to use either her father's or husband's last names, struggled to enforce

'the age of consent,' and was India's first practising lady doctor; Kashibai Kanitkar, who secretly educated herself and became a novelist; Krishnabai Malvadkar, who edited a women's magazine called *Simantani*; and even an 'ordinary' housewife like Lakshmibai Sardesai, who wrote a memoir. Several of them are mentioned in Kosambi's book, *Crossing Thresholds* (2007).

6 Anandibai got her medical degree in Philadelphia in 1886, the same year that Kadambini Ganguly, another Brahmin girl from Kolkata, became the first woman to graduate from the Bengal Medical College.

7 Indeed, even within the subcontinent in very recent years, the writings of Taslima Nasreen have been banned, burned and have evoked death threats on the author.

8 See their website: 'Ramabai Mukti Mission', last modified 22 December 2011, accessed 17 January 2012, <http://www.ramabaimuktimission.com/index.html>

9 Perhaps, we might discern a similar pattern in the Dalit movement half a century later when, after the initial conversation of Dr Ambedkar and his followers to Buddhism, education and government jobs are seen as a more direct route to social empowerment than conversion.

10 Some portions of my analysis of this text appeared earlier as the 'Afterword' to the latter edition.

11 Abigail McGowan uses shoes as a starting point in her essay on nineteenth century Maharashtrian women as consumers who had access to and control over goods.

CHAPTER 7

1 An earlier version of a part of this paper was presented at the seminar on 'Swami Vivekananda's Impact on the West' held at the Center for Indic Studies at the University of Massachusetts-Dartmouth, on 27-28 July 2004. Portions of this paper have been used in my Introduction to the *Penguin Swami Vivekananda Reader* (2005) and in *The Cyclonic Swami: Vivekananda in the West* (2005).

2 In this section, I closely follow *Vivekananda - A Biography* by Swami Nikhilananda, which in turn relies heavily on the more extensive *Life* by the Eastern and Western disciples. Quotations attributed to Vivekananda or his interlocutors are paraphrased or derived from Nikhilananda. The date of birth is disputed, but 12 January 1863 is now the most accepted

date, coinciding with the auspicious Hindu festival of Makarasankranti that year.
3   See Howard Zinn's *A People's History of the United States* for an account of social inequity in the USA
4   This was published as *The Penguin Swami Vivekananda Reader* in 2005.
5   See *Kali's Child: The Mystical and the Erotic in the Life and Teachings of Ramakrishna* (1998).
6   See the works of Michel Foucault, particularly *The Order of Things* ([1966] 2002) and Hayden White's *Tropics of Discourse* (1986), possibly the most extensive discussion of the idea.
7   See, for instance, Karl Popper's *The Logic of Scientific Discovery* (2002) and the notion of 'paradigm shifts' in Thomas Kuhn's *The Structure of Scientific Revolutions* (1962).

CHAPTER 8

1   A second edition, with an enlarged Introduction, was published in 2010 by Rupa and Co. Portions of this chapter appeared in my Introduction to this volume and its earlier edition.
2   Sir Edwin Arnold (1832-1904) was an English poet and translator. He was principal of the British government college in Pune, and later, in 1873, became the chief editor of the *London Daily Telegraph*. He is best remembered for his epic poem *The Light of Asia* (1879).
3   See J. J. Wilhelm, Ezra Pound in London and Paris: 1908−1925 (1990): 'When Pound was invited early that fall to the house of the Indian nationalist poet Sarojini Naidu, he was doubtlessly expecting to spend most of the evening discussing poetry with the charming 'Nightingale of India', but Sarojini had been prevailed upon by the already mentioned Mrs Mary McNeill Fenollosa to arrange the appointment so that she could look over the young American poet for the job as literary executor of her husband's estate.' (Wilhelm, 1990, 129)
4   This is in keeping with the general romantic fascination for the 'innocent' and 'natural' past, a longing best epitomised in Schiller's 'On Naive and Sentimental Poetry': '[On natural objects, and later on ancient poets who were in touch with nature] They are what we were; they are what we ought to become once more. We were nature as they, and our culture should lead us back to nature, upon the path of reason and

freedom. They are therefore at the same time a representation of our lost childhood, which remains eternally most dear to us...'

CHAPTER 9

1. Though it was not the house in this photo, another of the Rushdie family's homes in Solan, Himachal Pradesh, after protracted litigation, was restored to him. This goes to show that no matter how hard we complain, all homes are not lost to us after all. It is a different matter that Rushdie, of course, never returned to live in India, though he has lamented its loss in so many novels and other writings.
An earlier version of this paper was first presented as the inaugural address at a seminar on 'Home and the World: Literary and Cultural Encounters in Colonial and Post-Colonial India,' University of Calcutta, Calcutta, 17–19 December 2002 and subsequently published as 'Home and Away: Colonialism and AlterNativity in India,' *New Literatures Review*. 40 (Winter 2003): 116–130.
2. First published in a special issue of *Critical Inquiry* in Autumn 1985, this essay has been reprinted several times in feminist and post-colonial anthologies before reappearing in Spivak's own book *A Critique of Postcolonial Reason: Toward a History of the Vanishing Present*. Benita Parry's 'Problems in Current Theories of Colonial Discourse' and Henry Louis Gates, Jr.'s 'Critical Fanonism' are examples of two critiques of Spivak's essay, as is Erin O'Connor's 'Preface for a Post-Postcolonial Criticism.' It is, however, Edward Said who inaugurates the 'worldly' turn of the text in *The World, the Text, and the Critic* published two years before Spivak's essay.
3. The lines are from Annapurnashtakam by Sankaracharya: '*Mata cha Parvati Devi pita Devo Maheshvara/ Bandavah Shiva bhaktascha svadesho bhuvanatrayam*' (My mother is Goddess Parvati, father the Great Lord/My relatives are devotees of Shiva, and the whole universe is my country). I have translated *svadesh* as my country; it could also be translated as 'my home'; *bhuvanatrayam* means the three worlds, the earth, the nether worlds, and the heavens, thus referring to the entire universe.

4   'Neti neti' is a Hindu chant that means 'not this, not this' or 'neither this, nor that'.
5   See Poonam Arora (1995) for a fascinating discussion of Devdas and the problem of masculinity in Indian cinema.

CHAPTER 10

1   An earlier version of this paper was delivered as the Hamid Lakhani Lecture, Department of English, Saurashtra University, Rajkot, on 20th March 2003, and published as 'Sri Aurobindo's "The Renaissance in India"' in *Critical Practice*, 10.2: (June 2003): 74-86.
2   See the works of Michel Foucault, particularly *Power/Knowledge* (1990) for a comprehensive analysis of the nexus between institutions of power and the production of knowledge.
3   For instance, consider how some of the lower-castes appreciated colonial rule. Describing the attitude of the Namasudra community to the British government in Bengal, Sekhar Bandyopadhyay, writes: 'they [the Namasudras] began to aspire for greater patronage from the colonial government, which at least theoretically made no distinction of caste. This very aspect of the new regime made it appear, in their perception of history, as a definite improvement over the traditional rule of the discriminating high case Hindu Rajas. Any political movement against this government was, therefore, interpreted as attempts to end this egalitarian rule...' (Bandyopadhyay 2005, 4).
4   There so many examples of this: several first nation people in Canada, native Americans in the United States, and indigenous communities in Australia, not to mention the original inhabitants of the Carribean islands, the Caribs.
5   See Peter Heehs' *The Lives of Sri Aurobindo* (2008) for a well-researched if controversial biography.
6   In her Booker winning novel, *God of Small Things*, Arundhati Roy explains her idea of the 'History House': 'history was like an old house at night. With all the lamps lit. And ancestors whispering inside. 'To understand history', Chacko said, 'we have to go inside and listen to what they're saying. And look at the books and the pictures on the walls. And smell the smells." (Roy 1997, 52).

7   The debate remains inconclusive to this day. For an interesting comparison between the European and the Bengal renaissances, see Chaudhuri (2004).
8   This has been extensively documented not only by Kopf (1969) but also by Stokes's earlier classic *The English Utilitarians and India* (1959). It took more than a century before a more liberal approach to India emerged in C. F. Andrew's works, one of which was called *The Renaissance in India: Its Missionary Aspect*.
9   Generations of Marxist historians, notably Susobhan Sarkar and his son Sumit Sarkar, have also written on the idea of the renaissance in India. For a discussion see Dhar (1987).
10 'The subject matter of the book was written in a way of appreciation of Mr. James H. Cousins' book of the same name' – this acknowledgement occurs in the front matter (no page number) of the 1920 edition of Sri Aurobindo's series, published as a little booklet.
11 Perhaps this is only possible because there is something in the texture of Hinduism that allows it. Nirad C. Chaudhuri takes the argument too far, however, when he argues in a section titled 'Worldly Character of Hinduism,' that Hinduism's 'main object is worldly prosperity...the religion is for the world, and there is no unworldliness in it...everything religious is involved in the world' *Hinduism: A Religion to Live By* (10).

CHAPTER 11

1   My special thanks to Doug Allen for sending me this quotation and for his perceptive comments on an earlier version, which was originally presented as 'Still Searching for Svaraj: India after Gandhi' at an international conference on 'Gandhi, Non-Violence, Modernity' at Humanities Research Centre, Australian National University, Canberra, 1–3 September 2004 and published in *The Philosophy of Mahatma Gandhi for the 21st Century* edited by Douglas Allen (2008).
2   See, for instance, Michel Chossudovsky,'"Manufacturing Dissent": the Anti-globalization Movement is Funded by the Corporate Elites.' (http://www.prisonplanet.com/manufacturing-dissent-the-anti-globalization-movement-is-funded-by-the-corporate-elites.html)
3   Perhaps, I have overstated the case here. To give one example, in the last three years, I notice a sudden proliferation of car stickers and windscreen covers with Gandhi's photo and the quote 'There is no religion

higher than Truth.' This unexpected and unusual resurfacing of Gandhi suggests that there is something perennial about his legacy, something that suddenly erupts into our everyday and often contrary reality. The best example of the most recent eruption is Vidhu Vinod Chopra's hit film, *Lage Raho Munna Bhai* (2006) where a lovable Bombay hoodlum gives up *dadagiri* (goon-ishness) for *Gandhigiri* (Gandhianness). The entire movement of Anna Hazare against corruption in 2011, too, has definite Gandhian overtones.

4   See, for instance, 'Why Do India's Dalits Hate Gandhi?' by Thomas C. Mountain, the publisher of the *Ambedkar Journal* (http://www.onlinejournal.com/artman/publish/article_603.shtml).

5   The term '*navya*,' which actually suggests the possibilities of renewal and reinvention, is often used in the tradition, for instance, *navya nyaya*. My friend Professor A. K. Singh explains this flow of tradition in terms of *avirbhava* (full manifestation), *antarbhava* (a sort of internalisation) and *punarbhava* (reappearance). He also likens, metaphorically, the flow of tradition to a combination of Ganga (perennial stream), Narmada (resurfacing after disappearing), and Saraswati (going underground but still existing).

6   I spell svaraj with a 'v' not with a 'w' as Gandhi did because it is *my* notion of Svaraj that I speak of even as I engage with Gandhi's. The difference in spelling, actually bringing the transliteration closer to the Sanskrit pronunciation, is simply a symbolic gesture to suggest that each of us must own up to our own idea of Svaraj (see my book, *Decolonizaton and Development: Hind Svaraj Revisioned.*)

CONCLUSION

1   Benedict Anderson's *Imagined Communities: Reflections on the Origin and Spread of Nationalism* shows at length the importance of print media in the creation of national consciousness.

2   See, for instance, R. J. Moore's pioneering study, *Liberalism and Indian Politics, 1872-1922* (1966), Uday Singh Mehta's *Liberalism and Empire* (1999), or Peter Robb's more recent *Liberalism, Modernity, and the Nation: Empire, Identity, and India* (2007).

3   For instance, Nicolas Dirks' *Castes of Mind: Colonialism and the Making of Modern India* (2001).

4   See my own account of the Gandhi-Ambedkar debate in *Altered Destinations: Self, Society, and Nation in India* (2009). It was D. R. Nagaraj who offered the first comprehensive way of trying to reconcile the two. See his book *The Flaming Feet: The Dalit Movement in India*, (2010) first published in 1993. Also see Valerian Rodrigues' more recent analysis 'Reading Texts and Traditions: The Ambedkar–Gandhi Debate.' (2011)

5   For an account of the major Muslim thinkers of this period, especially their relation to modernity, see Valerian Rodrigues' 'In Search of an Anchor: Muslim Thought in Modern India' (2011).

INDEX

A Forgotten Anglo-Indian Poet, 80
A Journal of 48 Hours of the Year 1945, 141
Abhijnanasakuntalam, 323
afterlife, 5, 15, 76, 152, 352
ahimsa, 364, 365, 367
Ahmad, Aijaz, 126
Akhanandananada, Swami, 206
Ali, Asaf, 357
Alphonso-Karlaka, John, 81
Alter, Joseph S., 2
Altered Destinations, 373
Amarnath *darshan*, 208
Ambedkar, Bhim Rao, 150, 356, 378-380
America's Coming of Age, 1
An Appeal to the Christian Published in Defence of the Precepts of Jesus by a Friend of Truth, 39
Anagol, Padma, 163, 164, 181
Anandamath, 63, 64, 121, 126, 127, 135, 138
Anantha Murthy, U. R., 14
Aurobindo, Sri., 5, 9, 13, 61, 122, 123, 126-127, 129, 219, 231-233, 235, 249-250, 273, 298, 311, 317, 319-320, 324-325, 333-345, 370
authority, 2, 4-16, 22, 25, 30-31, 38, 44, 47, 78, 138-139, 147-149, 152, 161, 167, 171, 182-183, 189, 227, 253, 352, 370, 372-376, 378-379, 382
Autobiography, 173, 369
Azad, Maulana, 299

Bagal, Jogesh Chandra, 129
Baig, Tara Ali, 252, 253
Bande Mataram, 126, 127, 135
Bandyopadhyay, Chittaranjan, 121
Banerjee, Krishna Mohun, 6, 33, 43, 94
Banerjee, Milinda, 60
Banerji, Brajendra Nath, 141
Banerji, Sunil Kumar, 129
Barthes, Roland, 12
Basu, Lotika, 264
Baumfield, Vivienne, 232
Bayley, C.A., 83
Beauvoir, Simone de, 155
Benares Recorder, 128
Bengal Chronicle, 78
Benjamin, Walter, 286

Besant, Annie, 226, 245, 249, 276, 335
Bhabha, Homi, 75, 117, 118, 242, 285, 286, 289, 290, 291, 295
Bhagwat,Vidyut, 155
Bhakti Yoga, 203, 231
Bharati, Subramanya, 5
Bianca or A Young Spanish Maiden, 141
Bishbriksha, 140
Bonglish, 9
Bonnet, Alastair, 21
Bose, Amalendu, 105
Bose, Jagadish Chandra, 6
Bose, Subhas Chandra, 5, 6, 298
Bradley-Birt, Francis, 80, 81, 82
Brahmo Sabha, 24, 40, 42
Brahmo Samaj, 32, 40, 44, 86, 173, 190, 298, 335
Brajagana Kavya, 111
Brooks, Van Wyck, 1
Buckingham, J.S., 74
Burke, Mary Louise, 233
Buro Shaliker Ghare Ron, 110
Buruma, Ian, 21

Candide, 331
Carey,William, 36, 45, 322, 386
Chakrabarty, Dipesh, 3
Charulata, 302, 304
Chatterjee, Bankim Chandra, 5, 9, 21, 61, 63, 93, 120, 121, 122, 123, 124, 125, 126, 127, 128, 129, 131, 132, 134, 135, 136, 137, 138, 139, 140, 141, 142, 143, 146, 235, 298, 311, 325, 333, 340, 341
Chatterjee, Joya, 327

Chatterjee, Partha, 85, 146, 165, 287, 303
Chatterjee, Reena, 46, 47, 50
Chattopadhyaya, Harindranath, 277
Chaudhuri, Nirad C., 123, 129, 304, 327
Chaudhuri, Rosinka, 60, 388
City of Dreadful Night, 321
colonialism, 4, 5, 10, 20, 21, 22, 24, 25, 28, 34, 47, 51, 59, 65, 72, 94, 95, 97, 98, 102, 115, 117, 118, 121, 129, 130, 135, 138, 139, 140, 147, 166, 167, 176, 182, 248, 255, 260, 267, 269, 276, 293, 296, 297, 298, 303, 307, 310, 315, 317, 318, 319, 320, 326,328, 330, 338, 347, 372, 373, 377
Cousins, James H., 264

Dalits, 188, 236, 301, 308, 309, 310, 356
Dalmia, Manju, 82
Daruwalla, Keki, 249
Das, Sisir Kumar, 129
Dasgupta, R.K., 81
Dass,Gaur, 102, 104, 106, 108, 109
Datta, Akshay Kumar, 6
Dawkins, Richard, 366
De, Bishnu, 101
Deb, Radhakanta, 6, 31, 33, 122
Deleuze, 13–15
Derozio, Henry, 5, 9, 31, 58–91, 93–94, 265, 323, 345, 388
Derozio, Poet of India, 80
Deshmukh, Nanaji, 353
Detroit Evening News, 228

INDEX ■ 401

Dev, Narendra, 357
Devdas, 303
Dharmatattva, 121
diaspora, 117, 118, 290, 295
Durgeshnandini, 129, 140
Dutt, Kylash Chunder, 141
Dutt, Shoshee Chunder, 141
Dutt,Toru, 141, 162, 265
Dutta, Narendranath, 298

Ekei Ki Boley Sobhyata, 110
Eliot, T.S., 21, 80
Erasure of the Euro-Asian: Recovering Early Radicalism and Feminism in South Asia, 90
Ezekiel, Nissim, 249, 258

Fanon, Frantz, 98, 130
Foucault, Michel, 2, 11, 12, 316
Friend of India, 38

Gandhi, Mohandas Karamchand, 4, 5, 7, 9, 11-13, 20-21, 32, 33, 44, 73, 173, 231, 241, 243, 245, 248, 249, 250, 268, 277, 279, 308, 311, 312, 351, 352, 353, 354, 355-370, 376, 379, 380, 381
Gandhi, Gopal Krishna, 73
Gandhi's Philosophy and the Quest for Harmony, 376
George, Rosemary Marangoly, 290
Ghare Baire, 288, 290, 294, 301-304,
Ghosh, Amitav, 123
Ghosh, Gautam, 76
Gita, 33, 115, 122, 369

Gita Govinda, 322
Godse, Nathuram, 352, 353, 357
Gokhale, Gopal Krishna, 6, 32, 173, 187, 235, 245, 257, 276, 376
Guattari, Felix, 13, 14, 15
Gundappa, D.V., 375, 376

Harijan, 352, 356
Hastings,Warren, 26, 84, 121
Heidegger, Martin, 286, 289, 303
Hindutva, 352, 357, 358, 366, 367
Hinglish, 9
History of British India, 330
History of Indian English Literature, 81
Hitopadesa, 322
Holstrom, Lakshmi, 178

Imaginary Homelands, 284, 285
India Gazette, 62, 73, 74, 77, 80, 88
Indian Field, 141
Indu Prakash, 126, 333
Inglish, 9
Institutes of Hindu Law or the Ordinances of Menu, 322
Iqbal, Mohammad, 5
Iyengar, K. R. Srinivasa, 62, 81

Jalal, Ayesha, 288
James, William, 203
Jameson, Frederic, 125
Jayawardena, Kumari, 90
Jinnah, Mohammad Ali, 245, 380
Jitatmananda, Swami, 232
Joshi, Anandibai, 153, 163
Jussawalla, Adil, 249

Kalidasa, 66
Kamala, 162, 163, 164, 165, 177
Kapalakundala, 140
Kapoor, Kapil, 326, 330
Karma-Yoga, 203
Kaviraj, Sudipto, 127–129, 139
Kesavadasa, 271
Khan, Paunchkouree, 128
Khilnani, Sunil, 6
Khristayana, 181
Kipling, Rudyard, 321
Kopf, David, 4, 316–319, 324–327, 344
Kosambi, Meera, 150, 157
Kotnala, M. C., 35, 37, 39, 41, 53
Kripal, Jeffrey J., 214
Krishna Kumari, 110
Krishnacharitra, 121, 138
Krishnakanter Will, 140
Krishnamurti, J., 54, 219
kshatriya, 204

Lal, P., 249
Lal, Vinay, 21
Lalita, K., 154, 181, 300
Lane, Dorothy F., 181
Life of Alexander Duff, 325
Lohia, Rammanohar, 357

Macaulay, Thomas Babington, 7, 10, 45–501, 167, 182, 296–297, 329, 377
MacLeod, Josephine, 225
Madhaviah, A., 153, 177–180
Madhusudan Dutt, Michael, 5, 9, 43, 93, 101, 105, 112, 120, 129, 296, 297, 323, 345
Madhusudan Rachnavali, 102

Madras Christian College Magazine, 177
Mahabharata, 121, 189, 328, 376
Margalit, Avishai, 21
Marx, Karl, 212, 330
Maya Kaman, 110
McCutcheon, David, 75
Medhavi, Bepin Behari, 156
Meghnad Badh Kavya, 111
Mehir Muneer, 252, 253, 254, 260
Mehrotra, A.K., 249
Midnight's Children, 142, 284
Mill, James, 330
Mishra, Ganeswar, 132
Mitra, Pramadadas, 197
Mitra, Surendranath, 190, 196
Mohamet, Dean, 61
Moore, Thomas, 74, 106, 261
Moraes, Dom, 292
Mukherjee, Meenakshi, 125, 129
Mukhopadhyay, Bhudev, 128
Müller, Max, 204, 207, 222
Mund, Subhendu Kumar, 128

Naidu, Sarojini, 5, 9, 174, 239, 240–280, 393
Naik, M.K., 75, 81

Nandy, Ashish, 3, 308
Narayan, Jayaprakash, 357
Nashtanir, 302, 307
Navajivan, 352
Nehru, Jawaharlal, 5–7, 219, 225, 231, 240–242, 245, 248, 250, 252, 277, 280, 299, 353, 369, 370
Never at Home, 292
Nikambe, Shevantibai, 166, 167,

168, 169, 170, 171
Niranjanananda, Swami, 204
noumenon, 211

Oaten, E.F., 81
occidentalism, 19-23, 28, 317
On the Education of the People of India, 50
Oriental Renaissance, 331
Orientalism, 3, 4, 63-65, 69, 75, 79, 315, 316, 317, 327,329, 343
Other, 10, 23, 97, 98, 99, 117, 119, 194, 264, 265, 299, 358, 365

Padmavati, 110
Panikkar, K. M., 226
Pantulu, Pandit Veerasalingam, 244
Paranjape, Makarand R, 246, 255, 256, 259, 261, 266, 267, 279, 373
Parel, Anthony J., 376
Parthasarathy, R., 61, 114, 249
Patanjali, 203, 367
Patwardhan, Achyut, 357
phenomenon, 211, 222
Pieterse, Jan Nederveen, 319
Pinney, Christopher, 75, 76
Pollock,Sheldon, 83
Prabhananda, Swami, 235
Prabuddha Bharata, 207, 213
Prarthana Samaj, 40, 173
Pre-Raphaelites, 260, 264
Provincialising Europe, 3
Punjlish, 9

Rachel L. Bodley, 153
Raichaudhuri, Tapan, 227
Raja Yoga, 203, 231
Rajagopalachari, C., 6, 225
Rajan, Rajeswari Sunder, 76,179
Rajasingha, 140
Rajmohan's Wife, 61, 124-132, 140-143, 146
Rajyalakshmi, P.V., 270
Ramabai, Pandita, 148-150, 153-161, 169, 173-175, 249, 391
Ramakrishnananda, Swami, 196, 206, 220, 229
Ramayana, 189, 197, 297, 328
Ranade, Madhav Govind, 6, 376
Ranade, Mahadev Govind, 150, 173
Ranade, Ramabai, 6, 32, 150, 152, 156, 173-81, 249, 386
Rasika Priya, 271
Ray, Rajat Kanta, 373
Raychauduri, Tapan, 123
Robinson, Andrew, 302
Rolland, Romain, 225
Rough Passage, 61, 114
Roy, Modhumita, 10
Roy, Rammohun, 4, 5, 9, 19, 20, 21-55, 58, 77, 85, 86, 94, 121, 123, 146, 161, 190, 233, 295-297, 310-311, 325
Rushdie, Salman, 284, 285, 289, 291, 394

Saguna, 162, 163, 164, 177
Sahib, Bibi, Golam, 303
Said, Edward, 3, 49, 315
Sarkar, Jadunath, 327
Sarkar, Tanika, 123
Sarkar, Sumit, 49, 396
Sarkar, Sushobhan, 29, 32, 43

Sarmishtha, 110
sarvodaya, 119, 277
Sastri, Srinivas, 6
sati, 42, 53, 59, 68, 70, 71, 72, 76, 77, 78, 79, 158, 159, 161, 177, 179, 269
Satthianadhan, Krupabai, 162, 177
satyagraha, 245, 354, 364, 376
Savitri, 61–62, 273
Schawb, Raymond, 331
Sen, Amiya, 235
Sen, Keshub Chandra, 32–33, 190, 298
Sengupta, Padmini, 252, 253
Seth, Vikram, 61
Shakuntala, 322
Shinde, Tarabai, 154, 173
Shiva, 189, 208, 287, 394
shudra, 204, 233
Sil, Narasinga P., 225
Sivananda, Swami, 204
Smart, Ninian, 227
Smith, G., 325
Smith, Vincent, 25, 29
Smriti Chitre, 180
Songs by S. Chattopadhyaya, 253
Speeches and Writings of Sarojini Naidu, 247
Spivak, Gayatri Chakravorty, 289–291
Sri Ramakrishna, 40, 44, 116, 190, 221, 297, 298, 346, 390
Stri Purush Tulana, 154
subalterns, 308
Sundari, Varada, 241, 243, 275
svaraj, 7, 22, 27, 28, 29, 55, 119, 152, 165, 181, 218, 293, 295, 296, 310, 311, 319, 332, 359, 364, 366–370, 375, 376, 382, 385
Swarupananda, Swami, 207

Tagore, Devendranath, 190
Tagore, Maharshi Debendranath, 50
Tagore, Rabindranath, 5, 76, 140, 249, 288, 290, 291, 292, 294, 299, 300–308, 332, 340, 341, 370
Tagore, Surendranath, 290
Tamlish, 9
Tharu, Susie, 154, 181
The Bird of Time, 245, 247, 254, 256
The Broken Wing, 245, 247, 257, 258
The *Collected Works*, 370, 387
The East Indian, 58, 88, 323
The Fakeer of Jungheera, 59, 60–62, 74, 80
The Feather of the Dawn, 247, 258
The Golden Gate, 61
The Golden Threshold, 239–241, 245, 247, 251, 254, 255, 256, 272
The High-Caste Hindu Woman, 153, 156, 157, 158, 169
The Home and the World, 290
The Human Cycle, 233
The Idea of India, 6
The Indian Gazette, 39
The Indian Opinion, 352
The Language of the Gods in a World of Men, 83
The Life of Vivekananda and the Universal Gospel, 225
The Location of Culture, 75, 285

The Lyric Spring, 270
The Nation and Its Fragments, 287, 391
The Oriental Herald, 74
The Oriental Renaissance, 331
The Oxford Book of Mystic Verse, 256
The Politics of Home, 290
The Precepts of Jesus – The Guide to Peace and Happiness, 37
The Renaissance in India, 319–320, 324, 333–345
The Revelations of an Orderly, 128, 141
The Sceptred Flute, 247
The Second Sex, 155
The Story of a Hindu Life, 163
The Tempest, 332
The Uncanny, 285
The World and the Home, 286
The Wretched of the Earth, 130
Third and Final Appeal, 39
Tilak, Bal Gangadhar, 6, 122, 188
Tilak, Lakshmibai, 156, 180–181
Tilak, Raghukul, 247
Tilottama Sambhava Kavya, 110
To India – My Native Land, 323
Tolstoy, Leo, 203
tradition, 4–5, 8, 11–13, 15, 20, 22, 25–26, 28–29, 32, 38–39, 45, 48–51, 54, 60, 66, 72, 77, 79–80, 84, 90, 101, 114, 115, 121, 123–124, 132–133, 136, 137, 140, 155, 158, 164–165, 172, 174, 177, 187, 197, 201, 212, 222, 226, 252, 259, 260, 265, 267, 271, 276, 280, 285, 296, 298, 301, 333
Travels, 61, 89
Trevelyan, C.E., 50
Tuhfut'ul Muhawahhiddin, 36
Tyagananda, Swami, 212, 213

Udbodhan, 207
Upadhyay, Brahmabandabh, 6
Upadhyay, Deen Dayal, 353
Utpaladeva, Acharya, 364

Veerangana Kavya, 111
Verghese, C.Paul, 81
Vidyasagar, Ishwar Chandra, 6, 111, 112, 189, 324, 389

Visions of the Past, King Porus, 109
Viswanathan, Gauri, 181
Vivekananda, Swami, 5, 9, 13, 157, 186–236, 297, 311, 332, 333, 340, 345–346, 392

Weber, Max, 11
Wigley, Mark, 286

Yates, William, 37
Young India, 352, 387